CW00553798

Banzai, You Bastards

by
Jack Edwards
in collaboration with
Jimmy Walter

Dedication

This book is dedicated to the men of Kinkaseki and Kokutsu (our jungle camp): those who died (either there or later as a result of their treatment there), those that survived, and those who passed through; and to those who faithfully waited and prayed for our return.

Printed by Professional Printer
Published by Corporate Communications,
704, East Town Building, 41, Lockhart Road,
Wanchai, Hong Kong.

© Jack Edwards

All rights reserved. No part of this publication may be
reproduced, stored in a retrieval system, or transmitted, in any
form or by any means, electonic, mechanical, photocopying,
recording or otherwise, without the prior permission of
Jack Edwards and Corporate Communications Ltd.

ISBN 962-7290-03-3

Acknowledgements

Words of course are insufficient to thank Colonel J.F. Crossley, MBE, TD, JP, DL, who was and is "the Major" and "the Man of Kinkaseki". His leadership, example, and courage helped us to survive. Further, I wish to thank him for the use of his camp records and reports compiled in 1946/47.

A special thanks to Mrs Nell Homer for allowing me to use excerpts from the diary of her late husband, Major B.M. Wheeler, MBE, IMS (She remarried after his return and subsequent death). The Major was known and will be remembered as "the man sent by God". He kept his diary at great personal risk and it voices the hopes, fears, and thoughts of all of the prisoners during those terrible days. But perhaps more importantly, it represents the memories and love of a wife or sweetheart that kept him and so many others going.

A separate thanks to Anne Wheeler, Major Wheeler's daughter, for the use of her research material for the documentary film "A War Story", a testimonial to her father and his incredible medical feats in appaling conditions.

I travelled to Canada to help in the launching of "A War Story" where I spent a memorable week at the home of the Wheelers' eldest son Harry and his wife Bette. At the showing of the film I met Alan and Ken Wheeler, the rest of Major Wheeler's family. The encouragement and support of both the Wheeler family and the Maclennan family convinced me I had to write this book as a memorial and tribute to the rest of the men from Kinkaseki, particularly the rest of the medical team, Captain P.G. Seed and our invaluable medical orderlies. How can I ever thank Corporal David Donnelly, BEM, RAMC, who not only helped saved my life at Kinkaseki, but also accompanied me back to Taiwan to make the film and assisted in telling the story during many long "blathers".

Thanks must also go to George Harrison, who travelled with us back to Taiwan and whose service as medical orderly, and whose friendship and drawings (which also illustrate the text) helped so much during our captivity; Sergeant Jim Bingham, who received a mention in despatches after the war for what he did as a PoW and the use of his precious nominal roll of the men held at Kinkaseki (found at the end of the book); Arthur "Trumpeter" Smith, the cheerful poet and the "Rabbie Burns" of Kinkeseki, for the use of his immortal song "Down the Mine Bonnie Laddie" (Only those who were there can know what he did for morale); Les Davis, my companion and confidant until the bitter end who helped in so many ways and who read the final draft making useful proposals; and Geoffrey P. Adams, my friend and the author of "No Time for Geishas", for his encouragement and the use of a phrase from his book; John Dodd, my nephew and godson (he was given my name when he was baptised in 1943 because he was my family's hope and faith that I would return even though I was "missing, believed killed"), for their understanding when I volunteered to return to the Far East in Dec. 1945 to assist in the War Crimes Investigations and Trials.

All surviving prisoners from Taiwan owe their lives to the US Navy and Marine Corps who rescued us and cleared the mines for the HMS "Belfast" and HMS "Bermuda". They carried away those who were too ill to travel on the first evacuation. We are particularly indebted to former Lieutenant of the watch, L. Henry Taylor from Hartford, Connecticut, USA, who navigated the lead destroyer USS "Thomas J. Gary" through the minefield for the dawn landing of the Marines. he has very kindly allowed me to publish some photographs and a personal letter to his son from that time.

Thanks also to those in Hong Kong: Ted Thomas, my publisher and head of Corporate Communications, a leading PR firm in Hong Kong; Tim Hamlett, our literary consultant and editor; Jimmy Walter who collaborated with me to knock my original text into shape, and whose father, Jim Walter, put the considerable facilities of his corporation in the USA at my disposal to help finally obtain from the National Archives (Military Archives Division) Washington, DC, a copy of the original Japanese extermination orders I found whilst on War Crimes Investigations in 1945/46; Andy Neilson, my old friend and supporter in Hong Kong; Mrs Sylvia Wong Lee Suk Kuen who struggled for hours with my handwriting to produce the first typed draft; Mrs Samantha Lam Hui Sui Ha who helped with secretarial work (both ladies worked not for personal reward, but just because they wanted "to help tell the story"); and last but far from least, thanks to Polly Tam Pui Ling. Polly's constant attention, assistance, encouragement, and devotion during months of writing carried me through the completion of the story of Kinkaseki and Kokotsu.

Editor's Note

Jack Edwards has an old soldier's affection for the details of rank and regiment, and for the benefit of other old soldiers these details remain in the text. Readers who are unfamiliar with the abbreviations used will find a list of them and their meanings in Appendix C. Two points may need some explanation: British artillery regiments use the ranks of Gunner (Gnr) and Bombardier (Bdr) instead of Private and Corporal (Cpl) respectively. Regiments in the British Army have a number, an indication of their branch and sub-branch of the service, and a name — usually indicating a geographical affiliation. Thus the full name of the unit to which Jack Edwards was attached is the 155th Field Regiment, Royal Artillery, the Lanarkshire Yeomanry. "Field" indicates that they were equipped with field guns, as opposed to anti-tank or anti-aircraft weapons. The regiment may appear in brief as the 155th Field, The 155th RA, or informally as "the Lanarkshires".

Malayan names have as far as I can discover remained the same since the war. Readers should note that Slim River is the name of a place as well as of the river it stands on. Taiwanese names are more of a problem. During the war Taiwan was a Japanese colony, and all names were Japanese. They are now, of course replaced by Chinese ones. Generally I have stuck to the versions then in use. Taihoku is now Taipei and Kinkaseki is now called Quinkashee. I have used the modern spelling for Keelung, then written Kiirun but pronounced the same. Neither Jack nor I is familiar with the standard ways of rendering Japanese speech into the Western alphabet and I have not sought to impose an arbitrary consistency. If this is occasionally confusing, readers will only be sharing the uncertainty of the original hearers.

Colonel Freddie Crossley (on right) with Harold Payne, President
National Federation FEPoW at a re-union.

Foreword

by
Colonel Freddie Crossley
MBE, TD, JP, DL

I should like to congratulate Jack Edwards on producing a very detailed and very accurate portrayal of the conditions and treatment of prisoners of war, in the notorious Kinkaseki mining camp in Formosa. I hope this book will help to dispel the mistaken belief, based on such films as "The Bridge over the River Kwai", that there was only one place where the treatment of prisoners was inhuman — the "Railway of Death".

The original number of men in Kinkaseki was 524. Over the years this varied up to 900 at some periods.

As the Senior British Officer in the camp, I had the task of dealing with the Japanese Command on all matters affecting life in the camp. I must pay tribute here to the men in the camp for their cooperation with me in this difficult job. Without their help, assistance and discipline it would have been an impossible task. The men working in the mine even agreed to share their rations with their sick comrades, for the Japs had a rule: no work no food. Various raiding parties were arranged on the Japanese stores from time to time, but here again it was fully understood that any food which we managed to lift was taken to our cookhouse and shared by all.

I should like to record my thanks to the others — named or not in this book — who helped with the day to day running of the camp. These included the few officers who were left with me at Kinkaseki, and all members of the various committees which were formed to assist in the organisation. Not least of these was the secret committee named in this book who were fully aware of the extermination order and had to work with the knowledge of that terrible death sentence and threat to all our lives. They had to plan what we could do to survive, or to take as many of the Japs as possible with us when the time came for what they termed the "extreme measures" for our "final disposition".

This book was not written with the "box office" in view. It is a true account of what happened. I trust all who read it will remember and reflect on the depths of human depravity in time of war, and the heights of human endurance, courage, conduct and spirit which ensured that one day this story would be told.

Freddie Crossley

Preface

Of the 50,016 United Kingdom forces captured at Hongkong, Singapore, etc. in the Far East by the Japanese, 1 out of every 3 died or was missing. This compares with 142,319 taken by Germany and Italy with only 1 death out of every 20 in the PoW. camps of Europe.

To the Japanese we were not men. They frequently told us we were "nothing", "expendable", and referred to as "animals for work today in the mine". We were below their.contempt. We had surrendered. Their insane warrior code, the *Bushido* of the *Samuarai*, demanded they either die in battle or take their own life. Thousands, though not even a large minority, did. The *Banzai* charges and *Kamikaze* aircraft were prime examples of this depravity. Those who were prison guards were not the best nor the brightest. The best and the brightest were in more important positions. As a consequence, our guards and their leaders looked down on us with even greater disdain in order to justify their own position. These factors largely account for their cruel and brutal treatment of us.

Some may ask why I have let 42 years pass before writing our story. The answer is simple: I was so traumatized by the experience that every time I sat and tried, the memories would cause such intense emotions that I was unable to continue. Even now I find it difficult to read parts of the drafts. The discovery of Doctor Wheeler's diary and the trip back to the mine on Taiwan when making the documentary film, "A War Story", helped to lay to rest many ghosts and renewed my determination to write the story of the suffering of the men in the mine at Kinkaseki.

War, either battle or prison life, brings to the surface the bravery and courage that exists in some men. Prison life brings even greater emphasis since there is no hope of victory, only survival. There are no weapons to lash out at your captors with; no place to retreat to, even for a moment's respite. On the battlefield you are fit, equipped, well fed, motivated, disciplined, in touch with news of home and the world (and they make sure the news is encouraging), and feel that "it can't last forever". In the Japanese prison camps we were starved, sick, unarmed, exhausted from hard labour under hellish conditions, harassed and humiliated 24 hours a day, nearly naked, and beaten daily. When sick we knew since there were no medical supplies the chance of survival was slight. Worse was watching your mates die in ghastly, ugly circumstances, a terrifying picture of what you would probably become.

It is little wonder that in every camp there were cowardly and mean men determined to live and saying to hell with everyone else. All men in such conditions are scared. The brave and couragous are able to overcome these instinctual emotions. The average can merely keep them at bay. The weak succumb. Thankfully, those in the last category were small in number. The vast majority looked after their mates. That was the system that allowed us to survive: knowing that if you looked out for your mate when he was in difficulty or sick, he would do the same for you. Knowing that someone cared, the love of one individual for another, is what enabled us to survive.

Courage and bravery in battle is rewarded by Victoria Crosses (VCs), Distinquished Service Orders (DSOs) and Military Crosses (MCs) if you're an officer, and VCs, Distinquished Conduct Medals (DCMs) and Military Medals (MMs) if you're one of the "other ranks", NCO or lower, even though it is the same act of courage or valour. But for acts of cool bravery and years of endurance in prison life there are few decorations; only the Member of the British Empire (MBE) and British Empire Medal (BEM), or "mentions". There were only three men decorated out of all the men who died or survived Kinkaseki. I saw both battle and prison. Neither were easy. But to my mind there were many, many more deserving of recognition than were decorated from Kinkaseki. The daily torments of the mine, the constant hunger and pain, the incessant beatings and harassment made courage, self-respect, and mutual esteem between the men a necessity. Those who did not have it, those who did not look after their "mucker", usually perished. The unwritten law was that you did nothing to harm your mates. The worst crime was to become "Jap-happy", to go along willingly with their orders or try to ingratiate yourself with the enemy. In those extreme conditions of despair and degradation we turned to each other for reassurance that life was worth living and that we **could** survive. This book is my attempt to record the ultimate courage, bravery, and love of their mates that occurred under these worst of all possible conditions, acts known only to those who were there.

Lastly I felt impelled to tell of the massacre plan, the plot to leave no traces of the atrocities of our captors. It is important that people know that the atomic bomb saved far more lives than it took, that it saved far more suffering than it gave, and that it was used on a people possessed and controlled by an insane code. No, not all citizens were believers in that insanity. But they supported those in control, and those in control were believers. Their military was. They were cruel, brutal, and uncaring because of their irrational beliefs. The revelations of the Tokyo War Crimes trials where my evidence was also used showed the Japanese brutally murdered six Million civilians. It is now overlooked that this was about the same number of Jews slaughtered in the Holocaust by the Germans. Every year now the anniversaries of Hiroshima and Nagasaki are used by peace and anti-nuclear groups to hammer home their message of the horrors of war. The Japanese have cleverly turned these annual events into world-wide media propaganda vehicles to try to show how badly they have suffered, and their citizens who survived those bombings still suffer. They attempt to make the Allies the criminals in a heinous crime. Their Ministry of Education has recently altered the history books and refers to the savagery of the "Rape of Nanking" as "an unorganised act committed in a state of utmost confusion", describe their invasions as "movements" or "expansions" and make the West out as the villian.

The world continues to be reminded of the Nazi atrocities and attempted genocide of the Jews. The USA, European nations, and Israel relentlessly track down, pursue, and bring to trial Nazi war criminals such as Dr. Joseph Mengele, "The Angel of Death", Adolf Eichman, Klaus Barbie, "the Butcher of Lyons", and John Demjanjuk, "Ivan the Terrible". Even now Jewish organizations and the American press are closely scrutinizing the war time activities of the Austrian President, Kurt Waldeim, his actions trivial when compared to the heinous crimes of the Japanese War Criminals, long forgotten. After the initial trials of those caught at the end of the war, there has been little or no investigation nor pursuit nor trial of those that escaped. Why? Why has Japan never paid the same type of compensation that Germany was forced to pay?

Table of Contents

Fate

She swirled the cup. I watched her, amused and curious as young boys are by mystics and such. It was all in fun. She wasn't a real mystic. She was only our neighbour, a friend of my mum.

The tea leaves settled. She stared.

"I see you in uniform, surrounded by wire!", came the prophecy.

I smiled, snickering inside. After all, there was no war on. World War I was long over and everyone knew it was to be the last one. The Germans would never be allowed to try that again. And I certainly wasn't going to be a prison guard. Maybe a soft job with the postal service, surrounded by telephone wires.

We talked and laughed about it, little realizing how well my fate had been foretold, right down to the tea leaves themselves, for they would be my last prison.

The Return

The road looked the same. Black wooden houses and huts cluttered the mountainsides, bamboo pipes connecting them like a spider's web. Stopping half way, we wondered how we had survived that terrible march on the first day, let alone three long years in the hell-hole. Our emotions were swelling, still strong after years of slumber.

When we arrived at the mine head, we found the old sheds and sidings still intact, yellowed by the fumes of sulphuric acid. Our skin and clothing had been that same colour almost 40 years ago. On entering the tunnel, the warm, musty smell instantly brought back the old revulsion and fear. Relief flowed through us as we surfaced. The mind and the body never fully recover from such prolonged horror.

We found the old camp gate still standing. Everything else was gone, overgrown like a forgotten grave. Part of the parade ground was being cultivated by the present miners. Well, we fertilized it well on our runs to the latrines.

As we had a thousand times before, we climbed the steps. From the top, we again thanked God for our survival. Looking down on "Boot Hill", the memory, if not the bodies (they had been exhumed after the war), of our unluckier fellow prisoners reached up to us. Later we laid some wild flowers on the site and stood in silence. The villagers told us of ghosts, and how they refused to settle or even approach this site, even though it was one of the few flat places available for construction. Perhaps my comrades' spirits refused to rest, incensed by the lack of respect from their countrymen.

It was a long, emotional day. That night my mind drifted back. It had all started with an unlucky number.

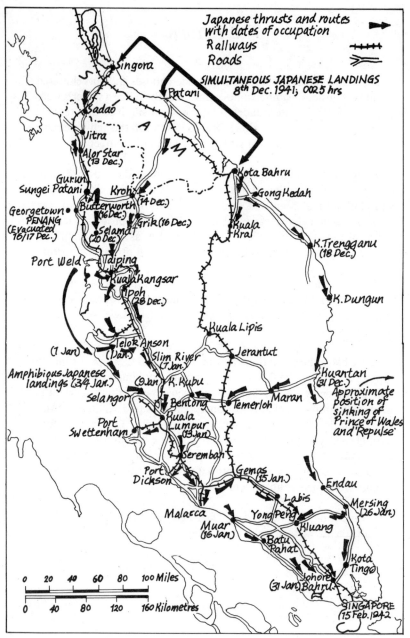

Map shows route of the Japanese attacks down Malaya and places of main engagements fought by 11th (Indian) Division mentioned in first three chapters.

CHAPTER 1

"Unlucky for Some"

From Jesus to modern day bingo players, the number 13 has been "unlucky for some." The chorus of groans and moans echoed in the factory room at Lanark. It was March, 1941. My signal section of 32 men, down from 36 due to the desertion of four of our number, was drawn from every corner of the British Isles. You could hear Cockney, Midlands, Yorkshire, Lancashire, Irish, Scottish, and Welsh curses as our section officer announced that the number 13 would have to be painted on all boxes and kit bags. We were busy packing them with our khaki drills and colonial sun helmets, christened "Bombay Bowlers" in the British/Indian army. The drills were shirts and special shorts that folded down so they could be taped around the ankles as a protection from the number one killer in the tropics, the mosquito. The shorts were known as "Bombay Bloomers". The topic on everyone's lips was, of course, our unknown destination. The favourites, due to our kit, were the Western Desert or Iraq. We were wrong about everything but our luck. Even there, we were wrong in the degree. "Unlucky for some" would be unlucky for all.

I was their Sergeant. My name is Jack Edwards. I'm from Wales.

Whistling and singing, we marched cheerfully to the dock that cold grey day, bringing up the rear of the 155th Field Regt, RA, (the Lanarkshire Yeomanry) all unaware that most of us would never see home again. There happened to be a great number of factory girls spilling out at lunch time to see us marching off. We started resurrecting the songs of the last war, "Pack up Your Troubles", "It's a Long Way to Tipperary", and "Good-Bye-Ee", to name a few.

"Where are you going?", someone from the crowd shouted.

"We're off to see the Wizard," one wag started up. All of us picked it up and continued, "the wonderful Wizard of Oz." We waved our

1

arms, singing with gusto the hit tune from the movie we had seen only that last month. Little did we know that, in our version, the Yellow Brick Road would lead us into the clutches of the worst of the yellow man's army.

We boarded lighters and were ferried out into the Clyde to board the "Strathmore", a P&O liner. As we drew alongside her, the khaki clad figures lining her rails greeted us with cries of, "There's tons of reek on board." Reek, we learned later, is Scottish for tobacco or cigarettes. In an endless stream, verses of "Hi Jig a Jig, Fuck a little Pig, Follow the Band", came from a lighter packed with Highland Light Infantry as they passed by. Laughter and songs, what a contrast to the days ahead!

Our convoy was huge and consisted mainly of liners such as the "Stratheden", the "Strathnairn", and the captured French liner "Felix Roussel". There were "Castle" boats and three funnellers as well. HMS "Ramilles" and other escorts shepherded us out to meet another convoy out in the Atlantic. After a few awful days of rough weather, we turned south.

The daily news of British reverses in the intensifying fighting in North Africa led us all to believe the Western Desert was our destination. We continued south, however, calling at Freetown where our escorts changed. The well known outline of the HMS "Nelson" took over, and we docked in the dark of early morning at Cape Town several days later. The fairyland lights of the city beckoned us like the Sirens of Greek mythology.

The morning route marches the next day through the suburbs of Cape Town were welcome, the exercise a great boon to us after being cooped up on board for so long. Shore leave in this beautiful city, backed by Table Mountain, was like Nirvana after a cold, blacked-out, bombed and rationed England. The memory of Dunkirk still weighed heavily on us all. We could not get ashore fast enough.

The warm welcome the Afrikaners gave us was fantastic. Many waited at the dock gates in their cars to offer rides and the hospitality of their homes. My turn came as I was standing in the queue for a cinema. A car drew up and a lady called out, "Any of you boys like a home-made tea and a bath?" Myself, my corporal, Herb Harvey, and two others quickly accepted.

Like hundreds of others, we were taken to a cosy flat near Sea Point. Our host was Mrs. MacDonald, whose eldest son was away "fighting in the north with the South African Army". Her daughters came home later, one from an office, the other from High School, and helped their mother entertain us at tea. The youngest, Yvonne, was a Rugby enthusiast. When she discovered I was Welsh from Cardiff, she bubbled over, Cardiff being among the best teams of the day. For our two remaining days in Cape Town, the family treated us like, well, like family. Yvonne introduced me to the Newlands Rugby team, who in turn treated me with lavish hospitality. We exchanged addresses, and they kindly wrote to our families, reassuring them of our welfare. It was the start of a friendship between Yvonne and I which continued until her death, and continues even now with her husband and family.

The huge convoy was split up as we left Cape Town. Now we were only five ships with one escort. Boring endless days of PT classes, lectures, and "bullshit" inspections followed. One officer, with nothing better to do, conceived the idea of having everyone store and fold their winter greatcoat, a vital item in the tropics, in such a way that all the buttons were showing. This meant the coats had to be taken down, the buttons cleaned, refolded, and then stored in a pile every day! With officers like that, it's a wonder we eventually won. Morale, while not low, was not high.

A little luck came our way when a call came for signallers with visual Morse-code reading experience. "Herbie", L/Cpl. "Tug" Wilson and others from my section, myself included, then stood watches on the bridge, manning the Aldis signal lamps. It was great up there in the fresh air doing something worthwhile, away from the endless fatigues, soul-destroying inspections, PT classes and drills without arms. Our tasks were simple: to relay the speed from the ship in front to the ship behind, usually "K8" or "K10", denoting eight or ten knots. This was day duty only, as we were blacked out at night, being still in the shipping lanes and vulnerable to submarine and surface-raider attacks. Eventually we docked in Bombay on a muggy day in May. We struggled ashore, sweating, laden with our equipment. We were greeted by the Indian volunteer organizations, all ladies, handing each of us a mess-tin of hot sweet tea, one of the few sweet memories of the years to come.

3

Our stay in India was a brief three months. Our home that night was a taste of what our home would be for the next four years. We were taken, packed in trains, to Ahmadnagar. On our arrival at 2:30 am, guides in clean, starched, and ironed khaki drill uniforms escorted us to our quarters. The guides looked so smart and regimental as we marched through a barbed wire perimeter to take over some old buildings covered with black-painted Italian slogans, "Viva Il Duce" and "Viva Italia". Only then did we realize that we would be staying in the just vacated Italian PoW barracks. It was then I remembered the tealeaf reading of my youth. A cold chill swept over me.

We trained and worked hard for the next three months. Later on we moved to Kirkee to continue our training. Our only worry there was the 155th Field Regiment. They were equipped with 4.5" howitzers manufactured in ... 1919! Our section officer, Lt Martin Kepple, drew up an intensive training programme for my signal section. It was not popular, but we all worked well together. One of my main aims here was to try to ensure that every man could drive any lorry or motorcycle with which we might be issued.

The constant night and day exercises with the artillery and a brigade of infantry in open plains and scrub country were obviously intended to prepare us for desert warfare. Moreover, we were instructed to paint our vehicles and dye our tents to blend with desert terrain. The tents proved to be a problem until we hit upon hanging from tree branches to dip them in huge drums of dye. Finally the officers were satisfied.

After weeks of this we entrained and made our way to Bombay. There it was back aboard a ship, the "Ekma", with two battalions of Gurkhas. No convoy this time. After a few days at sea, it was obvious we were not on our way to Africa. Port Swettenham, Malaya, was our destination.

We arrived in the dark, early hours. Again we marched through a barbed wire perimeter, this time into a transit camp used in the past for Tamil labourers heading for the rubber plantations.

After a short stay while vehicles and guns were unloaded, we headed north in convoys through miles of lush green country and rubber plantations to reach our base at Sungei Patani. Here we lived in wooden huts in the midst of one of the dense rubber plantations. It was hot,

4

humid, mosquito-infested, and generally unpleasant. The sun barely broke through the dense canopy of rubber trees, but this didn't lessen its sweltering effect. We had little time to contemplate our surroundings, though, as everything had to be repainted: the tents, the vehicles, the guns, even our tin-helmets; this time to match the jungle. Ah, the efficiency of the army.

Back in Scotland I had been nick-named "the Wee Sarge" due to my enormous height of 5' 7"! My helmet came back with the legend "The Wee Sarge, if lost please return to S7" neatly printed on the inside by one of the section wags. S7 was the signal truck and office where my kit was stored.

The news at this period was not good. There were reverses for the British everywhere: Greece, Crete, Egypt, and at sea where we had just lost one of our most famous battlecruisers, the HMS "Hood". The Japanese were making ominous moves. We were kept at a high state of readiness but were restricted in our movements, allowed only on certain estate roads, warned against cutting down any branches, and prohibited from digging slit trenches anywhere on these huge estates.

As we got on with our training, we watched and criticized our parent regiment. The 155th Field Artillery was tagged a "real bunch of bullshitters" since they seemed to be endlessly cleaning and polishing their guns and vehicles. They had been a Territorial regiment, the Lanarkshire Yeomanry, and had been forced to give up their horses, much to the annoyance of the "County-type" officers. Their CO, a monocle wearing, charismatic character, Lt Col A. Murdoch, even had cavalry spurs mounted on the vehicles and gun limbers, partly severed to denote their "broken spurs". He had christened them the "Tally-Ho" boys and had it painted on their vehicles. We "signals" used to love to poke fun, shouting "Tally-Ho, you bastards" as they passed by. Some wags trained an unknowing Chinese boy who brought the daily newspapers to shout this, which he did as he entered the officer's mess, much to the annoyance of those assembled. A human explosion of swear words, normally used by the rank and file, ensued, the CO blasting the morning air.

Sungei Patani was the last army base before the Malaya/Thailand border. North of here was the small town of Jitra where the 2nd Battalion East Surreys, the 1st Leicesters, and a battalion of Punjabis

5

were preparing defensive positions.

The current rumours had it that in the event of a Japanese declaration of war and an attack from Indo-China on Thailand, we would cross the border. Our exercises, however, remained defensive in nature, confined to the plantation roads.

After several false alarms when we packed our vehicles and small kit only to unload, we finally received orders to move up to the border. Lt Kepple showed me maps of the Thai border area. Our objective appeared to be Singora on the Isthmus of Kra.

We, of course, knew nothing of the new phases this world war was entering. Huge Japanese convoys were even then converging to strike ashore at Singora, Pattani, and Kota Baru on the east coast, south of our position. The "Prince of Wales" and "Repulse", with no air cover and an escort of only four old destroyers, were heading north from Singapore to intercept the Japanese convoys. Further east, Japanese divisions were bearing down on Hong Kong. In the Pacific a huge Japanese fleet of aircraft-carriers and battleships was heading for their date with infamy at Pearl Harbor.

We moved off into pitch darkness, our lights dimmed, the warm tropical rain pouring down. Moving slowly north through the endless rubber trees, the vehicles, guns, and limbers slithered in the mud.

Suddenly, the whole of our convoy was illuminated by a pair of powerful head-lights as a large sports car rounded a bend and brought our lead vehicles to a halt. Our leading motorcycle riders shouted to the car driver to dim his lights and go slower because of the long column of vehicles. From the car a white-dinner-jacketed, irate European shouted, "Who the hell do you think you are to give orders? I manage this rubber estate!" Eric "Plonka" Clack, a Yorkshireman from my section, replied "Tha won't manage bloody estate for long when the fucking Japs reach here! Dim your bloody lights!"

"Japs? The Japs would never dare to invade! You bloody uniform types are just out mucking up the countryside hoping for a skirmish!" The attitude of this ill-tempered Britisher was typical of what we had already found and would find again in the weeks to come. Many civilians could not believe there was a Japanese threat, and what a threat it was to their way of life.

When we reached Jitra, we found some of our poor fellows laboriously digging slit trenches and tank ditches as defences, and watching them fill up with the incessant rain. In the pouring, steaming downpour and mud, we waited.

CHAPTER 2

"Little Men on Bicycles"

The debacle of the Malayan campaign and the fall of Singapore has been told in many different narratives as seen through the eyes of senior officers and military historians. However, to the ordinary soldiers who fought from the Thailand border to Singapore Island, only to be ordered to surrender, the historical descriptions of that terrible experience have always left a bitter taste. It has been called "Britain's greatest military disgrace". Young historians, writing on the 40th anniversary of the campaign, headlined articles with captions such as "70,000 Empire troops surrendered to 25,000 little men on bicycles after the 'Repulse' and 'Prince of Wales' were sunk." Here is my ground level account of the events from 8th December, 1941, to 15th February, 1942.

Empire troops in the north of Malaya, where my little signal section was in action, consisted of the 11th and 9th Indian Divisions. Both were under strength and short one infantry brigade each. Neither had tanks. Our "armour" consisted of a company of armoured cars, 1930 vintage, manned by very gallant Malayan Volunteers. The far superior Japanese Zeros swept our lumbering "Brewster Buffaloes" from the sky after the first few days, leaving us naked from the air. The depleted 11th was in the northwest Jitra area, while the 9th defended the Kota Baru area over on the east coast, bearing the brunt of the main Japanese landings.

In the south of Malaya was the 8th Australian Division, also short a brigade and necessary support troops. The only reserves available were one brigade of Gurkhas, the 28th, all young inexperienced battalions who were destined to write their names in glory in the weeks ahead.

On Singapore Island were three much depleted and under-strength British battalions, the Gordons, the Manchesters, and the Loyals, all engaged in rear defence and airfield guard duties. These three regular battalions had been a long time in the Far East on garrison duties, though with little jungle training in the "up-country" of Malaya. All had high sickness rates.

The "little men on bicycles" were in fact the crack, seasoned 5th, 18th, and Imperial Guard Divisions, supported by full divisional artillery, first-line aircraft, tanks and, in reserve if required, two fresh divisions from the Japanese mainland. According to their records, they used 125,408 men, 7,320 vehicles, 179 tanks, 11,516 horses, 354 army planes, 180 navy planes, and 30 seaplanes. There is no record of how many bicycles! Moreover, they had a navy in uncontested control of the sea after the first few days.

After the first few weeks of fighting at Jitra, there were only sufficient men left to make up one composite brigade out of the 6th and 15th Indian Brigades. Out of the only two English battalions in these Indian Brigades, the 2nd Surreys and 1st Leicesters, there were only enough men left to make up a single battalion, thereafter to fight as the "British Battalion".

The Jitra battle was spread over five days from the 8th to 13th December. My section was constantly in action. We strove to keep communications going between the OP's (Observation Posts) and the field guns and HQ, and HQ and the hard-pressed infantry. The Japanese attacked without pause, both day and night, infiltrating around positions which held them and overrunning road blocks on the main road with tanks. Fear of being cut off spread quickly when we heard that the Japanese had broken through at Kroh on the frontier and were driving for Sungei Patani behind us. The whole division might be lost.

Our two methods of communication were field telephone cable and despatch riders. Wireless sets were useless, as reception was impossible through the dense jungle and rubber plantations. I was particularly lucky with my four despatch riders. All had been keen motorcyclists before the war. Two of them, the corporal in charge, Len Savage, and Les Davis had been trial riders, and volunteered by joining up through the famous "Green-Un", the nickname for the motorcyclists' magazine. The others were "Plum" Warner and J. "Kapp" Kappelhoff, also excellent riders, full of guts, hard workers, and cheerful characters to boot.

9

The remainder of the section was split up between linesmen, wireless operators, and drivers; and let's not forget Frank Gill from Liverpool, our cook. As the wireless sets were useless, their operators were pressed into service as linesmen. They had to run their telephone cables in any direction and over any obstacles to get through. Our two largest vehicles, S6 and S7, carried the section's stores, charging engine, accumulators, and two field exchanges. We always carried one spare in case the other was destroyed.

During our training in India we had worked hard, constantly practising against the clock, perfecting a system that connected up quickly on arrival in position. We were a happy section and everyone "pitched-in" no matter what "trade" he was. The first thing the drivers did on arriving at a position was to camouflage their vehicles with nets and foliage, and start digging slit trenches. "E.J." Morris, an irrepressible Welshman from Penclawdd near Swansea, always competed with the other drivers, "Jimmy" Gibson and Dave Taylor of Halifax, to dig the quickest and best "funk hole". "E.J." was proud of his wagon, a Dodge with winding-gear on the front. Being a truck-driver in civilian life, he became the "authority" on driving and maintenance in our section.

The Japanese advanced quickly around the flanks of our main defences, and we soon heard the artillery firing over open sights to defend themselves. With the heavy rain and constant firing, the 4.5" howitzers sank so deep into the mud that their tow vehicles became bogged down trying to drag them out. "E.J." went forward, and by chaining his Dodge to some trees, used his winch to assist dragging the guns out; all this amid machine-gun, rifle, and mortar fire as the Japanese closed in.

That night, Japanese infantry were heard coming around the flanks threatening our HQ. I was told to arm every man I could, and we went forward to stop them, protecting the HQ and field telephone exchange. We had only nine rifles and two .38 revolvers between the twelve men I took up the track into the rubber. With Johnnie Griffiths, previously an infantryman in the "Gloucesters", as my Lance Corporal, we positioned ourselves in pairs to cover what we thought would be their lines of approach.

We were all tired, having had little sleep for three nights. It was a pitch black, moonless night with hordes of mosquitoes making us even more miserable. Though we heard mortar and heavy rifle fire to our right and left, no Japs came toward our position. At approximately four o'clock we heard noises of men approaching from our rear. With rapidly beating hearts we turned and challenged. Thankfully, it was a very young, nervous officer leading a patrol of twelve Gurkhas. I was very relieved to see them as they had rolls of barbed wire and had been sent to guard the paths we were watching. However, he was more relieved and pleased to see us. He told me he would prepare a defensive position but wanted my men as reinforcements.

We stayed with the Gurkhas and held the position until dawn broke. Then we were ordered back to our normal job as signals at HQ.

That afternoon the HQ came under heavy machine-gun and mortar-fire. Again my "rifle platoon" formed a defensive perimeter while the vehicles moved out to the road leading out of the rubber estate. I remember feeling very scared and wanting to run as I saw those vehicles pulling away, leaving us to face the on-coming Japanese. Thankfully, the threat to our front subsided, and as more Gurkhas came up, we rejoined our trucks and HQ on the move back.

We reached the main Jitra Road, which was under shell and mortar fire. The infantry was coming back looking very tired and dispirited, covered in mud and soaked to the skin.

As we turned off into a rubber estate, we were told to set up HQ and that lines would be required to the guns and infantry positions. Our Section Officer had gone off on a motorcycle to try and locate Cpls Lush, Lynch, and Moore, and Signalman Barber, who were laying field cable to the guns.

There was very heavy firing on our left and forward of us as we rushed to our respective jobs. A barrage of mortar bombs burst among us. It was obvious we had been spotted and the Japanese, instead of being miles away, were close at hand.

Through the trees, running away from the sound of the fighting, came Indian infantry, their eyes ablaze with fear. One red-faced, sweating, British officer was shouting and firing his revolver into the

11

air, trying to stop them and restore some sort of order. It was useless, and a frightening spectacle to us — the first time I was to see soldiers scared, running in full retreat.

Immediately my men turned to me for orders. "Let's get the hell out of here too", was the cry. But nobody moved, and we carried on with our tasks.

As we were going to experience many, many times in the next two months, the Japanese had infiltrated troops in behind our positions and quickly exploited the surprise this caused. We did not stay long as it was obvious the front was coming back fast; vehicles and guns were passing us on the main road back to Alor Star.

Again we were ordered to pull out, just as our Section Officer arrived with the missing linesmen. They all had alarming, but good luck, stories to tell of their cable laying trips.

In the growing dusk, we moved down the road to the bridge which had to be crossed to reach Alor Star. As we reached this area we were heartened to see defence lines of British infantry, Leicesters and Surreys, formed to hold the bridge-head. A troop of the Lanarkshires' 4.5" howitzers were already firing up the road. Here Lt Eustace, later killed in the last days of fighting at Singapore, uttered words which I was never to forget. As my truck drew near, he saw me and shouted, "Sergeant Edwards, do you know where you are heading for?" This would become one of the ironic catch-phrases in the years that followed.

I shouted, "No! We are only following the CO and HQ." Back he shouted, "You are withdrawing to Singapore with what's left of the llth Division! And there is bugger-all behind us all the way!" I was flabbergasted. I thought he was mad.

He went on, "I'll bet you never saw Bob Hope and Bing Crosby in the 'Road to Singapore'."

Again I shouted, "No".

"Well" he replied, "It won't be quite the same, but you will certainly see the road! And there isn't another unit behind us!"

12

We moved on into the dark, crossing the bridge being busily prepared for destruction by the Bombay Sappers and Miners. On to Alor Star airfield we went in the dark. It was raining, again, as we tried to scatter our vehicles on the airfield, avoiding piles of boxes which we found out later contained gelignite to blow up the run-way. The aerodrome and buildings had been evacuated two days previously. God knows what would have happened had any of the trucks from the regiment struck one of those boxes accidentally in the dark.

Mortar-bombs were still falling on the fringes of the air-field. Heavy machine-gun and rifle fire continued in the vicinity. Some of my section went to see what was left in the way of food in the bombed buildings and came back loaded with tins of food and cigarettes. They told me everything had been left: food on tables, clothing hanging in cupboards, training manuals, equipment. It was as if someone had waved a wand and the RAF had disappeared. The comments, from those of us who had experienced Dunkirk, where the absence of the RAF was very noticeable, were, "Rare as fucking fairies!"

"Disappeared like fucking fairies too!", came a Yorkshire voice in the dark, giving vent to all our feelings.

We had hardly settled the vehicle positions when fresh orders arrived that we were moving again, off the airfield as quickly as possible.

The increasing incoming fire made it obvious that the Japanese had followed the withdrawal from the Jitra line down the main road with their tanks and lorried infantry quicker than expected. They were also closing in on our flanks. In the dark and confusion some vehicles ran off the concrete airstrip and aprons on to the surrounding grass verges, sodden after days of heavy tropical rain. Our stores truck, with "Gibby" Gibson, went in and sank up to its axles, and to make things worse the engine refused to restart.

We were ordered to follow the other vehicles and leave a small group to try to restart or tow the stores truck. If they failed, they were to destroy the truck and jump in the last vehicle to get away. We did not know where we were going. It was now one o'clock. All vehicles and artillery seemed to be heading south. We were on "The Road to Singapore".

13

My Section Officer Martin Kepple kept a diary of the campaign and buried it at Changi when he was shipped out to Taiwan. It was recovered at the end of the war by another officer. His notes describe so well the chaos, confusion and changes in orders the night of that withdrawal.

"Mortor bombs landing around RHQ, infantry withdrawing around us ... much confusion. Set out to find cable parties, without avail ... fortunately they came in shortly afterwards."

"Saw CRA (Commander, Royal Artillery) on side of road ... he seemed quite calm, so assumed in spite of confusion everything was alright! Suddenly he jumped into his car and disappeared South!"

"All over the aerodrome were large cases of gelignite, obviously as land mines ... fortunately went in and out of these ... only discovered later what they were ... settled at aerodrome only to find vehicles on move again — stores truck stuck up to its axles ... went to find out what was happening ... at entrance John (John Brocklehurst, Adjutant, 155 Field Rgt RA) said we were going to Alor Star Village ... Mike Wilmer appeared and said, 'Do you know where you are going?' I replied, 'Not really.' He then said, 'Sungei Patani, Ipoh, Kuala Lumpur and Singapore!' He later gave me a serious answer that we had to go to Gurun."

The withdrawal from Jitra in the darkness, chaos and confusion, finding an aeordrome abandoned with no attempt made at demoltion or destruction of stores and runways was going to be the pattern of events down the Malayan Peninsula. The depleted brigades of infantry were going to have to fight and fall back, time and again. The Japanese quick follow-up down the main road at Jitra with tanks and lorried infantry coupled with thrusts around the undefended flanks and coast-line would be repeated time and again.

The Gurun line did not hold long. The Japanese proved expert and fast at rebuilding the blown bridges over the rivers. A longer withdrawal was ordered to give the diminishing, exhausted troops time to reorganize on a natural obstacle. My section found itself in a long valley between the hills below Ipoh at Kampar in tin-mining country. The artillery of the Lanarkshire Yeomanry were now supporting a Gurkha battalion, covering the hills to our left and right. The main force of

14

what was left of the division was holding the main road down to Tanjong Malim and Kuala Lumpur. We held Chenderriang from 22nd December to 5th January. We heard here that our llth Divisional Commander, Major General Murray-Lyon, had been replaced by Brigadier Paris. The llth was now only a composite brigade made up of the 6th and 15th Indian Infantry Brigades.

We held the position, the regiment performing well, giving covering fire and again shooting over open sights when the Japanese broke through. Our communications, though difficult to install, were good. We had to lay cable up and down a twisting, narrow road through the valley and into the position. We even managed to connect to the abandoned telephone exchange of a tin-mining company. One of our OP officers was delighted to get right through to Singapore on the field telephone! (A conversation I would have given anything to hear.)

Penang had by now been evacuated. We heard, with horror, that hundreds of launches and boats had been left undestroyed. The Japanese quickly made use of this armada and staged landings along the west coast. They were coming ashore in strength south of us at Telok Anson. This meant some troops had to be withdrawn, both from the Kampar position on the main road and from our front, to try to repel the landings.

The Japanese attacks increased each day. They had complete control of the air, continually bombing and machine-gunning anything that moved on the roads. My section's linesmen, L/Cpls Lynch and Lush, Smith, Moore and "Jimmy" Barber, worked like heroes, non-stop, to continually patrol and repair the telephone cable breaks. The despatch-riders also took tremendous risks, driving their motor-cycles up and down the valley roads. Every vehicle moved as fast as possible, always with a look-out to spot the low-flying Jap planes. They came in so low now, you could clearly see the grinning crews.

We spent a miserable Christmas in this valley. We were under constant fire, but morale was improving as the line was holding. As New Year approached, the Japanese pressure increased and all of the section except DR's wireless and exchange operators were pressed into service as linesmen or infantry guard pickets. On one dawn "stand to", in a lonely position in the hills, we were confronted with movement in the nearby jungle. The four of us prepared to fight for our lives, but were shocked to see a party of about 80 native pygmy "Sakai" tribesmen and their families on the move away from the fighting. They were armed with spears, blow-pipes, and parangs, and looked a fearsome sight. They were obviously as scared as we were, however. After one look at us with our rifles, they fled back into the hills.

The CO of the Lanarkshire Yeomanry, Lt Col Murdoch, and his regiment were mostly Scots who insisted that Hogmanay was to be celebrated, in action or not. He ordered all guns to open fire at 23:58 and again at 00:02. This "regimental gun fire" was ordered to celebrate the arrival of 1942. It was to be a disastrous year for the Regiment and the last year for its CO.

The regiment withdrew from this position after several more gallant actions, and went into a "hide" in another rubber estate near Slim River. This, evidently, was the next "line" to be held above Kuala Lumpur. What was left of 12th Brigade had come over from the east coast to fight in the centre with the remains of 28th Brigade of Gurkhas. We heard the Argylls with 12th Brigade had put up a tremendous fight and had several successful ambushes to their credit.

At Slim River another disaster befell the 11th Indian Division. The Japanese attacked, in early morning and in great strength, down the main road with heavy and light tank regiments, fresh infantry following in lorries and on foot. This was their big advantage. The Japanese always had fresh troops up-front. The Indian and British troops were always exhausted, fighting and falling back. Many, like my signal section, had not had a proper night's sleep since the start of the fighting. Moreover, since we knew we were retreating, our morale was low. The Japanese morale must have been terrific: forward, always forward.

The attack at 2:30 am was led by light tanks followed by the heavy tanks keeping in time with the infantry. The first troops, Punjabis and Argylls, met them with rifle-fire, gallantly trying to stop this juggernaut. The tanks were through them in no time, and then on to the Gurkhas who were resting, thinking they were in reserve. At 0800 hours, Lt Col Murdoch called our Section Officer, "The Japs have broken through ... We go into action at once!" The brave CO of the Lanarkshire Yeomanry set off up the road on the back of Bobbie Warwick's motorcycle, followed by our "Plum" Warner and the trucks of our advanced signal section.

16

Within a mile of crossing the Slim River Bridge, they met the Japanese tanks head-on. The Colonel, Warwick, "Plum" Warner, and the following trucks were caught by bursts of machine-gun and cannon fire. In the hail of fire, Craig managed to turn his line-truck around, and quickly headed back down the road, warning everyone following. The Lanarkshire Yeomanry reacted immediately. One 4.5" howitzer was stationed to meet the tanks, and, with a well-directed, point blank shot, stopped them. The gun immediately came under intense fire. Keen, the gun Sergeant, was instantly killed. Captain Brown, the officer in charge, lost his leg, but survived the war.

There is no doubt that if it had not been for this courageous act the whole Japanese advance over the bridge and on to Kuala Lumpur would have been far more successful. Those who were there said that if those tanks had had sufficient fuel, they could have kept right on going to Singapore. This was truer than it might appear as behind the Slim River Line was only the understrength 8th Australian Division. The only possible reinforcements were just arriving at Singapore after nearly three months at sea: the 53rd Brigade of the ill-fated 18th British Division.

The disaster at Slim River was followed by the evacuation of Kuala Lumpur. Despite desperate and gallant fighting by the Australians at Gemas and the Indians and British at Yong Peng and Ayer Hitam, the inexorable withdrawal to Singapore continued.

On that terrible day my signal section lost Cpl Harvey, L/Cpls Frank "Tug" Wilson, Tom Lynch and Bill Lush, and Signalmen Brook, Druett, Moore, Mason, Smith, Sheringham, Scott, Saunders, and Warner. All ten were posted "missing in action". Some turned up later after fantastic adventures, as prisoners in the notorious Pudu Jail in Kuala Lumpur. Others got sent back to Changi after capture. Sadly, too many were never seen again.

My signal section, now badly depleted after these losses at Slim River, had been reinforced by signallers from the signal section of the 137th Field Regiment. They also had suffered badly at Slim River and in the fighting on the coast, where thousands had been cut off by the rapid advances and infiltration of the Japanese Imperial Guard Division.

We got a rest, at last, in a "hide" about five miles from Johore Bahru.

17

We were sitting in a circle, checking equipment, charging batteries, and cleaning rifles, when suddenly a rifle went off.

One of my L/Cpl replacements from the 137 was sitting with his back against the wheel of a truck, cleaning his rifle. He had been in Dunkirk and was very depressed. For days he had been saying there was no hope for us. "We will never get away from Singapore like that", was his continual moan. He had shot himself clean through his boot, blood and bone spurting out. We applied a field-dressing and took him to the nearest Advance Dressing Station. A young, over-worked, harassed medical officer took one look. "Self-inflicted", he said. "Dump him in the corner. He can wait." We never saw him again, but I am convinced his hope that he would get away in a hospital ship was never realized.

We crossed the causeway that linked Malaya to Singapore. We believed, as we had been told so often, that Singapore was a fortress. Fields of fire would have been cleared, barbed wire put up, and trenches and strong points prepared. Just the opposite. Nothing had been done on the northern shore facing Malaya and the fast closing Japs.

The rear-guard came over that night. Appropriately, it consisted of what was left of the 9th and 11th Indian Divisions. The 28th Brigade of Gurkhas was down to a battalion of less than 700. One Indian Brigade could only muster 27 men. What was left of the Surreys and Leicesters, the "British" battalion, finally made it back. Last but not least, and doing it in their regimental tradition, a company of the 2nd Argyll and Sutherland Highlanders piped over to the strains of "Jenny's Black E'en" and "Hieland Laddie". They were watched impatiently by the squads of Royal Engineers who had been busy drilling and preparing holes to blow the massive causeway. At last, we thought as we crossed, there would be a barrier the Japs could not infiltrate around.

CHAPTER 3

"Fortress Singapore"

As Lt Eustace had so accurately predicted at Alor Star, we had seen "The Road to Singapore", travelling the whole 450 miles in just 53 days. We had lost Malaya to a brave, resourceful, clever enemy. The Japanese use of small launches captured at Penang to tow strings of barges filled with infantry meant they could land, remain hidden, and attack at will, wherever required. It was this uncertainty, never knowing whether they would appear at your rear, which was one of the most demoralizing factors to the British and Indian soldiers in that withdrawal down Malaysia.

We were tired, wet, dispirited and hungry as we took up positions on Singapore Island. The landing of the remainder of the 18th British Division brought only a little cheer to those of us who had survived. They had arrived in liners flying the American flag. Rumours that the Americans had landed troops spread rapidly. Another rumour which gained wide belief was that Roosevelt had promised, "I will blacken the sky over Singapore with American planes."

Well, the sky was soon to become black, but not with American planes. The huge oil tanks at the Naval Base and on the northern shore of the island were soon set on fire by bombs and shell fire. Great, black clouds hung over Singapore like a pall. Prophetic; Singapore was a dying city.

The next morning we were laying telephone cable to an OP on a hill overlooking the Straits of Johore. The causeway to the mainland was below us. We had heard rumours the causeway was to be blown that morning. This we wanted to see. Eventually, with a tremendous explosion and clouds of debris, the demolitions were fired. As the smoke cleared away we were shattered... dumbfounded by what we saw. There was only a pitifully small gap. We had hoped for a complete demolition or at least a wide breach. My cheerful, hardworking driver from South Wales, "E.J." Morris, summed up the feelings of thousands of the soldiers who had watched.

"Sarge", he said, "The fucking Japs will spit across that. It won't stop them an hour." He was right, of course.

On 8 February, after days of continual bombing and shelling, we suffered a heavy artillery bombardment and constant straffing by Jap Zeros. The Lanarkshire Yeomanry's RSM, "Left-Hand Down" Scullion, our old 1914-18 war veteran, described it as "just like the bombardment on the Somme". With a fearsome barrage of thousands of shells came the Japanese, landing over to our left on to the Australian positions.

In the few days prior to the landing, our OPs could clearly see the Japanese moving on the opposite bank of the straits. Our artillery gunners were frustrated. Orders had come down to conserve both 4.5" and 25 pounder shells. A limit was imposed on the number of shells per gun which could be used, depending on the target spotted. The attitude of our High Command seemed to be: conserve and prepare for a long siege. The regiment's officers were furious at this negative approach. It was infuriating to spot Jap parties and be told the guns could not engage. Worse was to be on the receiving end of the very accurate Japanese artillery.

Although our front near the causeway held, we were ordered back as the Japanese had broken through the Australians and were turning to cut the Bukit Timah Road back to the town.

The situation to us seemed incredible. The Japanese even had a spotter balloon floating over Johore on the opposite shore. There was not one plane left to shoot it down! At least some of the big coast defence guns, 9.2 and 15 inchers, had been turned to fire north. Their shells were dropping on to the Japanese massing opposite the causeway and those landing along the North-East coast.

We fell back again into positions around the reservoir area and found units of the 18th British Division, the Norfolks, Suffolks, Cambridgeshires, and Northumberland Fusiliers coming into action alongside the remnants of the 9th and 11th Indian Divisions. They had been rushed in from the northeast coast where our high command had expected the attack.

My men worked hard, as always, trying to ensure communications

20

between OPs, guns, and the infantry strong points. Trying to lay lines along the roads was a nightmare of avoiding low-flying planes, artillery and mortar fire. It was worse for our despatch-riders, soon nicknamed "the suicide squad."

Laying forward with Driver Craig, Lance Cpl Lynch, and "Jim" Barber, we were suddenly confronted with about 30 Australians running out of the trees to our right. They looked terrible, dirty and dishevelled, and were cursing and shouting at us.

"Get the fuck out of here. The Japs are right behind us! Every bastard officer has left us and gone for the boats!", they screamed as they ran past us.

I tried to stop a corporal, asking him, "Where are you running to?"

"To the docks you stupid fucking Pom," he cursed at me.

Jim Craig, infected by their panic, shouted, "Let's go Sarge. It's Slim River all over again. They've broken through!"

I sent him back down the monsoon drain, telling him to warn some military police we had seen about 400 yards down the road. L/Cpl Lynch, Barber, and I decided to wait and see what happened in the next five minutes. No Japanese infantry followed up. The men in that group were obviously a bunch of stragglers still coming back from the carnage of the Japanese landings two nights previously. We continued forward, found the OP, laid and connected the phone, and reported what we had seen.

I often wondered how far those Australians ran that evening, if they reached the docks, and how many men they managed to panic on the way back. This conduct disgusted me and shamed the vast majority of Australians who bravely did their duty opposing the landings. These cowards were typical of the small groups of undisciplined, leaderless Empire troops found running for the small boats at the docks in an attempt to escape this doomed island unlike the vast majority fighting and dying against overwhelming odds.

Our HQ position was now in a square of houses off the infamous Lavender Street, a well-known "red light" district. In the centre was what remained of a tennis-court, now criss-crossed with slit trenches, Our guns were to the rear of us, firing over our heads. We were under constant attack by low flying planes, shell-fire, and mortars, as well as rifle fire from nearby snipers or fifth columnists.

I remember we were delighted to see the arrival of a Bofors gun at the corner of the square. It was in constant action against Japanese planes, which were swooping low, machine-gunning anything that moved. The gun's regular "clunk, clunk, clunk" as it fired its clips of five rounds, stood out amidst the crescendo of noise. One moment remains in my memory, when a Jap plane had its tail shot clean off by this gun. We all stood up out of our slit trenches, waving our helmets and cheering. It was just like a football match when a goal is scored.

The next afternoon at 2 pm, Kepple called me and said, "We are packing in at 4."

Just those six words. We were dumbfounded and couldn't grasp just what he meant. For one mad second I thought the Japs must have had enough and were evacuating the island! Of course we knew we had been pushed back into the city, and that our ammunition and water supply were critical, but I couldn't understand why we had to surrender.

We waited for four o'clock. The fighting seemed to be subsiding in our sector. What would happen to us, we wondered. We couldn't expect much mercy from the Japs, especially our division after fighting them hard all the way down the peninsula.

Four o'clock came at last. We waited a few minutes, then stood up out of our holes. There was the scream of incoming mortar shells, and we flopped. They burst about eight yards in front of us, but luckily a truck between us and the bursts of shrapnel saved my group.

Then the whole front opened up, the firing fiercer than ever, our Lanarkshires' guns answering the incoming barrages.

Several of the regiment's officers said we wouldn't give up. There was talk of forming a square around our HQ with what was left of our artillery. I heard that although most of the officers were for it, the padre and medical officer were against it. They argued, "What use is it for us as a regiment to fight on, if the rest of the garrison is going to

22

surrender?"

Firing seemed to gradually diminish and at 7:30 pm stopped altogether. Even the sniping ceased. Some of our artillery gunners coming into our position told me they had used the last of their ammunition. Then, against orders from "the top", they blew their guns with the last shell. The silence seemed eerie after the mad racket of the past weeks, the situation somehow more frightening. We were warned that any move from our positions would be treated as desertion. We were to "stand to" with our rifles. If the Japs came down the road marching with an officer, we were to let them pass. If they came in skirmishing order, we were to fight on.

At 2:00 am Cpl Savage comes back from a journey as despatch rider. He tells me he knows where there is a boat that could hold at least ten of the section. We discuss our chances. "It will be too late once the Japs reach here," he argues. I say that we survivors of the signal section should stick together. Back and forth we debate our options and obligations. "Our orders are to hold the position," I say. Others argue that it's a soldier's duty to escape rather than be taken prisoner. At last, we decide. We stay together and wait for morning. We spent a peaceful night for the first time in nearly three months of fighting. But there was little sleep. Each man had his own fears of what tomorrow would bring.

Next morning we were ordered to pile our rifles as this, we were told, was part of the surrender terms. My section and all the Yeomanry men near us decided against it and deliberately disobeyed orders. We smashed our rifles, revolvers, wireless sets and equipment, and buried them in the slit-trenches. We all wondered what they would be thinking of us at home, what judgement they would pass on us. Would the truth of what had happened ever be told? Each of us thought of our families, wondering if we would ever see them again, and what the future would bring.

We formed burial parties for the dead, soldiers and civilians. While we were doing this the Japanese arrived, armed to the teeth with rifles and bayonets. They ignored us, but struck out at civilians standing nearby. One rushed at a group with his bayonet fixed. There was a scream as one Chinese obviously had not moved fast enough. Bodies were lying about, stinking, covered in flies, rotting in the sun. We hurried with the burials. "Basher" Gore, Haslam and Buttifant were burying two Chinese when suddenly a car loaded with Japanese pulled up alongside. They jumped out, laughing, obviously pissed from drinking. They pointed their tommy-guns and rifles at us, motioning at our wrist-watches. We looked over at RSM Scullion nearby.

He shouted, "You'd better hand them over boys, or take the consequences!"

Life is sweet so we handed them over. One Jap I noticed had about six already on his arm. They laughed, shouting with joy, just like children. They jumped back in the car and drove madly off, leaving us to our grisly task.

Then just across from us, another Jap appeared carrying a captured Bren gun over his shoulder. He was leading by a rope a group of about 30 or 40 Chinese, all with their hands tied. Several other Japs walked alongside, clubbing at the shuffling line. The Chinese waved and shouted something at us. As we watched, the last man in the line managed to slip his hands free and cleverly fell into a monsoon drain. The Japs, obviously more interested in what we were doing, didn't notice. He wriggled away to live another day. We had heard bursts of machine-gun fire all morning from the edge of a creek nearby. We knew this was where this group was heading.

"Look at the poor buggers", said Basher. "They'll be mown down by one of our own bloody Bren-guns!"

We discovered later that this was going on all over Singapore: executions by machine-gun, bayonet, and rifle-fire, as well as decapitation by swords. We felt powerless, waiting in fear to see what would happen to us.

We had not long to wait. Orders were given that all British troops would be concentrated in the Changi area, and that we were to march there right away. As we assembled, parties of Indian troops marched past us. Then came the Gurkhas, still marching proudly, heads high.

As we marched away from our last position off Lavender Street, I thought of the waste it had all been and the graves of our dead, symbols of the stupidity of war. We made our way, carrying what we could, in a long column along the roads leading to Changi. All along the way was the litter of the fighting: dead soldiers lying about, and bombed out trucks, still holding the charred corpses of men killed in the last days' fighting. It was horrible.

We talked of the surrender and who was to blame. Those of us who had fought from the border had realized Singapore was doomed. Who had ordered the 18th Division in to be sacrificed to the Japs? We passed a group of civilians who smiled at us, one Indian woman crying and wailing, "Poor British, poor British!" One wag in our column shouted, "Don't worry Ma," and started to sing "Here's to the next time." After a nightmare daylong march in the heat of the sun, we reached Changi. Exhausted, we fell to the floor in the area we were allocated.

A few days later, all the British troops left of the 9th and 11th Indian Divisions were ordered by the Japanese to move into the civilian jail at Changi. We had marched past this huge, fortress-like jail on our way to Changi. Now what was to happen to us? Why had they chosen us? We guessed it was because we had fought and delayed them all the way down Malaya. We were packed into the cells, assembly room and workshops, wherever there was space to lie down. The Chinese and Malay criminals had all been released in the last days of the fighting. The Japanese only posted guards at the main gates, and left us to make our own arrangements for space, cooking, water, etc.

The next day we knew why we had been selected. They marched us out on work parties to the beaches near Changi. There, lying grotesquely entangled in rolls of barbed-wire, were hundreds of bodies of Chinese men (civilians), women and even youngsters of all ages. Their hands were still bound together on long ropes. They had been herded together into the water, and then either shot or bayoneted. Our task was to cut them clear of the barbed-wire, drag them off the beaches, and bury them in mass graves that others of our party were digging. This gruesome task went on day after day for nearly three weeks. The smell was appalling since most of the bodies were decomposing in the hot sun. This was Singapore's first taste of the "Great Japanese East-Asia Co-prosperity Sphere", a phrase appearing on posters everywhere in the streets.

The killings went on for three weeks. When the last of the victims had been buried, we were ordered to return to the area we had originally

25

occupied. As we left the prison we saw, to our horror, lorries arriving bearing interned civilian men, women and children, the jail's new inmates.

We moved into hutments which had been badly damaged in the fighting. We set to and repaired the roofs and walls, and eventually all had cover. Now the Japanese had started to issue rice. This, and whatever tinned food could be found in this old barracks area, was all we would receive. Medical Officers started to give opinions on how long we could exist on the meagre rations of boiled rice. The effect on our stomachs, not used to an Asian diet, soon became apparent. Diarrhoea became prevalent and quickly turned to dysentery. The digging of more and deeper latrines became urgent, and this task was kept going night and day. Luckily, long earth augurs had been found in the Changi area and were quickly put into use.

The latrine areas were sited as far away as possible from the main camp. "Latrine guards" were put on duty to ensure that the men used them properly and replaced the covers to keep the flies down as much as possible.

At this regular gathering place, it became common to squat and exchange information. The camp rumours became known as "bore-holes". The latest "bore-hole" was always more optimistic than the last: "The Americans have landed at Penang", "There is a revolt by the Malayans up-country", "Train-loads of Japanese wounded have been seen coming across the causeway". Some of the "bore-holes" were so optimistic and so well believed that we heard that over in the Australian area some Aussies were climbing a water tower every night, optimistically looking for signs of a battle!

Changi PoW camp quickly became organized. The Roberts Barracks area was turned into a hospital. Water pipes and electric power were restored. Every effort was made to improve morale by organizing lectures, classes and concerts. The only depressing sight was the frequent funeral processions, a stretcher on two wheels with a small escort heading for the rapidly growing cemetery. Thankfully, none from my section were so honoured. I only had to visit the hospital, where Gibson, Earnshaw, Clack, Simpson, Hanford and Raymish were in with dysentery. It was crowded with patients. Every inch of every corridor, balcony, and room was covered with the sick or injured. The stench was overpowering, but the doctors and orderlies endured it, working themselves to a standstill. The dysentery epidemic was the first of the many diseases and illnesses we would suffer. Worse was to follow.

To go outside the wire of the compound on work or funeral parties, you had to have a pass, a white cloth armband with Japanese characters, worn by the officer in charge. The "outside" work parties were popular despite the labour involved: chopping down and rooting up trees, and loading them on trailers which were then pulled back to camp where the wood would be used for fuel. Each unit of PoWs had its "transport". These were the chassis and four wheels of old army trucks fitted with tow-ropes. The peril of going "outside" the wire in parties was that you were exposed to passing sentries and patrols.

By now the Japanese had succeeded in persuading many Indian soldiers to join the "Indian National Army". This was the brainchild of a Japanese Intelligence officer, Major Fujiwara Iwaichi. He recruited Indian officers to lead the army to support Subhas Chandra Bose, a long time advocate of Indian independence. Major Fujiwara had formed a unit of Intelligence officers (a *Kosaku*) operating in Thailand prior to the invasion. He quickly got to work in northern Malaya after the battle of Jitra on the captured Indian troops. The propaganda was aimed at getting Indian soldiers to join greater Nippon in "liberating" India to the "Great East Asia Co-prosperity Sphere".

Major Fujiwara, in explaining his goals in this ideological warfare, briefed his own unit as follows:

Keeping in mind His Majesty's concern for benevolence that extends not only to our troops but also to enemy soldiers, we must impress His concern about indigenous people and the enemy, especially prisoners of war, and build by inducing them to co-operate with us in building the foundation for a new friendship and peace out of the ashes of war.

We have to spread the Imperial benevolence and our friendly message to the enemy until we make them our allies. The strength of the Japanese Army should not be dissipated as we fight but it should be consolidated by gaining the support of native people and friends from the enemy camp. We must impress on them that

27

this war is a war of righteousness aimed at freeing indigenous people and PoWs and helping them achieve their national aspirations and happiness.

After the War Major Fujiwara became Lt General Fujiwara Iwaichi in the Japanese Self Defence Force!

Major Fujiwara recalls in his memoirs that he met a Sikh officer, Captain Mohan Singh, with the first Indian troops to surrender after Jitra. Captain Singh became the founder of the Indian National Army (INA). After the fall of Singapore, the INA grew in strength. Tremendous pressure was put on Indian officers, NCOs, and men to join the INA instead of becoming PoWs.

Armed with British rifles and in British uniforms, but with Japanese armbands, they were used to guard the gates and perimeter wire, and patrol the roads in the Changi area. The majority appeared to be Sikhs. We knew that other Sikhs, as well as Jats, Dogras, Rajputs, Mahrattas, Pathans, Punjabis and, of course, Gurkhas, had remained loyal rather than accept the manifest advantages of joining the INA. The renegade Indian recruits quickly seemed to want to show their new masters how they could degrade the British. The slightest hesitation in bowing in salute to them or obeying their orders meant a slap across the face, a punch, or sometimes the boot or rifle butt.

It was on a working party to collect timber that I experienced my first "bashing". Our young officer in charge had not saluted and called us to attention quick enough. He got a fist in his face and then the boot. We were all lined up and slapped. A big Sikh was obviously enjoying himself and the slap he gave me knocked me sideways. My cheek burnt, but I knew my pride was hurt far worse. That face slapping was the first of a long line of similar incidents I was to receive in the next three years. We were going to "lose face" even more.

Just as life seemed to be a little more pleasant, with lectures or concert parties at night, we received orders to march the next morning. It was now May, and we had been prisoners for three months. Already there were signs of deficiency diseases. The first to hit was a form of scrotum rash, a mass of red and white pimples around the groin. It was loathsome, extremely painful, itchy, and spread rapidly. Not knowing what it was, we christened it "Changi Balls". The name changed, depending on the camp: "Bukit Timah Balls", "Java Balls", or "Kranji Balls". There was no cure except an increase in vitamins in our diet. It caused real misery as you had to march or walk bow-legged.

We set out that morning in the hot sun and marched past the Changi jail. Despite the slaps, kicks, and rifle butts of the Jap and Sikh guards running up and down the column, we waved and shouted to the pitiful white arms which waved at us through the barred windows.

It was a nightmare of a march. All day the pitiless sun beat down on the concrete road. My Cpl Len Savage had a nasty leg ulcer which grew from about half-inch across to a suppurating mass by the time we reached the old Kranji wireless station near the Johore Causeway.

We were told that next day, and every day, we would be required to march to Bukit Timah hill for road work. The Japanese had decided to build a road up the hill and a memorial on top, commemorating their victory! We paraded daily at 6:30 am after an unpalatable meal of rice. We christened it "cargo rice" because it was brownish in colour and appeared to come from the sweepings in the rice warehouses at the docks.

The march from Kranji to Bukit Timah hill took us past a PoW camp for Indian soldiers who had not joined the INA. The first morning, through the wire, we could clearly see many Pathans, Dogras, Gurkhas, and Mahrattas, all from regiments who had fought with us so courageously down Malaya. It became a ritual to try and smarten our step by singing and shouting "Teekai Johnnie" as we passed each morning and night. It was great to see those Indians springing to attention and saluting as we passed.

Road making was heavy work. We were organized in work parties under very junior Japanese NCOs, hardly ever seeing an officer. The sergeants or *Gunsos* seemed to wield immense power wherever we went as PoWs. However, as the work force was so large, and the number of Japanese supervising the work limited, we soon found plenty of opportunities to rest or sabotage when not being watched. Usually there were about 200 men working with chunkels and rattan baskets. The earth was dug by the hoe-like chunkel, pulled into a basket, and then carried and dumped where required. We quickly organized the parties with look-outs at either end of the group to keep watch on the supervisors. As soon as the Jap turned his back or walked away, work would cease. On the old Army cry for "Tombola" or "House", of "Eyes down, first number", all would immediately start again, the cry meaning that the Jap had turned.

Work was slow until the Japs started a system of marking off areas to complete before a rest period would be given, or offering a promise of an early return to camp as a reward. However, we quickly discovered that each day the section of work required was made a little longer. The Japs, of course, became more annoyed with the slowness of the work, and many beatings were given. All the supervisors were armed with bamboo poles or handles from tools, and lashed out at the slightest pretext. One particular incident I recall seeing was a small Japanese lining up a group of prisoners for a "bashing", but realizing they were too tall for him to reach. He forced them to stand in a ditch in order to reach their faces with his fists.

We quickly found it was fatal either to show by your actions that you despised them for hitting you, or to avoid their blows by shielding or ducking. Those who did suffered worse. Some were tied cruelly with wire to the trees alongside, then beaten and left for hours in the sun. We found it was also fatal to fall to the ground during a beating. Boots quickly came in to your ribs. The only slightly successful tactic was to try and "take it", putting your feet apart, arms to your sides, and answering *Hai* (Yes) to any shout.

The new road gradually progressed to an area within 20 yards of the main road. This had to be built up with mountains of earth dumped from thousands of baskets. Then huge mounds of stone flints were brought by lorries and dumped on the main road. We would form into a long "crocodile" of prisoners, and, two to each basket, carry the flints to the top and dump them on the surface.

It was like a scene out of some Biblical film of the building of the pyramids. On one side of the hill was the long trail of men carrying the baskets with flints. On the other side was a queue making their way down. Again, it was impossible with the thousands of men involved for the Jap sentries to watch everywhere. As our own people were filling the baskets, we could get away with a light load. Then, on the way back down, we would dawdle as much as possible. It became a point of honour between my partner, "Basher" Gore, and myself to carry as little as possible. We were even daring enough, when the Jap's back was turned, to sometimes carry away only five stones, dribble them out on the way up, and join the downward queue, thereby not even tipping one on the road surface!

Anything like this gave us a tremendous morale boost, well worth the effort of the constant watching and the risk of a bashing if caught. And it broke up the endless hours of boring slave labour.

Rumours continually trickled through. Any item was seized on, dissected, discussed, and argued about. One morning, however, we had real news. A car stopped on the main road near the huge mound of flints. The driver, obviously an English internee, got out and lifted the bonnet, scratching his head. The car contained Japanese officers. The driver was a former Public Works Water Engineer helping to restore the island's water supply. He fiddled with the engine and called to one of our officers for help. They appeared to be deeply engrossed, discussing the problem. Eventually, after a few minutes, the car started, and the English internee drove off with a shout of "Good luck" and a thumbs-up sign.

In about a minute the news had reached the group I was working with about a quarter of a mile away: there had been an American victory in a big naval battle in the Coral Sea. Such news would be passed, man to man, down the line until the thousands of men in the camp all knew. It was a tremendous uplift. News was like life-blood to a prisoner. Any and every possible source was tried.

About this time, the road was reaching completion. A steam-roller arrived one morning to flatten out the surface of loose flints and earth. There was consternation and then an uproar as the first steam-roller drove out onto the new road. It started to sink before it had moved ten yards. Down it went to its hubs in the loosely packed earth and small flints. We just howled with laughter. This only added to the temper of the Japanese supervisors who turned on us with rifles and staves. We were beaten, ordered into huge groups, and then given ropes to pull the roller out. Eventually, with the assistance of the second roller and a couple of trucks, the job was done. But the road surface was ruined.

To our amazement, we were not called out for road work for two days. The rice ration was cut, but we were glad of the rest.

When work started again, we found a complete change of Japanese supervisors. These were the Japanese engineer battalion who had fought down Malaya, rebuilding the blown bridges so quickly. Work parties were re-organized, the food improved, vegetables were brought in, the bashing stopped, and work proceeded in a far more organized manner.

Among the engineers were several who could speak some English. One was fluent, with a strong American accent. He told us he had been born in the USA, but was in Japan in 1940 and had been conscripted. Many amusing incidents occurred through "the Brooklyn Kid's" (as he was nicknamed) contacts with the prisoners. One day he was escorting a party of prisoners in a truck going into the city for stores. The prisoners were in the back, while the "Kid" sat alongside the driver in front. The prisoners were discussing the prospects of scrounging some food when the truck stopped. These men had no knowledge of their escort's linguistic ability.

One said, "I wonder if this little yellow bastard in charge today will stop somewhere for a woman; while he is in there we can nip off and find some grub."

Later the truck stopped. The "Kid" appeared around the back of the tail-board and drawled to the stunned prisoners, "Say you guys, this little yellow bastard has pulled up, but not for a woman. Now you get to hell out and find some food!"

Two days later, my pal in 155th Field Artillery, Sgt. Johnnie Ford, told me an officer was taking a small party to do fatigues in a drawing office for this Engineer Unit and asked would I like to volunteer. Several of us jumped at the opportunity of a change of scenery and an escape from the drudgery of the road work. We were taken to an old colonial house near the Singapore Golf Course and McCritchie Reservoir, where the Japanese had decided to erect a Shinto Shrine and bridge as a memorial to their dead and the conquest. It was to be called the Shonan Shrine.

When we arrived we found, to our surprise, that the garages of the house and ground floor rooms were stacked full of bags of cement. Our first job was to move the whole lot out and clean the rooms and garage. Every bag had to be man handled about 200 yards to a storage hut. We cursed our luck and repeated the old army phrase, "Never volunteer!"

However, once this job was completed, the next three weeks were like a dream and proved to be the best period I ever spent as a prisoner. The NCOs in charge of our group were surveyors, engineers, or draughtsmen, and did not shout and scream or bash. They gave their orders, and let us organize the daily work. At night they would come amongst us, give us their unwanted rations, sometimes the odd cigarette, watch us at our card-games, and try to exchange English phrases for Japanese. We gave them all nicknames. One, a very short, amiable draughtsman, was fascinated by the keeping of the score in "Solo Whist", especially the continued reference to "plus" and "minus". He heard these words so often, everything became "plus" or "minus" to him. As he was shorter than the rest, we christened him "Minus". Even when it was explained, he took no offence, but walked around pointing to himself saying *"Minus San Jotoh"* (Mr. Minus, very good).

"Minus" loved to look at snapshots of wives or children of prisoners, and borrowed some to return the next day with very well drawn likenesses. I discovered later from G.P. Adams, who wrote "No Time For Geishas", that their Commander was also a good man. G.P. Adams described their commander, Colonel Yasuji Tamura of the 5th Engineer Regt, 25th Army Division, as a real officer and gentleman — praise indeed from a Japanese PoW! He also commented on the difference in attitude from this unit to other Japanese units we were to meet. However, that brief period of three weeks was going to be like an oasis in a harsh desert. It was well we knew nothing of our future.

Soon we were ordered back to Changi camp. We had heard that large parties had been leaving for an unknown destination, "up-country" in Thailand, while others were leaving the docks in ships. Only two days after settling in the old hutments at Changi, a new Japanese Commandant took over the PoW camps, and we had to parade for an address. His name was Lt General Fukuei Shimpei. He harangued us through an interpreter. I can only recall one phrase, "We will treat you well (a long pause) I think." One day later, we were to learn what he meant by "I think". We were assembled by our own commanding officers and told that he had ordered that every man must sign a parole document which would bind them on their promise not to make any attempt to escape. If we did not sign these "no escape" forms, we would be subjected to "measures of severity". These were not enlarged upon but we, who had buried the thousands of civilians massacred and seen the daily display of severed heads on the bridges in Singapore City, had a fair idea of what he meant.

Our Senior Officer gave us our option. "Any officer or man wishing to sign, take one pace forward."

Not a man moved. Next morning the first blow struck. All PoWs in the Changi area, except the wounded and hospital cases in Roberts Barrack area, were ordered to be in Selerang Barracks square area by 1300 hours. We took all we could carry or load on our trailers: cooking equipment, wood, and all the rations we could move. It was a fantastic sight. Thousands of men laden down, pushing or pulling the trailers and water-carts. Anything that had wheels was pressed into use.

The square at Selerang was bounded on each side by two barrack blocks, and surrounded by a monsoon drain. In peace-time the whole area had been the home of the Gordon Highlanders, roughly 800 strong. Into the square and surrounding buildings were crammed more than 17,000 men. On the other side of the monsoon drain were INA Sikh guards supported by Japanese guards every 50 yards with machine-guns. We were warned that anyone crossing the drain would be shot. The brutal treatment meted out to those even approaching the edge of the drain was enough to convince us that they meant it. There was only one water-tap. It was amazing how each unit settled on to its allocated area of the square. We found ourselves on the roof of one of the blocks, and immediately tried to erect some form of cover from the sun and rain. The command structure was marvellous; discipline in each unit held. An area was cleared in the concrete square to dig latrines. Other areas were set aside for the medics to work on the sick. We were warned to use only the latrine area being dug. Everyone worked in relays, digging like mad into the concrete. Huge queues of men formed to use these latrines, shepherded by the MPs amongst us. Although the work of digging the pits went on night and day, each man could only have a few seconds to use the area.

Somehow fires were lit, food organized, and the meagre ration of water boiled and issued. Conditions were terrible. You could barely move, let alone sit. But morale was tremendous. That first night singing broke out, and it was taken up all around the square despite the appalling stench, heat, and hunger.

Next day all the senior officers left were ordered to Betin Kusa beach at Changi to witness the execution of four men caught outside the area. The Japanese claimed they were attempting to escape. The four were an Australian, Cpl Brevington, and three British privates, Fletcher, Gale, and Waters. They were shot in a horribly bungled execution by a Sikh firing party. The Japanese warned our officers that this was an example of what would happen to all of us, if we did not sign.

This action, however, seemed to stiffen everyone's resolve, and the "measures of severity" continued for three days. On the third night, after the threat by the Japanese that they would move the 5,000 wounded and hospital cases in with us, urgent meetings took place.

Conditions were now becoming impossible. The urine and excreta pits were constantly filling, flies were everywhere, dysentery and contagious diseases were increasing, and the first deaths had occurred. Lt Colonel Holmes of the Manchester Regt, now the senior British officer, finally signed on behalf of us all.

In signing he stated, "I am doing this under duress and on the direct order of the Imperial Japanese Army, to save further loss of life and suffering."

The word passed around in the dark was, "It means nothing, just another scrap of paper!"

That night the square again erupted in all the old army songs, ending with "Land of Hope and Glory". The cry was, "Sing up boys, sing louder so the women and kids in the jail can hear us!"

We did. The so called "Selerang Incident", or "Black Hole of Changi" as it was called by those who were there, ended the next day at 1:00 pm. Lt General Fukuei Shimpei had won the day, saving his and his army's precious face. Year later he was shot by a firing squad after a war crimes trial which I had the pleasure of attending and giving evidence to.

35

I made a rough drawing on the spot and carried it through many searches, eventually concealing it in a piece of bamboo which I buried. I dug it up after the war and it was a useful piece of evidence. In 1976 I returned to the same spot on that roof and gave a copy of the drawing to an officer of the Singapore Defence Force who escorted me that day. It now hangs in the Officers' Mess at Selerang Barracks. After the war I discovered that a hidden camera had also recorded that day, and these faded prints are proudly displayed in the barracks. Below them is a brief description of what happened as a reminder of the courage and fortitude of the men who were executed and incarcerated at Selerang in 1942.

Large parties of prisoners were now leaving the Changi area weekly. Our turn was bound to come. One day, out of the blue, a consignment of supplies arrived through the South African Red Cross. We were told it had arrived at Singapore on a ship bringing Japanese diplomats being exchanged from Lorenco Marques. We had tinned milk, cocoa, and Marmite. Some men were lucky enough to obtain khaki South African bush hats. The Marmite, because of its great value in helping with the now thousands of serious malnutrition cases, went to the hospital at Roberts Barracks.

Some Marmite, however, came back to working parties. My group was told one day that all men with "Changi" or "Bukit Timah Balls" would get one dose of Marmite. We sufferers formed a queue before the MO (Medical Officer), who was issuing a small amount with a spoon on to the outstretched finger or tongue. The MO exploded as one man, instead of eating the Marmite, rubbed it all over his scrotum like an ointment! Although these small doses had little effect in my group, I heard that the Vitamin B-rich Marmite saved lives up at the hospital.

In 1948 I was in hospital still being treated for chronic amoebic dysentery and various other nutrition deficiencies, and was given Marmite in my diet. I told this story to the ward sister, who phoned the local Marmite representative. He appeared at my bedside a few days later with a box-full of bottles. He said the pity was that he dare not use the story in an advertisement as no newspaper would print it! Today, I still eat Marmite and recommend it to anyone recuperating from illness!

Our few days interlude of better rations and some mugs of cocoa with tinned milk ended all too quickly.

Then we were told we were to be part of a group of 1,000 men to be sent to Japan for "light work". The instructions were that even the unfit in our group would go in order to bring the number up to the magic 1,000. So the words "light work" appeared true. The group was made up of the 80th (Anti Tank) Regiment RA, 155th Field Regiment (Lanarkshire Yeomanry), RA, 5th Field Regiment, RA, some 11th Indian Division Signals, and other RAOC and RAMC officers and men. My group was split up, but I took with me my Lance Sgt, "Basher" Gore, Cpl Savage, Lance Cpl Davies, and Signalmen Jim Barber, Frank Buttifant, Coates, "Plonka" Clack, Leslie Davis, Gill, Gilboy, Gibson, Haslam, Hanford, Kappelhoff, E.J. Morris, Sheldrick and George Smith. My section had become really scattered. Counting Lt Kepple, the Section Officer, there were now only 18 of us left out of the original 37 who had left Scotland.

On orders of the Japanese, we were paraded for a glass rod anus test. This was grotesquely funny to watch, but painful and humiliating to take part in! The 1,000 of us had to line up, drop our trousers, and bend down while white-coated and masked Japanese went through the charade of carrying out this primitive medical test. Obviously, it meant nothing to them as no records appeared to be kept. They, like us, were obeying orders!

With what we could carry, we were paraded for what we thought was the long march from the Changi area to the Singapore Docks. Again came a surprise: a convoy of trucks. We were packed in like sardines, but set off to the cheers and farewells of our comrades remaining. Despite the crowding and uncertainties of the future, we were in high spirits. As the convoy was halted near the prison, we burst into song and sang our hearts out, refrains of "There'll always be an England" and "The Yanks are coming!" pouring out for the benefit of the internees, whose thin arms waved to us through the prison cell bars.

On arrival at the docks, we were pushed into lines to file on to a ship. Inside we were herded into big steam baths where we were sprayed and hosed down. Then off the ship we filed to sit down on the filthy dockside and dry off in the sun. Soon we were sweating and as dirty

37

as ever. Obviously someone was obeying orders. Just then, the skies opened and down came the torrential monsoon rain. We huddled together, miserably trying to make what shelter we could with our bundles and blankets.

At last, to the accompaniment of the usual barked orders, screeches, curses and rifle butts, we were shepherded in single file onto our transport. It looked a real rusty old tramp, the sides patched in several places. As we were pushed and stumbled past the deck house, we saw a plate giving her name, "England Maru". It also said that she had been built on Clydeside in 1905! The 1,100 of us were split up between four holds. We were pushed down ladders through decks containing Japanese soldiers until we reached the bottom of the hold. Our hold was about 50 feet square with a very low ceiling dropping to only four feet around the edges. Ours was typical of the other three, filthy and verminous, with cockroaches and bugs everywhere. The walls and floor had the remains of dried horse or mule excreta, obviously from the last cargo. It was dark, the only light coming from two very dim light bulbs, supplemented by sunlight filtering down from the open hatch above during the day. Into this space they crammed 256 of us. Those first in were lucky and found some straw mats under the hatches. My section ended up in the square below the hatch, open to the pouring rain. This area was a mess of wet mud and filth.

CHAPTER 4

"Clydeside Built"

The boat sailed very soon, but only to move out to midstream and anchor. We sweated and tried to sort out some space for each man. The latrines were on deck, consisting of a wooden shack slung out over the sea. You climbed out and squatted. This was terrible as diarrhoea was rife. The sentries insisted on only one man going out at a time and we had to queue up the ladders to reach the deck.

Eventually some food appeared, and again the arrangements were chaotic. Two buckets were lowered down to us on ropes, one small bucket of rice and approximately two quarts of a watery vegetable soup. This, twice a day, would be our ration for 40 men for the length of the voyage. Thank God we had some tins of meat saved from the South African Red Cross. We were now told to ration this carefully amongst syndicates of twelve men.

We lay in the harbour for three days, the sun beating down and making the sides of the hold unbearably hot. Conditions inside were like a pressure cooker. Everyone sweated as we sat or stood close to each other, dressed only in shorts. As soon as the rain poured down, we in the centre of the hold would be jostled as those in the side deck spaces tried to bath in the rain or catch the drops in containers. The only drinking water supplied was lowered in buckets. It tasted like warm, brackish, boiler water with a flavour of salt. It seemed to make you more thirsty. The rain water tasted like wine by comparison.

The medical officers accompanying our party were Major B.M. Wheeler, a Canadian of the Indian Medical Service, Capt Peter Seed, attached to the 155th Field Regt RA, and Captain Blair, attached to 5th Field Regt, RA. They had arranged for Seed to look after Nos. 1 and 2 holds, Blair No.3, and Wheeler No. 4.

Before the ship got underway three days later dysentery broke out,

39

and everyone was covered in sweat rashes. This was inevitable with the humidity high, our clothing constantly soaked from sweating, unwashed bodies, and the temperature in the holds constantly between 95° and 100°F.

The only respite was two short periods on deck, one in the morning and one in the afternoon, or the regular climbs up the ladder to the revolting latrines. The troughs by now were piled high with faeces and completely saturated with urine from users. Despite our fears of torpedoes from American submarines we prayed for the ship to sail, hoping the conditions would improve with sea breezes.

The Japanese soldiers above us had some ventilators rigged, which blew what breeze there was into their sections. Some of them, by their eyes, seemed sympathetic at our plight. One of them attempted conversation, and my little knowledge of Japanese, picked up from "Minus" at the "Shonan Shrine" work, came in very useful. As I passed one soldier, back and forth to the "chicken coop" (our nickname for the the wooden deck latrines), I enlarged my vocabulary. He told me we were headed for Japan, which was winning the war "everywhere". However, after several days, he added, "Americans now in North Africa." He brought us back firmly to reality as he indicated that American submarines were active between Singapore and Japan.

At last we sailed. Our hopes of being redistributed around the ship before sailing were dashed, however, as we remained confined in our holds.

On deck that night, we counted five ships in our convoy with what looked like a destroyer in the lead. We were obviously sailing north, up the Malayan coastline. Sailing out of Singapore there was an alarm as a mine went up, but otherwise all seemed peaceful, the sea placid under a copper-coloured sky.

The many Scottish lads in the Yeomanry kept up our spirits by saying "Dinna worry, she's Clydeside built. She'll stay afloat". However, we didn't dare think what would happen if a torpedo tore into her side. With all her patches of rust, she would disintegrate, drowning us like rats in a trap.

A few days later we dropped anchor off Saigon and were allowed on deck to be hosed-down like cattle, queuing up before laughing Japs who directed the jets of seawater over us. While there we saw passing nearby a patrol boat with Frenchmen in white uniforms, and the French tricolour floating over its stern. It gave us a lift to see these free Europeans, and the flag of our allies, but when we tried to shout and wave the Japs quickly bashed and pushed us below into the tomb-like hold. The Japanese would not allow us to sing, and we spent our time talking on every subject under the sun, or playing cards with packs made by those who loved this wonderful time consumer.

There were two padres on board, and eventually the Senior Officer, Lt Col E.W. F. Jephson, 5th Field Regt, RA, arranged for one or the other to visit each hold every night. The sight of the padre standing in the middle of that stinking crowded hold, praying for deliverance, was an inspiration, our faith our only solace.

As we left Port St Jacques, Saigon, conditions got worse. The wind rose and the temperature dropped, but the relief from the heat was spoilt by the twisting, bucking, and turning of the ship as we hit heavy seas. To add to the dysentery cases, we now had suspected cases of diphtheria and typhoid. When our MOs told the Japs about the typhoid, they at last became interested. They allowed the worst of the dysentery sufferers to be carried up on deck to lie nearer the "chicken coop". This saved them the long drag up the ladders, but left them exposed to the worsening weather. The rain came in torrents, but it was cooler than in the south. As the waves got higher, spray swept the decks, pouring down our hatch. The conditions in our hold now resembled a Hogarth painting: a nightmare mass of dirty, unshaven, soaked men, blankets, and bundles. Everyone prayed the old rust-bucket would stay afloat. We were alarmed to see leaks around some of the old plates. Even the most optimistic had ceased to make jokes about "Clydeside workmanship".

The first death occurred the next night. He was unceremoniously buried over the side, at least out of his suffering. Others were dying. Major Ben Wheeler, one of our medical officers, whom I was to come to know much better later in captivity, kept a secret diary. He wrote about one dying patient:

At present the two padres, like vultures, are hovering around him. The RC chap seems well in the lead, more persistent or a

41

better product to put over. I don't know which. Perhaps it helps him, I don't know. Personally, I wouldn't want it.

At long last, we anchored off Taiwan (sometimes called Formosa), and my friendly little Jap soldier told me we had reached a port in the south of the island. While we talked that morning, his comrade attracted his attention, and I was able to steal his army plastic soap container, quickly sliding it into the pocket of my tattered shorts. It contained a small piece of precious soap. I later buried the container because it had Japanese Army markings. If it had been discovered in searches, it would have been good for a bashing or worse. In February 1946, on my return to Taiwan to give evidence and assist in the apprehension of Japanese war criminals, I dug up the container. It is still a treasured reminder of those terrible days.

Then Japanese medical staff came on the ship in white coats and masks. We were herded on deck and farcically sprayed with some disinfectant. Again we were subjected to the indignity of the glass rod stuck up our bottoms.

We sailed in the afternoon, again heading north up the coast, and that night another man died. He was buried at sea also, but not until later. Major Wheeler recorded:

A nightmare operation with the Japanese Cpl in charge insisting that disinfectant be thrown everywhere. This led to words with Lt Col Jephson, who was bashed and dragged off with a rope-halter around his neck, over the corpse waiting to be dumped in the sea. It was done in the most brutal manner, and only by the Grace of God were the men handling the body restrained from falling on the Cpl.

We in our hold knew nothing of the events on deck. In my little group of Cpl Len Savage, Les Davis, Frank Buttifant, Frank Haslam, George Smith, and myself, we were worrying about and nursing Johnnie Griffiths. He looked ghastly, his throat swelling. Moreover he had a high fever. Our MO, Captain Seed, knew what it was, but did not tell us — diphtheria. That was to be a terrible nightmare of a night, as we headed north into the wind and churning seas. Thankfully it was our last one on the hell ship "England Maru". I was worried also about "Basher" Gore, who had been up and down those cursed ladders to the "chicken coop" so many times with dysentery. He was very weak.

Again the ominous "13" struck. Major Wheeler wrote in his diary in November, 1942:

<u>Friday 13th</u>.

> We are on the way again and disembark tomorrow morning.
> The typhoid died last night — again we buried him at sea — only
> one now who may not make this night but I am hoping and trying
> — nothing could be worse than this has been — Netty (his wife),
> I begin to wonder for the first time if I will ever see you again.

Early next morning we docked at the north Taiwan port of Keelung. There was a cold and steady drizzle of rain coming down from the low clouds hanging on the hills around the harbour. We were pushed into a line and, with our soaking bundles, we stumbled down the gangplank. At least, we thought, we had reached land safely. At the bottom of the gangway were a squad of Japanese armed with disinfectant sprays and wearing the inevitable face-masks and white coats. We were pushed, punched, and butted to turn around while we were sprayed from head to toe. Quickly we were formed up in lines of six and marched off the dockside into what appeared to be a town square.

Here, it seemed, the whole population had been turned out to see the spectacle of the British prisoners which the all-conquering Imperial Japanese Army had taken at Singapore in their conquest of Malaya. There were huge groups of schoolchildren in uniforms, and hordes of what appeared to be police. Even the townspeople seemed to be dressed in the same sort of uniform clothing, including a peaked cap. The din of the chattering, shouting crowd echoed around us. The soldiers poked and shoved at us with their rifles until we were halted in the middle of the square. We looked a sad spectacle, shivering in tropical shirts and shorts, filthy, unshaven, many supporting comrades who could barely walk after the ordeal of that voyage.

We were lined up, checked, counted, and counted again by an endless stream of Japanese NCOs and officers. They counted us so many times I lost track. Some men just sat down in their exhaustion but, to the seeming delight of the huge crowd, the guards quickly moved in and kicked them to their feet. Then we were divided. It appeared the 5th

Field Regt, RA, and 11th Indian Divisional Signals were to be one group. The 80th Anti-Tank Regt, RA, and 155th Field Regt, RA, were to be the other. My section, attached to the 155th, moved off with them. We were marched to the railway station and boarded train-carriages, all with wooden shutters closed down tight. At least there were wooden seats inside, and we collapsed on them, relieved to be away from that jeering crowd and inside, out of the incessant drizzle. Those of us who had a dry change of shirt in our packs quickly stripped, dried ourselves as best we could, and changed.

After about an hour and a half we stopped at a small station called "Zeho". Here, again, outside the station were assembled thousands of the local population and excited, yelling, schoolchildren. We were lined up, counted, and then, mercifully, on the cry of *"Yasumay"*, allowed to sit where we were on our bundles. One small bread-bun was distributed to each man. This was like manna from heaven. I immediately thought of the miracle of the five barley loaves and two small fishes in St John, and prayed, with thanks, for this miracle. We had had nothing to eat or drink all day, and quickly munched down these dry buns. Our spirits rose, as we hoped that this was a sign that our luck was changing and our treatment would improve. How wrong we were!

We were formed into columns of six to "march to new campu", according to the interpreter. He was a very short, fat, pleasant-faced Japanese, we estimated in his 60s, and resembled in stature and size the cartoon figure "Pop" in the "Daily Sketch". This, of course, he was immediately christened.

Poor Johnnie Griffiths, his throat swollen, looked ghastly. Len Savage and I decided to get to the front of the column with him, in the hope that he would be seen and not forced to march. We split his kit, and helped him between us. Others were doing the same. Les Davis, Buttifant, and Haslam were assisting Dennis Hanford and "Basher" Gore.

What was ahead, we knew not. The road we were on was a rough mountain road, leading into rain-clouded hills. It wound up and up for nearly eight miles. Fortunately, at the beginning we knew nothing of the march ahead. The cold rain seemed to increase as we staggered up the road. To add to our misery our guards, now ably abetted by black-uniformed police with bamboo poles, seemed to become more angry. Here we first heard the cries in Japanese which were to blast our ears for the rest of our years of captivity:

Bakeroo!	Stupid!
Damme — Damme!	Foolish idiot!
Hyaku! Hyaku!	Hurry up!
Koora!	Hey, you there!
Nani Suru Ka?	What are you doing?

These words would be screamed at us if we straggled out of line or stopped to relieve ourselves. The diarrhoea and dysentery cases were hit while they squatted in the grass and bushes flanking the road.

The road passed through small villages of black wooden houses, which appeared to be fed with water by long bamboo poles. In every village and hamlet were groups of civilians watching us, but now we could tell from their eyes and expressions that they pitied us. Johnnie Griffiths could not speak any more, but stumbled on between Len and I to the first halt. We sank to the road exhausted.

After what seemed another endless nightmare, we reached the top of the hill and could see, down in the distance, the sea and a cluster of buildings. This was our destination, Kinkaseki. The appearance of many of the civilians, in black, wearing mining helmets, carrying lamps, made us fear that ahead was a mine where we would be forced to work.

The down-hill march was easier at least, and after a few more terrible miles we turned a corner, to be greeted by the noise of children's voices in excitement or derision. I remember wondering what was going through their minds as they watched their first examples of the British Army, a ragged, dirty, unshaven, hollow-eyed, straggling column of stumbling men. Our Japanese and Formosan guards reacted to the yells of the huge audience by redoubling their screaming, shouting, pushing and prodding of us towards the school playground. Herding these white men like cattle, they must have felt proud, like Roman Emperors of old parading their spoil and prisoners before the welcoming citizens.

We lined up on the playground, flanked by the thousands of onlookers and children. The mighty Dai Nippon was giving the evidence of their Imperial Army and Navy's invincibility. We begged a guard to let us put Johnnie Griffiths on the floor, but he refused with a slap and a kick at us both. The sneer on his face was one we would come to know well.

Then as our names were called from a sheet we had to run into the school hall and line up facing a platform. Just as when getting into that railway carriage, we were thankful to get inside, out of the cold and incessant drizzle. Immediately we were ordered to give our word not to escape, and told that each of us would be required to sign a form. Our Senior Officer called out saying, "It means nothing. Remember Selerang." He signed for us all, under duress.

Then "Pop" introduced us to the Camp Commander, the *Buncho Dono* as he was called. He looked what he turned out to be, a pompous, self-important man. In an immaculate uniform, highly polished riding boots, and white gloves, his hand at the hilt of his *Samurai* sword, he struck a Napoleonic stance. He looked what he must have felt, the overlord and task-master of 525 defeated white men. Drawing himself up, he launched into a bombastic speech. "Pop" did his best to interpret and put the right emphasis on the right words, but failed miserably, to our amusement. He extolled the glories of Dai Nippon and the "Great East Asia Co-Prosperity Sphere". He told us the American and British navies had been swept from the seas, that not a British or American plane was in the sky, and our armies were defeated everywhere. The invasion of Australia was imminent, he said.

"When we have captured Australia, then we will give you bread and meat to eat." "Our main concern," he went on, "is your health. You must take care of your health so that you may return to your loved ones big, strong men."

That struck us, after our experiences so far in Singapore, on the voyage, and during that hellish march, as funny. His words, "Take care of your health", became one of the most used sarcastic comments among us in the years to follow.

We were then pushed into squads of 30 men, the officers and warrant officers in one squad, sergeants and corporals in another. Then a squad leader or *hancho* was appointed by the Japanese officer in charge, by the simple expedient of naming the one on the right of the line. My section was split again. Len Savage, "Basher" Gore, and I were

46

separated from poor Johnnie Griffiths, who was now being helped by Les Davis, Frank Buttifant, "Joe" Haslam, and "E.J." Morris.

By the time we left the school hall it was dark, but still the rain came down. We were to find this day was typical of that mountainous area. It has the highest rainfall in Taiwan. We were pushed on up a seemingly endless flight of rough stone steps, and then through a wooden fence into the camp which was to be our home for the next two and one-half years. There were wooden huts which, with their electric lights on, looked inviting. Through the windows we could see two long wooden platforms topped with straw matting, and a walk-way down the middle. We were ordered to strip completely, and our boots and personal items were taken from us. We were given, instead, some old Japanese uniforms, patched and threadbare, and a pair of wooden platforms with straps for the feet. We were told these were *Gaita*, and we slipped and shuffled as we tried our first inexperienced steps in this traditional Japanese footwear.

At last, at about 2:00 am, after another long harangue from the camp commander (now nick-named "The *Buncho*") we were led to our huts and given two rough, thin army blankets. But before we could sleep, the *Fu Shimbun* or "Night Vigilant Guard" had to be arranged. Japanese regulations were that two prisoners had to be on duty during the night. We were told their job was to watch for robberies and fire, and that they would be held responsible for all men in the hut. If any man went to the latrine, he had to report first to the *Fu Shimbun* who would keep a record until he returned. There was drawing of lots in my squad to decide where this rotation would start and who would be first on duty. This nightly *Fu Shimbun* duty became a periodic curse in the years to come.

We rolled out our blankets and fell on them exhausted. We were not allowed to go outside the hut, we could not communicate with the other squads, and we had no news of how poor Johnnie had made that climb up to the camp. Eventually we slept, exhausted after the long day's privations, wondering what the morning and future in this camp would bring.

CHAPTER 5

Kinkaseki

The strident blast of a bugle, banging of wooden sliding doors, and screams of *Koora!* and "Show!" abruptly woke us the next morning at six after only a few hours sleep. We soon discovered that as the bugler put his bugle to his lips, a Formosan guard would be poised, ready to burst into each hut, his rifle with fixed bayonet in hand. They would dash in, screaming, shouting, cursing, lashing out with their rifle butts at the bundles of blankets huddled together in lines on the platforms. Those a little slow rising were lined up and slapped. Others were punched. The "bashings" at Kinkaseki had started; the Kinkaseki "Reign of Terror" had begun.

From then on, at every conceivable opportunity, the guards would find an excuse to hit us. It was either a succession of smacks across the face, punches, or the rifle butt on the run. We christened them "the Runabouts" or "Goons". They seemed to be the lowest type in the army. Very young, they jumped at the commands of the lowliest Japanese privates, who did not hesitate to slap them. Face slapping seemed to be allowed from officer down through NCOs to privates in the Japanese Army. The Formosans were below privates and as we soon learnt, we were the end of the line! These young Formosans could expect and demand instant salutes from us. We had to come to attention and bow immediately, if we saw or passed a guard. Also, if a guard entered the hut, it was the duty of the first prisoner who saw him to shout *"Keree!"* (Salute) and bow. Then all the hut had to immediately come to attention and bow. These young "Runabouts" revelled in their power, and they loved to rush into the hut, trying to catch prisoners too slow in bowing and coming to attention.

We learnt fast, that first morning, not to venture outside the hut. Every sentry had to be saluted by coming to attention and bowing. A visit to the latrines became a nightmare, as two sentries had to be passed. This meant two bows on the way there and two on the way back! For the many men with diarrhoea, who sometimes had to go every hour, it was torture. Often they would be running, very difficult in the wooden *Gaita*, and a sentry would be hidden around the corner of a hut, not noticed. The first you knew was the scream *"Koora Nani Ka! — Bakeroo Keree Nai Ga! Koora!"* We soon discovered this was about the lowest form of shouting to attract an inferior. It roughly meant "Hey You, What are you doing, stupid, why don't you salute!" You would then be slapped, punched or kicked, as the mood took the guard, mostly depending on which guard stopped you.

The first news I got that morning was depressing. Poor Johnnie Griffiths was dead. Captain Seed had, evidently, asked for serum for him that night but had been refused. He then carried out an operation with no anesthetic or surgical equipment. He had made an incision in Johnnie's throat in an effort to disperse the fluid which was choking and killing him. Griffiths was the first of many men to die as a result of that ghastly sea voyage, the march up the mountain to Kinkaseki, and lack of drugs and proper medical facilities.

The Japanese refused to allow us to make a cross for his grave, and instead supplied a wooden stake with his name in Japanese *Katakana* characters. To add to our despair, the only padre in the camp was an RC who refused to read a burial service because Johnnie was Church of England! A small party of six was allowed to carry his corpse up the hillside about three miles from the camp where, to our horror, the Japanese officer indicated terraces would be made for future burials. Only a hole approximately 1 foot deep was allowed to be dug, using the usual chunkels and baskets, with accompanying yells of *"Speedo, Hyaku"* from the guards.

Later, L/Sgt. Gore and I were called to the prison office, where the Japanese interpreter told us through the orderly officer that an "enquiry" would be held into Johnnie's death! In this farce we were ordered to sign a statement written in Japanese, which we could not read, that evidently indicated he had died of pneumonia. The real reason, we knew, was malnutrition, ill-treatment, and exposure, ending in diphtheria. We both protested, but Captain Seed, standing next to us, said, "Go ahead. Sign. It will look worse on the day of reckoning." "Pop" obviously did not interpret or did not understand, otherwise we would all have been beaten badly.

49

During the next few days we were finger-printed, given numbers, and photographed like criminals. We were told that we must learn Japanese (*Nippon-go*) so that we could number-off, carry out simple orders, and memorize our camp numbers. Mine was 159, *Itchee-Go-Koo*. We were paraded, screamed at, shouted at, slapped, kicked, and "bashed" — their form of advanced teaching. We learnt quickly under our cruel "Runabouts." In order to satisfy these screaming imbeciles, we had to learn the following:

Atsumarei which meant	"Line-up", or "Parade"
Bango	"Number off"
Kashira hidari	"Eyes left"
Kashira migi	"Eyes right"
Kashira naga	"Eyes centre" or "Eyes front"
Kyotskee	"Attention"
Mae sumei	"Quick march"
Nori	"As you were"
Tenko	"Roll call"
Yasumay	"Stand at Ease"

It was all confusing for us, and a mistake by anyone caused an explosion. There were many bruised faces, split lips, and cut shins that first night. I had always resolved on the "England Maru" to learn as much *Nippon-go* as possible. That day only increased my resolution.

Between these drills, we were forced to do physical exercises, Japanese style, and had to imitate not only our instructor's actions, but also his cries in Japanese. In one of these exercises, a swinging of the arms and trunk with a loud shout which sounded to us like "You saw", we had our chance to let off steam. The back rows of prisoners would chant "You saw" and then, quicker, "What", to be followed by a few choice explicative phrases describing our tormentors. This "reign of terror" in the first weeks of the camp was also suffered by the party which had left us at Keelung, containing Major Ben Wheeler.

Wheeler, like many of us, had found a way when we were stripped and searched to shuffle his kit, piled on the floor in front, to save his secret diary. There he tried to carry on his daily conversation with his beloved wife Nell (Netty). Some of his terse sentences, at that time, convey his feelings:

15th November 1942.

I am afraid there is no hope for one patient, poor chap. I could say a lot, but how this got through the search I don't know, so may be next time, and it is perhaps better to generalize in this diary. I am busy all day. Medical personnel are recognized as non-combatants, but that is all. If this doesn't turn my hair grey, nothing will. Called at 6:30 am for roll-call, again at 7:30 pm then bed. Sentries on all sides — have to wear clogs — just how one would picture a concentration camp — some slapping, etc, I do not like, I want to go home!

21st November 1942.

Guards — gleaming bayonets — screaming guards — ferocious bayonet practice under our noses — men getting beaten up, for what? Real beatings too — still, it will improve as they get to know us and we will adjust, even as we did on the boat and nothing could be any worse than the nightmare of one or two nights on the boat.

Major Wheeler, like most of us, was still optimistic that nothing could be worse and conditions were bound to improve.

In that first traumatic week, we evolved the nicknames of the Japanese officers, guards, and the Formosan "Runabouts". The second officer in camp we called *Ashida* (tomorrow), simply because in reply to any request, he replied *"Ashida"*. Another officer was called "Rubberneck". He was a slim, bent, cruel faced officer, who had the habit of twisting his head as he talked. One was named Suzuki. He wore his uniform loosely, but when he stripped for PT you could see he was strongly built, and knew it was wise to keep away from him. The other orderly officer was a complete contrast. Tall, good looking, always immaculately dressed, he seldom lost his temper, and we christened him "Flash Harry".

The Sergeant Major was a typical martinet and needed no label. His assisting sergeant became well known to me. Because of the pose he adopted, feet wide, head up, pouting, hand on sword, he was labelled "Napoleon". I quickly discovered he knew a little English and was very keen to learn, so I decided to try to cultivate a relationship with him. He strutted about the camp, and was proud to tell everyone his sword was over 300 years old. The sergeant in charge of stores was called

51

"Smiler" or "Goldie" for his habit of showing his gold teeth while grinning.

The "Runabouts" were also given nicknames: "The Christian", because he sometimes sang little bits of hymns to impress us; *Rampu* or "Lampo", because one day he bashed us all while pointing to the lamp, *Rampu* (he was an ugly vicious character who seemed to grunt instead of talk) and "Scarface" or "The Mad Carpenter", because he had an old scar on his face, and was in charge of the prisoners assigned to carpentry repairs (he had a violent temper and a vicious punch, as I found to my cost in the first days).

There was much discussion among us of why the Japanese had brought us to this remote camp in the mountains. It was obviously to work, but at what? Some thought factory or road work, but the largest group felt as I did, though hoping we were wrong — mining. We could see a minehead in the mountains behind our camp. Every morning and night there were hundreds of workers with mining helmets and lamps passing over the paths in the hills above the camp.

The food was an improvement over the grub on the boat, although the rice ration was never enough. It was supplemented at morning and night with about half a pint of watery vegetable soup. The trouble was the rice was tasteless and had to be served up in new wooden buckets, so the smell of the new wood injected itself into the rice. To our now many sick, mainly with diarrhoea, dysentery, upset stomachs, and the worsening effects of malnutrition, the diet was useless.

Up one flight of steps above the camp there was one hut set aside for what the Japanese called "the hospital". Here Captain Seed, the young RAMC doctor, with L/Bdrs Black and Wallace, the orderlies, and a volunteer officer, Captain George Hinton of the 155th RA, worked hard to nurse the sickest prisoners. They had divided the hut into one large and two small cubicles. Of the two small cubicles, one contained the worst of the dysenteries, the other the prisoners in the most critical condition. That last cubicle became known as the "Death Hut". Whoever went in seemed to die quickly. It was clear already that many of our comrades were slipping away. Either they could not eat or could not retain the tasteless daily rice. "Basher" Gore was a good example. He was fading away with dysentery, the flesh seeming to drop from his body.

The "bashings" went on daily. Everyone was on edge. The main guard, which consisted of Japanese troops, seemed to be trying to outshine the Formosans, who they clearly despised. The Guard Commander, a bullet-headed, well-built Jap NCO we nicknamed "Mussolini", proved a real brute. His "rounds" of the camp huts were dreaded. Watches were set in each hut so his progress could be plotted and word passed as warning. He would rush in with his patrol, a guard at either end of the hut, his beetle eyes everywhere. If he saw one prisoner slow or anything out of place, like the small wooden tables used for meals not stacked properly, all hell would break loose. He loved to run at the offending prisoners with his rifle-bayonet pointing at their throat, screaming. He revelled in making you flinch. One day, Cpl Len Savage, in a moment of cold hatred and with his typical courageous manner, did not flinch. The bayonet went through his clothing, causing a wound. He was lucky he was not killed.

Mussolini's rounds were dreaded by all, especially the squad *hanchos*, for whom any discrepancy or slowness in the *Keiri* meant a bashing. It was a sight to see men swarming to the latrines to squat and wait until his passing.

Even at meal times, you were not safe from a bashing. We were forced to squat cross-legged Japanese style, to eat our meagre rations. Sentries would always enter just as you began to eat. Anyone not squatting properly was beaten, the whole hut standing to attention until the guard had vented his spite and decided to let you continue eating.

Another camp catch phrase, "How you feel now?", was born through an incident which illustrates the minds of our jailers. After Griffiths had died of diptheria, we decided it would be best to burn his clothes. We placed them in the area by the camp incinerator to be burnt. At the same time, someone had thrown some rice grains, left in the mess-tin, on top. We knew nothing of this until suddenly that night about 15 minutes before the evening "meal" at 7:00 pm, we were hurried out of our huts to cries of *"Atsumarei"* (line up). The parade square in the centre of the huts faced the high ground which led up to the hospital. There was also a separate flight of steps to the Japanese quarters, administrative office, and the "Holy of Holies", the *Buncho's* quarters. We stood in the cold wind and usual drizzling Kinkaseki rain, shivering, wondering why the assembly had been called and waiting for something to happen.

Eventually, down the stairs to the terrace above our heads came "Pop" and four guards with rifles and bayonets. A box was placed in the middle of the terrace. Then, after what seemed an eternity, the *Buncho* slowly descended the stairs, dressed immaculately with sword, white gloves, and high riding boots. He slowly mounted the box and eyed us disdainfully. After a moment, he began to speak. His voice was sharp, showing he was obviously in a temper. He spat out his words, making it extremely difficult for poor "Pop".

He started by calling us English barbarians, and saying we had no right to be alive. If we had been honourable men, we would have died in battle! It was only through the "August virtues and kindness of the Japanese Emperor" that we were alive, as no Japanese would dare disgrace himself, as we had, by becoming a prisoner of war! Suddenly he ordered us all to strip to the waist. We did. Those moving slowly received the attentions of the guards. We shivered as the biting cold rain and wind hit us. His speech raged on. He said we had thrown away clothing and, worse, rice, "the blessed food of Nippon". This was a crime, and we would pay.

He asked, "How you feel now? Are you cold and hungry?" At first no one dared to respond, but the inevitable fists and rifle butts brought the response he wanted. "Yes", we yelled. He smiled, an evil sardonic smile, and knew every one of the suffering prisoners before him was watching his face. "You will stay cold and hungry until you learn it is wrong to throw away food and clothing!"

Then, while we stood and shivered, he continued his harangue about the "divine food", rice, sent by the Gods so Japan would never starve. Then followed another phrase, which was to be repeated sarcastically, time and again by prisoners, "You will learn to love the rice, relishing and worshipping each grain." He went on, "It will save your lives, if you wish." He finally turned and left us standing. We remained for a further hour, men collapsing, but no one was allowed to carry them off that parade ground.

There was no food that night or the next day. After that, all rations were cut by half. Eventually, a 155th RA Sergeant stated he had thrown the rice away. He was beaten up and sentenced to five days in the cells.

These wooden cubicles were like inverted large size coffins, only 5' high by 2'6" wide, with a hole in the corner for use as a toilet. The Japanese called these cells, located at the rear of the main guard room, the *Eiso*. We christened them the "Ice-box." A man shut in there had nothing, not even a blanket. It was impossible to lie down and each hour when the guard changed, it was usual to either beat up the prisoner or force him to take up an unnatural position. For the slightest infringement and with no enquiry, anyone could be sentenced to a period of solitary confinement in the *Eiso*. You were pushed in as you were, dressed often only in the lightest clothing, to freeze in the bitter cold of a northern Taiwan winter. One hour the guard might make you kneel facing the wall, the next, stand on one leg, the next, squat legs crossed with arms in the air. Frequent checks meant that if you were caught not in these positions, you received another severe beating. It was a refined method of torture, at the whim of the guard commander on duty. Men came out of that "Ice-box" broken in health, shivering, bruised and battered, and invariably a hospital case. Captain Seed would put them in with the infected cases in the hope that the Jap guards would leave them alone.

Another incident happened two days later which shocked the whole camp and depressed us even more. The Japanese suddenly found they were 15 photographs short. The missing photos were all of men in the hospital, very ill. They had not paraded with the rest of us for the finger-printing and photo session. That night at about 6:30 pm they were all dragged out on to the parade ground in the cold rain, and lined up to the usual screaming and shouting. We were all confined to our huts, forced to watch what followed from the windows.

"Rubberneck", the Japanese sergeant, appeared with the NCOs in charge of the Medical Section, the "Sanitary Squad". The sergeant commanding the "Sanitary Squad" was a particularly brutal Jap who always had a *Kendo* fencing stick made of split bamboo in his hand. We nicknamed him "Sanitary Syd". His two NCOs were called "Lan-Cho" and "So-So". "Lan Cho" was very squat with glasses, had an evil grin and a temperament to match. "So-So" was a peasant type with a kindlier personality. "Rubberneck" ordered the prisoners to strip to the waist and hold their arms in the air. Captain Seed's intervention to try and explain what had happened only seemed to inflame "Rubberneck" and the sergeant more. They bashed all those miserable, thin, sick men, and threatened *Eiso* ("Ice-box") for disobeying orders. After an hour of beatings and forced PT exercises, several men collapsed, only to be kicked back to their feet again. Eventually, after an intervention by our senior officer, they were led back into the administration hut to be photographed. Japanese regulations had been broken! There had to be victims. Now face was saved!

Of those 15 men, 10 would be dead within the next two weeks, one of them the invaluable regimental medical orderly of the 155th Field RA, Lance Bdr "Joe" Black.

The camp was now organized into squads, each squad with its leader or *hancho* and deputy *hancho*. Our squad leader was Company Sergeant Major Harry Dubock of the 80th Anti-Tank Regt RA. Because I was learning Japanese and could help him, Harry asked me to stand next to him at roll call, or *Tenko* time to help.

The officers were in one hut with the four Class I Warrant Officers. A small number had volunteered to act as camp administrators. Here we struck very lucky and the officer who became Personnel Administrator, and later Senior British Officer, Major J.F. Crossley, 80th A/T RA, turned out to be heaven sent. We were surprised when we first saw that the Major had taken this task because there were two officers senior, Lt Colonel Napier of the 80th A/T and Lt Colonel Fasson of the 155th Field RA.

I remember the first time I met the Major. It was on the occasion when we had to sign the statement about Griffith's death. I looked at his appearance, and my hopes that he would be a good leader fell. He was only of slight build, wore glasses, and did not look soldierly. We were to discover this Yorkshireman had immense strength of character. He became known to us all, simply as "The Major", the man we could turn to with any problem in the years to come. To those of us who survived, he will always be "The Major; The Man of Kinkaseki".

The adjutant was Lt J. Cross, also 80th A/T RA. Lt M. Brown 155th Field RA, Lt R.W. Hellyer, RA, and Capt J.E.R. Francke RIASC took on other jobs in the administration.

CHAPTER 6

The Hellhole of Kinkaseki

The first signs that our worst fears about work were true appeared the next week. Into the camp came a supply of black cardboard mining hats and carbide lamps. We then knew our work would be mining.

"Sanitary Syd" seemed to hold tremendous authority in the camp. He and his two henchmen were supposedly medical corpsmen in the Jap army, easily recognized by an insignia over their breast pocket which looked like the figure W. "Syd", clearly, was "in charge" of all the medical and hygiene side of the camp. It was he who decided who was sick and could "lie down" in the hospital. His visits to the camp hospital were dreaded by Capt Seed and Capt Hinton, Wallace, and the orderlies. Always there was an interrogation over why there were so many sick followed by screaming of *Nani Ka, Bugeiroo*, and the inevitable slapping.

To decide who was to go to work in the mine, "Syd" held a full camp medical inspection. He chose for his "consulting room" a large draughty hut standing apart on its own, containing a concrete bath we had up to then not been allowed to use. We had to file into the hut and strip completely in front of a desk where he sat, flanked by "So-So" and "Lan-Cho". Alongside him was his Japanese sword and bamboo fencing stick. This was Syd's "court", and his stick, his "sceptre". As each man stood in front of him naked, it was obvious that the sight of the thin bodies and size of the penis caused the most comment and amusement. Any sore, bruise, or rash on a man's body seemed to give them great delight. "Lan-Cho" and "Syd" sneered and made obvious obscene jokes to each other. "Syd" would see red and fly into his worst temper if any man said he had diarrhoea, then most prevalent.

Immediately, "Syd" would shout "How many times today?" The unfortunate prisoner would reply. Then, to "Lan-Cho" and "So-So"'s great delight, "Syd" would pick up his stick and whack at the head and shoulders of the suffering "offender" that number of strokes. As this parade was to decide who was to work in the mine, and so many had diarrhoea in that file, those really "on the run" to the latrines had the choice: tell the truth and get bashed, or say nothing and be listed "fit" for work.

Poor "Basher", ahead of me in the queue, was one who answered truthfully. His powerful frame was now wasted away, his bones sticking out. He had never recovered from the voyage. I did not even hear his reply. I only saw that maniac, "Syd", beating him, crying "this is *jotoh* medicine", meaning "very good" medicine. "Basher" later collapsed. That night I had to carry him up those stairs to the camp hospital, now dreaded by all. Most of those who went up came down head first, dead.

"Syd" had evidently decreed that anyone in the hospital with dysentery or diarrhoea would be put on a diet of garlic and two cups of rice gruel a day! This was his "cure". He regarded everyone who was sick as a malingerer, and anyone disagreeing with his diagnosis was beaten.

I was horrified the next day to see that "Basher" had been put in the "Death Hut". At the first opportunity, we went up to see him. It was pitiful, all those men lying there, all close to death. You could see it in their faces. "Basher" pleaded with me for water. I got a friend in the cook-house to fill a water-bottle with boiled, warm water. That night, concealing it under my shirt, I ran the gauntlet of the sentries to get it to him. He only sipped a little, and asked me to lay the warm bottle on his stomach. He was obviously in pain and hallucinating. I tried to cheer him up.

"Come on Basher", I said. "Get well. We're going to work soon, in the mine. We are bound to make contacts down there, and maybe get better grub."

He opened his eyes, and seemed to look past me. He said, "Jack, when did 'Plum' come into the camp?"

I realized he was delirious, talking about "Plum" Warner, one of our despatch riders, "missing" at the battle of Slim River back in January.

His eyes closed, and I held his hand. I thought he was dying right in front of me. But then, he looked me straight in the eye and said, "Oh! What's happened to Plum, there's blood all over his throat!"

I did not answer. I just gripped his hand, and begged him to fight and hold on. I had to be back in my hut by *Tenko*, so I pulled my hand away. His eyes opened once more. I put my thumb up and said, "Goodnight Basher. See you tomorrow. We may start in the mine then. We'll be working together soon."

He shook his head and said, "You'll make it, Jack. You'll make it."

I never saw him again. By the time we came back from our first day's work at the mine, "Basher" was dead and buried.

The afternoon of my visit to "Basher", we were told that the next day a party of 50 men from my hut, the Sergeants' Squad, would be required for work in the mine. Harry Dubock, our *hancho*, called for volunteers rather than detail this fatigue party. I decided to "volunteer" with the group who made up our "table" for meals, Jim Ferguson, John Waugh, Jim Watson, and Davy Dewsnapp, all gunner sergeants from the 155th Field Regt RA. That night we were issued black cardboard helmets, canvas shoes, a threadbare short-sleeved green shirt, and shorts. These were to be our mining clothes! We were told our name and number-tag, a piece of white cloth with our name and camp number, had to be fastened to our shirts for which purpose we were each given a safety pin.

Next morning, we were given little wooden boxes which contained boiled rice. This was our lunch, the *bento*. Then we were lined up, given carbide lamps, and instructed on how to regulate the supply of water flowing on to the carbide to produce a flame. We were checked and counted several times, each of us having to shout out our names and numbers in *Nippon-go*. Facing us was the Sergeant Major and our escort of four guards, armed with rifles and bayonets. After a short lecture from Suzuki, interpreted by "Pop", we set off for the mine.

"Pop", in this lecture, had again made one of his usual mistakes. His interpretation was, "He say, you are now going to work in the mine behind you". We naturally turned round to look for the mine in the hills at the rear of the camp. An explosion from Suzuki of *"Bugeiroo"*

59

made us understand quickly that the mine was the other way, behind his back, not ours!

We marched out of the camp at 7:00 am, and up about 250 rough steps to the brow of the hill. In the distance below us, we could see the mine head, railway, and hundreds of trucks. To reach the mine we had to clamber all the way down to sea-level on a very rough path, reinforced in some places with stone steps. In the inevitable morning drizzle, we slipped and slithered. It was treacherous and steep, our Japanese guards cursing, as we did, as we made our way down. We never thought that first morning, 22nd December, 1942, that we would be doing it daily for the next two long years. There were 831 rough steps on that steep hillside!

At the mine head, we saw the cage-shaft and a cable railway to the top of the hill. We said to each other, "Don't worry. When we go back to camp, we'll use that." We were destined never to use that cable-railway. I had my first ride on it when I returned to make a film in March 1980!

We marched through the mine sheds and across the many sets of railway lines, packed with rusting red mining trolleys full of ore, waiting to be taken away. Other long lines of empty trucks were being pulled by small electric trains into a tunnel in the mountainside. On our left was the open grey sea, and over that horizon, we all knew, was freedom. The wind coming in from the sea even smelt of it to us.

Here, we met our new "task-masters" for the first time. The mine *hanchos* were all dressed in green uniforms with black mining helmets, white stripes painted on the side. On the arms of their uniform was a white patch with two black hammers crossed. Each of them carried a long hammer in one hand and a brass carbide lamp in the other.

The whole set-up was military. Each of the white stripes, we found, denoted a rank, and we christened them either "four-bar, three-bar, two-bar, or one-bar" *hanchos*. The four-bar was obviously the big boss. They bowed and saluted each other. We were again counted, and finally, with great flourish, the Jap Sergeant Major and his sentries handed us over.

We were then marched to the mine entrance and were halted right outside the tunnel, facing what looked to us like a doll's house with vases, paper flowers, and signs in Japanese. This, we were told, was a shrine, and we must pray here for our safety in the mine! We were called to attention with *"Kyotskee"* and then, to an order which sounded like *Sack Obo*, we were instructed to take our hats off. Then we heard *"Sai Kerei"*, which meant we all had to make a low bow while the mine *hanchos* accompanying us shouted what evidently were set prayers. This would also be required when we returned from work, to "give thanks for our safety"! This ritual became a daily occurrence, and we invented our own chant which we mumbled as we bowed to that shrine. There were many versions, all obscene, but the favourite was "Please Hirohito keep the bloody roof up today because there are no fucking timbers!" Some men though, while bowing, prayed silently for safety, peace, freedom, and the sight of our loved ones again.

In single file, we were pushed and marched down into the dark unknown that first morning. The damp, musty smell met us, that smell which reduced my pal "Gordie" Williams to tears when he revisited the mine with me 40 years later. Oh, that long walk in the same dark, dreary tunnel every day. We got to know every loose plank and broken sleeper as we picked our way in the pitiful pool of light from our sputtering carbide lamps. Your eyes had to be always on the ground, watching every step, except for the occasional glance to keep away from the overhead electric power lines. Our path was between the rails on which ran the trolleys which carried the ore out to the mine head. We knew now that it was a copper mine.

I consoled John Waugh and John Ford, walking in front and behind me, "At least it's not a bloody coal mine. We can use naked lights and there should be no gas and less accidents!"

Below us, and sometimes alongside, were drains full of water. It was easy to slip from a broken plank and fall in. The drain was the only latrine. Men had to continually stop and squat over the drain, their lamps illuminating the grotesque scene. The word for diarrhoea was *gerri-gerri*, and the often heard cry was, *"Hancho, gerri-gerri, OK Ka?"*

After marching about three quarters of an hour, we reached an adjoining tunnel, turning off to our left from the main tunnel carrying the trolley lines. Warm air hit us, coming from this tunnel, and we found ourselves climbing down very rough steps under a low ceiling.

61

Water dripped down, quite warm. Each flight was about 200 steps, and after two flights tunnels led off in different directions. But down we went, getting hotter and hotter. After four flights, we found another tunnel with two sets of trolley-lines and could see a cage operating to the surface. Instead of stopping, as we hoped, down we were taken again, the steps becoming rougher and the ceiling lower until we were nearly bent double. There were cries of pain all around me as others, like me, caught backs or arms on the jagged walls and low ceiling. I will never forget that first morning. I thought we were descending into hell. The sweat was pouring from us; our knees were shaking. We were all feeling the effects of our captivity, and were unaccustomed to such exertion.

At last, after climbing down nearly 800 steps, we were turned and walked along trolley lines past the cages on that level. This led into the lowest level in the mine. Here we were lined up and assigned to various holes and given tools, a chunkel and a two-handled bamboo basket. A demonstration by the one-bar *hancho* of how to fill the basket came next. You scraped ore with the chunkel, then you tipped it into the trolley, and pushed the full trolley to the assembly point near the cage. Each working hole was allocated a number and a direction, north, south, east, or west. As we pushed the trolley to the assembly point, a checker would record how many we filled.

That first morning I worked the Sgt John Ford, a cheerful Londoner. The one-bar *hancho* visited our hole once in the morning and, with his long hammer, tapped the roof over our heads. He dislodged some loose or hanging stones, pointing out that this was *Abunai-O!* (dangerous).

We worked away, quietly filling the trolleys (which we called "bogies"), and pushing them down to the cage where we collected an empty one. At 12 o'clock there was a loud knocking on the air pipes and shouts of *"Yasumay"*, time to rest and eat.

Back we came to the assembly point, where we could wash off the worst of the sweat and dirt in brownish water from a wooden tub filled by a bamboo pipe. Then we were taken to a cooler tunnel which was timbered and obviously used as a store by the civilian workers. There we ate our *bento* of cold rice and vegetable tops.

The tasteless cold rice and bits of green which we had carried in our boxes had been left nearby, wrapped in our green shirts. We were horrified to find them alive with cockroaches, crawling all over the pile. They had even got inside the loose fitting lids. We brushed them away and stepped on these loathsome creatures, but the cold rice was still like a banquet to us ravenous prisoners. After an hour, the one-bar *hanchos* re-appeared and began banging the overhead pipe with their hammers, shouting, *"Roeki, roeki"*. Back to our holes we went.

After what seemed a long time, but was only two more hours, the "knocks" on the pipe came again. To the cries of *"Yasumay"*, we returned to the assembly point where we were lined up and counted again. Then they had us swill off in that putrid water, and dress to return to camp.

As we moved off towards the cage shaft, I said, "Never mind. It's better than camp. No bashings, and we will ride up to the surface". The last of these hopes was quickly dashed as we turned off in single file up the "Jockey Tunnel" (you had to bend over like a jockey, or be no taller than one) and those terrible stairs. It was bad coming down that first morning, but it was a real killer climbing out that night. You forced your legs forward. No one spoke; you needed all your breath.

At last the top, and gradually the cold air coming on to your face made you realize you were getting close. In the distance there was the semi-circle of daylight. We halted at the entrance for the *Sai-keiri* to the shrine. Never was I so relieved to see the sky as I was that first night.

After being counted again, we were handed back to the Sergeant Major and our guards. Off we set, to climb again that 800-foot steep grade up the mountainside. We dragged ourselves up, pushed and prodded on by our guards, who would not allow us to pause and take a rest. On top, before the descent back to our campsite, there was a panoramic view of the sea behind, and the mountains and valley in front. In the distance we could see the rough road we had travelled from Zeho on the day of our arrival.

I paused, faced the sea, took deep breaths, and pointed out the road to Johnnie Ford, struggling along beside me. "Never mind, Johnnie," I said. "One day we'll go back down that road again — free men."

He replied, "Well Jack, that's one day nearer victory, one more day they can't make us do again!"

We had, naively, discussed the situation during the day. As the party was only 50 and there were nearly 500 available for work in the camp, we thought we would be worked in relays with rest days in between.

Down the steps we went, past some wooden shacks from which we were watched with obvious pity by the local civilians. We filed onto the camp square where we were counted and searched. Even the *Buncho* turned out to watch us. We knew every eye of the prisoners in the huts was on us. Through "Pop", we were asked by the *Buncho* how we felt. Were we tired, and how did we like the work? The only response by some of our party was that the rice was cold and covered in cockroaches. The *Buncho*, the orderly officer, and guards all thought this was uproariously funny. The *Buncho* drew himself up in his usual pompous manner and shouted, "You will get used to the cold rice *bento* and the work!"

We were grateful to be dismissed at last, and literally fell on the platforms in our hut, exhausted. Those who had stayed behind in camp plied us with questions. After trying to wash off the dirt in the thin trickle of cold water that came from a wooden conduit, we had our supper, gulping down the warm rice and watery soup. Then we stretched out to ease our aching bodies on the platforms. Barely had we done this than the "nightly blitz" by the guards and "Runabouts" began. It was forbidden to lie down before 9:00 pm "lights out", and woe betide anyone who was caught breaking this rule. The fact that we had worked outside in the mine that day made no difference. Into the hut tore *Rampu* and another "Runabout" we called "Little Tich", one from each end, demanding their bows and *Sai Keiri*. Always someone was caught, and a bashing delivered.

After the meal, I said to John Waugh, "I am going up to the hospital to see how Basher is getting on."

As I was making my way out of the hut, Len Savage beckoned me over. "Sarge," he said. "Basher died this morning... We buried him this afternoon... He asked that you be given his ring!"

He handed me a simple ring in the form of a crucifix, which I had

64

last seen when I was holding his hand that previous night. So much had happened since then, the journey to and from the mine and the troubles of that day. I was shattered.

What a miserable end, I thought, for a gallant, courageous Englishman, a good soldier and comrade. We had been close since we first met. His regimental number was 2581810, mine 2585881. My first day in that mine ended with the depressing realization how your friends were dead and buried so quickly.

To our dismay, we found our hopes of rotation were fantasy. We were ordered back to the mine the next day. The original 50 of us from the "NCOs' hut" worked daily until Christmas Day. We were joined by an additional 100 who were left behind on higher levels on our way down into hell. In the weeks that followed we were gradually joined by more parties until the whole camp, except for the sickest men, the officers, and a handful kept for in-camp fatigues, was working "in the mine behind you."

That Christmas Day, the first of our captivity, we sat at "lunch" time with our cold rice *bentos* and thought of our families gathered at home. Inevitably, the talk went to food, the subject we tried to avoid. Talking about it only aggravated our aching pangs of hunger. But talk of home brought the taste of roast potatoes, pies, turkey, and pudding to your mouth, and here we were, thousands of miles away, forced to work deep below sea level in Taiwan, treated worse than coolies.

Still, that day as we reached the long dark tunnel, I started to hum a carol. Quickly, my pals Johnnie and Jim joined me, and soon the whole line was singing. It was a moving and eerie sound. With only the bobbing, sputtering carbide lamps to light our way, "Silent Night" and "Oh Come All Ye Faithful" acquired such a poignancy, to me and others there, that now we cannot hear those familiar tunes without tears running down our faces. We feel no sense of shame, just great loss.

The *hanchos* tried to quieten us, but one, who had evidently attended a missionary school, shouted out, "Ah So! Merry Christmasu!"

We returned that night to find that our Camp Commandant, as the interpreter told us, "in his deep sense of kindness and respect for our festival and work in the mine, has allowed eight pounds of pork meat bones for the soup that night!" This meant some taste in the stew that night. Also, we found the officers had been allowed to purchase one small orange a man. This was our Christmas treat. As another "great concession", we were to be allowed to sing for half an hour before roll call, any song except the National Anthem!

We gathered in the largest hut and sang all the old songs and carols. The Interpreter, Orderly Officer, and guards attended to check we did not sing "The King". We ended with "Pack Up Your Troubles", "Tipperary" and, everyone standing, "Land of Hope and Glory". We had decided previously to end with that great, stirring, patriotic song, and did we let the lines rip.

"Land of Hope and Glory, God who made thee mighty, make thee mightier yet!" We roared out the words!

The Japs could do nothing. Major Crossley told them it was a hymn of praise and sung with Christmas carols. It was a moment to remember, and always in future, whenever we were allowed to sing, we ended with that anthem. We discovered years later that it became the same procedure in nearly every Jap PoW camp. "Land of Hope and Glory" has now become the anthem of the FEPoW (Far East Prisoner of War) Association. It is sung with reverence and fervour wherever we gather for reunions, and the tears that moisten every face are tears of fierce pride.

CHAPTER 7

The Rice-Ball Racket

So 1943 came, and many were the hopes that we would not see another Christmas like that. But life in Kinkaseki only became worse. "Don't worry. It will be over by next year," said the optimists.

The only news we received came from the Japanese in their announcements, and it was all bad. According to them, we were being pushed out of Egypt, the Germans were about to enter Moscow, and they were scoring resounding victories in the Pacific, with the American fleet all but finished!

There was nothing but gloom and despondency, and the sickness rate increased. With malnutrition diseases, beri-beri and dysentery spreading, every few days another died.

Jim Watson, a dour Scot, asked me one day, "Jack do you ken, with three dying a week now, what our chances of survival are?"

I had already done my calculations, but had made up my mind that I was not going to think or talk about depressing, negative subjects. Always, when I sat with pals, on *Yasumay* in the mine, back in camp, or on the long walk in the tunnel, I refused to discuss depressing thoughts or, the most maddening of thoughts, food. To avoid talking about food was a constant battle. No matter what topic you talked about, food would creep into the conversation. Some men tortured themselves, discussing menus or meals they had had or planned to have. Others dreamed up recipes. Those with thoughts and hopes for the future seemed to want to start chicken farms or go into pig breeding. It was mental torture to me, and to many others, to listen to such talk.

The daily mine party was now increased. They forced every man possible into the copper mine to increase production. Captain Wakiyama, the *Buncho*, thought up a scheme to force more sick men out to work and increase output by those already working: the "rice-ball racket" and the *presento* parades". Every day, the mine *hanchos* would mark the work sheets with a circle (*maru*) or cross (*kakeru*) next to our PoW camp numbers at the end of each shift. Those with a circle would be known as "diligent workers" and receive a reward at parade (we called it the "presento parade") and two rice balls extra, while those with crosses were lazy and would be punished on return to camp. Those in camp sick would have the basic ration, but later their ration was cut in half. It became obvious to us and Major Crossley, on checking the amount of rice ration received daily from the Jap quartermaster for cooking, that the rice saved by cutting rations to the sick was used to make up the extra rice balls for the "diligent workers".

We were paraded when we came back from the mine, and had to wait for Wakiyama and "Pop" to stand before us on the square. Then the numbers of the "diligent workers" were read out. "Pop" would interpret.

"He say you outstanding working record and give you three piece cigarette."

Other times, it was "three piece orange". The second week, he announced, the first PoW squad to get 70 percent of its number working in the mine "Would allow to write letter home to love ones."

Those with the red circles were delighted. Two extra rice balls at night and a cigarette. It was like manna from heaven. However, for the sick it meant less rice. After these schemes started, men thought twice of trying to be allowed off work for illness.

The *kakeru* (black cross) men really caught trouble. Instead of being dismissed from the parade, they had to remain. Lined up, they were screamed and cursed at by the Orderly Officer and sentries. Then they got, of course, a "bashing". Some nights they were forced to run around the square and up and down the steep flight of rough steps to the hospital. Other variations were standing on one leg or with both hands in the air holding a stone. Those who sagged, stumbled or dropped were beaten again.

The Major quickly called a meeting of all squad leaders and told them that by going along with the "presentos" and, worse, the "rice ball racket", we were playing into the Japs' hands. Still worse, he pointed out, we were denying our own sick comrades their normal rice ration. The end of it would be that we ourselves would suffer, for who could escape illness or injury for long? He would protest to Wakiyama, but we could do more if we could only persuade our squads to co-operate by pooling all "presentos" and, more important, rice balls.

Harry Dubock, I, and others in our squad had already decided to do this. After much argument with those who were short-sightedly only concerned with themselves, we secured a majority vote to break up our rice-balls, put them in the communal bucket, and serve out an equal ration of rice to all in our hut. There were arguments galore the next day, both in the mine and in the huts, from those who felt they were entitled to the extra rice balls because they were working in the mine. In some huts small groups of six or eight prisoners, who were close comrades, agreed to pool their extras.

It was a cruel and vicious plan, setting one group of prisoners against another, and it produced a very black period in the camp. In every community there are short-sighted selfish people. Prison camps and hard times cause this cancer to flourish in some. There were those who were only concerned with themselves. They lived up to the oft repeated army phrases, "Fuck you Jack, I'm all right" and "I've got my paddle". (This last phrase had evolved in Malaya when we were always retreating. The comment then was, "We are up shit creek without a paddle", which meant, of course, to be in real trouble.)

But against the greed of the selfish minority was the selflessness of the vast majority, who cared about their "muckers". (This word, "mucker", meant your close comrades; those you "mucked in" with. The unwritten law was, "You look after your 'mucker'.")

For nearly four weeks the "presento parades" and "rice ball racket" continued. Gradually with the increasing number of sick, the sight of those being "run up the hill" and beaten at night time, and the persuasion of officers, NCOs and hut leaders, we reached full agreement. Every night in each hut, the rice balls were broken up, and the "lobber-up" "lobbed" (rationed out) the rice. This was a task given to the most trusted in each squad. He had to try and judge how much rice to put in each container. Using a small measuring bowl into which he dropped or pushed it — it made a big difference because rice bulk

69

could be easily compressed — he doled it out.

In every hut a group would watch to be sure no favourites were played. In our squad, we called them the "shite-hawks", the name given to the vultures in India who hovered where we had trained. Usually the "lobber-up" managed to serve the ration so there was a little left over. This became known as "*leggi*-rice". (*Leggi* was the Malayan word for more and *leggi* meant extra food to any PoW) Each man stood in the same order as in roll call (*Tenko*). On numbering, your roll call position became your "*leggi* number". The extra each night, while it lasted, would be given to the next men on the list. Every man knew his "*leggi* number" as well as his name.

Full agreement and the impossibility of checking every rice-ball issue broke the "racket". Although the *marus* and *kakerus* (circles and crosses) continued to appear on work-sheets, the "rice-ball racket" and "presento parade" systems were gradually ended.

The "blitz" on the sick in camp continued, however. Captain Seed, George Hinton, and the orderlies never knew when "Sanitary Syd", "Lan-cho", or "So-So" would enter demanding to examine prisoners.

The visits of "Syd" were the most feared. Always armed with his fencing stick, he would demand to know what was wrong with each man. He struck and beat the doctor, Captain Hinton, and the orderlies whenever he was not satisfied with their replies. Often he would order patients to their feet and dole out his prescribed medicine, a hit, a slap, or a poke with his *Kendo* stick.

A few weeks later, we were again paraded and a whole lot of regulations on the punishment of groups was read to us. In future, we were told, if any man in a group of ten prisoners committed any offence, all ten would be punished. It was specially emphasized in the case of an attempt to escape: if one attempted, all ten would be "shot to death!"

The Japanese were very quick to show us they meant to carry out their threats. The next day the Camp Commander himself, Wakiyama, strode into the hospital hut and caught two patients sitting up, playing cards. He exploded. Because there were seven men lying together in that cubicle, all had to be punished. The seven men, all dysentery cases, were all hand-cuffed together. Their misery, in being beaten and then having to drag each other to squat on the latrines, was indescribable. This went on for three days. In the two weeks after this punishment, four of those men died.

No one was spared. At night time when we came back after *tenko*, when you hoped for an hour's peace before lights-out at nine, the "Runabouts" and guards were always prowling and looking for trouble. One night they burst into our hut and caught one of our squad lying down, a crime before "lights out." As he was in my punishment group of ten, we were all stood to attention outside in the cold, beaten-up, and hand-cuffed together for two days. The only time the hand-cuffs were removed was to allow us to go to work in the mine. We slept, ate, and "chain-ganged" to the toilet together!

We were to discover later the reasons for the "punishment groups". Two men had broken out of a camp in the south of the island at Taichu. They had been quickly captured, tortured, and executed. Private L.C. Carvell, an RAMC medical orderly at that camp, wrote these notes of that attempt to escape:

On the 28th of February, 1943, two of our prisoners, Private Johnson of the Manchester Regiment and Coleman D. Grierson, USN, escaped just after 8:00 pm roll call. The two squads that they were from covered their escape until the following morning. On being reported, the night-guards (*Fu-Shimbun*) from each squad, comprising 18 men, all went to the Nip officers and civil police for interrogation. This went on all morning, the Nips getting no satisfaction from any of us. At lunch time we were sent back to our squads for food. No sooner had we received it to eat, then the Japs rushed in and made us get into squads and stand to attention. We had to stand stiffly to attention then for 6½ hours, and if we even closed an eye or moved a finger, we were immediately beaten with a 4 foot length of bamboo, approximately 3 inches in diameter. If we asked to go to the lavatory, we were beaten again and told to keep quiet. Some of the men had diarrhoea and dysentery, and therefore no option but to stand there and relieve themselves. The stench was terrible. Every half hour or so the Nips said that if we told them everything, we would be released immediately. Needless to say nobody spoke, and eventually after 6½ hours we were released.

There was not one man that did not collapse on the floor after this ordeal. They let us get on with our food, and we thought it was finished. But at 9:00 pm, the night-guards were once more called, one at a time, to the Nip office. I went there about 12:00 pm and had to make out a statement concerning the escape. I was then slapped a few times and sent back. Sgt. Forsyth, RAMC, and Sgt. Pickles were put in prison because they were the two squad chiefs. The following day they were released, and they told us they had had to stand at attention all the time they had been inside. In the afternoon the guards were called once more for interrogation. When my turn came, I went before four Nip officers and the interpreter. I was once again asked to tell them what I knew about the escape, and when I told them I knew nothing, five of them immediately started beating me up with a wooden sword, a metal sword, bamboo stick, leather belt, and the other, fists and boots. When I came to I found that I had been thrown outside in the hot sun, and had been lying there for nearly an hour. As soon as I was able to crawl, I was sent back to my squad where I found all of them had had the same treatment given them. The interpreter came in and told us everything was finished with and that we would not be called up again; it was only a matter of time before they caught the two prisoners.

On March 4th we knew they had been caught because we saw food going into the guard-room. On the 6th everyone was paraded, and the two poor devils were led out for us to see. They were bound with rope and wire, and led like dogs with a lead around their necks. We were told they were going away to serve their sentence, and that we would never see them again.

A few months later I was shown graves by one Jap. He told me they dug their own graves and were beheaded. A Formosan told me they dug their own graves and were shot. They were definitely tortured and then murdered because their graves, marked with their numbers on a stone, lay just outside the English and American cemetery at Taichoo.

That short but explicit testimony was used at the war crimes trial I attended in Hong Kong in 1947.

What is not recorded is that the whole camp at Taichu suffered. A

British officer, held responsible, was imprisoned in solitary confinement for 30 days, tortured and beaten, and died very soon after release. Every camp on Formosa suffered the backlash of that brave but foolhardy attempt to escape. Kinkaseki, the "Hell-Camp of Taiwan", was no exception.

That attempt was the only one on Taiwan. Very few escapes were recorded in the Far East, and the successful ones were only in the early days of captivity. Unlike the prisoners in Europe, you were quickly spotted once outside because of your white face and your size. The jungle and sea surrounding most prisoner of war camps was far more effective than the electrified fences, walls, or barbed wire of compounds in Europe.

CHAPTER 8

The Officers' "Work Parties"

The officers had not been ordered to work in the mine, but were made to work in camp on tasks like building steps and straw sandals. They had to make a certain quota per day, otherwise their rations would be cut also. They came in for very brutal treatment from both the Japanese guards and "Runabouts", who entered their hut when they pleased, just looking for an excuse to beat up an officer. Those who were tall seemed to be particular targets.

Major Crossley recorded the following incidents during that time:

30th January, 1943.
    Two WOs severely beaten because some men were caught singing.

2nd February.
    A Taiwan soldier known as "The Nasty Carpenter" went into the officers' billet and there was a terrific beating-up. Many officers were knocked completely out.

8th February.
    The most brutal and severe beating up, as yet. Eight Taiwan soldiers (the "Runabouts") entered the officers' billet and made straight for Captain A. Sewell, MC, RA. They proceeded, each in turn, to beat him for an hour, and finished up with a sentry with rifle, holding the butt end, hitting him on the head with the bayonet. The officer concerned was in a very bad way when this brutal, savage beating was finished.

    Immediate protests were made, and the following day, Lt Col Fasson and Capt Sewell were seen by Wakiyama. Subsequently, these Taiwan soldiers were paraded and slapped across the face themselves by Japanese guards. (Capt Sewell was a tall, courageous officer who had won the Military Cross in Malaya.)

16th February.

Eleven men who, through no fault of their own, had no mining lamps were kept standing to attention for four hours and beaten if they moved. They then had to work digging all day in the camp with no food or rest.

18th February.

Inspection of the whole camp. All Taiwan soldiers appeared with sticks, and beat up all the sick men left in camp after the mine workers had left. In the afternoon a small party was taken outside the camp gates to work and was passing through the gates when Gnr Bilham fell out to fasten his clogs on. By the time he had finished, the party had gone and the gates closed. Ten minutes later the party returned, the Jap officer in a terrible rage, sent for Gnr Bilham, who was immediately knocked senseless by Taiwan guards. The Personnel Administrator went out to argue with the Jap officer re this, and pointed out that no matter what the man had done, there was no excuse for such brutal and inhuman treatment. Eventually, the Personnel Administrator was allowed to take Gnr Bilham back into the office, and that evening the Jap officer made a half-hearted apology. "There was a misunderstanding," he said.

20th February.

The Camp Commander walked into the prisoners' cook-house and ordered four of the cooks to beat each other with fists for half an hour. The Japanese NCO of the guard ("Mussolini") had a terrific day, beating up all and sundry.

21st February.

Mine workers with crosses severely beaten up, then made to run up and down the hill.

26th February.

... After returning from work, the P.A. was sent for by the Japanese Officer and told that he had broken all camp regulations by writing a letter of protest to the Commander. After a long discussion with the officer who, incidentally, had checked each item of the report, he said it would be attended to.

(There is no doubt that the condition of the men did improve from this date, but, as will be seen later, very much at the expense of the officers.)

28th February, 1943.
Major G.M. Stewart was severely beaten by the Guard Commander. The beating lasted for about ten minutes, and the Major sustained injuries to the ribs. The reason for this was that the Major, while taking exercise, had been walking with his arms behind his back, and not swinging his arms as the Guard Commander thought a soldier should.

On the 25nd of February, ten officers were ordered to prepare for work at the minehead. On that same day the Personnel Administrator, Major Crossley, decided to submit to the Camp Commander, Wakiyama, a previously written letter of protest at the camp conditions:

To The Camp Commander   22nd February 1943

I wish to bring to the notice of the Commander the following instances of inhuman treatment which is, at present, being meted out to Prisoners in this camp:

1. Feb. 18th. At 1200 hrs, No. 69, Buchanan, was in the men's billet when some Nippon soldiers came in and searched the kits of men who were working in the mine and found a pair of green trousers. For no reason whatsoever, they immediately turned round and beat Buchanan with a stick until he was unconscious. This man was sick in the billet at the time, and for 24 hours after this attack, he lost all power of speech. The effect of this may have lasting and serious effects on this man's future health.

2. In No. 12 Squad hut, in the morning (of that same day), all occupants were ordered to go outside the hut. Lt Col Napier and Fasson were sitting on a form outside this hut, when along came the Commander of the Guard and knocked them both off the form with the butt of his rifle.

3. At 1400 hrs, a Nippon sentry entered the hospital and beat up a man who was lying seriously ill with dysentery.

4. Feb. 19th. At 1945 hrs, the NCO of the Guard hit five men of No. 10 Squad for lying on their beds. These men had been working in the mine all day, and permission was given, by you, that all men who had been working could lie down after supper.

5. At 1955 hrs, Lt Brown had just entered the billet after leaving the Office and commenced to make his bed when the NCO of the Guard entered. Upon seeing Brown, he immediately knocked him out with the butt of a rifle.

6. At 2030 hrs, a sentry went into No. 12 billet, and, by signs, told everyone to get into bed. As most men had been caught by this trick before, none got into bed. And sure enough, within three minutes, three sentries came in to beat up all those who were found in bed.

7. While we were taking supper in the officers' billet a few days ago, seven different Nippon soldiers entered the billet, all within 15 minutes, and in each case we were forced to leave our meal and salute. This form of persecution takes place regularly in all huts.

8. On Feb. 10th, we had waited for two hours to proceed with a funeral. The Nippon soldiers were in a great hurry, and it was with the greatest difficulty that I was able to obtain permission to hold a service over the body. Even then, the Nippon soldiers stood at the door of the bathroom where the service was being held and continued to shout, "Speedo, Speedo, Speedo", throughout the service.

The very few examples which I have given will, perhaps, help to show you the conditions under which our daily routine is carried out. The present state of the men in this camp is one of nervous tension, for no-one knows at what moment he will be knocked off his feet or for what. I submit that, if it is the intention of the Nippon Army to continue this treatment, then all prisoners will become mentally unbalanced within the next few months.

Another typical example has just occurred while I am typing this letter. The Commander of the Guard walked into the Office and with the butt of his rifle knocked me straight off the typewriter and almost through the window of the office. I now request that you will investigate the above instances and ensure that we may be treated at least as human beings.

[signed]

PERSONNEL ADMINISTRATOR.

The ten officers taken to the minehead were ordered to work on the surface of the mine, turning over scrap metal in tanks of acid water. That night the officers decided they would do other work, but not the job allocated, as they felt it was helping the Japanese war effort. The PA told the Officer i/c Work that the work was not suitable for officers.

It was clear, on the day after, that the Commander was in a furious temper. In his rounds of the camp two incidents happened which showed his unpredictable savagery.

The Japanese had erected a large map of the world along the wall of one of the huts facing the parade ground. All areas in the Far East then occupied by the Japanese were painted red. Most of China, Indo-China (Vietnam), Thailand, Malaya, the Phillipines, Java, Sumatra, all the islands to Hawaii, and all the islands to Australia had tin Rising Sun flags nailed in them. Poor Gnr Myson, a bit of a half-wit employed in the camp sweeping up and doing odd jobs, happened to be sweeping the small square as Wakiyama, in all his majesty, approached on an inspection round. Myson immediately placed his broom against the wall map in order to come to attention, arms to sides and bowing in the prescribed fashion. Unfortunately, as Myson bowed, the broom slipped and fell, taking with it the tin flag from Java.

The Commander was no longer interested in Myson's salute. He had seen the flag of the Great Japanese Nation knocked to the ground by a broom used by a common British soldier, a disgraced prisoner of war! He exploded, shouting and ranting at poor Myson, who was then set upon by the accompanying sentries, beaten, and kicked to the ground.

All the officers and men remaining in camp that day were ordered on parade and given a long lecture on the seriousness of the awful crime Myson had committed. The offended flag was then ceremoniously hammered back into Java. Then each officer had to go forward, salute, and salute again, before returning to the ranks. A further harangue followed, and Myson was sent to the *Eiso* for ten days. The PoW Duty NCO, Lance Cpl Hanford, from my Signal Section, was also sent to the "Ice-box" for one day for allowing such a "terrible crime" to happen while he was on duty.

That night, when we came back from the mine, we heard of the day's events and saw another astonishing sight. One of the ducks the Camp Commander kept in one of two small bamboo pens was fastened on the square. The poor bird was quacking away, its wings tied to two large stones! Before we could be dismissed after the usual roll-call, we were told of the flag incident. Then we were told the duck was being punished for breaking Camp Regulations! In his stilted English interpretation, "Pop" explained that the duck had "escaped" from his compound and was being punished "according to regulations", a warning to us all!

These incidents show the mentality of Wakiyama, the Camp Commander, who had supreme power over our lives. His "mind" defined the daily conditions in which we suffered and some died.

On February 28th, all the remaining officers decided that they would not work in the mine, and on March 2 they submitted the following letter:

To: The Nippon Officer i/c Work,
    PoW Camp No. 1, Taiwan.

Dear Sir,

All officers, with the exception of those unfit, have now had an opportunity of working on the copper sluicing tanks at the mine. They have now unanimously decided that this type of work is a direct aid to a Nation at War with King and Country and cannot therefore be carried out by officers holding the King's Commission.

It is a well known fact that the Code of Honour of Officers of the Imperial Nipponese Army to their Emporer and Country is of the highest standard and we feel sure that they would not, under any circumstances, deliberately do anything in the nature of forcing British Officers to break their Code of Honour and their Oath of Allegiance to their King and Country.

The Regulation expressly forbidding Officers to do this type of work is contained in our Manual of Military Law which I understand is in your possession.

We all appreciate the thoughtfulness of the Camp Commander in providing us with this work on the grounds of health and we much regret the trouble that has been caused as we fully realize his difficulties under present circumstances.

I am, Sir,
Yours respectfully,

W.E.S. NAPIER,
Camp No. 362, Lt Colonel.

Counter signed — Squad Chief No. 12 Squad.
James F.H. Fasson, Camp No. 166. Lt Col

The above letter was returned later in the day by the interpreter, who said that all officers who agree with it, must sign it. The following letter was substituted:

To: The Camp Commander,
    PoW Camp No. 1, Taiwan.

Sir,

We the undersigned having fully considered the work of sluicing copper at the mine, are agreed that it is of such a nature

that it contravenes the Regulations set out in the Manual of
Military Law for British Officers holding the King's Commission.
Therefore, under these circumstances we are unable to continue
this type of work.

We are, Sir,

Signed	Lt Col	Napier	Lt	Hill
		Fasson		Hugo
	Major	Sanderson		Hudson
		Pedley		Hellyer
		Stewart		Brown
		Crossley		Mclean
	Capt	Francke		Cross
		Hope-Johnstone		France
		Rook		Kepple
		Bartelot		Mcknight
		Mackenzie		Davies
		Stewart		Smith
		Sewell		Ford
		Anderson		Porteous
		Tabeart A.E.C.		

Squad 12. 2nd March, 1943.

The Camp Commander said he did not understand what was meant
by "direct aid", so the following letter was submitted:

To: The Commander,
    PoW Camp No. 1, Taiwan.

Sir,

In accordance with your request I respectfully submit a brief
summary of the regulations in the Manual of Military Law as it
effects officer prisoners of war.

It is laid down in minute detail in the Manual of Military Law
what work officer prisoners of war may or may not undertake
(on a voluntary basis only).

In general they are as under:—
PoW (officer) shall not be required to engage
in any work which is of definite assistance to
the actual military war effort of the enemy (even
on a voluntary basis).

e.g. MUNITIONS and all their subsidiaries.
RAW MATERIALS, obtaining and processing of same
(oil, minerals, etc.)

The following are some examples of work for which an Officer PoW may volunteer (for which he will not receive working pay).

Gardening — Vegetables for extra food for PoW personnel.

Gardening Horticultural. Example — Landscape within Cemetery.

Poultry Farming for PoW personnel.

Administration — Office etc. within the camp.

Should any officer undertake any work which is in the nature of an aid to the enemy military war effort he is subject, on returning to his country, to Military Law, under which he would by tried by Court Martial for Treasonable Conduct and on conviction would be liable to be sentenced to DEATH, or imprisonment for life.

I would point out that on the cessation of hostilities on return to his own country every officer must appear before an Official Military Court of Enquiry which enquires into his conduct while a prisoner of war.

> I am, Sir,
> Yours respectfully,
> James H. Fasson, Lt Col
> Camp No. 166
> Chief Squad 12.

On the 3rd March, all officers were ordered to parade. The

Commander harangued the parade for about an hour, and stated that their refusal to co-operate was tantamount to a declaration of war. He then read out the list of officers who had signed the letter and the following sentence:

These officers have often declined insincerely the propositions made courteously by the Nippon Army and furthermore submitted paper full of insolence and openly expressed their intention not to co-operate with Nippon Army.

On account of such discourteousness and disobedience on their part they are sentenced to be imprisoned indefinitely until they show repentance.

Because the "Ice-box" was too small to take more than one prisoner and Myson was already in the cell in the guardroom, the officers' billet was stripped of blankets, clothing, and light bulbs, and turned into a prison. Guards were posted inside and the officers were forced to stand, kneel, or squat in whatever position the guards decided. Their rations were cut to two rice balls per meal and only a small amount of water to drink. During the morning and evening when all prisoners were in the camp, parties of these officers were periodically forced to clean out the sumps of the toilets with scoops and buckets.

It was obvious to us that the Japanese were trying to degrade our officers in front of us and drive a wedge between the officers and men. Luckily, they had need of Major Crossley, Lt Brown, Captain Seed, Captain Hinton, and the others appointed by them to administer the camp and look after the sick and dying in the "hospital". These officers were allowed out of the "punishment hut" to continue their work. Unshaven and shivering with cold, they looked dreadful, but were our contact and inspiration. The men, in my hut and others, responded by smuggling rice and clothing through these officers. We assured them of our support and loyalty.

On the 7th of March, "Pop" conveyed a message that the officers should submit a letter of apology to the Camp Commander. Accordingly, the following letter was sent:

To: The Commander,

Sir,

The officers agree to the working conditions as shown in the Treaty regulating the work to be done by officer PoWs.

We wish to add our apologies for any discourtesies and misunderstandings which may have occurred.

I am, Sir.
Yours respectfully,
G.B. Sanderson, Camp No. 407
CHIEF SQUAD 12.

(Lt Colonel Fasson had been relieved of his command of the officers' squad, and Major Sanderson replaced him.)

The result of this apology: the officers had again insulted the Nippon Army and rations were cut to one rice ball per meal on the 9th of March. By this time many officers were becoming seriously ill through exposure and lack of food.

On the 16th of March, "Pop" gave Major Sanderson a typed letter which he said should be submitted to the Camp Commander. He pointed out that if the letter was sent, all would be well and the officers would not be asked to work (a Jap face-saver). In view of the serious condition of some of the officers, it was decided to sign this letter.

NOTE: Every word of this letter was written by the Japanese.

To the Commander,

We are indebted to the Commander as he has accepted our request pleasantly and gave the work to ten Officers to begin with when we voluntarily applied for it. However, all of us have contended the work as it gives a direct aid to the country now at war with our country and submitted it to the Nippon Officer in charge. He suggested us to stop work on the following day so that we can fully discuss the matter, and at the same time he required us to make definite reply on the day till 15 hours on whether we stop or to continue it. We have replied him to continue the work.

On 2nd inst. we have again reported him to stop the work, this we now see showing ourselves totally lacking consciousness and insulting Nippon and her soldiers.

We are ashamed for what we have conferred and decided on the 2nd inst. and feel sorry to Nippon, Nippon army and the commander and exposed our blunder to our NCO and men. We are entirely refrained from the work since and recollecting the teaching Commander gave us. We must restore our honour and worrying how we could do so.

We attribute all mistakes in the past to our fault and would request the commander to clean slate this unpleasant incident and allow us to resume work at earliest opportunity.

Immediately the following reply came back:

Perusing the letters wrote to me by your officers I find all:

1. Of them consider the work in the copper sluicing their main point and expect to be released as term of exchange you resuming to work there.

2. Commander of the camp heard very often of your work on so called "voluntary basis" and knows very well how it is sloven and irresponsible, he did not imprison you to enforce you to work, in overlooking the stipulation of International Law.

3. In refusing to work you gave some false legal points as excuse and I gave you an explanation on the International Law because your dubious principal will bring you nothing but contempt of other party, therefore requiring you an introspection, remember, I do not seem to demand you to work.

4. Commander of this camp extremely hates you though itself indicating as not to "co-operate in industrial activity in enemy country" you entirely forget a favour by which your lives in the battle field have been narrowly saved from danger, and still maintain hostile attitude if so you can determine that this camp is also the same as battle field and we Nippon Army will treat you with same feeling as yours.

The only ground gained by this letter was a reduction in the hot water ration. It was quite obvious by this time that the Commander had no intention whatever of releasing the officers, having merely created an "incident" for his own purposes. Therefore, no further letters were submitted.

On the 17th of March the Camp Commander commenced interrogation of each officer separately. This continued until the 20th. At the end of an interview, the officer was ordered to write out on paper whether he was willing to work.

On the 20th of March at 1700 hrs, the Commander came into the detention room, stood on a chair, and stated that he was not yet satisfied, as some of the stories told by the officers did not agree. Immediately, Lt Colonel Napier stepped forward and told the Commander that he would accept full responsibility for the whole incident. The Camp Commander thereupon sentenced Lt Colonel Napier to a further five days imprisonment and Lt Colonel Fasson to a further three days, the remainder being released.

The following notices appeared on the Camp Notice Board:

28 Officers, Prisoner of War
While being imprisoned on account of disobedience are released today as they have shown remarkable repentance.

Lt Col Fasson
While being placed in an important role as liaison officer concerning petition made by all officers PoW for their work. He neglected to convey the wishes of the Nippon Army to them causing the incident enlarged unnecessarily. For such reason he sentenced to be imprisoned for three days.

Lt Col Napier
For the reason he has made a false statement against the enquiry of the Camp Commander he is sentenced to be imprisoned for five days.

20th March, 18 year of Showa.

The incident with the officers ended but, it was clear, Wakiyama was furious with them. Despite Major Crossley's protests, the camp "reign of terror" continued. Even on the so-called *Yasumay* days, one in ten when the mine workers were given a day off, the Camp Commander ordered cleaning of the huts and the camp, and "air raid" practices.

The "air raid" practice really gave the guards and "Runabouts" a perfect opportunity for beatings and making our lives even more miserable. We were herded out of our huts and made to run back and forth to various assembly points while the Japanese "fire precaution" squad turned on the hoses. Various huts were their targets, and everything inside was soaked. Always the hoses would be turned on a group of prisoners, supposedly in error, but this we knew by the cries of delight from the guards to be deliberate. Always after the "air raid" practice was over, we were told these were precautions "for our safety", but that there would never be an air raid. They were really intended as fire practices!

During that black period, all the news we received was depressing. It came in the form of either "News Announcements" from "Pop" or Japanese papers printed in English. Only a few copies of the papers were circulated. They were full of stories of great naval victories and the exploits of their air force, which they called their "Wild Eagles." Some of the exploits described were fantastic and caused us such amusement that we kept records:

NIPPON TIMES

AIRCRAFT CHANGES CONCEPTION OF WAR. JAPANESE AIRMEN DOWN TWO FOE PLANES BY HURLING RICE BALLS AT THEIR MACHINES.

UNDISCLOSED BASE IN SOUTH PACIFIC. BY TEIJIRO SHIRATORI (NAVY PRESS CORPS).

A complete change has come over the strategy of war. This is the age of aircraft. Whether in advancing bases in the war of supply or in the reduction of enemy positions.

Instances of the superhuman heroism of our Sea Eagles in the aerial battles off BOUGAINVILLE and GILBERTS were recently related by Vice Admiral XX commander of a Navy Unit.

It was at the time of the 5th Aerial Battle of Bougainville. A young First Sub Lt was starting out as the commander of a torpedo plane unit. Lt Commander XX, his supervisor, said to the young officer: "You have already had experience in patrol reconnaissance and bombing. When you return from the attack you will be fully qualified as a Squadron Leader."

The first Lt expressed his determination: "I don't expect to come back alive, I shall die gladly, I do not care for promotion." He meant what he said, he killed himself by plunging deliberately into an enemy aircraft-carrier.

A Japanese fighter plane was chased by two enemy machines. The Japanese pilot had exhausted all his ammunition. Nothing daunted however they kept on flying low over the surface of the sea, all the while hurling at their chasing adversaries anything and everything they could lay their hands on. The enemy kept up the chase. The Nippon plane was hit in several places. The machine caught fire. There was no hope but the airmen were set on bringing down the foe planes "Confound it!, if we have to die, they shall also!" They hurled everything left at the enemy, empty bottles, telegraph equipment etc. and now there was nothing left.

"We found it!" There were two rice balls covered with *nori* (black seaweed). The rice balls were hurled at the enemy. Mistaking them for bullets, the pilot of the chasing enemy fighter that was immediately behind lowered the control lever. The plane which was flying as low as almost to touch the sea surface, plunged into the water. The other enemy plane trying to dodge the "rice bullet" also crashed. The Japanese airmen therefore managed after all to send two planes to the bottom of the sea.

Crashing into a mountain on XX island their plane broke in two. The man who was in the front seat shared the same fate as the plane. The one at the rear was thrown clear and miraculously escaped death came back to report the "shooting down" of the two enemy planes.

Our Sea Eagles are the greatest exponents of self-sacrifice and every one of them are determined to fight to the last ounce of strength. We must have aircraft. Victory is decided in the air. The nation, with a united will, must keep fighting. With adequate air strength we can and shall win!

Vice Admiral XX
XXX Base, South Pacific
On an undisclosed date. XX hours.

With this was the following story, again from <u>NIPPON TIMES</u> of the same issue:

German U-Boats are operating in the upper waters of the Mississippi. They are engaged bombing bridgeheads. Terror amongst milkmen on New York waterfront owing to presence of U-Boats off there.

These stories were the only rays of humour that came through the endless reports of American and British reverses. The constant assertions that there would be no air raids and the story of the rice-balls bringing down American planes would lead, later in my captivity, to the worst beating I would receive.

Using every opportunity to learn *Nippon-go* by exchanging words and phrases with "Napoleon" or the one-bar *hancho*, my vocabulary was growing. The Japanese had ordered that the reports at roll call each night had to be given in *Nippon-go*. Poor Harry Dubock, a BSM of the 80th Anti Tank Reg RA, our *hancho*, found great difficulty in learning the necessary phrases. Every night before *Tenko*, when the Japanese orderly officer arrived, Harry would be in a panic trying to memorize the necessary words. I was his teacher. One mistake or hesitation by a Squad Leader in reporting meant a certain bash in the face, and poor Harry always seemed to be in trouble.

"Taff", he said to me one night, "There is only one way. You stand next to me and be number one (*Itchee*) in the roll-call. Then, if I should forget or go wrong, you prompt me".

The first night Harry made a mistake and I prompted him, we both got bashed! However, in our desperation, we thought of a way out. At the end of each hut was a blackboard and chalk. It was used by the *Fu-Shimbun* (Night-watchers) to write down the number of any prisoner leaving the hut for the latrine. On his return, the number would be rubbed out. This way any patrolling Japanese guard could check on an absence if necessary. Between us, we arranged to put the board facing where Harry stood to report, but behind where the Orderly Officer, Interpreter, and Guard Commander normally stood on *Tenko*.

Each night then I chalked up in romanization the words Harry had to say:

Dai-Ni-Han; Soin-Yon-Ju-Mei; Jiko San Mei; Itchee Mei Suijee; Nee Mei Bioyin; Genzai Sam-Ju-Nana Mei.

which meant:

"No. 3 Squad, strength of squad 40 men, absent three men, one man cook-house, two men hospital, present 37 Men."

Of course, he first had to call the squad to attention with "*Yotskee*", then shout *Sae-Kerei* for the salute, and then *Bango*, telling us to number off in *Nippon-go*.

All went well for the next week. We positioned the blackboard at the rear wall where the roll-call party of Japanese never turned to look as they entered the hut. Disaster hit us the night it rained. The Japanese rain gear consisted of a large hood and flowing capes. That night, the Camp Commander himself, the majestic Wakiyama, decided to attend roll-call with them. We knew nothing of the change. On the first blast of the bugle for roll-call all prisoners had to be inside their huts standing in line, so we didn't even see them coming.

I had the board chalked-up, ready, when in came the party. Instead of the normal three, there were six; Wakiyama had two escorts. To Harry's horror, they lined up in such a way that their wide hoods and flowing capes hid the chalked-up words. Harry started all right, but then began faltering, and then stuttering and mumbling as Wakiyama's anger grew. Two smacks from Wakiyama and the guard commander, and Harry said, "For Christ's sake Taff, take over."

I quickly bowed to the livid Camp Commander and reported the squad. "*Yosh,*" barked Wakiyama, and then he shouted at the Interpreter.

"Pop" looked at me and said, "*Itchee Go Koo*, he say, 'You in future, *hancho*, this squad.'" They stormed out. We picked Harry up from where he had been hit by the Guard Commander. That night was the start of more trouble for me caused by my learning *Nippon-go*. My object had been to pick up bits of information or news and keep myself out of trouble. However, the more I learnt, the more I was used as a go-between or interpreter.

CHAPTER 9

The Hammer and the Hot-spots

Production of copper ore is important to war efforts, and the Japanese supplied as many men as possible to the mine. We were not the only "impressed" labour. Parties of women and girls were brought below by the Formosans, and another large number of Chinese men were seen at the mine head. These Chinese, dressed in thin black shirts and shorts, looked very miserable and thin, and when the guards were not looking we waved at each other, putting our thumbs up and making the "V" sign, obviously feeling a sympathetic bond. We called them "The Black Sappers". One of our one-bar *hanchos* told us they were convicts and political prisoners.

The Intelligence report on PoW camps and conditions in Formosa compiled in October 1945 stated:

Kinkaseki Copper Mine

47.   The Kinkaseki Copper Mine was one with the largest output in the Japanese Empire and was a commercial enterprise, although regimented along military lines, with foremen and staff wearing insignia denoting seniority or rank. The mine was situated 1 mile from Kinkaseki prisoner-of-war camp, nearer the shore line with a hill between the camp and the mine.

48.   Although mining conditions universally are severe, it is emphasized that few can equal the hazards of this tunnel. There was no lighting (prisoners of war used carbide lamps), no props, rock falls were a daily occurrence, and down the steps there ran a stream of sulphurous, acid water. Passage through the tunnel, made twice daily by the prisoners-of-war, constituted a severe mental strain and a physical risk. In their underfed condition, often too ill to

work in the opinion of the Senior Medical Officer of the prisoners-of-war, the trials of this tunnel alone brought extreme suffering to the men.

49.   The Kinkaseki camp was estimated to be 400 feet above the level of the main shaft in the mine, and the main shaft 800 feet above sea-level. Below this mine shaft there were six levels at which copper-ore was worked. Each of these levels was 200 feet approx. below the preceding one, and thus the lowest level of working was below sea level. There was no ventilating system whatsoever in the mine. Heat and humidity was intense throughout, but at the greatest depth, whereat Chinese labourers refused to work, British prisoners-of-war were forced to. Conditions were so extreme that many prisoners-of-war collapsed while digging in chutes and were succoured by their comrades. The temperature in these chutes at the lowest level ranged from 130°F, and sulphurous water, in which the prisoners-of-war often had to stand while working, exceeded these temperatures. Many men experienced a delayed asphyxiation owing to lack of oxygen in the non-ventilated tunnels. In the very worst of the chutes, of the comparatively fit men, none could work for more than 5 or 6 minutes without collapse.

50.   Bearing in mind the frequent despatch to work of men so ill they had to be helped to the mine, and their inevitable collapse in the lower depths, and their journey up the almost perpendicular shaft back to the mine's main tunnel, thence by tunnel to the camp, the ordeal was an ultimate in brutality.

51.   Throughout the course of the prisoners-of-war's use in the mine, no medical attention was permitted in the mine. Ranging from light injuries, collapses of the sick, to the maimed or killed in the mine all were without medical relief until the camp was reached at 1800 hours. Early departure from the mine was forbidden, no matter what the reason.

The Camp Commander, Wakiyama, was determined to supply as many miners as possible for work. Each morning as we paraded for work, men would plead to be allowed to be sick, others would collapse. However "Sanitary Syd" and the Jap guards were unmoved. Kicks and clouts with sticks forced those who collapsed to their feet. Helped by their comrades, they struggled over the hill to the mine shaft.

More men were becoming ill. Others were literally losing all will to live, even refusing the rice when they were sick, so great was their dread of the mine. It was not only the brutality of the climb back and forth to work and the hard labour in dangerous, hot, acid conditions that they dreaded. In February and March of 1943, the quotas of "bogies" (trolleys) of copper ore began to be stepped up ruthlessly, and two far more sinister forms of brutality started. Their use as punishment first started on the lower floors of the mine where the hottest and wettest working holes were. They were to become the greatest fear at Kinkaseki — "the hammer" and "hot spots".

The hammer carried by each *hancho* had a long wooden shaft about four feet long and two inches thick, tapering down to the metal head. This was, supposedly, their "safety hammer", used to tap the roofs of our working places and bring down loose stones. This was also the symbol of their authority and became the instrument they would use to force up ore production.

Each morning when we reached the assembly point and lined up in our "Jap-happys", a piece of cloth worn on a string around our crotch, we were harangued and given our quota of trolleys (bogies) to fill. Instead of "one-man, three bogies", now the one-bar *hanchos* called for "one-man, four" or even five or six, depending on the hole to which you were assigned to work. Then came the threat, "*Speedo, Speedo. Speedo Nai — Hammero.*" That night when we finished work, we were to learn what "*Speedo Nai — Hammero*" meant.

The "one-bar" *hanchos* were all Formosans, and, although one or two showed some compassion for our plight, the large majority were brutal bullies. Each level had its "two-bar" *hancho*, always a Japanese. They were, in some cases, men who had done military service. These were the strict, disciplinary NCO type, always screaming and shouting at their underlings.

At night when the "two-bar" checked the output for the day, those not completing their quota had their numbers called out. These men had to step forward, were ordered to *Yotskee* (attention), and were punched to the shouts of "*Kura — Bakeroo! Nani-Ka No Roeki!*" (You, stupid, why no hard work!) Several men were knocked to the ground, but worse was to come. They were forced to turn and hold the air-pipe over our heads, while the one-bar *hanchos* flogged them with the hammer's shaft. That first night each was given six strokes across the back and buttocks. Every blow caused every man to wince with pain. I was one of the unfortunate ones. Those watching often suffered seeing very sick comrades collapse in agony. Then we were told, "*Asta No Speedo Again Hammero!*" (tomorrow if you do the same again, the hammer!). The walk back and climb up those steps that night was worse than ever.

Word spread from squad to squad. That night Major Crossley, looking at the bruised, cut backs of the victims, promised us he would protest. His protests were laughed at by Wakiyama, and the use of the hammer for floggings quickly became common practice on all levels in the mine.

The "hot spot" or "punishment hole" treatment began at the same time. Most levels had particularly hot working-holes where it was impossible to fill the required quotas. To get into one of these holes, you had to climb up a shaft alongside a chute, down which you would throw the ore to be collected in the bogie. The working-hole was at the top of the shaft and had to be reached by climbing rotting old wooden ladders, some as high as 40 feet. These working-holes were blasted out by civilian workers, and varied from only 2 ft 6 in high to quite large caverns, depending on the dynamite blast and fall of the roof. The heat radiating off the sides of these holes was terrific, and acid water poured down on you as you climbed up the ladder. The air was so foul that your naked lamp often went out through lack of oxygen.

We found the only way we could work these holes was to do it in shifts of two, four prisoners always being detailed. The first two would go up with the best of the lamps, one lamp left at the chute hole and one near the ore to be cleared. We would try to finish five baskets of ore each. By the time you reached the fifth basket your head would be drumming as you gasped for breath, sweat streaming from your body. You then flung down your chunkel and basket and staggered to the ladder to be replaced by your two mates. With your heart pounding, your one thought was to get at the water that filled the drain alongside the bogie rail. Here you sat, feet on either side, scooping up this filthy, sulphurous water and pouring it over your trunk as the steam rose from your body. You used your filthy sweat rag, now dyed yellow by constant immersion in the acid-impregnated water, to sluice and wipe your face. The sight of men working in searing heat, dripping acid water, panting and steaming, was like a scene from Dante's Inferno; still a recurring nightmare for all who worked there.

Each hole had its Japanese number. The worst hole was *Itchee ku nee kita* (192 North). Every man in our squad dreaded to hear his number followed by *Itchee ku nee kita*, an assignment to hell.

Each of our mine *hanchos* was quickly given a distinctive nickname. Among the most notorious and hated "one-bars" was "Patchy", so named because of patches on his coat. "Goldy" had two prominent gold teeth. "The Frying-Pan" was so named because when working on his level, you were either in the "frying-pan or the fire"; there were so many hot-holes. "Pan-Face" had a flat face. "Laughing Boy" always smiled with a malicious grin. "Sammy" had a nasty growth on his arm which seemed to affect his whole personality. He swung his hammer and flogged viciously.

The Japanese "two-bars" had another notorious "*hancho*" known as "The Eagle" or "Don-R". He had beady eyes and had been a wrestler. "The Eagle" loved to show his strength and prowess, and he thought nothing of felling a prisoner with a wrestling throw and kicking him while down. He told us he had been in the Army and was a reservist. He was a stickler for discipline, and woe betide any prisoner who did not bow quick enough at the shrine when so ordered when "The Eagle" was near. On one occasion he heard me muttering as I bowed and must have guessed my remarks were not "prayers". He knocked me completely out with one swing. Like everyone else, I detested "The Eagle" and prayed that the day might come when I could revenge myself on him.

Another hated and feared "two-bar" was the infamous "Ghost". Each *hancho's* lamp was far better than ours. Theirs had a large brass reflector. Because of the light, we always knew when they were coming and made sure we were working. The "Ghost" discovered this and would blow his lamp out and creep up in the dark on prisoners resting between baskets or bogies. He would then scream, "*Yasumay nai! Nani-ka! Bugeiroo!*", his hammer flying.

96

To fill a "bogie" (a rusty, iron trolley on four wheels approximately 4' × 2½' × 3') took 50 baskets of ore. Each basket had to be carried from the face and tipped into the chute. Then the prisoner assigned as "bogie-pusher" would release the ore from the chute into the bogie and push it to the check-point. In holes where there were long "carries" to the chute, a wooden wheel-barrow was sometimes provided. In others where there was no chute, you carried to the bogie and pushed your own bogie to the check-point.

At the check-point, which was near the cage going to the surface, an old man or a boy sat by a blackboard. As the bogie was pushed past, the prisoner pushing called out the working hole number and the "checker-boy" marked the board. On some levels, the bogie had to be tipped into a chute which, evidently, fed a large storage hopper near the cage level.

All the *hanchos* on all levels were now using the hammer and hot-holes regularly as punishment. Even when you were able to avoid punishment yourself, it was sickening to have to stand by and witness the beatings and floggings. The scene of filthy, near naked men lined up with their hands holding the pipe, the tunnel lit by the flickering carbide lamps, the crack of the hammer on wasted bodies, and the groans and cries is another of the Kinkaseki nightmares that will live with me forever.

Captain Seed and Major Crossley, seeing the bruised and battered bodies each night and knowing that many of these men would be condemned back to the same foul holes next day, were distraught. They did their utmost to persuade the Japanese to allow more men off sick. This, of course, proved futile.

In the mine when the Japanese struck a good seam of ore, there would be more visits by the "one bar" and "two-bar" *hanchos*. Even the "three-bar" would come to flash his lamp and say "*Jotoh ko-saki*" (Very good ore). We learnt the low-grade material, *Hi-saki*, a red, earthy, coloured stone we sometimes had to move, was no use in their refining process. The *Ko-saki* was easily recognizable; it was bluish gray with flashing pyrites.

The only timbering was carried out in the main tunnels near the cages or check-in areas and some of the "bogie-runs" which led to the work-holes. There appeared to be no consideration for safety, and with our poor lamps and rapidly deteriorating canvas shoes, accidents occurred often. Roof falls became frequent. We quickly learnt to move fast when we heard the roof moving or felt dust or small stones falling on our shoulders or backs. Many men slipped, stumbled, and fell on the slimy, soaking floors or when walking or labouring in water. Daily now there were cuts or bones broken, and with no first aid we had to help each other until we got back to camp at night.

Captain Seed discovered that if a prisoner had a mine accident and he could show a broken arm or leg or cuts, the Japanese allowed him to "go sick" and stay in camp. With the terror the mine now held for every man, the thought of an accident took on a different meaning. I will never forget when Harry Dubock broke his arm.

As I had four years of first aid experience in the Boys Brigade and spoke some Japanese, the *hanchos* sent for me if a prisoner was injured. One day I found Harry nursing his arm, sitting in the filth of the drain, trying to clean the dirt away from an ugly gash in an obviously fractured arm.

"Taff," he chuckled, "I've done it! I've bloody well done it! My arm is broken! With any luck, I'll never come down this fucking mine again!"

That was his reaction! With what looked like a serious compound fracture which must have been causing intense pain, Harry was delighted. Such was the terror of the mine. His accident had been caused by a rock fall. We had no first aid equipment at that time, so we had to use urine as a disinfectant to cleanse wounds. We bound him up, immobilizing his arm as best we could, to wait for our return to camp that night.

There were many men who contemplated, planned, and caused self-injury. No one could blame any man for trying to gash a leg or arm in the hope of gaining a respite from this daily hell. It was only sheer fear of permanent damage that stopped men from just putting their legs alongside the face and pulling the sharp stones down.

The Japanese must have been concerned about the low number of workers they could force into the mine. One year after being taken prisoner, every man was showing some evidence of malnutrition. The appearance of more huts outside the camp boundary, built by civilian workers, confirmed the rumours we had heard of more prisoners coming to work in the mine.

The official record kept at that time shows the following:

	Average Daily Sick	Average Daily Working
Jan., 1943	162	287
Feb., 1943	159	298
March 1943	125	351
Apr., 1943	124	328
May, 1943	206	257
Jun., 1943	183	291
Jul., 1943	167	289

Those just "sick" were serious hospital cases. Among the daily working were many who should have been in hospital, but had to hobble along or were carried each day by their comrades! In those first six months we also had deaths due to roof falls in the mine, and again the peculiar out-look of the Japanese showed in the different way they treated these deaths.

A prisoner killed in the mine was allowed to "lie-in-state" overnight in the hut that had a concrete bath. Paper flower wreaths were sent from the Mine Company, and a dish of fruit or rice-cakes was placed on the corpse. The squad of the unfortunate prisoner had to provide two men as "Vigilant Guards" all night long. The squad would rotate two men every hour. The burial parties were formed by two of the officers and men left for in-camp duties. To show the state of mind of prisoners then, terrible arguments broke out when it was discovered that the burial party ate the fruit or rice biscuits. Those of the dead man's squad who had provided the "night-watch" and had to go into the mine next day would grumble at the "vultures" benefitting by their comrades' death.

There were signs of several men having mental trouble. It worried our group at night, as we sat and talked in the brief half-hour between roll-call and lights out. I was very lucky to have comrades such as Cpl Len Savage and Sgt. Jim Watson, Johnnie Waugh, Jim Fergusson, and "Big Sam" Lockhead. We all tried to cheer each other up during that period, talking of anything which would take our minds off the horrors of the camp and the terrors waiting for us in the mine each day.

We looked forward to seeing new faces in the camp, hoping it would maybe mean some news. Perhaps there would be more so-called "fit workers", and perhaps the Japanese would be more lenient with the sick. Our troubles with sickness and beatings were being experienced in other camps, and Major Wheeler, still in No. 6 Taihoku camp, recorded in his diary:

December 16th, 1942

This is, I think, mentally, one of the worst days I have had. It all seems so hopeless — can't get through to the Japs — no medicines, pushed about on some new thing daily with no chance to do much, even with what we have — no dropping in the sick — many new avitaminoses — not surprising. A large proportion of the men will never be fit to work under these conditions and believe it or not, although the Jap Medical Officer did a Schick test on us all, they haven't even read it — 72 hours! I didn't used to harbour hatred and revenge, but now! Daily it mounts. Pray God I don't go — mental I won't, but even for my nature this is hard to take, and to think only of the day!

Was up too long this pm but got a lot done and drained about a gallon off Brown with ascites. TB I am afraid, poor chap — wonder whether it is better to go on draining him or not to prolong it — not for the likes of me to judge where there is life, and so on, so we will keep him alive as long as possible, even under these conditions.

In Major Wheeler's camp those in the "hospital" suffered the same as in ours. His diary on 1st March, 1943, is explicit:

It is hard to know what to put here that will be of any interest afterward — so many things that were unreal have now become so commonplace. The worst of all for me of course, is trying to do something for the sick with no tools — not even the authority to give them rest, and worst of all, having to send out sick men so that more sick men may be allowed to stay in. As the Padre says, there is no use worrying, one can only do one's best, but that does not make it any more pleasant.

I do not think I shall ever forget the screaming and screeching, the first few nights after we arrived. They carried on bayonet practice beside the hospital, off and on all night. Even when they shout orders, one would swear at least two people were being murdered and it shakes one even now a bit. It is more of a highpitched scream. They still do a lot of slapping and more on occasions, but here again we seem to have come to look on it as normal. Yesterday one of the sentries at the corner of the hospital spent most of the morning slapping or striking people whose bow did not please him; no love taps either, as he knocked a tooth out of one.

March 15th, 1943

Little new — beri-beri going up and many severe. Rations continue low, almost a new low. Flies are starting — soon dysentery I fear — things could not be more ideal for its spread. Sick men's rations, especially hospital, cut again. I am afraid and I am not being pessimistic, things are bound to get worse with the general level of health going down and down. We now have 128 beri-beris on the list. All with definite symptoms and many more who have not reported. However, we will get through — I am sure a lot is happening.

Major Wheeler's hope in March, 1943, that "a lot is happening"referred, of course, to the war. The hope, always in all of our hearts, was that the tide was turning. Fortunately we knew nothing of the continued Japanese and German successes at that time, or that it would be nearly 2½ years before those who survived would be free.

In Kinkaseki, to add to our misery even at night, the Japanese thought up a new order. From 9:00 pm to 6:00 am, when we tried to "escape" from our surroundings in sleep, no man could pull the blanket up over his head. Despite the still cold nights, heads must show! Also, we had to sleep head to toe, alternating along the wooden platforms. Those with the heads out nearest the walk-way were easiest seen and got woken the most. Nasty guards like "Lampo", "Scarface", "The Mad Carpenter", "Tich", and "Goldy" were notorious. If your head was not showing, they would bang your head with the butt of a rifle. You would wake to find them screaming at you with rifle and bayonet poised; from a dream of home, back to that nightmare. Immediately, their shouts would wake up the whole hut. After first being slapped, you would usually be made to stand for an hour as punishment.

Poor Wylie, who happened to be the Squad *hancho* on duty one night, committed the unpardonable crime of walking in front of the Japanese Camp Sergeant Major. The Jap exploded and hit him savagely on the head with his *samurai* sword. Gnr Wylie was lucky to survive. Knocked to the ground, he was dragged off by other prisoners to have the horrible gashes stitched.

Then, on April 13th, a miracle happened: Red Cross parcels arrived in the camp to be shared on the basis of one between three men. The Japanese made the distribution of the life-giving powdered milk, chocolates, and other items to us difficult by insisting on opening every tin, probing the contents, and inspecting the back of every label before it was handed over for sharing out. This was typical of their attitude, but we were pleased to see their reaction to the food the tins contained. The guards expressed surprise that Britain, a defeated nation, could still provide such food for prisoners. The food, comments, and envious eyes of the "Runabouts" on the chocolate and high-protein food did wonders for our morale during the week we made it last.

The weather was becoming warmer and the rains began easing as the summer of '43 approached. Then another event happened to boost morale. A small group of men arrived from a camp in the south called Heito. They brought news of their camp, of who was there, and a little optimistic news of the Russians throwing back the Germans. But more importantly, they also brought some Royal Army Medical Corps orderlies. These men would prove a great help, especially with Captain Seed sickening. Into Kinkaseki came Cpl David Donnelly and Lance Cpl Thompson, both to prove of immense value in the years to come.

A few weeks later we heard that a new Commander-in-Chief for all PoW camps in Taiwan had been appointed and would be visiting the camp on 11th July. "The Major" always took advantage of any opportunity to try and improve conditions or obtain more information. He asked through "Pop" if a party of the officers could be allowed to go up the hill overlooking the camp to tidy up the cemetery for the visit.

At the same time, he tried a different method to improve the situation of the sick by writing direct to our Camp Commander, Wakiyama, bypassing the Medical Sergeant, "Sanitary Syd". In his letter the Major drew attention particularly to one man, Sergeant Baker, who should have been in hospital, but was still struggling, carried to work in the mine. To our surprise, Wakiyama replied that Baker could be put in the hospital that night when the mine-party came back.

This attempt by the Major back-fired. Two days later "Sanitary Syd" was walking through the hospital and saw Sergeant Baker. He became crazy with rage, beat him up, and ordered him out. Then he slapped all the rest of the patients and beat up the doctors, orderlies, and the Major. Such was the power of "Sanitary Syd". He, like other Japanese sergeants and sergeant-majors we were to encounter later in our captivity, seemed to wield immense influence and power, and often their officers would ignore such disregard of their orders.

Every morning now as we walked out of the camp up the hillside we could see progress on the new huts and a new fence being built around the camp. The rumour was that all of us who had been working for six months would be replaced. This started because the men from Heito camp looked so fit compared to us. They were not as thin, and outdoor work in the sunshine of the much warmer south had given them a tan. We, with our skeletal bodies, white and stained yellow from the acid water of the mine, looked awful to them.

CHAPTER 10

" Take Care of Your Health "

In July, 1943, the new PoW camps' Commander in Chief arrived. All but the sickest prisoners in the hospital were sent into the mine. We miners did not see him, but Major Crossley told us squad leaders that the new commander had made a speech in which he said he sympathized with our position, but, "We must take care of our health so that we could return to our homes after the war". His echoing of the phrase from that now famous speech we had heard from Wakiyama on the night we arrived did not amuse or comfort us.

"Take care of your health — too bloody true," Len Savage replied to me when I told him that night. "Those bastards don't intend to take care of our health. They will work us all to death in that mine."

Poor Len, over six feet and a big man, was suffering, going down rapidly, his legs swelling with beri-beri. So far in that camp I had lost "Basher" Gore, Johnnie Griffiths, and "Kapp" Kapplehoff, another of my courageous despatch riders from the Malayan campaign. The rest from my original signal section and their replacements in Malaya were showing deteriorating health, some worse them others. Dennis Hanford looked ghastly, as did Gibson, one of my drivers recovering from an amazing operation by Captain Seed.

Gibson was dying of what appeared to me a bronchial cold, and one night I was told Captain Seed was going to make a final attempt to save him. While others held him down, Captain Seed scratched his chest and dabbed in iodine to relieve the congestion. It must have been agony for "Gibby", who showed me his criss-crossed chest a few days later.

At Taihoku No. 6 Camp, Major Wheeler, still keeping his diary, was recording his problems with the Japanese NCOs in charge of the "sick" and the hospital. He wrote:

6th May, 1943

What a week it has been so far! Monday for me was one of those sickening, unreal days which used to be so common but which, of late, have been only occasional and usually not so bad. The sick parade was a bit bigger than average but all genuine and a number of very sick men. Along came the Lance Cpl, absolutely white with rage, screaming at me for giving them tickets, then shouted for them, lined them all up, shouting in Japanese; then each in turn had a good slapping with a long wooden roller. For some reason he picked out one of the sickest, an acute gastritis and struck him until he collapsed. One officer with malaria collapsed with a temperature of l05.5 degrees. They were lined-up in the mid-day sun with no hats. Another collapsed. There was some more slapping. A Lance Cpl finally OK'd four men who even to him were obviously unfit for work. The rest were put to work in the camp and sent out next day. Some had temperatures from 100 to 101, many with advanced beri-beri with oedema.

Tuesday not so bad. Naturally few reported sick — poor devils yesterday. Byrne died in the evening — acute rheumatic fever? Today, so far, has been quiet — may it continue.

16th May 1943

The past two weeks or so have been most difficult in the Medical Inspection Room with practically no sick being allowed on the sick list and the Lance Cpl sending one man after another to work. Fortunately, on the whole, our health is a little better but I am afraid that we cannot be lucky forever and one of them is going to pass out one of these days.

I have written a long letter to the Camp Commandant pointing out all the difficulties etc. and asking that I be allowed some authority but from past experience I have little hope. 150 of our fittest men have been picked (fittest according to the Japanese, no attention being shown to me) and are supposed to be leaving but no details so far.

Major Wheeler was obviously fighting the same battle with Japanese NCOs as Captain Seed, trying desperately to keep the sickest men from being sent out to work, and striving to get some authority on medical decisions which affected life and death. The frustrations and agonies of the doctors and medical orderlies were shared by the Senior British Officers in each camp as they saw their men slipping away, day by day. Major Wheeler's protest letter met the fate of Major Crossley's letter. He ruefully wrote:

May 20th 1943

The Japanese Medical Lance Cpl continues to be most difficult. I have no acknowledgment of my written protest and likely won't have, I suppose, as I never have before.

May 24th 1943

The Lance Cpl is particularly hostile to me these days. He saw my letter all right — demonstrated how he tore it up and threw it away, so I am sure it did not get to the Commandant. Also demonstrated how he would cut my head off, so all in all, I don't suppose it will make any difference — it may make him more difficult but one can only try and hope.

Major Wheeler did not know then that his days facing that lance corporal were numbered. He was to be ordered to accompany the party of 150 "fit" men to Kinkaseki.

In Kinkaseki, the nightmare went on. Anything that broke the tension or torment of those days and gave some hope was seized on by all. One improvement and, perhaps, sign that something was happening was that prisoners no longer had to parade with the Japanese on the 8th of every month. This parade was hated and feared by those in camp. It was called to read out, with great solemnity, the "Imperial Rescript", the wording of the declaration of war by Japan on the USA and Great Britain. All Japanese paraded in full uniform, bayonets fixed, officers in riding boots, belt, white gloves, and swords, the pathetic prisoners standing at the rear. Each word was intoned gravely, as coming from the Great Highness, His Imperial Majesty, Tenno Heinka Hirohito. The Rescript was kept rolled in a box, and always carried above the head by one of the officers.

Summer came at last to Kinkaseki, and instead of the perpetual low clouds and drizzling cold rain it brought blue skies and sunshine, raising our spirits.

In August the old fence at the side of the camp was pulled down to reveal about a dozen new huts. Again our hopes rose, as we believed new prisoners arriving might replace the sick and those of us who had survived the eight months since mine work started.

On the 10th of August, sure enough, into the camp came 100 men from Taihoku, most of them from the 5th Field Regiment, RA. The rest were from the llth Indian Divisional Signals, Royal Engineers. With them came a great boon, Major Ben Wheeler, the Canadian doctor of the Indian Medical Service whom I've quoted before, and a medical orderly, Lance/Bdr George Harrison. These men looked fit and well and had suntans, although they had suffered from all the usual malnutrition diseases.

The party from Taihoku had arrived during the afternoon while I had been down the mine, and I remember the tremendous lift in spirits I experienced that night when I saw them. At least they would bring news of the world outside our fence. They brought rumours that the Germans and Italians had been defeated in North Africa, that the Americans had re-taken the Aleutian islands, and that Mussolini was about to resign. Strange now to look back and realize that the rumours and news were almost always good, regardless of reality; we wanted to and would believe anything to build up our hopes.

Major Wheeler faithfully recorded his impressions of the move from No. 6 Camp, Taihoku, and his thoughts on Kinkaseki:

August 10th 1943

Up at 0400 hours and lined up at 0600 hours with lots of shouting — worse — I was made to carry at least 40 pounds. The whole camp was up and gave us a good send-off. Marched to Taihoku about three miles then entrained and after one change and at about 1200 hours we arrived at a station, not knowing what was ahead. What was ahead was a six to seven mile walk or rather climb, on a rough, rocky mountain road, winding and climbing all the way. I shall not forget it. The last long climb I started to stumble and fall — legs just gave out — however, I was able to pass on some of my kit and got there in a vertical position — we only had one five minute rest the whole day.

Our new home is a real prison — dismal — perched on a steep, rocky slope, led up to by stone steps, surrounded by a high brick wall. Who should we find but the 155th Field Regt and 80th Anti-Tank Regt we left at the boat. Captain Seed is looking fit but he has, I am afraid, had a worse time even than we, and things are worse, far worse, than with us. 33 deaths including one officer, the Dental Orderly and his Regimental Nursing Orderly.

Men are working in a copper mine and almost without exception are pale, sick and discouraged looking, especially compared to us with our tan. Their troubles seem to have been the same as ours but the work (hell they tell me) has made the difference.

August 12th 1943
Began trying to know the patients — some 40 — most chronic, several mine injuries, a few severe. The hospital has no beds, no mattresses and only two blankets per man. At present they are all on boards with certainly no more than 1½ foot per man. To examine one you have to climb on the platform and shift the next man.

August 13th
One beri-beri, Rigby, died.

August 18th
Sweeney of the 155th Field Regt killed in the mine today. I went down to collect the body — little but flesh and broken bones, poor chap.

Great doings in the camp — all officers but those employed in the camp and 100 more men, unfits and TBs are being sent off. The Japanese did the picking with no reference to us, of course, and some of the worst are not included — still, it will be a big help. The Padre, Father Kennedy, and the dentist, Captain Badgett, are being sent off, but we are keeping some things for extractions.

August 23rd, 1943
Another death — Smith — beri-beri — inanition — starvation — or what have you — just gave up and who can blame him.

Things go on and on — rumour has it that more of the old men will go — I hope so. There is hardly one of the originals that does not look like death — the mine must be a hell, let alone climbing to and from it.

Major Wheeler's terse diary comments were so true. We must have looked like death to them. We had got used to the sight of each other, our skeletal bodies, stained yellow now with the washing in the mine water, but it was wise not to look in a mirror. In any event, shaving was a luxury enjoyed once, maybe, in a month, using a communal razor. Soap was non-existent, and we used a soft clay we had seen coolies in the mine use to try and wash off the worst of the dirt.

The rumour that all the original survivors would leave Kinkaseki and be replaced had started due to what we called "The Thin Men Parades". The Japanese had ordered us all to parade one night for a "medical inspection". As we lined up, we saw with dread that it was "Sanitary Syd" and his two hench-men doing the inspection. "Syd" was armed as always with his *Kendo* stick.

When we realized he was picking out men who he thought could not work much longer in the mine, all of us prayed and hoped we would be chosen. As Major Wheeler records, he simply picked out those who looked the thinnest. These were sent away with the TB cases. Amongst those to go were several of my signal section: Eric Clack, Frank Gill, Dennis Gilboy, Jimmy Gibson (of the scratching operation), Dennis Hanford (a TB case), Eric Mulliner, George Smith and Lt Martin Kepple, our officer. All were ill and would have been hospital cases anywhere else in the world. We envied them. They would be leaving Kinkaseki, travelling over the mountain on the road we could see every night on our way back from the mine.

A few days later another 100 men came into the camp. They were a mixture of Manchesters, Loyals, and Royal Artillery, all from Heito camp. They brought more rumours and the sad news that out of 504 in their camp 51 had died. Equally sad, 90 percent of their camp had malaria.

With more so-called "fit" mine workers in the camp, Major Wheeler, Captain Seed, and Major Crossley decided to take this opportunity to try to get more control of the number of men allowed off sick. They argued that if they could control who stayed in camp sick, they could cure more of the sick and the mine would be ensured a steady supply of "fit" miners. They won, and a miracle happened. Major Wheeler's diary recorded the incident:

September 6th 1943

Are one's prayers being answered? The Nips have given us 70 white cards for sick, to be given or taken as we see fit, and five red cards for lying down cases — less than they had (not always used) themselves, and with 31 cases in hospital, sounds a reasonable number. In reality, it is grossly inadequate as there are close to 50 who cannot possibly be sent down the mine by us, leaving very few cards really to play with. However, we can keep in the worst and one cannot realize how big a step forward it represents without having seen and experienced the former brutality and chaos. Will be able to keep records now too, if they will only not interfere too much.

Despite the constant efforts of Major Crossley, Major Wheeler and Captain Seed to improve the situation, there was always "Sanitary Syd" ready to pounce and cause brutalities as only he could (again from Major Wheeler's diary):

September 22nd

One day the Medical Sergeant sent out ten of our permanent sick, most of whom had to be carried back in the evening, but we have got them back on cards now.

The Medical Sergeant here cannot be described. He is an animal, as they all are, but a good many degrees lower — still these days his visits are infrequent.

With the arrival of more men, the camp was re-organized from its original 12 squads to 22 squads. I was still Squad Leader (*hancho*), and my squad consisted of Sergeants, Lance Sergeants, Bombardiers and Corporals. Our squad name was *"Dai ju-go han"* (Number fifteen squad). I was persevering with my *Nippon-go*, and another close friend in my hut, Sergeant Dick ("Tiffy") Sheppard, was also hard at work learning it.

110

We tried to make contacts in the mine with civilian workers, when we were not being watched. Our main object was to obtain news of the war and its progress. Gradually, on our working level in the mine, the "NCOs' floor", we established good contacts. My best came through a most peculiar incident. If the "bogie" tracks were broken or the sleepers got rotten, civilian workers came to repair them. Similarly if the wooden chutes were damaged by falls of rock, carpenters would arrive. These *daikoo*, as we came to know them, were poor coolies, and though mostly friendly were scared to talk. However, one afternoon I was amazed to hear one of them humming and singing the hymn, "Onward Christian Soldiers" (in Taiwanese). I squatted by him, sang a little, and soon we had shaken hands. In my limited Japanese I discovered he had been to a Christian school. He was obviously very anti-Japanese, and his news of the war's progress seemed too good to be true.

He indicated, by signs and drawing maps in the dust, that the Americans were taking islands south of the Philippines. He claimed American and British forces were in Italy. The Russians, he indicated, were pushing back the Germans from Moscow. His news certainly gave us a boost, and I carried these good "bore holes" back to camp that night.

At about this time, the "two-bar *hancho*" on our floor, a Japanese who we had christened "Blackie", suddenly decided to make me a "Mine *hancho*". He gave me a large sledge hammer and told me my job in future would be to go from hole to hole, breaking up *oki ishees* (big stones) so they could be lifted into bogies or put down the chutes. To me this sounded great. I would be off production, not having to turn out a set quota of bogies, and I would be free to move about. The trouble, I found out that first night, was that he was going to hold me responsible for the overall performance of my squad. After those who had not completed their quota got their "bashing" and "hammer flogging", I got one too!

We discovered that "Blackie", so-called because he always looked dirty and unshaven, was a drug addict. If he had his long thin pipe and was squatting, puffing, he was a very contented person. This was probably the main reason why on this floor we were able to start a "racket" which became known as the "phantom bogies". Not only did this save us work and beatings, but it drastically cut production of copper ore on our floor.

111

The checkers at this time were always elderly men or young boys. Clearly, the Japanese were conscripting all eligible men for the fighting. As the day wore on in the mine, the checkers became less attentive. They invariably sat on pieces of board on the floor alongside the blackboard, and unless the "two-bar" Japanese foreman was about they seldom stood up to look at the ore as the bogie passed.

In my new job as *hancho*, I now could go around on our level with no problems. I found a hole nearby the hot-hole chute where we could fill bogies with *Hi-saki* (poor ore), and do it easily in the cool. The only problem was that this ore was brown coloured, while the *Ko-saki* was dark grey or bluish grey. The solution was simple. We filled the bogies ¾ full with *Hi-saki*, and then pushed them on to the chute containing *Ko-saki* to "top off". The first day we tried a "phantom", I worked with Johnnie Ford, John Waugh, Jim Ferguson, and Jim Watson, who were working the hot-hole in two-man shifts. Our "bogie-pusher" was Bombardier Glendenning, also of the 155th RA. I was the look-out. We hoped that if the checker boy looked in, he would see what appeared to be a full bogie of *Ko-saki*.

I followed Glendenning down with his first that day, and helped him to get it going fast. It went like a dream. As I let go the front around the corner of the tunnel, out of sight of the checker, Glendenning, head-down, went past him, calling out the hole number, "*Minami itchee hatchee shee*" (South, 184). The checker did not budge from his board.

We were elated. And so was born the first of our "phantom bogie" schemes. Not only did it save "bashings" and hard work, but it provided less *Ko-saki* production for the Japanese war effort. The effect on morale on our level was tremendous.

Next we tried another method, "building bogies". This entailed finding old pieces of pit-props, wood, or baskets to "build" a central pyramid in the bogie. We would then surround and cover it with *Ko-saki*. As long as these passed the checker to be tipped into the communal chute, there was no problem, as these large chutes were fed from all holes on the level.

We got a tremendous boost from these activities, and I blessed the day my *Nippon-go* had got me appointed as a mine *hancho*. In my wanderings from hole to hole, supposedly to break up big stones, I searched for easy "fill" sources of *Hi-saki*, or old workings where timbers could be used.

Always I would try to "chat-up" the checker boy and establish friendly contacts with him and the civilian workers. With our production figures on this level now being produced easily, "Blackie" and our Formosan "one-bar" became more human and the beatings eased. Not so on the other levels where the "Ghost", the "Eagle", "Frying Pan", "Pan-face", and "Sammy" kept up and increased their vicious floggings.

However, our period of comparative peace, about two months, came to an abrupt end one night. A break-down in the cages caused a back-up in bogies. The cages were about 300 yards from the checker and the assembly point. At the assembly point there were electric bulbs. The last bogies down that night came to a stop under the glare of the electric lights. To our horror, we saw tell-tale trickles of brown mud coming from the sides of bogies. Another bogie, on stopping, jolted against the long line of waiting "bogies", and the contents just collapsed. The carefully built pyramid inside could not cope with the sudden jolt. "Blackie", standing by with his powerful lamp and his hammer, scraped at the top of the ore, the one-bars doing the same. They all exploded together.

"*Bugeroo, nani ka*", they screamed. "*Damme, damme, sukoshee bogies. nani hi-saki, ko-saki nai ga!*" (Stupid, what is this, Damn you, what is this poor ore, no good ore?)

The whole of my squad, "*Ju-go han*", was lined up. I, "*Itchee go koo*" was "*Damme, damme*", and we were slapped, beaten, and harangued. Then "Blackie" said "You *itchee go koo, hancho*, You *hammero!*"

It was clear he wanted me to use the hammer on my own squad. In other levels and in the camp the Japanese had tried this method of punishment, forcing one prisoner to hit another, and sometimes forcing a PoW squad *hancho* to hit his own men. It had never happened with me before.

My pals Len Savage, Johnnie Ford and the others all said, "For Christ's sake, hit us Sarge! Better you than him."

Instead, I tried a different approach. I stood against the pipe, hands up, and said in my best *Nippon-go* that I was responsible. "Blackie" reacted violently. He gave me a number of strokes across the back and shoulders. The next thing I recalled was a terrible pain in the head and blinding flashes. "Blackie" had floored me. I was told later he seemed very upset as he did not even flog the squad. My belief is that he did not flog my squad or beat me further because I offered to accept responsibility. He was an ex-Army Sergeant. Whatever the reason, "Blackie" never touched me again. Three days later we had a change of working levels. My squad, *"Ju-go han"*, was moved to one of the higher levels to work on "The Eagle's" floor.

Years later I found I had been made an honourary life member of the Duchy Far East PoW Association due to a speech that Len Savage had made recounting that incident. That he would remember touched me deeply.

We found another way to vent our feelings, though not as practical as the "phantom bogies". With the flame on our carbide lamps, it was possible to burn marks on the rusty sides of the "bogies". "Tiffy" Sheppard, Len Savage, and I delighted in burning large "V" signs and "...-" on the bogie sides. Great was our joy if we happened to see these bogies on the surface. Even better, sometimes we saw these "V bogies" (as we called them) being pulled by the little steam engines along the mountainside tracks.

Our new level in the mine had a notorious reputation for hot and dangerous holes. With the "Eagle" as "two-bar", and "Sammy" and "the Beast" as "one-bars", life became very unpleasant again. Strange though it may seem, the "Eagle" one morning told me I was *hancho* and gave me the same job as before. The checking system on this level was the same. The checker this time was a very elderly man who loved to sit on his board. We prisoners called these flat pieces of board *"shushin* boards" (sleeping boards). All civilian workers, "one- bars", and "two-bars" had them, usually in some cool deserted spot on the various levels.

Accidents were happening more often. The canvas shoes the Japs provided for work quickly broke, being rotten from the constant climbing and working in water. We were often down to just the sole tied on with string or strips of cloth. It was easy to slip and fall in the dark. Your sputtering lamp blew out if there was any sudden gust from either an explosion or an uncoupled air-pipe.

Our worst accident on this floor happened to my close friend, Johnnie Ford, *"Itchee hatchee ray"* (180). One morning, working in a hot-hole, he slipped and fell into the chute, blacking out in the extreme heat. It was agony to get him out as he was 30 feet down. We had to release two bogies of ore before out came Johnnie's legs. He was alive, but unconscious, with a terrible gash on his head. I cleaned his head as best I could and argued with the "Eagle" to let him return to camp. After a nightmarish discussion, they finally agreed to let him return, and we pushed him to the cage on a wooden flat-top bogie. We despaired that day as we worked, waiting for the time to return to camp and see if Johnnie would live.

Miraculously, he lived. Major Wheeler performed a fantastic operation with no anesthetic, using dental forceps to remove bits of bone. Johnnie was ill for weeks, but survived, a testimony to his courage and guts, and the skill of our doctors and medical orderlies.

Major Wheeler recorded the brief details of his work at that time:

October 13th 1943

I am lousy for the first time but am waging war and as they haven't yet had time to dig in, I shall win. I turned my ankle the other day and have been hobbling with a stick since but it is improving.

Things go on as usual. I am busy these days, which is a good thing and passes time. The last two accident cases have been fractured skulls, the last one extensive, and we had to remove bone down to the brain over an area of about 1½ inches in diameter on the forehead. Our methods, etc. were very primitive I am afraid, but so far, only two days after, he is doing well, which after all is the main thing. There is certainly plenty of experience here in minor surgery and some not so minor! — very useful experience too, as opposed to the other camps where everything was skin, beri-beri, or gastrointestinal. We have constantly here between 20 or 30 injuries on the sick list or in hospital. One is constantly amazed at how well most of them do, all things considered.

October 23rd 1943

I must say I don't know what to write in here — everything seems to go on much the same and for the last two weeks or so we have not had even a decent rumour, though plenty must be happening. Surely God it is not going to go on and on!

Had two more serious fractured skulls, the last one yesterday. The worst with a bad tear in the longitudinal sinus and had to plug it with gauze. Tried to take it out today, hoping it would have stopped, but no luck. Hope it will eventually or I hardly know what the answer is. These injuries are certainly an experience, things of course one would not have to touch normally and with the best of instruments, but we have to do our best here with what we have and I am continually amazed how good our best has been. The last is doubtful, still with luck there is no reason why he can't come on. I must say it will take a lot to shake me after this.

Another death, beri-beri, a few days ago — 37 years old — and another who will not last for more than a few days — what the score is going to be when the cold weather comes and all these thin, debilitated men, I don't like to think.

November 3rd 1943

Things go on and on — not any real change though I am very busy. Seed has what appears to be an amoebic hepatitis and I have him in bed on some Emetine which we fortunately had. He seems to be coming around but it will be some time before he will be back at work. Serious accidents and all kinds of accidents continue — two fractured sternums and a foot in the last week.

Another 100 sick have been picked out to leave and this time they let us do most of the picking so it is a good selection and will get rid of the worst who can walk. Knowing the Japs, of course, one wonders if they will be any better off. 60 are said to be going to a camp where they won't have to work but our friends have a peculiar conception of no work. On October 31st the orderlies sent 38 men to work off the sick list, 25 of the worst; many had to be helped there let alone work. I am gradually getting them back on the sick list, however luckily such does are not so common now and too, I suppose one is getting callous after a year of it. God knows one can't help it. Wonder if we will slip back to normal on release.

Am having a great time now trying to get some kind of frames made for the two fractured sternums who have to lie on their backs. Bed-pans, wash bowls, etc. are the big things.

Had an air raid alarm for the first time. I think one is safe in saying it was the real thing. No news, no Red Cross. Tomorrow will be wee Kenneth's birthday and he will be a big boy — five years — he was such a grand age when I saw him last. Still, I can be, and am, thankful that they are all safe at home and the war, the real war, can't and won't touch them. Nell, when are we going to be together again, when will this all end?

The enemy, that is time, moves but slowly — two days and a year of this behind us — something to have survived.

November 14th 1943

A year in Taiwan, and believe me a year we shall not forget. Today it rained a little but almost since the month began we have had a steady drizzle or down-pour and it has turned cold. Men are soaked and chilled morning and evening and have to put on their wet clothes and soggy rags of shoes again next day. Lots of colds, bronchitis, tummies and some pneumonia. Injuries in the mine keep on averaging one a week or so — fractures — with any number of other serious wounds, sprains, abrasions, etc. Do not think there is a day without something.

November 25th 1943

Two deaths today — one killed in the mine, lived a few hours — would have lived some time though his condition was hopeless had I not, well, suppose one can only say put him out of his misery, but no one can tell me I was wrong. The other was a beri-beri of long standing.

These accidental deaths, though, keep coming and coming. Last week had a compound fracture of both legs, with many other cuts etc. This week a death - next week what? The conditions under which the men have to work must be unbelievable. How

117

those that have been here a year have stuck it, I don't know. Of course half have been sent away as unfit by Jap standards even, and 40 of the originals have died, two killed in the mine and only about two-thirds remaining are fit, even by the standard one has to use here.

Seed is still down and has been, except for two days, so I am really pretty busy going steadily from 7:00 am to 7:00 pm.

CHAPTER 11

A Farewell Song

As the first year of mine work at Kinkaseki came to an end, we survivors were becoming fewer and fewer as each "thin man party" was formed. Those of us left prayed, hoped, schemed, play-acted, and would have done anything, in fact, to be put in one of those groups leaving. So many were carried out that a saying, which spread to every camp on Taiwan, was born: There are only two ways out of Kinkaseki, "feet first or head first!"

Those of us who were left clung closer together, and although friendships were made with the incoming men from other camps, few were cemented like those among the "original miners." Even the *hancho* in the mine differentiated us, and using our numbers (1 to 525) would put any new miners with us older miners so we would "teach" them.

We taught them, all right, every method we could to avoid a "bashing" or the "hot-holes".

Despite bashings when caught, the "phantom bogies" were still being run. We devised a new method to stop production by blocking the chutes. This, though successful, caused me a few "bashings". We would manhandle the largest pieces of stone we could to the chute, and then drop them in. As they fell, often one would catch some of the wooden struts and cause a block. The "bogie-pusher" below could not "draw off" the ore in the chute, and those working in the hole could only work until the chute was full.

Their method of clearing the blockage, a piece of dynamite tied to the end of a long bamboo pole, often put the chute out of action. Since my job as a "mine *hancho*" was to break up these large stones, every time we had a blockage it invariably meant two explosions: one in the chute and one from the "Eagle" or "Sammy", venting their spite on me!

Then on 2nd December, when we came back from the mine, we found the in-camp men in a state of excitement. It seemed rumours had been circulating all day that Camp Commandant Wakiyama was leaving. Although his leaving had not been announced, the whole camp had been ordered to assemble when we returned. We lined up facing the platform, still filthy from the mine, and eventually down came the usual procession: Wakiyama in full uniform, sword, riding breeches, boots, and white gloves; the Orderly Officer with his red and silver sash; and "Pop", trotting along in the rear.

We waited on his speech scarcely breathing, listening closely as "Pop" interpreted, sentence by sentence.

"He say", began "Pop", in his high pitched tone trying to imitate Wakiyama's haughty manner, "Today I make speech of farewell to you all."

The sigh of relief from the starving, filthy PoWs in front of him must have been audible.

He went on to say that when he first got to know us, he thought we were a lot of uncivilized barbarians and had treated us accordingly. We should never forget we were prisoners-of-war, kept alive only through the "tender mercies and august virtues of the Imperial Japanese Emperor (*Tenyo Heinka*), the all highest Hirohito." In fact, he went on, we should have all been killed in battle, as no Japanese soldier would dishonour himself by being taken prisoner.

"We have treated you well, I think," he said, "according to the great *Bushido* warrior code and spirit of the *Samurai*. Therefore, you must take care of your health so you may return one day to your home. When I was a boy, the Japanese were helping the British to win the 1914-1918 war. At that time the British soldiers had the spirit of *Bushido*, were very brave, and had good marching songs full of spirit."

One of those songs he remembered was called "Tipperary." He asked if we would do him the favour of letting him hear it again!

We were dumbfounded. Soon we found voice and the old marching chorus our fathers had sung, in vastly different circumstances, resounded around the camp. Never had I, or any others there on that occasion, sung "Tipperary" with such feeling or enthusiasm. We would have sung it 40 times to get rid of the bastard. It sounded like a "Te Deum" and, today, all those who survived feel pangs of deep emotion and a genuine tear of pride when hearing that tune. It is funny how the music from all the old songs we sang there in Kinkaseki can still find and release such intense emotions after so many years.

Our new commandant arrived the next day. He looked much older and far more human than Wakiyama. We just hoped for the best. He came from Shirakawa No. 4 Camp and had been Commandant there. His reputation had been very bad. That camp was occupied by senior officers, amongst whom were Sir Shenton Thomas and Sir Mark Young, previously Colonial Governors, Lt General Percival, GOC Malaya, and Lt General Wainwright, an American army general who had taken over as GOC in the Philippines from General MacArthur. In that camp he had been given several names: "Poxy Percy", "Old Sourballs", and "The Grouch".

Major Crossley in the camp records noted the following:

2nd December
     Camp Commander changed. Loud cheers from all! With this change of Commander a new phase commenced during which it was possible for the P.A. (Personnel Administrator, Major Crossley) to submit various requests which in most cases were granted or at least considered.

Major Crossley, after a meeting with Major Wheeler and the older squad *hanchos* (collectively known as the Camp Committee), decided to try to improve conditions by petitioning the new Commandant. During the meeting, he told us he would try to cover every possible aspect. The following letter was than sent:

Sir,

     "We have commenced our 2nd year working in the mine with another dreadful, and this time fatal, accident due to a fall from the roof. This month already 45 men have sustained injuries while working, two of a very serious nature and one fatal.

     I beg of you to consider very seriously some of the following

121

suggestions and observations which I am positive will help to reduce this appalling damage to men's lives and bodies.

Many of these suggestions have been mentioned on several previous occasions but unfortunately no action has been taken by the Company. I do not understand why because it has always been our impression that both the Nippon Army and the Company were anxious to avoid these accidents.

It is now established without doubt that the chief reasons for accidents have been due to:

1.   Bad lamps.
2.   Bad boots.
3.   No inspection of working places by *hanchos* after blasting.
4.   Ladders broken or in bad repair.
5.   Unguarded chutes.
6.   Blowing out of lamps through blasting.
7.   The "fear of being beaten with the *hancho's* hammer".
8.   Fainting spells caused by working in very hot places.

The following suggestions would help to obviate some of the above:

1.   Bad Lamps: The bad condition of lamps was reported about six weeks ago. On this occasion many new lamps were issued and a new system of daily issue at the mine head was introduced by which all men were receiving good lamps in working order. This however now seems to have dropped off and unservicable lamps are being issued again.

2.   Boots: Generally speaking the condition of boots is now fairly good and the *jika tabi* is definitely the best and safest footwear for the mine.

122

Instead of men having to wait until a certain date before new boots are issued why not allow each squad *hancho* to inform mine *hancho* each morning the number of men whose boots are so badly worn as to constitute a danger? These could then be replaced immediately for there would only be a few each day.

3. Roof Testing: The mine *hancho* who are presumably very experienced men can tell immediately whether a roof is safe or not.

After blasting has taken place or before commencing work should not the roofs and workings be examined by the *hancho* and if it is considered unsafe to proceed, men should not be allowed to commence work?

4. Ladders: Several accidents already have occurred through ladders coming away from the wall or having treads missing. There are at least 20 or 30 prisoners working in the mine daily who are experienced carpenters and joiners: could not these men be employed in repairing and renewing these ladders in the mine in an effort to save the lives and limbs of their comrades?

5. Unguarded Chutes: Many men lately have fallen down the chutes which are level with the ground and not marked in any way.

Useful suggestions as to the types of guards which could be used on these chutes have already been submitted by the men, and these could be put into practice by the same joiners squad.

6.	Blowing out Lamps:	When blasting takes place or there is a leak in the air pipe, lamps are unavoidably blown out. The men have no means of relighting them and one of the men has to start off in the dark and try to find the *hancho*. The result of this can be seen in the Camp Hospital where one man now lies with both his legs broken.

Is it not possible to issue each group with a box of matches which could be handed back to the mine *hancho* at the close of work?

7.	Fear of the Hammer	Pyschologically this is indirectly responsible for causing the biggest percentage of accidents, for the following reasons:

The word *speedo* coupled with the threat "No *speedo*, hammer" is shouted at the men. This on the face of it does not appear very harmful, but having seen the mutilated and bruised bodies of some of the prisoners returning to this camp after a beating in the mine there is no doubt that any man with any sense will do everything possible to avoid such brutal and degrading treatment. Men do not always take the care necessary when moving from one place to another as a result of this *speedo*, with the result that one false step brings him to the bottom of 30 or 40 ft chute. In the case of lamps being blown out, the men are told by the Camp Authorities to stay

124

where they are until the *hancho* or someone brings a light. This sounds all right but if they do this then they will also receive a sound beating for not turning out the required number of bogies.

Punishment for laziness or bad work should surely be carried out and controlled by the Nippon Army in Camp.

8.   Sickness

Many men through working in hot places have temporary fainting fits and "black-outs". Again if they are unfortunate enough to have one of these at the top of a chute, then down the chute they go and another man is carried back into camp seriously injured.

On 26th Oct., 869 Taffs submitted a letter stating that he had had a very serious illness in the Military Hospital at Heito from which he had been lucky to recover. After working some weeks in the mine in a hot place, he found that fainting and dizzy spells were becoming frequent, and therefore asked for a change into a cooler working place. No reply was received to this request and five days later he had a fainting fit at the top of a chute falling at least 30 ft. This man now lies in hospital seriously injured and it is unlikely that he will ever be able to work in the mine again.

Very frequent changing of men working in hot places and a more reasonable amount of work demanded of those men would help.

9.   <u>Medical Attention:</u> As there are no medical attention and supplies in the mine whatsoever the following suggestion is submitted:

There are many men in the work parties who are trained in first aid for the field. Could not there be one officially appointed for each of the floors who could be supplied with the necessary medical requirements to render first aid to the men? This would save loss of blood and prevent dirt from entering wounds etc.

There is one more special point I wish to bring to your notice: (See diagram below)

On No. 2 floor there is a tunnel through which 80 or 90 of the working party have to pass daily on their way to working No. 176. Frequent falls have occurred in this tunnel and the men have to climb over the fallen rock bending down as they run because the roof is so low. They are always instructed by the *hancho* to run when passing through this tunnel. Evidence of the lowness of this tunnel can be seen from the men's backs, which are all scratched by the stones on the roof.

The men in this particular part have a constant fear that this tunnel could collapse one day and will be the scene of another tragic accident.

It is understood that this fault will be quite easily remedied if the loose stones from the fall were removed from the floor and the tunnel timbered. All of

126

which could be done by the prisoners themselves.

In all the above suggestions there is little or no cost or trouble to the Company whatsoever, merely a question of organization, and I feel sure if these suggestions are given a trial the result will be very gratifying and a benefit to the prisoners and Company together and will help the men to feel more confident and safe at their daily work.

The result was miraculous. The request for medical attention to injuries in the mine was granted the following day, and other significant small changes followed. Major Wheeler dutifully recorded the miracle:

December 9th

Three deaths in the past 24 hours — one a beri-beri with diarrhoea that has seen so many off. One with pneumonia and one with dysentery of sorts.

Weather remains fairly cold with usually rain, but so far not felt it half so much as last year. Things are much more quiet with the new Commandant and yesterday had orders to send two orderlies with first aid kit with the work parties. A step in the right direction except that they have not replaced the orderlies so we are very short-handed.

December 11th 1943

A miracle! Fresh milk for the hospital — 11 one quarter pint bottles arrived. The Jap orderlies drank three, leaving eight but one has had to live through this to realize how much of a miracle it is. They say it will come each day, we shall see! Also allowed me one orderly Harrison in place of the two down the mine — the war must be over, if it only were!

The following week we were also allowed to write off a PoW postcard to our families. It was a printed card on which you crossed out words, but at least it was something and improved morale.

Our second Christmas at Kinkaseki came near, and Major Crossley was determined to try and make it better than the last. He persuaded the Camp Commander to allow a concert to be arranged, to allow the miners to come back early from the mine, and for an improvement in food on Christmas Day. The officers were allowed to buy some bottles of tomato ketchup and a syrup-like drink which the Japanese called "New Piece" (we called it "Nu-Piss"). We were woken earlier than usual that Christmas morning, at 5:00 am, but we were in good spirits as we knew of the concert and, more important, an improved meal that night. For the first time, we actually burst into jubilant song on the way into the mine.

We finished work early and reached camp at 2:00 pm. The meal that night, rice and a stew with some definite traces of pork fat, was a big improvement. Also, the cooks had made a risotto of rice with pork fat which, to us starving men, tasted heavenly.

The concert was terrific. The officers dressed up and put on a sketch, and each squad provided one "entertainer". I sang "Phil the Fluter's Ball" and got a reception which would have been worthy of a professional entertainer. We ended our concert, as we always did, with patriotic songs: "Rule Britannia", the chorus of "Britons never, never shall be slaves" being roared out defiantly, and then, always the very last, "Land of Hope and Glory, Mother of the Free".

Morale was high that night. We had survived one year in the mine and another Christmas was gone. "Who knows," the optimists said. "It may all be over by next."

Major Wheeler noted:

December 25th 1943
Another PoW Christmas — infinitely better than last year in every way but!

It has rained all day but the men all in good spirits, having sing-song in the huts and to end the day we had an issue of tea with sugar in it! And so to bed, though I have a round of ½-hour guard duty to put in. All day, of course, I have been trying to picture home. I got out your photo, Nell and the boys and rearranged yours, one corner had got wet and mouldy, but otherwise kept well. I keep it packed away. I somehow do not like the idea of these animals looking at you. Not a happy day, I am afraid, for most of us — too many memories attached to it and perhaps it is better that it is not very much like Christmas to make these memories more vivid. Darling, God pray all is well with you this day, with our boys, with all the family — how I would like to have helped you fill the stockings — still I must not dwell on such things too much — the only way to get through this is to be as near normal as possible and live from day to day, meal to meal, good-night my love.

Major Wheeler's diary graphically recorded his feelings of that day and of his wife and family. They are symbolic of the thoughts of every man that Christmas night.

Before we slept, everyone prayed silently. I always tried hard to focus my thoughts on pleasant things before I slept, believing this would influence my dreams and instill in me the spirit to survive another day in that hell below ground — the mine. It was dreadful to be woken, often from a blissful dream of home, with the clarion call of the Jap bugler and screams of the guards as they tore into the huts. You woke with the knowledge of another slog over that mountain and the long climb down into the mine, never knowing what the day held for you, what you must do in order to avoid the "hammer".

The lines of men going sick, trying to obtain the magic White Card, grew longer. We had a new year to face. Rumours of Allied advances were improving, but we on Taiwan could see no evidence of an early end to the war. We shook hands with each other and wished for, not "A Happy New Year", but survival and an end to the war in 1944.

Major Wheeler wrote:

I have made no resolutions this year. What is there to resolve? Nor have I made any more guesses as to the end of all this. What is the use? We have nothing to go on — it may be this year — pray God it is — but just as likely from what we know, it may not. The only thing is to live from day to day the best way one can and that, on the whole, I think is becoming easier, partly due to improved conditions, but more so due to the fact that this life is becoming, or has become, real, natural, or how should I describe it, whereas all else seems so far away, almost like another world or dream. One thinks of home and all the rest as much, but it is not so sharp, not so clear, as it was at first, though I cannot put it into the right words.

Each man fought his own mental battle for survival. A lot depended on your immediate companions, both in the hut and the mine. Some were always gloomy and despondent. These men would "go down" the quickest; deterioration was rapid in body once the signs of mental instability or depression could be seen.

Some men started to save their morning rice in a container to eat cold when they came back from the mine at night. They seemed to get a sense of satisfaction from having a larger meal than the rest at night time. Others ate their rice slowly, grain by grain, to make it last until after the others had finished. Three men in my squad fell into the same habit of going to the latrines or washing while the rice was being served. They would wait to return to the hut and eat theirs when everyone else had finished. The crazy look in their eyes, as they glanced around trying to ensure everyone was watching them, showed they were cracking. We tried to talk sense into men like this, but it was useless. Often they would reply, "You are only jealous because we have more to eat at night time."

Other men had an obsession for cigarettes. They were difficult to obtain, as the rarely supplied cigarettes came from what the Japanese called "this canteen". Every day we worked we were credited with 10 *Sen* (about one penny). With this we could purchase "canteen supplies". Periodically, five cigarettes were issued to those working. I did not smoke, so I took mine below ground to exchange with civilian workers for salt or, if possible, a small orange. Smokers, though, craved their fags or "the reek", as the Scots called it. Great would be the excitement in the camp if cigarettes were issued. The cry would go out, "Reek up." Some smokers would cut their issue in half to make them last longer. Others would break up the cigarettes and, using a "rolling paper" (pages from Bibles proved best), carefully roll thinner cigarettes, thus doubling or sometimes trebling the number of smokes. This rolling of the tobacco with pages of Bibles or old hymn books gave birth to the phrase, "Any Holy Smokes?"

Those with a worse craving for tobacco than others exchanged their last valued possessions for their insanely treasured smoke. The tragedy was that when men reached this state, it was clear they were not mentally stable and had given up normal values. We had one sad case in my hut, in normal life an intelligent surveyor. He craved his tobacco. He started swapping his rice-ration for a thin cigarette. He progressively became more unstable. A friend of mine, Ben Slack of the Sherwood Foresters, tried hard to reason with him when he discovered the man had given away a signet-ring from his wife for three cigarettes — to no avail. The man died very soon after. Ben saw that ring on another man's hand in a different camp after the liberation in 1945. This man explained he had also bought it from another PoW, who had also died, for two rice rations, three months earlier in Shirakawa. Obviously the first purchaser of the ring had left Kinkaseki on a "thin man" party and had gone to Shirakawa where Ben Slack went also on a later party. Ben persuaded the third owner of the ring to part with it for some tinned food, and eventually returned the ring to the original owner's widow. Thankfully, she never knew the story of how the signet ring had twice been used for insane craving, both to be followed by death.

At the end of January 1944, another incident occurred which gave us hope that conditions might improve and that the fortunes of war were definitely turning against Germany and Japan. On the 29th, Major Crossley was sent for by "Pop" and told that the next day the Commander-in-Chief of all PoW Camps on Taiwan would be coming to Kinkaseki for an inspection and a meeting. Five officers and five enlisted men would represent the whole camp. Each representative would be allowed to put one question to the Commander. Furthermore, only these five men would be allowed to remain in camp. Every other man, except those with "Red Cards" (hospital cases allowed to lie down), was to be sent to the mine.

That night, "Pop" and Major Crossley told me I had been selected as one of the representatives. As the camp was now over 800 strong with the recent intakes from Taihoku, Heito, Karenko, and Shirakawa camps, I felt a big responsibility.

The five selected were all from the original 525 men who had arrived at Kinkaseki. I was pleased to see we included Patterson, who was in charge of the cook house, because he was one of the most trusted and knew the important aspects of our main concern: food! The Major quickly called a meeting of the men chosen, Captain J. Francke, Lt R.W. Hellyer, Lt J.T.N. Cross, Captain P.G. Seed (the doctor), and

131

we five from the ranks. He told us what question each of them was going to ask, and told us to go round the huts and come back with one question each. It should concern improving conditions in the mine. As the Major said, "You are below all day, know the conditions, know what best to ask. We officers don't go below. It is up to each of us to ask questions on different subjects with one object, to improve our conditions."

Eventually, after considerable argument in the huts, we finally obtained a consensus on the most important questions affecting the mine. We took them back to the Major who had to tell "Pop" early next morning. We had to ignore the most popular suggestion: "Ask him when he thinks the war is going to finish and that bloody mine will close down!"

Came the great day, the camp was roused early, and everyone sent to the mine. Those few left on duty in camp were made to clean up everything for the inspection. We five were told to be at the camp office at 1330 hours. We were ushered in by the guards to be seated at a long table. We were faced across the table by "Napoleon", "Pop", the Camp Commander, and the Commander-in-Chief of PoW camps. In front of each of us there was a placard with our PoW camp number, rank, and name in Japanese *Katakana* characters. There were also some small bowls containing biscuits, sweets, and cups for tea.

The conference began by each of us in turn standing up, stating our name, profession in civilian life, and present state of health. We were then each asked the same questions, "Where did you see action?" and "Did you see any bloody combat?" (The way "Pop" interpreted the last question made it sound as though he was using the word "bloody" as a swearword instead of the obviously intended adjective. It was all we could do to keep straight faces. Major Crossley, sitting next to me on the bench behind the table, gave me a warning kick.) Then he asked us, "When do you think the war will be finished?" Most of us said six to nine months. When asked why, we said we thought the end of Germany would come first and that would be followed by a peace with Japan. The Commander-in-Chief seemed highly amused by our replies and there was much laughter between him and our Camp Commandant. He stated in rebuttal, "Even if Germany does finish fighting and make peace, Nippon will fight on." He then asked "Who do you think will finally win this war?" We all answered, "The Allies, America and Britain, if there is no peace agreement first."

The Commandant then asked, "If Britain was surrounded by enemies would she give in? Would all British people give up fighting and raise their hands?" We all replied no. We went on to say Britain had not given up in 1940, and would not surrender as a nation. He then went into a speech pointing out the 3000-year history of the Great Nippon Empire and the spirit of *Bushido* and *Samurai*. He told us he believed the war would go on for 100 years, if necessary, as all Japanese would fight to the last man.

His next question surprised us. He asked, "Are you controlled by the Jews?" We all replied in the negative. He then said, "Nippon is the most fortunate of the nations as it has no Jews!"

Then, looking straight at me and pointing, he asked, "Do you still pray to your God?" I thought for a moment and replied, "Yes." Right back he asked, "For what do you pray?" Summoning up my courage, I answered back, "For my family, home, peace, victory for the Allies, and safety in the mine." Major Crossley took a sidelong glance and gave me a kick which I knew meant his approval. Again this answer caused much laughter, and later "Napoleon" told me I had answered "very brave."

Each of us was then allowed to ask our question. Captain Seed asked if it was possible to stop sending sick men into the mine, and for more drugs for the hospital. Major Crossley asked if the notorious No. 2 level in the mine could be closed down, and could a minister of religion be sent to Kinkaseki from another camp on the island. Capt Franke sought more clothing and shoes for the miners, and soap and some towels for all. Hellyer asked for more canteen supplies and some chickens to breed so that eggs could be produced for the sick. Lt Cross, the last of the officers, pleaded for some books, magazines, or reading material for the miners to pass the time when they were allowed to rest or were recovering from accidents. Patterson asked for a better choice of vegetables, a scale for issuing rations, and soya bean paste or cooking oil. We asked for more safety checks, better lamps, helmets, control of the blasting (which took place each day with little warning), and more rest days. I asked if men over 40 years of age and those who had completed one year working below ground in the mine could be sent to another camp to recuperate.

To all the questions the Commander-in-Chief gave non-committal replies, and he said he would consider our requests. He went on to say that all men and women in Nippon were working very hard and there could be no changes in our work in the mine. We must be content with our life as prisoners and we were lucky to be alive. He ended the conference by saying, "I think the war will last a long time. Do not do any reckless action as it will only lead to your ruin." We were then allowed to drink the tea in our cups, which we did, and quickly demolished the small piles of biscuits, a luxury we had not seen since the beginning of our captivity.

That night we told the men what had happened, and my group of comrades tried to analyze the Japanese Commander-in-Chief's comments. Major Crossley and Capt Seed both looked on the optimistic side, feeling the meeting was an indication that things might improve. Major Wheeler in his diary shared that optimism and recorded:

"The big day in January was an inspection by the GOC PoW Camps Taiwan on 30th January and the surprising thing was that he had five officers and four men to tea to be asked questions. Captain Seed represented the medical. I gather the atmosphere was almost matey. They discussed the war in general for half an hour or more and then each was allowed to ask him questions. He agreed to many of the requests but one has, of course, to wait and see. They said they would try to improve the supply of medicines. They said no sick were to be sent to work but we have been given no more cards and the orderlies have been ordered to see all the sick we recommend, and of course only OK a proportion, usually the wrong ones, so at present we are much worse off. They think that they got across to him that we are perhaps not getting all the rations meant for us (we feel sure the Quartermaster gets away with some) and he said rations would be investigated. Anyway, even if a great deal doesn't come out of it, there is a change in their attitude towards us and this is bound to be a good influence on the permanent staff here, I think".

In the next three weeks two definite signs appeared indicating that the Commandant's visit had paid a dividend. First, more cooking oil was given to the cooks. It was obvious our fears were true: the Japanese Quartermaster had been holding back rations. Secondly, into the camp came a supply of old British Army anti-gas capes for us to wear on our way to and from the mine. These would protect us from the never ending mountain rain of Kinkaseki. Major Wheeler wrote:

All the men have been issued with British anti-gas capes — what a tremendous thing — only we who have lived here and seen the men out in rain day after day, always wet, always cold, can realize. They still only have rags for their feet and that is the next greatest necessity. How their feet stand up, even as well as they do, I can't imagine.

February 15th 1944

Two whole long years behind us — at least we cannot be made to do them again but pray God we haven't two more to do, though this year I haven't so much confidence in the war ending soon, or this year.

February 15th was, of course, the anniversary of the cause of our captivity, the fall of Singapore. His words, "They can't make us do two years over again", were echoed each night by me and many others. Always, when we reached the head of the hill returning from the mine, I would pause with John Waugh, Jim Ferguson, or whoever was next to me. We would take deep breaths and say, "That's one more day the bastards can't make us do. One day more and one day less to do!"

CHAPTER 12

New Phantoms

In the mine now I was concentrating on establishing contacts with civilian workers to get bits of information on the progress of the war. My *Nippon-go* continued to improve, and I started to learn the simple Japanese *Katakana* characters. I found these were based on their five basic vowel sounds AH, E, OO(U), EH and O as opposed to our A.E.I.O.U. One lunch time, my Formosan contact in the mine showed me the first ten symbols. These were based on "soft" and "hard" sounds with a K and G sound. KA, KEE, KU, KEH, KO and GA, GEE, GUI, GEH, GO. As I had learnt Pitman's Shorthand, I suddenly realized that the system of strokes and vowel sounds was similar. Each day I practised and learnt more characters, fitting them to the vocabulary of Japanese words I was also gradually building.

We were lucky to have Lt W.M.G. Brown, who had lived in Japan as a boy and still had a good knowledge of the language. He also taught me, furthering our quest for information and sources of news outside the camp.

Daily I tried to obtain the confidence and friendship of the checker-boy who counted the bogies. I studied carefully the method used to record each bogie. After I had mastered the Japanese characters and system for counting, I decided to try out a new and more dangerous phase of the "phantom bogies". As each bogie passed, the bogie pusher shouted out his working hole number and the checker would put a stroke on the board. The counting system was based on fives, ①each stroke going to make up the final character. I decided to try to add some strokes first chance I could.

I will never forget the first day I tried out this new method. It was during lunch break. I went to the board and found the checker boy missing. I looked around and, seeing no tell tale miner's lamp

① See Appendix E for explanation and chart.

approaching, grabbed the chalk and quickly marked up three strokes for the hottest hole. After the break I went to the hole and told them to do three less than their quota. Working in 192 (*Itchee ku nee*) that day were three close friends, all 155 RA gunner sergeants, whom I could trust. That night we lined up as usual to be counted and have our production checked against our hole quota, with the inevitable "bashings" to follow. Our eyes were on the blackboard. As each hole's number was shouted by the Taiwan "one-bar *hancho*", the checker gave the total. 192 (*Itchee ku nee*) had its required quota, and the *Yosh* from "Sammy" (the "one-bar *hancho*") told us my ruse had worked.

Our success that day spurred us on, and I was able to pull more men in the squad into the new "phantom bogie" racket. We thought up schemes to lure the checker boy away from his board to give me more opportunities to chalk up "phantoms." With willing helpers like bogie-pushers Bombardier Glendenning, Sergeant "Chook" Lowther, and Sergeant "Tiffy" Sheppard, we devised a method of derailing bogies far enough from the checker to lure him from the board to investigate. While he would be shouting and probably hitting the "pusher" for allowing his bogie to become derailed and hold up production, I would be busy chalking up "phantoms".

After chalking up the bogies, I would hurry to the holes in question and ask, "What is your quota?" and "How many finished?" I would then tell them to have a "*sukoshee yasumay*" (a little rest) as they had one or two less to do for their quota.

The scheme was successful beyond my wildest hopes and became a daily routine on our level. It gave me a tremendous boost in spirit to be able to tell my pals working in the hot holes that they had less to do for their quota. There was a terrific lift in morale, as apart from less work and fewer "bashings", we were helping the war effort by reducing production.

Looking back now I realize the risks we took were big, but the thrill I got from the daily success of the "phantom bogies" was worth it all. It gave me an incentive to go into the mine each day. The constant, daily scheming to arrange "phantom bogies" certainly helped me mentally. This positive influence made the difference between "getting the rice down", as we called eating and therefore surviving, and giving up and dying. Like me, there were men determined to think positive, who would try anything to take their minds off the ghastly conditions and gloomy prospects of days, weeks, months, maybe years ahead.

George Harrison and Eddie Burch begged, borrowed, or stole scraps of paper for cartoon sketches and were able to portray even the grim conditions in the mine as funny. All the Japanese PoW camps had those special wits with their ability to find and convey the "black humour" of the situation, all of it reflecting their miserable existence and hatred for their captors.

Arthur Smith, a Trumpeter from the 155th (Lanarkshire Yeomanry) Field Regiment RA, was another of the talented characters at Kinkaseki who used his skills to lift morale. He was a gifted pianist, an excellent trumpeter, and a Scottish poet in the tradition of the immortal Robert Burns. He was always composing either poetry or songs.

Using an old Salvation Army marching tune, he composed what became known as "The Kinkaseki Miner's Anthem" or "The Taiwan Serenade". He first sang it to us in our hut one night in 1943, and it quickly caught on in every camp on Taiwan, being carried by the "thin men" parties. It was even sung in Japan later in the war. Arthur himself became one of the "thin men", but is still alive and full of spirit as I write this tribute to the minstrel of Kinkaseki. He did so much for our spirits and morale in those dark days.

"The Taiwan Serenade"

1.
There's a song in old Formosa,
that the Nippons loudly sing,
In the billets every evening,
you can hear the welkin ring.
Now they sing to British Soldiers,
who have travelled from afar,
To fight for King and Country.
Now your Prisoners of War.

CHORUS
Down the mine, Bonnie Laddie,
down the mine you'll go,
Though your feet are lacerated,
you dare not answer no;
Though the rice is not sufficient

138

and they treat you all like swine,
Down the mine, bonnie laddie, down the mine.

2.   Now the men were fairly happy
till one cold and rainy day,
When the *Buncho-dono* called them out
and to them he did say,
"Now I suppose you'll all be wondering
why you're out on this parade,
Because now I'm going to teach you
to sing THE TAIWAN SERENADE."

Repeat CHORUS

3.   You should see them with their chunkels
and with their baskets too,
Though the method is old fashioned,
to the boys it's something new,
But they'll work away with patience
till the dawn of freedom's day,
But until then the Nipponese
will all be heard to say.

Repeat CHORUS.

Arthur Smith had his serious side, and one day, moved by the
constant sight of comrades being carried out to be buried on the hillside
(we called it "Boot Hill" after the American westerns), wrote the
following:

GLOOMY TAIWAN

A dark and gloomy Taiwan
That overlooks the sea
Your rising hill with graves thereon
Forever frowns on me.
Our comrades rest
Within the breast
Of yonder mountain steep.
Unafflicted, unoppressed,
They sleep the blessed sleep.

Blow gently winds I ask of thee
Above the simple grave.
Be quiet thou angry sea,
Disturb not England's brave.
Oh willows droop your heads and weep,
Oh vagrant softly tread.
Disturb thou not the blissful sleep
Of England's glorious dead.

O frowning Hill
I'll see thee still
Though I be far away.
When shadows fall
I'll oft recall
Each dark and gloomy day.
When we began the ascent steep
Bereaved and sore distressed,
To lay our loved ones down to sleep
Within thy rugged breast.

Arthur had a good comrade, "Wee Willie" Gnr Williamson, a short, sturdy lowlander Scot from the Dumfries area. Always cheerful, he seemed to be able to crack a joke and see the funny side of any situation. Like many of the men of the Lanarkshire Yeomanry who came mainly from the southern counties of Scotland and Glasgow, Arthur and "Wee Willie" had come from tough backgrounds. It put them in good stead for the rigours of Kinkaseki and what would follow. It was their type that survived.

As the days dragged on, I realized how lucky I was to be with the nucleus of a regiment. In Kinkaseki we still had two sizable detachments left of the Lanarkshire Yeomanry and the 80th Anti-Tank Regt, RA. Both had traditions and a history of regimental pride which helped to keep them together. I found it strange that these same men who before the fighting in Malaya would always call being "regimental" a "load of bullshit", now had a tremendous fierce pride in their units. The Anti-Tank men were mostly from Yorkshire, many ex-Duke of Wellington's Regiment, and now proudly called themselves "Duke's Men". All the trappings of rank, badges, and uniform were gone. We found, as men in other camps all over the Far East were to, that discipline came from respect for the officers and NCO who rose to that grim occasion, the tradition of the regiment being their rallying flag.

The work in the mine went on apace on the other levels: the floggings and bashings continued. The improved conditions in camp and situation described below, however, told us the Japs were beginning to suffer.

What we called a "*Speedo* Drive" started. With the drive, accidents increased, the Japanese pushing after good seams of copper ore regardless of safety. Cave-ins now occurred regularly and the number of daily gashes and fractures increased. Major Wheeler recorded on 3rd March 1944:

> Two fractures again today — both of legs and nothing to work with, just for the want of a little plaster and X-ray — they both have a good chance of being cripples. Hope we are not starting another series of serious accidents, as we have been fairly free for the past two to three months.

Some of the worst accidents occurred after "blasting time", usually during the mid-day *Yasumay* period when we ate our cold rice. Often, when we left our working holes, civilian mine drillers would move in, drill holes into the face, and blast with dynamite. We dreaded returning to these holes, still reeking with the smell of dynamite and smoke. You never knew what to expect. The "one-bar" Taiwan *hanchos* were supposed to go in first to shine their powerful lamps on the roof and walls and tap at hanging and loose stones. When we first went into the mine in January, 1943 they usually did this job properly. Then, in 1944, they quit, sending us back in immediately after blasting without checking, but with the usual cries and threats; "*Speedo, roeki*", "*No speedo, hammero*", "*Wakata ka?*" (Hurry up! Work hard! No speed, the Hammer! Understand?)

With our dim carbide lamps we would climb up the ladders and then grope our way in, often stumbling over large pieces of stone dropped near the ladder head. Every man who worked in that mine had an accident of some sort and carries the scar today. Unlike many of my comrades, I was lucky enough to survive.

To add to our troubles, carbide for lamps was running short. They were only issuing one large or two small lumps for your container each morning. At lunch time there was another issue, but unless you were very lucky, only two lamps in any gang of four men would be working by the afternoon. Each night you had to hand in your lamp, and it depended on luck whether you got a lamp that gave a good light the next day. The lucky ones had thin pieces of wire to use as "prickers" to keep the jet holes clean. This was important as lamps frequently fell from the rocks where we hung them, and the jet then clogged with dirt. If a sudden roof fall occurred or, by bad luck, two lamps fell together, you were left in total darkness. You then had to crawl on the floor, "feeling" your way out, and climb down the ladder to the tunnel where you would call out for "*Denki! Denki!*" (Light! Light!)

Sometimes the "one-bar *hancho*" would come and look at the result of a blast, but most often it was a very brief flash of his light on the roof or wall, followed by the warning shout of "*Abunai-O*" (Dangerous) before he left you. As Jim Fergusson always used to say, "The bastard's got no need to tell us. We know bloody well it's *Abunai*!"

There were miraculous escapes on many occasions. I personally missed being crushed, maimed, or killed in three different holes on that dangerous level. One instance will always remain in my memory. I was breaking up a large stone with my hammer in a narrow, low, working tunnel which led off from a larger cave. There were only two men in the hole working with me, "Chook" Lowther and "Wee" Charlie Moorland. In order to swing my hammer easier, I told them to move back from the face so I could take a full backswing. My back was then to the face where they had stood. As I swung I suddenly felt a faint trickle of dust and a gust of wind like a cold breath on my shoulder, just as if someone had blown on it. I don't know what made me immediately jump and push them out, but, as I did, a huge slab of rock fell from the roof. The rush of air and dust blew out our lamps. We crawled out, shaking with fright. After we had had our lamps relit in the tunnel and recovered, Chook asked me, "What made you jump, Taff? Christ, if you hadn't, we'd all have bought it!"

I will never know what made me jump; the dust falling or, as I liked to believe, someone breathing on my shoulder!

Major Wheeler's diary kept a record of how the medical situation was worsening:

<u>March 19th 1944</u>

Three bad fractures in the last ten days. Still, we are left on our own resources — no plaster, etc. — an appendix on the 16th, sent this time to the Nip Hospital for operation, not without trouble, the first orderly would not even let us put him in our hospital!

The doctors and our medical orderlies did as he reports, working with their own resources. Splints were made of wood, the strappings from old webbing belts or equipment harnesses. But limbs were being saved and men walked again, although sometimes crippled for life. Lance Cpl "Mick" McLoughlin had his leg shattered. A hand-carved splint was strapped on his leg with webbing. The bone mended, but when the doctor tried to remove the splint, he discovered to his despair that there were complications. Years later, McLoughlin, who like all the men at Kinkaseki revered Major Wheeler, was to say of him, "He was so upset, I almost cried for him."

If you had to have a mine accident, then a wound at least meant a rest from the mine. Something to show the Japanese Medical Orderlies meant a certain "White Card". A bad injury of course could mean a "Red Card". In the 1914-1918 war, soldiers prayed for a wound that would send them out of the trenches and home. They would call it "a Blighty one" (Blighty being the slang for home). We became so callous that injuries were classed in this way. We hoped for and talked of getting "a White Card".

Captain Seed and Major Wheeler even resorted to putting a gash in the legs of very sick men so they could show a wound to the Japs, the only way they could save the men from the mine.

My "turn" for a "White Card" eventually came when a sudden fall of rock caught my leg, opening the flesh in a long, jagged cut to the bone. The medical orderlies, now accompanying us to the mine each day, bound me up. I staggered back up those terrible steps and over the hill that night, helped by my mates.

After dismissal, I joined the nightly line of miners on the sick parade, queuing up to see Captain Peter Seed or Major Wheeler. Filthy, broken, beaten men shuffled forward, praying and hoping for a white or red card. When Major Wheeler saw me, he said, "Look Peter, Sgt

Edwards has a beauty. I think he can look forward to at least four days *Yasumay*!" That was the way he dispensed what treatment he could give: always with a joke, a smile, and words of encouragement.

Captain Seed, in his quiet manner, also had a sense of humour. By this time all of us were suffering from beri-beri to some degree, and the tell-tale swelling in the ankles and legs was a common sight. The cause, of course, was malnutrition. The doctors had nothing to combat the diet deficiencies with. The rice and meagre vegetable top rations were insufficient sources. One night, a Scot in front of me put up his leg to Captain Seed and squeezed the flesh to show the tell-tale finger-prints, the first signs of the disease. "*Sukoshee* (small) beri-beri," he said. Captain Seed, without a trace of a smile, replied, "I have only got *sukoshee* medicine".

Captain Seed's most famous reply on sick parade came later and became legendary. It showed his true sense of humour and efforts to try and improve morale on that pitiful nightly sick parade. After Father Kennedy, the Roman Catholic priest, left the camp we had no padre to hold services. Captain Seed, an RC, occasionally tried to hold a Mass for the Roman Catholics in the camp.

That particular night he had the usual long line of desperate men, all seeking solace and a day's rest from the torment of the mine. Seed faced one of the most foul-mouthed men in the camp, a tall, skeletal man, and asked, "What is it? What's the trouble?" The man looked straight at the doctor and, in a loud voice, said, "Captain Seed, I'm fucked. I'm literally fucked. I've had it. I canna' do a day more in the mine." Seed looked at him coldly, and replied, so that all could hear, "I am sorry. This is sick parade. I'll take your confession on Sunday, if there is time. — Next!"

Those few words from Seed filled the long line of miserable men with laughter and a smile. Even the recipient of the rebuff walked away with respect for this remarkable doctor.

The Selarang Incident — photographed with a concealed camera and hidden till after the war by Tim Bowden, AIF, both actions putting him at great risk.

The Selarang Incident — sketch by the author, who smuggled this picture through the rest of his captivity, recovered from buried bamboo container, Kokutsu Feb 1946.

Another of Tim Bowden's shots of Selarang.

The "situation map" at Kinkaseki. Although the Japanese had surrendered when this picture was taken in Sept. 1945 the Rising Sun still "flew" over Borneo!

The mining camp at Kinkaseki — war-time photograph

Japanese troops in Malaya advance under fire — picture by a
Japanese war correspondent.

The Japanese fighting in a pineapple plantation during the Malayan
Campaign

Japanese in ambush position — Malayan Campaign

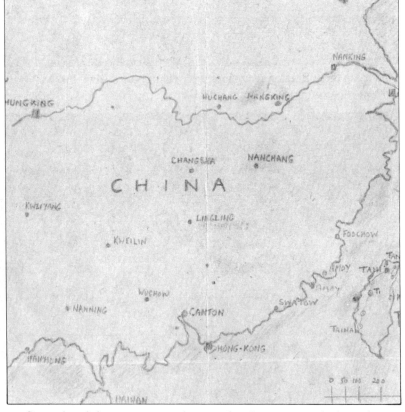

Secret hand drawn maps made on stolen Japanese work sheets by the author during captivity.

"The Beast" or "Sergeant Major".   "Rubber Neck"

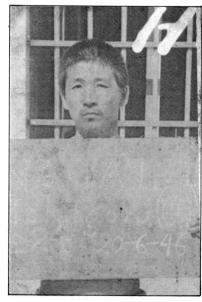

"Sanitary Syd"   "The Ghost"

"Goldie"

"Pan Face"

Captain Imamura

"Flash Harry"

" Blankets"

"The Eagle"

"BLACKIE" TWO-BAR HANCHO

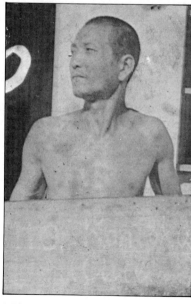

"The Frying Pan"

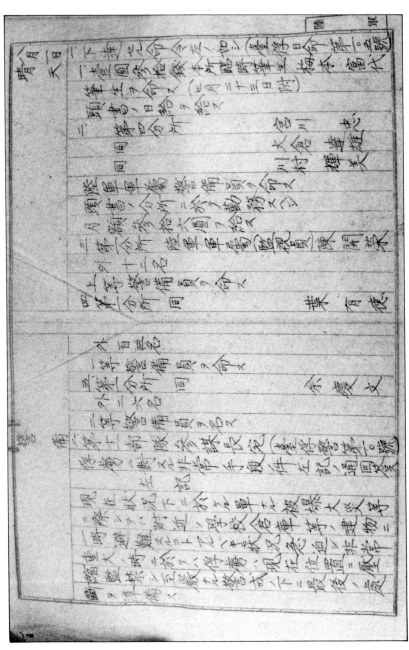

The Japanese order to "kill them all" and "leave no traces" (also facing page), The original is now in the US National Archives at Washington DC.

Additionally ____________
Clerk of the Court

處斷ノ時機方法左ノ如シ
一、時機
上司ノ命令ニ依リ實施スルヲ本旨トスルモ左ノ
場合ニアリテハ獨斷處置ス
イ、多數暴動シ兵器ヲ使用スルニ非ザレバ鎮
壓シ能ハザル場合
ロ、所内ヨリ脱逸シ敵戰力トナル場合
二、方法
イ、各個撃破式ニヨルカ集團式ニヨルカ何レ[illegible]
ニセヨ大兵爆破、毒煙、毒物、溺殺、斬首
等當時ノ狀況ニ依リ處斷ス
ロ、何レノ場合ニアリテモ一兵モ脱逸セシメズ殲滅
シ痕跡ヲ留メザルヲ本旨トス

警備三、軍司令官宛
憲兵司令官宛
臺灣俘虜收容所非常警備ニ關スル
第十一部隊トノ協議事項、基隆要塞
司令部トノ協議事項及各州トノ協議事
項、報告（通牒）ス

遺留四、第六分所ヨリ
七月二十七日死亡俘虜英國砲兵バートン[illegible]
ノ遺留品二點送付ヲ受ク

俘虜處罰五、第六分所ヨリ俘虜處罰ノ件次ノ報告接ス
一、俘虜英國陸軍兵長ナイト、チャールス同砲
兵エルドレット、ヘンリーハ不寢番勤務不確實
ノ科ニヨリ重營倉三日ニ處ス
二、米國陸軍兵ホーリー、チャールスハ作業中不從
順ノ科ニ依リ重營倉三日ニ處ス

	155 FIELD REGT R.A.			Bttr. SIGS SECTION	Bttr. R.A.H.
OFFICERS	CAPT. STEWART J.H.F. LT. BROWN J.H.G.				CAPT. SEED P...
W.O's	B.S.M. LOWTHER G.S. B.S.M. SHRIVEY D.A.				
SGTS	ANDERSON W.G. BINGHAM J. DAVIS E.G. DEWSNAP D.J. DONALDSON L.	HEAVER L.A. McPHAIL A. MITCHELL CB MURGATROYD J. SEPHTON R.	WARWICK R.D. WATSON J.L. WAUGH J.D.	EDWARDS J.O.	
L/SGTS	BRODIE J. BROWN J. FORD J. GOODMAN R.G. HARRISON T.	LOCHHEAD S. MILES R.C.			
BDRS	DOWNIE A. FERGUSON J. GLENCROSS W. GOUGH B. MATHER J. NORBURY F.	PATTERSON W.J. STEVENSON J.D.M. WYLLIE T.C.		SAVAGE L.V.	
L/BDRS	BEAN J.B. CARLYLE I. CARSON B. DOUGLAS J.C. DOWNIE J. FITZGERALD J.A.	POPPLE C. VACHER W.M. VICCARS J.V. WALLACE J. WHITE J.G.		DAVIES T.A. McLOUGHLIN M.G.	
GNRS	BAILLIE T.W. BARRIE W. (or 98 Fd) BLAIR D. BRANDON W.J. BUCKHAM J. BUCKTON T.E. BURNS H. CALDOW J. CAMERON W. CAMERON W.J.R. CAMPBELL A. CAMPBELL G. CAMPBELL W. CARMICHAEL A. CARROLL H.A. CARRUTHERS W. CARTER C.F. CARTWRIGHT D. COX F. DALGLEISH G. DALY R.W. DICKSON A. DOBBIE P.H. DOCHERTY R. EDGAR P.F. FLEMING W. (or Horn) GILL J.M.	GRAHAM J. GREEN J. HARVEY D.A. HAY W.L. HIDDLESTON A. HOLT W.G. HOPKINS G.L. JESS S. KANE J. (or 148 Fd) LARKIN F. LINDLEY P. MACKIE R. MARSHALL J.H. McCUTCHEON J. McEWAN J. McGHIE F.D.S. McGHIE R.G. McGILL R. McGUINNESS J.L. McLEOD J.A. MELROSE R.G. MILNE W. NASH R. NOTLEY W.R OGDEN J. OSTLER J.A. PATTERSON J.A. PICKLES S.	PLOWBRIDGE L. SCOTT J. SCOTT J. SCOTT W. SHIPLEY W. SMITH J.M.M. SOUTHERTON H.H. SWAN G.E. TELFORD J. TERRY E. TUCK S.H. TUTHILL G.W.T. VACHER G.W. VERE A. WALKER A. WARD T.B. WEARING G.W. WILLIAMS E. WILLIAMS G.H. WILLIAMSON W.B. HUFTON R.	BARBER G. BUTTIFANT F.J. COATES W.H. CRAIG J. DAVIS L.E. GIBSON W.H.G. HASLAM F. HORRIS E.J. SHELDRICK E.F. CLACK E.A. SMITH W.G. GILBOY D.	

66.

Nominal roll by regiments of men who were PoWs at Kinkaseki sometime during 1942-45 — sample page of original compiled on rear of Japanese mine works sheets

Feb 1946. Author digging up camp records buried during captivity.
MAJOR CROSSLEY, at rear, led war crimes investigation team to the
spot.

Japanese news sheet which provided the last instalment in the "Kinkaseki News Service".

Taken during War Crimes Investigations 1946. Author demonstrates how bogees were pushed in the mine.

The Kinkaseki Mine main tunnel. At this point, one quarter of mile from the entrance the investigation team refused to go any further. The actual work done during captivity was performed some ¾ mile further into the mountain and 800 feet further down.

Author re-enacts marking of bogees with carbide lamps. George Harrison, a Medical Orderly from Kinkaseki, looks on.

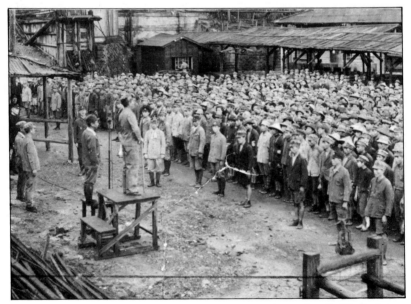

"Four-Bar" giving speech to civilian mine workers after PoWs had entered the mine at Kinkaseki

Inside the mine — official mine company photograph

Woman miner at work in Kinkaseki

Some of the "Black Sappers" (girls gang) at work in the mine.

Pushing bogies to the chute

"Boot Hill" — picture taken immediately after the war.

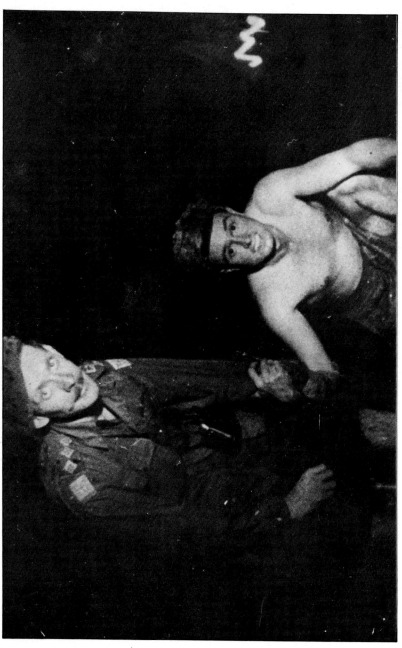

The author and Capt. J.T.N. Cross revisit the main tunnel at Kinkaseki in March 1946. This picture, used as evidence in War Crime trials, shows the depth of water in the main tunnel. Prisoners worked 800 feet below this level.

Japanese propaganda photo of prisoners "praying for peace" at
Kinkaseki in 1944.

"The Hammer" — post-war sketch by George Harrison.

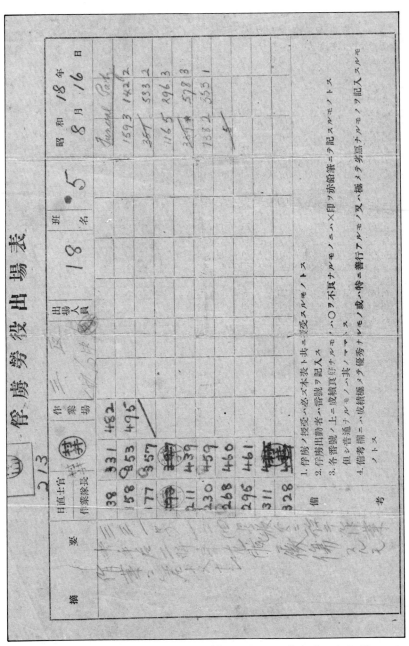

Japanese worksheet from the mine, with crosses and circles to indicate prisoners' work performance. List of numbers at right is of burial party for "Plonka" Clack at Matsuiyama.

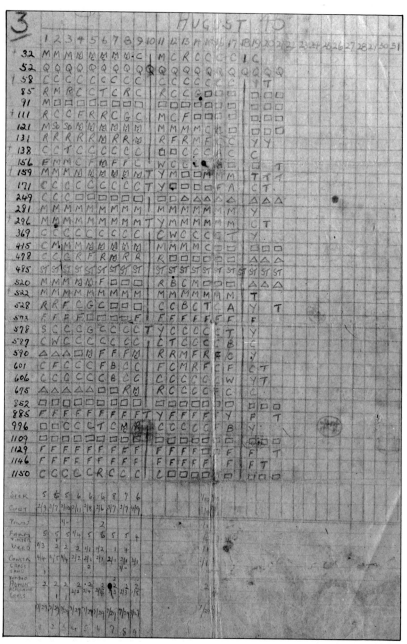

Other side of same sheet has working party roster from the Jungle Camp.
"M" is for "Madman" party.

Prisoners arrive on the docks to a warm welcome from Lt. Taylor's shipmates on the U.S.S. "Thomas. J. Gary".

The Marines carry one of us to freedom — picture by Lt. Henry Taylor USN.

Sailors carry a sick prisoner on board.

Our transfer by small boat to the USS "BLOCK ISLAND".

Rescued prisoners who survived Kinkaseki relax on the hanger deck of the Block Island.

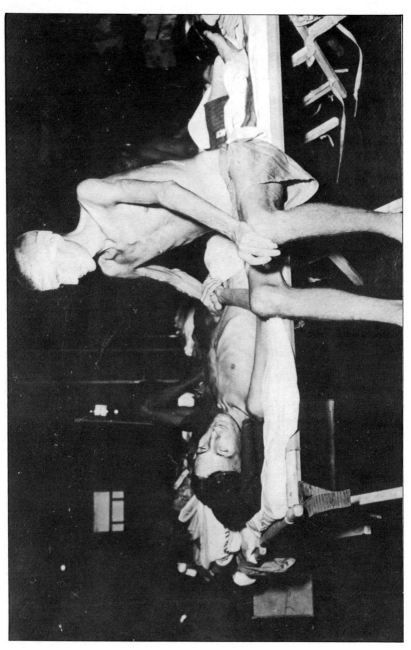

Two survivors from KINKASEKI on U.S.S. Block Island.

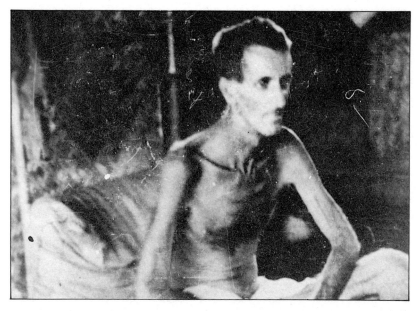

This and facing pages — typical condition of survivors.

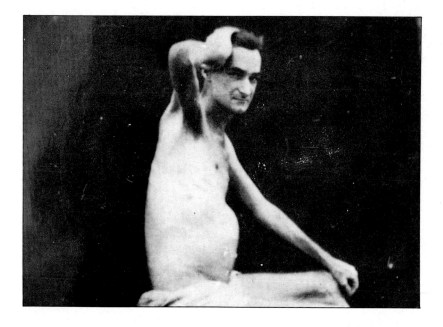

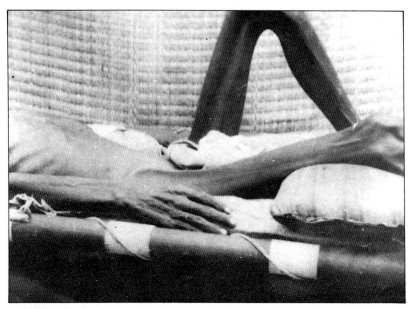

An idea of the condition survivors were in when rescued.

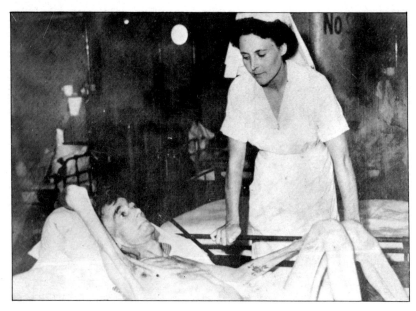

KINKASEKI mine survivor on hospital ship.

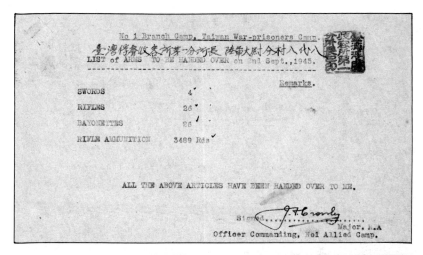

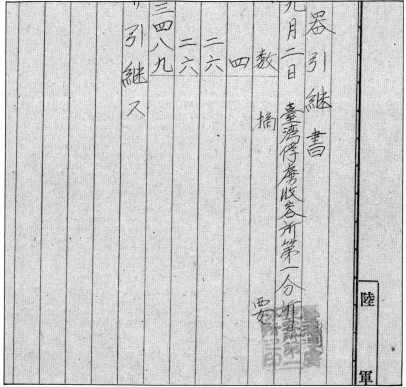

Copies of the receipts for the arms of our Japanese guards. Received at their "surrender" of No. 1 Camp, Taiwan, by the skeletal PoWs before the landings of the U.S. Marines on 5-6th Sept 1945.

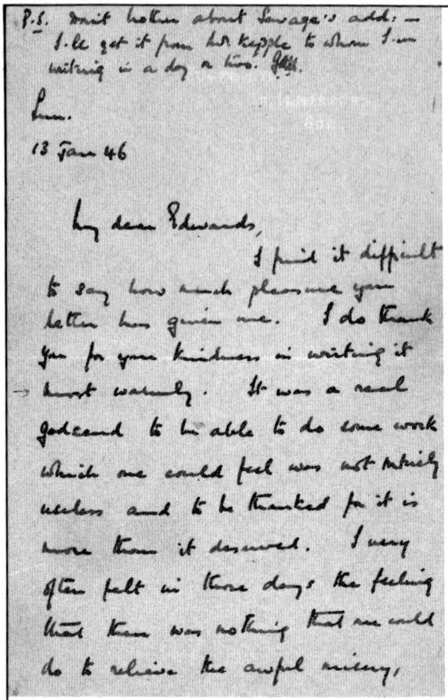

P.S. Don't bother about Savage's add: — I'll get it from Mr Kepple to whom I am writing in a day or two. [illegible]

Lon.

13 Jan 46

My dear Edwards,

I find it difficult to say how much pleasure your letter has given me. I do thank you for your kindness in writing it most warmly. It was a real godsend to be able to do some work which one could feel was not entirely useless and to be thanked for it is more than it deserved. I very often felt in those days the feeling that there was nothing that one could do to relieve the awful misery,

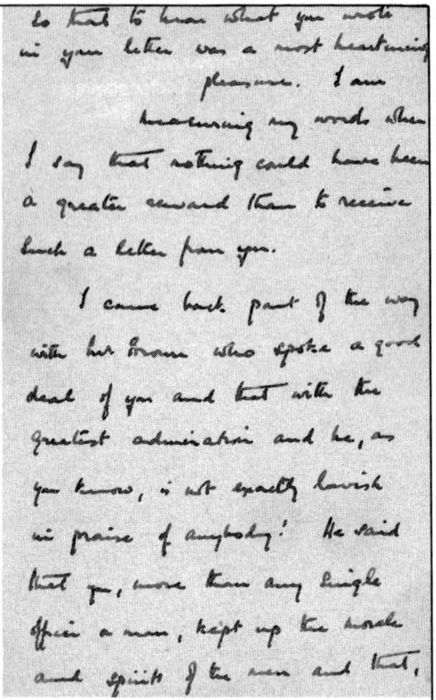

so that to know what you wrote in your letter was a most heartening pleasure. I am measuring my words when I say that nothing could have been a greater reward than to receive such a letter from you.

I came back part of the way with Mr Brown who spoke a good deal of you and that with the greatest admiration and he, as you know, is not exactly lavish in praise of anybody! He said that you, more than any single officer or man, kept up the morale and spirits of the men and that,

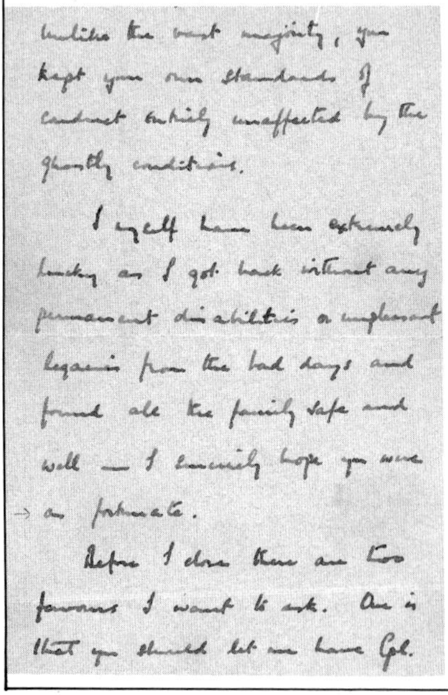

unlike the vast majority, you kept your own standards of conduct entirely unaffected by the ghastly conditions.

I myself have been extremely lucky as I got back without any permanent disabilities or unpleasant legacies from the bad days and found all the family safe and well — I sincerely hope you were as fortunate.

Before I close there are two favours I want to ask. One is that you should let me have Col.

It was a real godsend to be able to do some work which one could feel was not entirely useless and to be thanked for it is more than it deserved. I very often felt in those days the feeling that there was nothing that one could do to relieve the awful misery, so that to know what you wrote in your letter was a most heartening pleasure I am measuring my words when I say that nothing could have been a greater reward than to receive such a letter from you.

I came back part of the way with Mr. Brown who spoke a good deal of you and that with the greatest admiration and he, as you know, is not exactly lavish in praise of anybody! He said that you, more than any single officer or man, kept up the morale and spirits of the men and that unlike the vast majority, you kept your own standards of conduct entirely unaffected by the ghastly conditions.

I myself have been extremely lucky as I got back without any permanent disabilities or unpleasant legacies from the bad days and found all the family safe and well — I sincerely hope you were as fortunate.

Portion of a letter written to the author in Jan 1946, by Captain George Hinton, ex 155th Field LY, RA, who left Kinkaseki on the first "thin-men" party. Published specifically at the request of other Kinkaseki survivors aware of its existence.

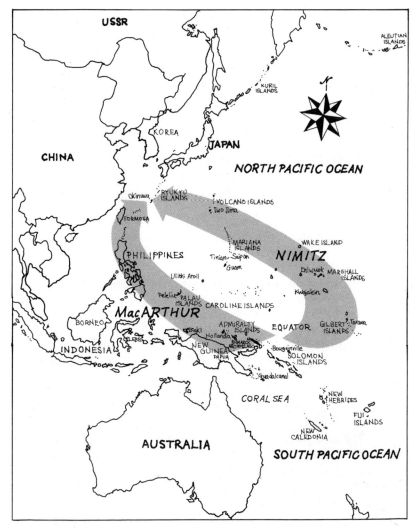

Map showing the "Island-Hopping" strategies adopted by the U.S. Marine and Carrier Forces of Admiral Chester Nimitz and the Army of General Douglas MacArthur. MacArthur resisted all suggestions of Nimitz and others that the Philippines should be "by passed" in favour of the invasion of Formosa. Formosa was allowed to "wither on the vine", bombed and starved, instead. This policy, which kept his famous promise of "I shall return", almost certainly saved the lives of the PoWs and the author on Formosa. They were to be massacred when the Americans landed.

CHAPTER 13

The Kinkaseki News Service

In May 1944 Major Crossley again decided to try to use the better atmosphere with the Camp Commander to improve conditions. He requested an interview between "The Old Man", the two doctors and himself to discuss improving the health of the camp, ostensibly to provide more mine workers. This, of course, was not his real motive, but the only excuse the Major found useful in establishing a dialogue on improvements.

The Major told the Commander that if the health of the men was to be improved, there must be more mental relaxation when they returned from the mine. There were few books or magazines, and nothing else to take the men's minds off the camp and mine. Furthermore, he told him that all the sentries had the habit of walking through the huts every evening and beating up men for the slightest infraction of the rules. The Major pointed out that the prisoners could not lie down or even sit with their backs against the wall. Playing of cards, a great relaxer, was also forbidden.

The doctors stressed the need for more drugs, better food, and some milk. They pointed out that when men were sick, the rations were reduced. He asked how they could possibly get men well enough to work under these circumstances.

"Pop" gave a faithful interpretation of their pleas, and the "Old Man" said he would consider them.

The result of the conference became obvious two nights later. The sentries stopped entering huts during meal times and left us alone for that blessed half-hour before "lights out". Then another miracle happened: a supply of books, some soft balls, and a football arrived from the YMCA. It was unbelievable, the effect on the minds of everyone was miraculous. In the evening the fittest prisoners would kick the ball about on our postage-stamp size parade ground. It was amazing how these changes and the improved weather of summer affected everyone.

But even more important for morale was the discovery of a fairly constant source of news. We had found a source and method of delivery at last!

From our earliest days in captivity, we seized on any scrap of information, any rumour to listen to, to dissect, to study, to argue about. Any hopeful word or sign was grabbed and expanded into a sign of an end to the war and our early release. Rumours in our camp now became known as "griff". "Tiffy" Sheppard and George Williams, another squad *hancho*, were now learning *Nippon-go*, and the three of us were constantly chatting up the "one-bars" and civilian workers in the mine. Always we would try to steer the conversation to the Japanese theatre of operations, but we found they would talk only about Germany, Russia and Europe.

Our only opportunity to talk was in the mine. Even there, the civilians were scared to be seen talking to prisoners, as they told us the *Kempeitai* (the dreaded Japanese Military Police) were everywhere. Every bit of news or gossip we obtained we carried back and related to Major Crossley. He encouraged me to seek out as many friendly contacts as I could. With my job of breaking up big stones, I was not confined to any hole and could wander around the tunnels, talking to the civilian workers, carpenters, rail-repairers, and the *Appah Mei* (blasting men).

At that time, Lt Brown had the idea of requesting the Japanese to provide the PoW Camp office with a primer on Japanese characters. The excuse concerned the order sheets to be filled out and returned to the Japanese. They were all printed in Japanese *Kanji* and *Katakana*. If we had the "primer", it would save interpretation. The interpreter provided a box of cards with basic characters and their Japanese romanization equivalents, i.e. *Nippon-go*. These proved invaluable in the development of the Kinkaseki News Service.

While discussing my contact and sources from the mine with Major Crossley and Lt Brown one day, they asked me to try and obtain Japanese newspapers. We badly wanted hard confirmation of rumours, coming from several sources we had, that landings had taken place in France by American and British troops. For several days my best contact, the hymn-singing worker, had drawn rough maps of Europe for me in the dust of the mine floor. He clearly indicated France, and to my question repeated again and again that "Americano", "Englando" "Boom-Boom" "Franceoo". I was satisfied between my limited *Nippon-go* and his limited English that the "Boom-Boom" did not mean just bombings. He excitedly told and indicated to me that *Toksan Heitai* (many soldiers) were in France. The news electrified the camp that night and I used to get my biggest thrill giving the "griff" to the boys in that pitiful hospital. Major Wheeler and Captain Seed always said to me, "Sgt Edwards, your good 'griff' is as good as medicine."

Major Wheeler secretly recorded in his diary:

June 17th 1944
    Big and continued rumours since the 8th of the second front having begun all along the French coast and this time I am convinced they are correct. It may be a long time before they reach Berlin or it may be only a few months but at least one can see the end of Germany in sight. And after Germany comes our friends. In fact I am sure they would like to get out now with what they can save but I can't see America at least talking of anything but unconditional surrender and longer though it may be, dearest, you will understand when I say I can wait a little more of it.

A few days later I succeeded in persuading my little Formosan friend to bring me a newspaper. It was very small, consisting of only two sheets. Later, in a quiet part of the tunnel by the dim light of my lamp, I eagerly checked the date and headlines using my limited knowledge of *Katakana*. It was that same day's paper and, sure enough, in the headlines was news of fighting on the coast of France and a little map with arrow indicators! I will never forget my euphoria and joy that day, hundreds of feet below ground in Taiwan. If only those men fighting in France knew what it meant to us! Quickly I made my way around the holes, spreading "the griff". The effect on everyone was the same: electrifying. It was the best news we had received since captivity.

Now my problem was to smuggle the newspaper back into camp. There the *Kanji* characters could be translated carefully by Lt Mike

Brown. Every night and morning when we lined up before going to and returning from the mine, we were searched by the Formosan sentries. Some were more particular than others, and if it was raining the search was often less careful; it depended a lot on the guard and the weather. In the morning they were mainly looking for pieces of carbide which we would try to steal to power our lamps in the mine. The amount given was never sufficient, so an odd lump was a great help. Furthermore, the native Formosan workers were rationed also, so a lump of carbide could be exchanged for a little rice, cigarettes or salt.

At night time, the guards would normally feel over your body and, sometimes, look in your old cardboard mining hat. I had got into the habit of standing arms apart, with my hat and sweat rag in one hand and open, empty *bento* (rice-box) in the other. I decided that I would fold the newspaper up small, wrap it in my old sweat-rag, and hold it in the hand with my cap. Luck was with me that first night, as it was in the future on every night that I succeeded in obtaining a newspaper. The Formosan "Runabout" on duty was "Lampu", the young, very ugly guard. "Lampu" had a foul temper, but he was very slow witted. As he approached me, I held my hands straight towards him. He pushed them apart with a cry of *"Bugeiroo"*, and pressed his hands quickly over my body. *"Yosh,"* he shouted, and pushed me forward. I was through!

Lt Brown had got Sergeant Jim Bingham, Major Crossley's assistant responsible for camp records, interested in Japanese characters, and he had quickly mastered the simple *Katakana*. That night after I had told the Major my news and handed over the paper, they worked on the details in the newspaper reports. About 8:30 pm, Major Crossley sent for me and gave me a synopsis of the news gleaned from the paper. He agreed to allow me to pass it on by mouth to other camp *hanchos*. It gave me a tremendous thrill to give out this *"honcho griff"*.

That night I tore up a portion of my gas cape to make a cover for my cardboard mining hat. If in the future I managed to obtain a paper, my intention was to fold it carefully and slip it inside this cover.

In the weeks that followed, my contact brought me several more news-sheets, and each night I followed the same drill at the searches. Others on different levels agreed to try, but Sergeant Dick Sheppard, on my level, was the only other who was successful in those early months.

So keen were the Major, Lt Brown, and Jim Bingham to obtain newspapers now that they would watch us closely as we returned from the mine. If they saw me make straight for the prisoners' office, they knew "a paper was in." If "a paper was in", this message would fly through the camp, excitement rising as we waited for "the griff".

I was eager now to obtain more newspapers, and enlisted more of my squad's help. The workers and "one-bars" had their midday meal in cool tunnels fitted out with wooden benches, tables, and cupboards for their clothing. Always after eating, they would smoke and read their news sheets, then usually lay down to sleep. It became necessary (and a great pleasure when successful) not only to visit the checker-board for the "phantom bogies", but also to watch the *meshee* room. Eventually, I found a time when the *meshee* room was not occupied, and using one of our "bogie-pushers" as a look-out I nipped quickly in, grabbed any newspapers left on the benches, and we were away, back to the working holes.

Success on several occasions made us more daring, and with the help of Dick Sheppard, Jim Brown, Jim Fergusson, and others, all willing to take the risk, we even went through the pockets of clothing left hanging up there.

As my mining hat rotted with the continued dripping acid water, I reverted to either folding the paper in my sweat-rag or just palming it in my hand under my empty rice box. I always made a point of thrusting my hands straight at the Formosan sentries. Not once did they look at what I held in my hands. They seemed content to search my body.

Each night as I came up from the mine, there in the camp office doorway I could see the Major, Lt Brown, and Jim Bingham, their eyes on me. They got to know immediately, by the expression on my face, if I had a newspaper or not.

All the effort of stealing and getting it past the guards would be amply repaid when I spread the latest news later that night. Jim Bingham, by now a close friend, would tell me the details. My first call was always at the hospital hut. All of us knew only too well that hope for the future and good news were vitally important to the sick. The look on the faces of those men when I had some good "griff" would light up my heart.

With both newspaper stealing and the "phantom bogie" racket, I had an even greater purpose to fulfil when I went into the mine every day. They became obsessions with me. Although I hated the place, dreaded the journey back and forth, was scared of injuries, and always fearful of being caught and beaten or worse, it became like a drug.

I can safely say that these "tasks" saved my reason and helped me to survive that dreadful place. No praise is too high for those who helped me steal the newspapers or create the "phantom bogies". We were all willing to share the risk. Lt Brown, Jim Bingham, and Major Crossley well knew the risks they took if caught working on the news-sheets by prowling sentries. Lt Brown, with his knowledge of Japanese, would have been arrested and possibly executed if the Japanese had got on to our news service. But we were lucky, and it continued to grow all through 1944.

Although the news in these newspapers was fairly accurate for Europe, the Japs' own fighting in the Pacific was only vaguely reported. It was only when we found items which admitted the bombing of certain Pacific islands by American planes, or "sea victories" by Japanese fleets over American fleets nearer and nearer to us, that we had confirmation that Nippon also was losing.

Major Wheeler faithfully noted any scrap of news, and from them derived hope in his regular out-pourings of his heart to his beloved Nettie. The following was prompted by the arrival of letters to the prisoners on 22nd June, 1944:

> Two letters today and one from Nell with snaps — the snaps, Honey, somehow they have made me feel nearer than since this all began — what real boys they are — I would only have recognized Ken — Harry has changed a lot, all his baby softness gone and of course Alan was a real baby. You look lovely, dearest, as always, though they did not get in your hat.

> I have studied and studied the snaps and I am afraid made myself a bit of a pest getting people to look at them, but I am so proud, and who wouldn't be? We certainly will have a honeymoon, Dear — you will have to meet me when I land and then on by ourselves — yes, Darling, how I love you and long for you.

Rumours of the second front continue strong. Also Germany out of Italy — odds and ends out here and raids on London with radio-controlled planes — surely at least Germany will be finished by the end of the year.

The news of the landings in Europe and the arrival of letters from home greatly improved the mental state of my fellow prisoners. Though some of the mail from home brought bad news, of deaths or marriage breakdowns, the large majority of it had an effect like that of Major Wheeler's. They were given a new lease of life, a reason to hang on. Sadly my pal, "Big Benny" Slack of the Sherwood Foresters, had bad news: the death of his fiancee. He was dejected and took it badly. He seemed literally to fade away and took to visiting the hospital hut every night to sit with and talk to the sick and dying. On visits with him I saw that in his own way he was trying to cheer up the sick. Still, other friends of his and I feared he had a "death wish".

Luckily in my close group of friends at that time was Cpl Len Savage, from my original section, and Bobbie McGhie of the Lanarkshire Yeomanry. Both Len and Bobbie were strong characters; Len always cheerful and Bobbie a real Christian. Bobbie practised what he preached, the love of God and the belief that we would come through if only we trusted in our faith. Gradually, poor Ben became sicker. Thankfully, he was put on one of the last "thin men" parties to leave Kinkaseki and survived.

Those months of summer in 1944 gave us hope. Again the unpredictable Japanese confirmed our news and belief that things were going the way of the Allies, this time in an amusing way.

On the morning of 24th June before the mine party left, we were suddenly all paraded for a speech by the Commandant. It was translated by the new camp interpreter who had just replaced "Pop". The new man, named "Koga", had an evil face and was nicknamed "Silas the Snoop" for his habit of standing near us and listening to conversations. His English was obviously not as good as that of "Pop", whose jovial face and appearance we were to miss. We were sorry to see "Pop" go; he had shown his dislike of our treatment clearly by his actions towards us, and we assumed he had been moved because of this.

The speech by the "Old Man" that morning was so incredible that

Major Crossley asked for a copy of it, saying not everyone could follow it and that he wanted to ensure all prisoners knew the Commander's orders! That night when I got back, the Major called us squad chiefs together to read it. I copied the speech and recovered it after the war from my hide-hole. Here is the translation:

I will give you a few advices. Of late, some PoWs are apt to violate the rules and regulations in the mine, showing an impudent attitude to the Mine *Hancho* or not fulfilling the work allotted to you by the Mine *Hancho*. Should such an attitude originate in presumption that your country is winning the war and that it will be over soon and the Allies victorious, it is a great mistake. Originally I did not want to speak of the war. It only helps to stir your peaceful minds during this camp life. But I am afraid you will happen to misact under the misunderstanding, and so, I will refer to it. It present how it will develop. You must not think that the Great Nippon or Germany will be easily defeated. This fact has been admitted both by Churchill and Roosevelt. In any rate, in the present war both Great Nippon and Germany will fight to the last man. Even if these countries will fall in temporary disadvantage, United States or Britain cannot win in the near future. Therefore, if you think the war will finish before long, you are mistaken. Even though the war would turn out unfavourably for us in this decisive stage of the battle, it should take a considerably long time until the war should come to an end. As long as the last Nippon man survives, we will not give Victory to the Allies. When the whole Nippon nation disappears from this earth, the Allies can only then gain victory. So even if the war would develop as you wish, your life as a PoW will continue for a pretty long time; that is a few more years. But as it is out of the question USA and Britain will give up the war, losing the fight during the decisive period, from this point of view, I am paying deep consideration how I am to return you fit and well to your land. Moreover, I have endeavoured to make your life comfortable and peaceful by issuing as good ration as possible in my power. This is not because the Axis countries are losing the war. Such a thought is very dangerous for you. In harmony with our kind treatment, you must reward us by discharging your allotted work and also obeying faithfully to our instructions. That is the only way you will be treated friendly here in this camp. That will also be the way you can lead a peaceful and comfortable life.

and then you will be able to go home safely. I believe it is the will
of God and also the duty of man.

Signed Capt Imamura Yaohashi
Commander No. 1 Branch PoW Camp Taiwan
19th Year of Showa, 19th June 1944.

That morning as we went to the mine, the only subject discussed was
the speech. As always, we analyzed every word and phrase seeking the
true meaning behind the *Buncho's* words.

"It must be coming to an end, Taff," said Johnnie Waugh to me.
"Why would he bother to lecture us?"

"I'll bloody believe it is coming to an end when I see American
planes," broke in Jimmie Brown, one of the Lanarkshire Yeomanry
sergeants who made up the bulk of *Jugo han* (15 Squad).

"All we can do is hope, pray and keep going," dour old Davey
Dewsnap suddenly said. He usually took no part in conversations in
the tunnel, only singing to himself on those daily marches.

The accidents continued. Our worst loss in one day occurred a few
days later on 22nd June, 1944. It happened one level below ours, after
the meal break as usual. There were only two men working this hole.
Both had become close friends and always tried to work together. They
were from the same squad and slept alongside each other. They were
destined to die together, crushed under a roof fall as they entered their
hole to begin work. They were Gnr Singleton, of the Royal Artillery,
and Marine Dunn, a Royal Marine who had survived the sinking of
the battleship "Prince of Wales"

This tragedy struck the camp hard. Both of these were cheerful men.
Their deaths dampened our spirits after they had been raised by the
Buncho's speech. Major Wheeler wrote that night:

Two more men killed by a rock fall in the mine today. Though
on the whole working conditions are better. Still, from what one
can gather, no real precautions are taken to prevent such
accidents. Everything one sees Japanese is slipshod and cheap,
poorly finished. How they have done so much against the US and

153

ourselves with so little is extremely hard to understand. However, all things considered, we are better off, those who have survived, this year than last.

I'll have another long look at my darling and our boys and so to bed. It has been a long busy day and I am on guard tonight.

The Major, who kept a rota for any additional duties required by the Japanese, told me my squad was on duty that night for the guarding of the bodies "lying-in-state".

There were groans in my hut as I had to detail the required number, and my number, *Itchee-go-ku*, was on the duty list as well. We always drew lots for the hour, and I drew one of the worst periods, from 2:00 to 3:00 am.

At a few minutes to 2:00, I and my companion for the hour were woken from sleep and told to be careful, as "The Mad Carpenter" was on guard near-by. We bowed carefully to this evil tempered sentry as we made our way across the moonlit square to the bath-hut. Tony, my companion, and I stood inside the doorway, out of the cold wind which even in the month of June still plagued those gloomy mountains. We went inside to stand and look at the crude wooden coffins in the hut; the only light came from the rays of the moon through the window. In front was the pitiful white paper flower wreath with black Japanese characters meaning "Nippon Kogyo Copper Mine". On top of each coffin was a small dish containing rice biscuits, "The food for the hungry ghosts". We had seen them putting fruit, rice, sake wine, and even cigarettes on the graves of soldiers in Singapore.

"The bastards!" said Tony. "They'll put food on them when they're dead, but won't give it while they're alive! What fucking hypocrisy!" Sourly, he went on, "Feed the fucking hungry ghosts! What the fucking hell use is that! By the centre, Taff, what I wouldn't do for one of those biscuits. Fuck the ghosts, I'm bloody hungry too!"

I pulled him away by the arm. "Let's go back to the door," I said. "It's no bloody use standing here arguing and cursing. We'll have that bastard 'Mad Carpenter' in if he hears us. Come away," I pleaded.

We went back to the door, and, shivering in the cold, argued about the hypocrisy and stupidity of it all. After about a quarter of an hour, Tony said, "I'm going back inside near the coffins!"

"For God's sake don't, Tony," I replied. "It's no use tormenting yourself."

After a few minutes, he came back. "Some bugger has had a tuck-in already," he declared. "We are fucking daft, Taff. Those rice biscuits will be eaten anyway by the in-camp burial party!"

We both went back in for a closer look. Sure enough, you could tell from the way the biscuits were placed, some had gone.

Back to the door we went discussing how hungry we were, the hypocrisy of it all, and whether it was really wrong to take the biscuits. Yet, to steal off the top of two crushed bodies...

Eventually Tony left me again, going inside the hut. This time he came back eating. "Christ Taff, they taste bloody marvellous," he said. "I couldn't resist one. Here, have a bite." I tried to fight my hunger, but could not resist. To bite a hard biscuit, after mouths of just soft rice; it tasted heavenly. After I had eaten it, I felt pangs of remorse. But I continued rolling my tongue around my mouth, savouring every crumb. It was wonderful to taste a biscuit after two years. I tried to soothe my conscience by telling myself I was hungry. I will never forget standing there in the moonlight of that cold miserable hut, fighting the desire to go back in and steal from off the top of those bodies.

Five minutes before the end of our hour, we both crept back in like thieves and took two biscuits each. We hurried back to the door, wanting to be away from those rough-hewn boxes, containing the two men we knew so well. They had died so violently, yet we were starving. That was the conflict. Looking back, it wasn't wrong. It was just that the harshness of our circumstances had instilled in us such fierce loyalty to our mates that we couldn't easily stomach taking anything from them, dead or alive.

Thankfully the time ended and Tony went for our reliefs. I was glad to hurry back to our hut. I climbed into my blanket, reached over, and tapped my mate, Len Savage, slipping one of the biscuits into his mouth. I sucked the other to make it last as long as possible. Len, bless

155

him, did not even ask me where the biscuit had come from. He knew. And I knew he would know how I felt.

We went to the mine the next morning as usual at 6:30 am, before the burials. That night Major Crossley sent for me and asked what I knew about the disappearance of so many rice biscuits that night. He said the Japs had been furious. He had been slapped, the prisoners' *hancho* on duty for the day had been beaten, and the burial party had had a terrible time. The Japs accompanying the party had taken it out on them. On burial parties the sentries were always in foul tempers. They would rush the scraping out of a hole, their cries of *"Speedo, speedo"* and *"Epai"* indicating when they thought the hole was deep enough, usually barely deep enough to cover the corpse. That day they had been absolute beasts. "Silas the Snoop", in his sneering voice, had told the Major, "Engirisu soldiers, worse than animals, steal from dead comrade". He held the Major, as Squad Leader and *hancho*, responsible. I felt terrible, as I had come to respect and revere this man. I could not tell him I had also stolen two biscuits.

After the war, I finally admitted to him that I had taken two of the biscuits. At last it was off my conscience! Well, almost. The bond between us is too strong.

As 1944 dragged on, more indications came that the Japanese were concerned about the propaganda aspect of their prisoners. It was suddenly announced that one day's rest from the mine would be given to the whole camp, and there would be an improved ration containing some pork bones from the mine company. Furthermore, we could hold a service to pray for peace! Miraculously, some musical instruments arrived, a violin, a banjo, and a piano accordion. These, we were told, were to accompany the singing of a hymn. We could not believe it: a day off, better rations, prayers for peace, singing, musical instruments!

It all became clear the next day. A party of Japanese photographers arrived to take pictures of the "prayer meeting". Photographs were also taken of "the prisoners' orchestra" and "the prisoners' doctors and medical orderlies".

Major Wheeler, as always, noted the event:

The Japs now have some peculiar game on in which we are all

156

to be photographed praying for world peace. Oh well it confirms one's certain knowledge that things are going the right way for us.

Big prayer today, the Nips taking pictures of "concert" party, men playing games, etc. What a false impression — if they only took the men coming back from work, the hospital, etc.

A few days after this propaganda exercise, we were told there was a Red Cross representative on the island, but unfortunately he could not visit the No. 1 Branch Camp at Kinkaseki. It was obvious to us why he was being kept away. The Major asked if we could at least send a letter to him. After some consideration by the Commander, this was agreed to. The doctors and Major Crossley drew up a detailed list of our medical needs and, after a few weeks, a small box arrived at Kinkaseki. In it was one item: bug powder!

There began to be other indications that the Allies were getting nearer and that Japan was really hurting. At night we saw the occasional searchlight in the distance and definitely heard planes, but no explosions. We assumed they were preparing for the Americans as they got nearer.

The Japanese still poured out their propaganda to us, announcing "Great victories at sea" by their "Glorious Imperial Navy and Wild Eagles." They put up on the camp notice board the following announcement:

STAGGERING LOSSES BY ENEMY TO OUR IMPERIAL NAVAL AIR FORCE, SUBMARINES AND GROUND UNITS

688 FOE WARSHIPS BLASTED BY NAVY IN TWO YEARS

	AMERICAN SUNK	JAPANESE	AMERICAN DAMAGED	JAPANESE
BATTLESHIPS	18	1	15	1
AIRCRAFT-CARRIERS	27	3	12	2
CRUISERS	92	3	56	5
DESTROYERS	79	23	47	12
SUBMARINES	147	11	62	5
WARSHIPS (UNIDENTIFIED)	6	—	5	—
SPECIAL SERVICE SHIPS	4	2	2	1
GUNBOATS	8	—	6	—
MINE-SWEEPERS	7	6	1	1
TORPEDO BOATS	35	—	7	—
SMALL WARCRAFT	21	3	26	1
CONVERTED WARSHIPS	3	2	2	4
TOTAL:	447	54	241	32

AIRCRAFT   Enemy Losses 6,874

             Our Losses   1,253   Planes not yet returned or self-blasted.

Figures since outbreak of war of Greater East Asia up to December 8th 1943 issued by Imperial Navy Information Bureau.

One week after that notice appeared another was put up with an even greater victory to report:

US LOSES 115 WARSHIPS IN 38 DAYS IN CENTRAL AND SOUTH PACIFIC AREAS

Staggering losses by enemy to our Imperial Naval Air Force, submarine and ground units between October 27th and December 3rd including the 6th Aerial Battle off Bougainville.

ENEMY LOSSES

Instantaneously sunk:

8 Aircraft Carriers	1 Large Destroyer
3 Large Cruisers	5 Cruisers
2 Large destroyers or cruisers	
1 Destroyer	3 Large-sized transports

"Just" sunk

4 Battleships	1 Battleship or Large Cruiser
7 Aircraft Carriers	2 Unidentified Large warships
5 Large Cruisers	3 Cruisers or large destroyers
6 Destroyers	10 Transports

Damaged

7 Aircraft Carriers	2 Battleships or Cruisers
(3 believed sunk)	
13 or 14 Large Cruisers	8 Cruisers or Large Destroyers
(1 believed sunk)	
5 Destroyers	
(1 believed sunk)	8 Transports
Shot Down	More than 641 planes

In the foregoing period, the Japanese losses are 2 Destroyers sunk, 2 Cruisers "slightly" damaged, and 165 planes not yet returned or "self-blasted".

These notices of their "great" war victories were received with "great" amusement. We got a good laugh out of their method of classifying results as "instantaneously sunk", "just sunk", and "believed sunk". Their claim of sinking huge numbers of aircraft carriers had the opposite effect to that they intended on our morale.

About this time, we discovered among the mine police, who stood at various points on the top level of the mine, one who spoke English with an American accent. By his attitude and comments as we filed past each night, it was clear he was friendly. With the growing indications of preparations for air raids — searchlights and a strict black-out of all huts at night — our spirits were rising. One night as we came in sight of him, a group of us broke spontaneously into, "The Yanks are Coming" and, pointing to the sea, "Over there... Over there... They're coming over!"

Instead of the reaction we expected, anger and possibly a face-slapping or beating, his face broke into a grin. He ran across the tunnel from his post, flashing his lamp at our faces and prisoners numbers. He said to me, "*Ah so, Itchee go-koo, ju go han, hancho*" (So, 159, 15 Squad leader). I was thankful he was smiling, but became worried after we passed, as he obviously knew I was a *hancho* in the mine and No. 15 Squad leader.

Two days later, as we were having our lunch in the "*meshee* tunnel", he appeared, called my number, "*Itchee go-koo*", and beckoned me. He was dressed in civilian clothing, not in his black mine police uniform. I shook with fright as I followed him. Speaking in perfect English, though with a strong American accent, he told me not to worry or be frightened, but to follow. I followed him and his bright carbide lamp through several tunnels until we turned off and crawled into what were obviously long worked-out holes. We then sat down.

He told me that he knew I had a fair knowledge of Japanese, was constantly talking to civilian workers, and I was trying to obtain information on the progress of the war. As he spoke I sweated, even though it was a cool tunnel. I was becoming more and more scared as I wondered how much more he might know of our "news service" and the "phantom bogies".

He went on, talking only about the civilian workers I had contacted. He then told me he was born in America, had come back to Taiwan in 1940, but could not go back because of the war. He then really staggered me by telling me the Japanese and Germans were losing the war on all fronts. He said there had been big sea battles near Taiwan, and that he believed the Americans would next invade either the Philippines or Taiwan. He then asked me how many British officers and men were in the camp, how many had died to date, how many were sick, and what we would do if the Americans invaded.

By now I was very scared and felt convinced he was one of the feared Military Police, the dreaded *Kempeitai*. I decided to play for time and told him I could not give him any information without first talking to the Senior British Officer in the camp. He looked at his watch and said, "OK. There is only 15 minutes to restarting work. You will go back, and I will meet you again tomorrow. Tell no one except your Senior Officer, or you will die!"

He led me back to within about 100 yards of the "*meshee* tunnel" and disappeared in the direction of the cages. That afternoon I was in a state of shock and disbelief, and very scared. I badly wanted to tell my closest friends, but knew I daren't until I had seen Major Crossley.

I told the Major the full story that night. He was astonished and worried that I was obviously being watched. However, after talking it over, he decided we should tell this Japanese the true state of affairs in the camp. The Major calmed me down and told me that if this policeman was *Kempeitai*, I would have been arrested long before. What had we to lose, the Major argued, by telling how many officers and men were in the camp and how many had died to date? He went on that I was to be very careful, and to continue to say that we knew nothing about the war's progress, except what the Japanese told us in their announcements or in the rumours we heard from civilians in the mine.

The next day at "*meshee* time" I waited anxiously for this mysterious Jap to appear, but nothing happened. Nor was he on duty in his usual place at the mine tunnel as we filed out that night. I told the Major on my return, and he advised me to lie low, suspending my "phantom bogie" and stealing activities. "Just wait and see," he said.

It was not until the fourth day after that meeting that this Mine policeman suddenly appeared, again calling me out of the "*meshee* tunnel". He led me to the same disused working, and we sat down. This time he produced from his pocket a *bento* and offered the contents to me. It was cold rice, but on top were small sardine-like fish and vegetables. In my starving condition, I did not even think, I just gladly ate it.

This time he told me he was pro-Allies, and that he had friends in Keelung who could get news of our condition off the island. He gave me more information of the war's progress, repeating his belief that the Americans would invade either Taiwan or the Philippines in 1944, maybe in the autumn.

I told him I had discussed his requests with the Senior British Officer, and gave him the details of the number of officers and men in the camp, how many had died, how many had left on sick parties, and the conditions in camp.

I asked him why I had not seen him for a few days and what he would do with the information. He said he had been in Keelung visiting his friends, and he would now go again and pass on my information. He then gave me some cigarettes, and, shaking my hand, told me not to worry. "I am not a *Kempeitai*," he said. "I am a friend. I want to help to end this war."

He led me back and left me at the same spot we had parted at before. As before, he walked away towards the cages. I returned to the squad, resting after their midday *bento*. I felt more relieved, relaxed, and happy after the feed of fish, having not tasted fish for years. I reported what had happened to the Major when we returned. All we could do was wait and see what would happen next.

Days went by, then weeks, then months. I never saw my mysterious Japanese again. He never even returned to his post near the mine entrance. Though I asked other Squad Leaders on different levels to look out for a mine policeman with his description, he was never seen again in the Kinkaseki mine.

In early 1945, just before the mine finally closed, I was told by one of my Taiwanese contacts that a spy had been caught and executed near Keelung. I wondered if it was my mine policeman or if there was any connection. One thing is certain, he was a friend and pro-Allies because no harm came to me as a result. But no news of our camp or its terrible conditions ever got off that island.

Major Wheeler faithfully recorded his thoughts and his hopes as the months of 1944 dragged by:

August 31st 1944
    Still plenty of rumours — the last big one is that Hitler has been

killed by a bomb. Stricter black-outs and occasionally an air raid warning that might be real. Have plenty of headaches in the way of patients these days, especially one poor lad whose back was broken on the llth. Complete paralysis from breast down and very little hope that there will be any recovery. He would be problem enough to nurse in a proper hospital but here!

The sad case he described briefly was poor Freddie Bradley, a Signaller who had come from No. 6 Taihoku Camp to Kinkaseki in the first draft of men. He had been a keen footballer and was a close pal of Harold Bowcott, a fellow countryman of mine from Wales. Like others, he had slipped and fallen in the pitch-black darkness into the chute. He went through agony as we raised his broken body from the pile of sharp rocks.

Luckily, the Medical Room had some plaster, received earlier from the Red Cross, and Major Wheeler and his devoted team of orderlies made a casing for the patient. Our camp carpenter, Freddie Thomas, scrounged sufficient wood from the Japanese to make a special bed for poor Bradley. Everything possible was done to nurse this badly injured man. Everyone tried to assure him that his back was not broken and that he would walk again. He had to lie on his back with his arms outstretched. Often, when we came back from the mine, Harold Bowcott and I would go and sit by him — Harold holding one hand, I the other. We did our best to cheer him up.

His wooden bed was built up so that he could look out of the high window. The orderlies, under Cpl Donnelly, nursed him and turned him daily. Nonetheless, his back gradually became ulcerated. Despite the agonies of pain and depression he must have felt, Freddie Bradley never complained, always putting up his thumb to us as we passed his window, morning and night. All of us knew he was gradually dying, but somehow his strong spirit and his raising of his thin white arms each day gave us strength also. Eventually the casing of plaster had to be cut away to relieve his pain. The sight and smell of his wasting torn back lives with me still. When he died the whole camp grieved, even though death had become common and ordinary to us. His fight was known by everyone in that camp. If ever a man fought to live and died hard, it was Freddie.

His fight for life was in contrast to so many others who were just giving up, not "getting the rice down" and wasting away, their eyes listless. Of the deaths at that time Major Wheeler wrote:

Another death — more to come I am afraid as there is no break. Starvation in a way and in so many cases just the inability to adjust to and live on this diet. This poor lad we had had on the sick list and hospital for months but could not save him. The intestines and stomach seem to get so sensitive that they cannot deal with anything solid, and as rice is the beginning and end of our diet, unless we are very lucky, many who are now and have long been on the downward path will not see next spring.

Even in the gloom caused by the death of Bradley and those dying of malnutrition, there were still small victories. Gnr Docherty was one. He too fell in the chute and was brought back from the mine, paralyzed from the waist down. Under Major Wheeler's instructions, Freddie made a wooden cradle for him. Major Wheeler and the orderlies persuaded other patients to constantly massage Docherty's legs.

"We sat there for hours, massaging that man's legs," Mick McLoughlin said years later. "Then one day his toe moved! I could have cried."

Later an exercise plank of wood was made and Docherty pushed on each end of the weighted plank every day. He finally walked!

Meanwhile Major Crossley was listening nightly to our reports of the mining conditions. Seeing the constant injuries and deaths, he tried again with the following letter:

To the Camp Commander

With reference to accident to No. 143 Docherty and No. 840 Livingstone, 14 Squad.

I feel strongly that both these accidents could have been avoided if more safety precautions had been taken by the mine authorities.

In November of last year I submitted a long letter in which the chief dangers of the mine, according to the reports of the men, were enumerated together with suggestions as to the remedy for

164

these dangers. I was assured at the time that this letter would receive very careful attention and that the Company would be asked to carry out these suggestions where possible. If the suggestions contained in paragraphs 5 and 8 had been acted upon I submit that these accidents would not have happened.

I am sure that you will agree that the boards which have now been placed across the top of the chutes, thereby preventing men from falling down, could have been placed there long ago, as was suggested in the letter referred to, approximately six months ago.

Docherty is now faced with the appalling prospect of being a cripple for life.

In an endeavour to reduce to a minimum this dreadful damage to men's lives and bodies I appeal to you, Sir, to insist that the Company carry out faithfully their obligations with regard to safety precautions in the mine.

Yours respectfully,

Personnel Administrator
19.4.16.

Then, at long last, came the first concrete signs that the Americans were coming and the war was close to us. On the 14th October we were paraded as usual for work in the mine, when suddenly the air-raid sirens sounded. Immediately we saw high overhead a flight of what appeared to be small single-engined planes, probably fighter/bombers. We were chased back into our huts by the guards, who were screaming, shouting, and clubbing us with their rifles. Orders were given for us to shut all windows, draw down the matting blinds, close all doors, and lie down on our faces. We were told, "lie down and don't look or you will be shot." The guards quickly slammed our hut doors and bolted to their posts. Then we heard, to our rising excitement, anti-aircraft and machine-gun fire, followed by loud bomb explosions. We got up and peeped around the blinds and through chinks in the wooden hut walls, excited as schoolchildren, anxious to see the planes.

Most of us were convinced that this was the real thing, an American air raid at last. We still had sceptics, however, who pointed out that only the previous day the Japanese had announced, "Big air raid practices next few days." They further argued that this was exactly what "Silas the Snoop" had said to expect: there would be explosions and gun-fire. These same doubters went on to ask if the planes were American, from where could such small planes have come? None of us even dared to think that an American fleet with aircraft-carriers could be that near northeast Taiwan.

After about two hours, the "all clear" siren blew, but we were still confined to our huts. Then suddenly, after what seemed to be about half-an-hour, the bells clanged, the guards began screaming and shouting, the siren wailed, and immediate sounds of gunfire and bombs told us "they" were back. Then at last, with a whoop of joy, we caught a brief glimpse of a diving plane with the white star of America on the side. The sight of this plane gave us a tremendous lift. We hugged each other with joy. At last there was evidence of a free man flying a plane over our camp. "It must be from an aircraft-carrier," we shouted.

All day long the alerts and all clears went on. We were only allowed out to go to the latrines, one minute at a time, during the "all clears". Smoke hung everywhere. We hoped it was from bombs, but then saw they had started fires on the hillsides, hoping the smoke would hide the mine buildings.

That night, as we had not worked all day, our rice ration was cut by half. Despite this, our spirits were high. At long last we had evidence that "The Yanks are coming!"

During that night we heard planes and faint explosions in the distance and assumed it was coming from Keelung harbour. "Let the bastards have it," was the cry on everyone's lips. "Think of those lucky free buggers, flying up there", one voice said. "They'll be going back to a feed of ham and eggs!" Even in the euphoria of knowing that freedom was that much nearer, you could never get away from thoughts of food.

Next day we were again kept in our billets. "God bless the Yanks," we shouted. "At least they have given us two days *Yasumay* from that fucking mine!"

166

Later that afternoon, following an "all clear" and a quiet period lasting two hours, we were ordered out of our huts onto the parade ground. The loud-speakers on the hills overlooking the little town above our camp were playing Japanese marching tunes, interspersed with announcements. "Napoleon", who spoke a little English, told Major Crossley, "Practice air raids now finishu, oru very successful, oru Nippon soldier very happy!" He spoke too soon, for just at that moment, back came the Yanks for another strike.

The system of warning was good, but at that moment caused us a a great deal of amusement. On the most dominant building in the small town was a tower with a flagstaff and loudspeaker. Look-outs could be seen posted there, and as the planes were sighted, a blue and white flag was hoisted and the loud-speakers started blaring, "Stage one" (in Japanese). This was quickly followed by "stage two" and a red and white flag. Finally came "stage three", a red flag, and the simultaneous warbling of sirens. The local ARP men would also ring bells and scream out, "*Kooshoo kayo, kooshoo kayo.*" Everyone was then running for the shelters, shouting, "*Tai-ee, Tai-ee*" (take cover, take cover).

We took all this mad chaos in as we were pushed into our huts to the screams of our guards. This ringing of bells, loudspeakers yelling, sirens warbling, and guards cursing gave us the utmost joy. We rushed straight to our vantage points, yelling and shouting, "They're off". As we spotted the swooping, diving planes, this time the sun clearly catching their silver bodies and white stars, we cheered and shouted. Then as we heard the bombs exploding, we shouted, "How do you like that with your rice, you fucking bastards! Go on lads, give it to them!" We could even feel the vibrations from the bombs this time, but there was no thought or fear that they would hit us! To know that at last someone was hitting back for us gave us our best feeling since we had been taken prisoner. We felt that every bomb dropped was a blow in retaliation for our persecution. This air raid, and those that were to follow, gave us the opportunity we needed to let off steam using curses and cheers. Then, as we heard the planes turning back for the sea, up went the cry, "There they go, only a few thousand feet up. Free men, back to good grub and liberty!"

When the last sounds had disappeared, we felt sad. We were quickly brought back to earth as the Formosan "Runabouts" and Japanese sentries tore into the huts. They were in a vile temper, and by now knew the British swear words we so often used to describe them. "*Kora, nani suru ka. nani,* fucking *ba.*" They hit out with rifles and fists, and kicked with their boots as they shouted their version of our favourite expression to describe them.

Nonetheless, our morale went sky-high, soaring with those white-starred planes.

We went to work the next day with lighter hearts than I had ever known, our excited conversations in the tunnel made even more happy as we saw the expressions of gloom on the faces of our "one-bars" and "two-bars". On the way down the hill to the mine head, "Napoleon", in charge of the guard that day, made his way near me.

"Edwardo, *Itchee go koo*" (Edwards, 159), he said, "*Oru mei* now happy *ka*?" (Air raid finished, everything OK Yes?) I mumbled agreement, replying, "*Meigwok shikoki bakudan abunaio!*" "*Oru finishu yoroshee!*" ("American planes bombing dangerous! All finished very good!") This was the mixture of Japanese and pidgin English that we communicated with. This time "Napoleon" made no remarks about it being a good air-raid practice. Nor did he make any attempt to deny they were American planes.

It did not "all fade out again", as Major Wheeler had worried. In a few weeks they were back, and one night there was a really big raid on what we believed was Keelung from the direction of the explosions.

That night will always live in my memory because it was also the night of the worst beating and punishment I ever received. During that raid, we lay head to toe in our blankets, listening to the bombs falling, and as always, everyone shouting out their own favourite expressions of pleasure and contempt for our captors. Each phrase uttered was interlaced with the most explicit swear words we could think of. We knew now that all the guards scuttled into the shelters and left the area around the prisoners' huts. We felt safe letting off steam.

After the raid and "all clear", they would pick on some of the huts for some "bashings". That particular night for some reason the guard commander, "Mussolini", entered our hut with two sentries. They all shouted and screamed, and wanted to know who was calling out during the air raid. Everyone tried to pretend to be sleeping, their heads under their blankets. The guards started to hit out, pulling men off the platforms and clubbing them with their rifles. They demanded to know, "Who was shouting during the air raid". When no one owned up, they got madder. Then "Mussolini" shouted the words I dreaded to hear, "*Hancho, hancho, Doko Ka*?" (Where is the Squad Leader?) I curled myself up under the blanket, praying they would go away. But it was no use. I stood up and said, "*Hai, watashee hancho*" (Yes, I am the Squad Leader.) "*Ah so ka. Kora, nani suru ka. Dameeda, bugeiroo*!" All the usual words were spat out at me as I was punched on either side of my face by "Mussolini". As *hancho*, he indicated I was responsible and should know who was shouting during the air-raid.

It was useless to argue with this ill-tempered Japanese NCO. Many had shouted abuse during the raid, including me. I made no attempt to point anyone out, only saying, "I don't know". This infuriated him more. After more punches, I was knocked down and kicked. "*Yosh!*" he screamed. "*Itchee go ku, hancho. Damme, Damme! Eiso! Speedo!*" I shuddered as I heard the dreaded word, *eiso*, the punishment cell or "ice-box", and all the beatings that went with it.

The two sentries dragged me off to the guard-room, "Mussolini" leading the way. I was dressed in my tattered shorts and nothing else. I shivered with fright and from the cold night air. It must have been about 2:00 am.

At the guard-room I was again asked who was shouting and given another "bashing", this time with a bamboo fencing stick. I pleaded, saying many were shouting, it was dark, I could not know who. "Mussolini" told me I was the *hancho* and responsible, and then made me kneel down. I was forced to kneel on the stony ground in front of the bench where the Japanese sentries sat, resting between their turns of guard duty. As soon as I knelt, I sank back on my heels, but was quickly "bashed" with the fencing stick and forced to the upright kneeling position.

It was agony. My knees were cut by sharp stones and my legs felt terrible from the strain of keeping my body upright. I dared not sway even a little. The watching sentries were in a bad temper from the raids, and were obviously enjoying my torment. The moment I attempted to move my knees and ease the position, I was walloped with the stick or a fist.

I gradually lost all sense of time and only realized it was passing when the guards changed. In the second hour, a bamboo stick was placed across the back of my knees, and the guards stepped on either side of the stick. The pain was excruciating. When the sadistic bastards tired of this, they moved the bamboo to my ankles, stepping on it again. To this day, I can't bear to go down on my knees. Even in church, I will crouch rather than feel my knees touch any obstruction.

Gradually I seemed to be drifting away, leaving my body. I had the distinct feeling that I was watching myself from a distance above my shoulder. I remember nothing after that, but I must have been close to death. My comrades in the hut told me I was brought back just before "reveille" at 6:00 am. When I came to, I ached in every part of my body. My face was bruised and my shoulders were criss-crossed with marks from the fencing stick.

That ordeal weakened me significantly. I was ill for weeks afterwards. I remember feeling that "my turn" was coming. A few days later, they told me another "thin man" party was going to be formed; I prayed hard each night that I would be on it.

CHAPTER 14

"Catch 22"

The next month there came a tremendous boon to our lives at Kinkaseki. We had heard rumours for some time that a narrow tunnel was being cut by civilian workers, direct from our camp to the main mine tunnel. It turned out to be true.

Major Crossley was sent for by Captain Imamura, the Camp Commandant, and was told the tunnel had been dug as a "short cut" to save us climbing up and down the hundreds of steps to the mine head. In future, we would parade in the camp, collect our lamps, and file straight into the tunnel. This, Imamura said, "was out of concern for our health." It certainly was a tremendous saving in effort and misery to us. The long, hard climb over the hill, often in pouring rain, would be avoided. We were delighted.

There was an iron door at the top, and inside there were wooden steps down a steep incline. We found we entered the main tunnel approximately half-way from the entrance to where the cages and beginning of the "jockey-tunnels" were. At the end of that first day, we counted 365 rough, wooden steps on this new route. We noticed further that the Japanese had also constructed a metal door where this tunnel joined the main level.

With this great improvement in our daily routine, the continuing air raids and the rumours of landings in the Philippines, our spirits improved. We were, however, still paying a great toll in the coin of sickness and death. It had been two years and nine months since we had been taken prisoner.

Major Wheeler's despair and hopes for next year were echoed by every one of us as we "soldiered on" in Kinkaseki:

Big stuff! Six days ago we were told 100 sick men were to be sent off — they allowed us to pick them out — said anyone who could stand and walk a few paces, so I acted accordingly and today they went. I don't want to see such a sight again — at least 60 of them were very sick men indeed, many colossal oedema, hardly able to stand without support, let alone walk. The upper parts of their bodies were skeletons. I only hope they are going to something better and that I haven't done the wrong thing in sending so many of the worst, but on the other hand a large percentage would not be alive after another winter here, so one can only hope one has acted for the best.

Captain Seed is sick again — has been slowly going down for months but finally got too much and have put him to bed. He seems to be coming around fairly well after a week — I hope so. He has had a hard three years and though we are very different temperaments, we have got along well together.

I did not make the "thin man party". More of my section left, my own little circle gradually getting smaller. Oh, how true was the Kinkaseki cry of "feet first or head first!" I prayed I would still go out on my feet; not carried, too ill to walk — or dead.

A few nights later, I was sent for after roll-call for a meeting with Major Crossley; a *hancho*'s meeting. These were now regular events. I did not feel any particular worry as I left my hut that night. When I got there, I found only Major Crossley, Captain J.H.F. Stewart, Lt W.M.G. Brown, BSM Dubock, and Sergeant Cameron.

The Major looked very serious. He told us that Lt Brown had been informed of a plan to massacre us all in the event of an invasion of Taiwan. Both a friendly Formosan guard and the Formosan youth who worked as a servant to the Japanese officers had told the same grim story. Lt Brown told us how "Big Head", the Jap officers' servant, had heard Imamura and the other Japanese officers saying, "If the Americans land we must kill all the prisoners." Lt Brown continued about how the next day "the Christian", the friendly Formosan guard, had told him, "American come, oru men die." Major Crossley had told Brown not to tell anyone else until he called a meeting, but to try to confirm the story. That very same day, "Big Head" had confirmed to Lt Brown that the Japanese officers had read this from an official paper. Both "Big Head" and "the Christian" were genuinely scared, according to Brown. Brown went on to say that he had the impression, as we were now getting from Taiwanese in the mine, that these two were trying to befriend us in case Japan lost the war. The Major put us on a solemn oath not to tell anyone else in the camp. He emphasized the seriousness of our position and the detrimental effect this information would have on the physical and mental health of many in the camp, not to mention those close to death.

He had picked us to plan what measures we could against this death threat, and we were to meet regularly from then on. The Major said, "We aren't going to just sit and wait! We are going to try and find out their plans: how and when they will do it! We are going to try to live! If we have to die, by Christ, we are going to take as many of those bastards as we can with us!"

The Major instructed the three of us NCOs to keep our eyes and ears open. He asked me to redouble my efforts to get news from my contacts and at stealing news-sheets.

"I need your solemn promises," he said, "to tell no-one outside this group." We all swore our secrecy, somewhat stunned by the thought of having survived so long and of having to endure so much more, only to face death at the hands of our captors.

"If this news gets outside us six, God knows what effect it could have on the rest of the camp," were the Major's final words that night.

I could not sleep, my mind going over and over the night's meeting. I badly wanted to tell Len Savage, now my closest friend. I knew I daren't. I had given my word. In any case, poor Len was a very sick man. His legs were swollen with beri-beri and his upper body was like a skeleton. To tell him might have killed him.

Fortunately, Len had obtained an in-camp job through Major Crossley. Len was an excellent craftsman, and while on "white card" had shown he could use a soldering iron and repair cooking utensils. The Japanese had recognized his usefulness to them, and Len worked in-camp repairing mess-tins and making old tins into drinking receptacles; repairing anything. He even managed to repair false teeth plates. Dear old Len, the prowess in his hands was to become even more valuable to us later in our captivity.

The following weeks saw many meetings of our small committee. Dubock carefully noted every sentry post, where arms were stored, and put forward a plan to take the arms store, if the time came. Brown continued to work on "Big Head", trying to obtain more information. Captain Stewart, an architect in civilian life, drew up a careful plan of the camp and then the mine tunnel, using my and Sergeant Cameron's descriptions of the tunnel.

We all put forward our views on when and how the Japanese would try to kill us if the Americans landed. We all thought it would come after heavy air raids on the island. We were on the coast, only about 14 miles from Keelung. This being the main harbour in northern Taiwan, we thought it would be one of the first and main targets. Therefore, we would probably not have much time between the invasion and when the Japs would have to make their move.

The next few days, along with Sergeant "Tiffy" Shepherd, I managed to steal two more news-sheets. After interpreting the reports, there was no doubt in our minds that the Americans were established and fighting in the Philippines. Our island would obviously be the next target for a landing on the route of islands the Americans seemed to be taking to Japan.

The Major asked me to check every aspect of the "shortcut" tunnel, especially the door connecting it with the main tunnel. I reported to the Major that both doors on the tunnel were similarly constructed and strong, being made out of old bogie panels. Both could be securely locked. Sergeant Cameron confirmed my findings, and at the following meeting we all decided that the real reason for building that tunnel was now clear. It was not as a short-cut "to improve and take care of your health", as Imamura had told Major Crossley, but a death trap for us, to be used when the Americans landed.

"That's the obvious place," Cameron and I agreed. "It's made to measure for the bastards to just shut us in and leave us to suffocate," Cameron said.

The Major, Brown, and Stewart all agreed. BSM Dubock, also doing an in-camp job since breaking his arm, was in no doubt either. More meetings followed, and then the Major put forward his plan. First, the three of us NCOs were to pick out the fittest men we could to form a "break-out" party. We were not to tell them yet, just choose them and report. Second, Cameron and I were told to try to find a method of stealing dynamite and detonators from the drillers' storage tunnels underground, and a place to hide them in the tunnel. Third, a container was be made and buried in the camp. It was to contain nominal rolls, brief details of what had happened, and where our remains could be found. The Major was determined that the world would know of Hell-camp Kinkaseki.

Our plans went forward on the theory that during the intensive bombing period that preceded any landing, there would be enough confusion for us to steal the dynamite and hide it in the tunnel. Then, before being forced in, a small group of the fittest men would escape to try and reach the invading troops. Those shut in would try to blow the bottom mine door and escape into the workings, hopefully to hide there until help arrived. It was a very optimistic plan, but we all felt it was all we could do, with the camp 90 percent sick and unfit for any sort of resistance.

Len Savage was given about a foot of bamboo to hollow out and told to make an air-tight cap for it out of old tins. He was only told that it was required to preserve and hide camp records in case we had to move from Kinkaseki in future. Len did his customary excellent job, especially considering the primitive tools and materials he had to use, and the container was ready for burial. The Major prepared a nominal roll of the camp, details of those who had left, the list of the dead, and a plan of the cemetery. He included a brief list of the worst of the atrocities, details of our plans, and what we thought would occur when the Americans landed.

The container was secretly buried under the sleeping platform in the officers' hut, within 20 yards of the entrance to that tunnel.

Only we six lived and worked with the knowledge that every day the Americans got nearer, was a day nearer our end. It is a tribute to that committee that all of us kept that secret, so much so that even today there are still Kinkaseki survivors who do not know the details of the horrible end which awaited us had the Americans landed or the "extreme measures" been deemed necessary by the Japanese. That tunnel which we had welcomed as a blessing and a hope that the Japanese were trying to improve our conditions, was for Sgt. Cameron and I a curse, a threat to our lives. We had to climb through it morning and night, knowing it could become our tomb.

Those last months of 1944 and the early months of 1945 were the blackest period at Kinkaseki in terms of deaths and sickness. The culmination of nearly three years of being on a starvation diet, being treated brutally, and the hard labour in the mine, was resulting in rapidly increasing illnesses, mental depression, and death. All of us were sick, some worse than others. Men dragged themselves back and forth to the mine like zombies. Everyone was exhausted. Major Wheeler, with Captain Seed now desperately ill, was working night and day with his still devoted team of medical orderlies: Cpl Donnelly, L/Cpl "Josh" Thompson, Parker, Fisher, Harrison, and little L/Bdr "Joe" Wallace of the Lanarkshire Yeomanry. Wheeler wrote of this time:

> The weight continues to slip — 57 kilos now, but I keep pretty busy, a bit more so with Peter (Captain Seed) being sick, though not so much, as I am afraid I am not so methodical as he — if there is work, I tend to rush at it and get it behind me, whereas he never changes or hurries his pace — still, I am on my feet most of the time from 7:30 am to 7:00 pm seven days a week. I must say I would like a break after two full years of the same routine, but as long as we are here I would rather keep going. Sometimes one hopes one is doing good — occasionally one really does save a life or cure a man but usually one cannot do anything but try to cheer and keep the spirit up.

November 7th 1944

> 83 cases of dysentery in the last two months, 29 in the last seven days! No deaths from it yet — but! So little to work with, so much wrong, so few cards. Still, we have seen worse and we no longer look for help but somehow do what we can and hope for the best. Two more deaths - both the old malnutrition, diarrhoea, oedema, etc. A slow starvation to death, poor devils. Many dread the mine so much they would rather die. There is no incentive to get well and not a few for that reason help things along, even to eventual death. One of the last was such a case.

"No incentive to get well". This was so true now for the vast majority of that camp. One day, over the corpse of one of my section, I asked Major Wheeler, "What did he die of, Sir?"

He replied, "'Disinclinitis'."

"What's that?"

"That's no more inclination to live," he answered. "And that's the most significant disease and biggest killer in this camp," he went on. "Don't you fall into that trap, Sergeant Edwards. Don't try and escape in your sleep or when you go sick. Remember always, 90 percent of your cure is up here, mentally," he said, tapping his head. "Only 10 percent is curing your body. Keep hoping."

It was true. You had to keep hoping. Even I, with the terrible knowledge of that damned tunnel, just had to keep on hoping.

A dysentery epidemic raged through the camp. The only medicine was a diet of rice water and, when the bowels firmed, a little powdered charcoal to try to prevent a recurrence. The orderlies spent hour after hour crunching burnt sticks into charcoal. Then they had the job of getting it down the reluctant patients' throats.

Another hut was cleared and set aside to accommodate the growing number of dysentery cases. The medical staff had the normal hospital hut, the small ward known as the "death hut", and this "isolation" dysentery hut to contend with. Captain Seed became even sicker, and the growing workload was taking its toll on Major Wheeler.

One night I was sent for by Major Crossley, but this time the meeting was not about the tunnel. He told us Major Wheeler had twelve dying men in the "small ward" and Captain Seed was sinking. Major Wheeler had told the Major he could probably save either Captain Seed or one of the other twelve men with what little drugs he had left. His dilemma was that if he gave them all only a little of the drugs, they would probably all die. Should he save the invaluable and only other doctor, Captain Seed, or one of the other men, or let them all take a chance and die? He asked Major Crossley for his help.

"I am tired of playing God in this camp. Help me make this decision," Major Wheeler pleaded. After only a short discussion, our decision was unanimous. I am sure it was what he wanted: "Give a little to all — let everyone have the same chance!"

177

Major Wheeler recorded about this time:

November 17th 1944

Damn busy with 100 cases in hospital, including 70 dysenteries etc. Captain Seed still in bed. Feel as though I am on a powder keg though, with so much dysentery. Many very sick men, etc. Hard to keep things in hand, what with the Nips interfering and shouting. Not so much as of old — no real authority and only a staff of seven orderlies, one Medical Officer, 100 hospital patients, 100 sick in camp, not to mention the daily sick. We do see life, or what remains of it.

November 25th 1944

Dysentery is falling off and the Nips have done comparatively a lot to help this time, why I don't know. I am still busy with lots of sick men, several near death. Captain Seed still sick — I wonder these days if I am going to be the same way as in the past four to five months I have dropped from 65 to 55 kilos and am finding it harder and harder to get down my food etc, etc.

One night we agreed in my hut that for ten minutes after the evening meal and roll-call was finished, we would each take turns talking on any subject we chose. There was only one condition. The subject must not be connected in any way with food. The "talks" lasted only about three weeks, but we learnt more about each other, as the men mostly talked about their past and civilian occupations.

There were more and definite signs now that the island was becoming isolated. In addition to the reduced rations, vital materials were not coming in. We were told one morning that in future only one carbide lamp would be issued to every four miners. The other three had to carry a very crude bean-oil lamp with a protruding wick. These lamps were very old, black, dirty, and gave a very poor light. As the flame could not be controlled, they just became gradually dimmer, finally going out as the day wore on. Furthermore, they were very easily extinguished by the slightest draught of air or quick movement.

Then we noticed lines of full bogies were piling up at the pit-head. Obviously, there were transport problems to Keelung. This led to a shortage of empty bogies to fill in the mine. But we were told each day to keep on filling the chutes. The quota system for holes was at last breaking down as no check could be made on work. Thank God! This meant the nightly floggings gradually ceased on all levels.

The Japanese were trying to use every piece of scrap metal they could, with old bogie lines being taken up on all levels. Then every day they ordered each miner to find a piece of scrap metal. At first we had to carry out pieces of old rails and bogie parts. But gradually it came down to any piece we could find, usually a rail spike.

Each day now meant another close friend falling sick and sometimes ending up with a "red card" in the hospital. If we had a pal sick we dreaded to hear, "They've put him in the small ward." The small ward contained two narrow platforms with five men on either side. We all knew it as the "Death Hut". Once in there your chances of survival were slim.

I will never forget the morning I regained consciousness to find that I was lying in the "small ward". My turn had come. Years later I was told the details of my illness and lucky escape from death.

All I could remember of that day in the mine was feeling ill with terrible stomach pains, faintness, and bouts of nausea. My pals, Jim Fergusson, John Waugh, and Jim Watson took turns helping me up the stairs that night. I recall sitting on the platform in my hut, but knew nothing further until I found myself in the "Death Hut". I had collapsed and been carried to the "small ward" by Cpl Donnelly. He told me 30 years later, when we found each other after the war, what had happened. At about 2 o'clock in the morning the duty orderly called him saying a worm was coming out of my anus. He quickly came to see, called Major Wheeler, and they drew it carefully out with string, weighted by a small stone.

I knew nothing at that time, only that alongside me there were men dying. The one on my right was from Liverpool, dying of dysentery. He was hallucinating, talking to his wife, clutching in his hand a photograph of her with a little boy. The poor devil on my left was from Yorkshire. Like me, he was suffering from worms. It was horrible to see what was coming from his skeletal body.

That first morning of horror was relieved only by the visit of Major Wheeler and Davy Donnelly. They crawled up on my bed space and, moving poor Eric on my right a little, cleaned me up. "For God's sake Sir," I said to Major Wheeler, "get me out of this place! What's happened to me?" As Donnelly cleaned me up, Wheeler smiled and said, "Don't worry, Sergeant Edwards. You will get out soon. All I can say to you is you've been lucky. Just have sympathy in future if you ever see an animal suffering from worms!" They moved on, attending to each of us lying in that miserable wooden hut. I lay and looked at the ceiling, listening to the babbling and sobbing of my companions who were obviously dying. On the next platform another man was ranting and raving about the Japs. It was a nightmare. That night my close friends, Len Savage, Les Davis, Frank Haslam, and "Colonel" Buttifant, all of my signal section, came in to cheer me up. Major Crossley, Lt Brown, Jim Bingham, and Harry Dubock of the committee also came, all encouraging me to fight and "get the food down".

Early the next morning, after two of my companions had died and been gently slid from alongside me, came what I remember as my turning-point. My eyes were closed, when suddenly a soft Scottish voice was saying, "Open your mouth Jack and have a wee sip." I looked up, and in the gloom of that cold morning saw the face of Bobbie McGhie. He was bending over me, my old friend who with his brother Fergus were now cooks. He was pushing into my mouth a spoonful of hot, sweet rice-water. God, it tasted good. As he spooned it into my grateful open mouth he said, "Come on Jack, you are going to get well. You've got to get out of here and down that mine again. We need you — for the 'griff'."

I gobbled the sweet rice-water hungrily, not answering. But I knew from those few moments that I was going to live. I had comrades who cared! And I had a purpose to get well.

Every night while I was in that terrible place, my friends came. Major Wheeler, Dave Donnelly, and the others crawled up alongside me to encourage me. Early each morning Bob McGhie, braving the sentries, smuggled sweetened rice-gruel to me. I learnt later that they had stolen some brown sugar from the store. Each day another corpse would be moved out, the space cleaned, and another dying man moved in. Truly it was the last stop before "Boot Hill", and a ghastly experience I will never forget. In the far corner were two men swollen up out of all proportion with beri-beri. Their testicles were like balloons. Each night

180

they became light-headed, babbled, cursed, argued and sobbed. One night they yelled such insults and threats to each other that I thought I was in bedlam. How I clung to life and my sanity at that time I will never know. I owe my life to Major Wheeler, Cpl Donnelly, Bobbie McGhie, and all my close friends who visited me.

The day after that mad glimpse of hell, I was moved out to the big hut we called "the hospital". Here we were also crowded, lying on platforms. But the atmosphere was far more cheerful. I felt I was getting well. Major Wheeler and the orderlies worked constantly, cleaning up the dysentery and diarrhoea cases, cheering you up, forcing the charcoal and rice-gruel down your throat. The Major's visits were looked forward to. He seemed to know everyone's name and number, and his cheerful words did more for us than his scanty supply of drugs. Captain Seed, who had done his best in the early days, now lay dying in a corner, slowly slipping away.

Major Crossley visited me constantly in the hospital, encouraging me to get well. He told me that on my discharge he had arranged for me to work on the in-camp stonemasons party for a while. Lt Brown and Jim Bingham kept me supplied with bits of news. "Tiffy" Sheppard and other brave souls were still managing to steal and smuggle in the odd-news sheet.

Finally I was discharged and spent two happy weeks working in-camp at making steps. "Kitty" Carlisle and a small group of sick prisoners, all ex-miners and "worn out" like me, worked on this so called "convalescent" work gang.

Just a week before Christmas I returned once more to the mine. I was greeted warmly by my Formosan friends below ground, and even received grudging recognition from the "one-bars" and "two-bars".

Christmas 1944 was dismal and pathetic. The Major managed to get us back early from the mine and persuaded the Camp Commander to give us a rest-day on the 1st January, a Japanese holiday. But the reduced rations, rising death-rate, and enormous number of men sick made us feel very sad. On Christmas Day the Major had me organize a choir, and with Sergeant Eric Scarborough playing his piano-accordion, "E.J." Morris, and a few others, we toured the huts singing, joined by the men in the familiar old carols. Some, however, just sat and stared, or openly wept. The worst time for us was in the hospital hut and the entrance to the "small ward". Here we sang "Silent Night" and "O Come All Ye Faithful." It was an awful moment. The smell of that place stung me as I remembered being there. The stench of death it was, lingering on, everywhere. It clung to every board in that hut.

Every day brought still more evidence that our island was soon to be invaded. The air raids were becoming more frequent. Work in the mine was still grinding along. But there was no place to put the ore we were producing except in the chutes. We were becoming more brave as the Japanese "two-bars" seemed to be disappearing. Many of them were reservists, and were obviously being called back to the army. The "Eagle" had gone, and several of the young "one-bars" had also been drafted. My contacts became more optimistic of the Allies winning the war, and were prepared to give us more news-sheets. I had been concentrating on finding a method of stealing dynamite and detonators. I had found the store and a way in. Major Crossley then knew that if the time came and we were shut in that tunnel, there might at least be a way out. All my Formosan contacts excitedly told me the same thing, "Philippines *moh sukoshee owaree*" (Philippines in a little more finished). There was no doubt in their minds; we were next for invasion.

Wheeler comments at this time:

January 27th 1945

We still get no official news but we do get bits and know that the Americans are at last on Luzon, the last of the Philippines, so with a lot of luck it may be only a matter of months now. Always providing:

1. We survive an invasion.
2. We don't die as so many are doing or
3. The Nips don't move us at the last moment.

Still I must not let myself get morbid at the end.

Unfortunately it looks as though prisoners are to be evacuated to Japan. One always hoped that they had left it until too late and even now the idea of a sea voyage in these waters is not too pleasant.

Nothing definite so far has been told us but from lists made, chance words and rumours, we gather that all sick (the worst sick) are being gathered in one camp on the island; less fit, along with all officers except a skeleton staff to be sent to Japan; men classified as fit in the camp anyway, are to be kept for the time being at least.

I, along with four other officers, are to remain. It leaves some unpleasant possibilities. Are we to make a last-minute dash when the Americans invade? Oh well, there is nothing we can do about it and there have been bad times before — one can only take what comes, at least the time must be months only, now.

13 deaths so far this month! The end I am afraid not yet. All but one (killed in the mine) directly attributable to malnutrition! An unpleasant task is mine, but one must not forget, though I myself know how little I can do, that the men have tremendous confidence and hope in one — strange, but it is a fact, so I suppose one does some good that way. How little a list of casualties tells the real story of war!

CHAPTER 15

The Mine Closes

The last draft of men, who had come from Shirakawa, brought back six of the first "thin men" party who had left us in early 1943! Among them were George Smith and Eric "Plonka" Clack, two of my signal section. We prisoners would joke that they came back for *leggis* (more). But really, it was shattering for them to be brought back. Eric Clack started to decline from the day he walked back into Kinkaseki. They brought us news from many camps on the island. Shirakawa contained many senior officers, Americans, and men from other areas. From them we first heard stories of the terrible atrocities and death rate on the Burma railway, later known as the "Railway of Death". Survivors had left Singapore and Saigon in Japanese "hell-ships", only to be torpedoed, bombed, and sunk by American planes. Several of the "lucky" ones had been picked up and off-loaded at Takao, a southern port. They brought cheering news of the destruction wrought by bombers in the south, but sad news of the deaths of many prisoners from the bombing of some camps.

Eric Clack had carefully copied some poems composed by a senior American officer at Shirakawa. They moved me so much, I copied them in my note-book. They summed up my feelings at that time:

A Prisoner's Prayer

or

How Long O Lord, How Long

How long O Lord! How long? No answer given,
Again this plaint assails the gates of Heaven,
How long O Lord can men endure the fate
Of blasted hopes, defeat and vengeful hate?
How long can spirit live and will survive?

And keep the flickering flame of life alive
In thralldom dark, depressed with ankering care,
How long can hope contend with black despair?

——

How long O Lord! How long? Foredoomed to shame
We're waiting still for help that never came.
Escaping death, alive, to wonder why
In living death, a thousand times to die,
Proud valour mute when base decision mocks
And rank degraded — yoke-mate to the ox,
Life's crowning goal of honoured high command
Now a coolie slave — a chunkel in my hand.

——

How Long O Lord! How long? For all I know
My loved ones may be dead, long months ago.
No letter comes, no word of love and cheer
For weeks and months and now another year.
How long O Lord! How long? Before the callous grow
On tender spots where heartaches pine me so?
When love's reward is bought but vain regrets
Must I grow hard and make myself forget?

——

How Long O Lord! How long, while ships delay
My precious years run out, my powers decay,
My birthright lost by ruthless time's decree
To lads who learnt their alphabet from me?
A rusting sword upon a garbage heap
God give me grace to smile when I would weep.
Eternal Justice! Righter of all wrong
Dost thou still live? How Long O Lord! How Long?

Written at Shirakawa, Taiwan by an unknown Senior American
Officer 25th Jan., 1944.

He followed this impassioned out-pouring of his frustration and
anger with the following, written obviously in remorse and hope.

Heaven's answer to A Prisoner's Prayer

Look up and read, the voice of Heaven replies
The signs and portents written in the skies,
Behold the stars still constant in their courses
Sincerely unaware of warring forces!
God's morning sunshine dries the evening dew,
The moon your loved one smiles at, smiles at you.
The mortal man knows not just how and when
God's purpose runs in small affairs of men.

———

The God of heaven who marks the sparrow's fall
Will never fail his people when they call.
Yon sombre clouds that screen the heaven above
Reflect the glowing spectrum of his love;
Celestial banner in the skies unfurled,
Repeating Heaven's promise to the world
His token now, as countless times before
That God will spare this wretched world once more!

Following these in my notebook, I wrote:

14th January 1945

At a black period, six men have died in four days. Two have
been buried this morning, there are more to go and no means to
stop them dying. One man of those six was killed in the mine.
How Long O Lord! How Long? As I wrote the above the time
was ll o'clock. By 2 pm one more man has died but the stars are
in the sky on those planes!

That same Senior American officer wrote another poem, preceded
by an explanation of why he wrote it, that "Plonka" thoughtfully
copied. It inspired me and everyone else I read it to:

When the Hong Kong PoWs arrived at Shirakawa, occurred
the following incident, the little silver tea-pot appealing to me as
a symbol of the unconquerable spirit and avenging might of Great
Britain.

The Little Silver Tea-Pot

They breed big men, where he was bred,
His eyes were blue, his face was red,
A short and bristling mustache,
The hue of desert sand.
A sturdy British Brigadier
A Nippon bayonet at his rear
He struggled with his tangled gear
And a little silver teapot he carried in his hand.

——

The battle lost, his prisoner's pack
With all he'd saved was on his back
But the little silver tea-pot
Was polished bravely bright
And in its cheerful, shining face
I read the history of his race.
And in my mind for just a space
There flashed a gleam of Union Jack — and all old England's might.

Several of us kept some sort of note-book. Others, like Major Wheeler, tried to keep a form of diary. With the shortage of paper and writing material, however, any daily record was impossible. All of us who kept any sort of notes hid them away carefully. In my hut I had made an excellent "hide-hole" by removing a board from the wall. There was a space between the board and the outer supports. In this space I kept my note-book, some maps I had made of Taiwan, a pair of Japanese *jikka-tabi* (split-toe canvas shoes) I had managed to steal, and a dirk from a Gordon Highlander. This dirk had been carried successfully through many searches by Harry Dubock, and he entrusted it to me for safe-keeping. The Major also knew of my hide-hole. That dirk was our sole armoury for when the Yanks landed!

The rumours that prisoners would be moved from the island continued through January and into February 1945. We now concentrated on wrecking the chutes by rolling in the largest boulders we could find. The "one-bars" and "two-bars" left in charge seemed to be losing interest in what we did. They would detail us off to our holes with the usual "*Speedo, roeiki*", but we knew they could not check what we did unless they just happened to come to our working holes. There was very little drilling and blasting. We were just clearing holes where there was still accessible ore to move.

In camp though, the deaths continued as more and more gave up the struggle. The incessant rain, low clouds, and gloomy atmosphere, coupled with the cold of the winter of 1944-1945, did not help.

While Major Wheeler had private thoughts and moments of depression which he committed to his diary, they were never passed on to others. To the nightly sick parade, the men in the hospital and the "death hut", his expression and words were always of hope. He was practising medicine with what he had available, giving words of comfort and encouragement to fight for life.

Captain Stewart, one of our committee, was now very sick and missing from our regular meetings. There was nothing more we could do, except wait and pray. We knew that if the Americans got near we could expect no quarter.

Gradually, word came out of who was going on the parties being formed to leave the camp. My own section and group of friends was going to be split again. Len Savage, Johnnie "Ack" Davies, Frank Haslam and "Ted" Shedrick were named for the "overseas" party. All we could find out from the rumours was that they would be going on a ship. There was only one place possible — Japan. They and we knew their chances of reaching Japan were very remote. We knew from information from other camps, our sources in the mine, and from stolen news-sheets, that few ships were getting through. The American submarines and aircraft-carrier fleets dominated the Pacific. The gloom which Major Wheeler experienced was felt everywhere in the camp. Friends were again being separated. Part of life in prison camp was that we shared everything. You shared the rice ration and the little extras, sometimes stolen or scrounged from below ground. You shared the "bashings" and floggings. You shared the hardships and burden of your "mucker". You helped him climb in and out of that mine. You shared his pack if he was too sick to carry it on a journey. You often shared his illness if he got dysentery, as we lay cheek by jowl. And ultimately? You might share the ground with him in "Boot Hill".

Len Savage was to leave in one of the ships. I was to stay. Len and I had been together so long that we both felt very depressed at the thought of parting. We decided to exchange pieces of paper with our wives' names and addresses and a brief message in case either of us survived what was ahead. Len was very pessimistic, convinced they would never reach Japan. I knew of the massacre plot and felt little hope myself.

All over the camp men were talking in groups, rumours of the leaving building up daily. Then the signal came that the party was definitely going, and the "boot store" was opened. As each party of prisoners arrived at Kinkaseki to work in the mine, all had had to hand in their footwear. You received in return wooden clogs (*geita*) for camp and, later, canvas shoes to work in the mine. We christened our old boots when they returned them the "Blighty boots". We had always dreamed and hoped we would wear them again to walk out to freedom and "Blighty" (home).

We all knew that the next day the party would leave for the port and the ship to take them God knows where. We had to say our good-byes that night, since we who were working in the mine would be gone before they left. It was very hard. Along with the four of my signal section, many old friends were going: Bobbie and Fergus McGhie, Eric Scarborough, Bennie Slack, dear old "*Itchee hatchee ray*" Johnnie Ford, with a hole in his head from that terrible accident (but still going strong). We shook hands, hugged each other, promised to meet "when it is all over" for "a slap-up meal". Food was still the first and last thought.

We were subdued that next day as we climbed down into the tunnel. We departed to our working holes but, as was usual now, did little work. I wandered the tunnels looking for friendly Formosan workers, scraps of information and, as always, the hope of stealing a news-sheet.

Wheeler wrote:

February 23rd 1945

210 men, including three officers, left on 21st of February. We are sure for Japan. I am afraid our turn will come and it will not get any healthier as the days pass. Things otherwise go on as usual: food, rain, sick, and so on. News, or rumours, seem good,

but not good or fast enough for one in this situation. Deaths this year still stand at 18 but I am afraid we are gradually working up to another bad period, though pray God not so bad.

His next entry was:

March 6th 1945

Nothing new dear, More letters in — some as late as October 1944 but none so far for me. Have Captain Seed in hospital now — poor chap. Have begun him on small blood transfusions — the last card I have. Rumours of our party never having left the island are strong. The Yanks visit us almost daily, at least once. They usually drop their bombs in the distance, I am glad to say.

Then on 9th March, three days later, came the day we had dreamed about, but thought would never come — work in the mine ceased! We came back from our levels as usual that day, climbing up from our areas, then along the main tunnel. We turned into the new "short cut" tunnel and handed in our lamps after the search. We then saw all the "one-bars" and "two-bars" assembled by the "three-bar", who we rarely saw. He made a brief speech. They all saluted and bowed and left. Some of the original "one-bars" smiled and waved as they were leaving. We wondered what it all meant. We were soon to know.

Major Crossley was told, "No more work in the mine for the time being." He immediately asked why. There was a long pause from the interpreter. After a discussion with the Japanese Orderly Officer, the interpreter said, "The lamps are in short supply now and required at another mine!"

The news went around the huts like a forest fire. "The fucking mine is closed!" "Thank Christ for that". "I'll never go down that bastard hole again!" These and even more choice words were echoed in every hut as we excitedly discussed this latest development and what it meant for us.

The Major called what was left of our committee together that night. He told us we would have to be on our guard even more now. We were cut off from our main source of news, our contacts, and the all important news-sheets.

Our euphoria over the closing of the mine ended quickly the next day. When the cooks went to collect the rice ration it was cut by half — now we would really starve. The Japanese were going to carry out our original Camp Commandant's infamous words, "No work, no eat". That day we were all put on in-camp work parties, making more steps or just endless cleaning tasks. Our best moment came when a party of coolies arrived to carry out all those old and nearly useless mine lamps. We waved our good-byes to those useless, spluttering lamps, thankful and rude comments flowing.

A few days later, everyone was ordered into their huts for a *tenko* and search. We watched as a large party of Formosan and Japanese sentries under "Napoleon" and the interpreter made progress from hut to hut. From the shouts, screams, and yells, and from seeing men being dragged out to stand on the parade-ground, it was obvious they were finding forbidden articles. Many men had kept small pieces of carbide in air-tight tins made by Len Savage. Others kept sharpened pieces of metal or bits of wire. Some like me had hidden old mine canvas shoes. Many kept some sort of note-book, and others, like Major Wheeler, a diary. All these were forbidden articles under the camp rules. It was obvious they were looking for trouble.

Into our hut they came. We were ordered to stand at the end of the sleeping platforms while they searched our kit behind. We were lucky as our hut was one of the last to be searched. We therefore had had time to put anything illicit in my "hide-hole". Still we sweated. The guards poked and prodded every blanket and pile of clothing, shouting and yelling. "Napoleon" gradually got nearer and stopped opposite me. Now I really began to sweat. So much was stored only a few feet from where he stood. He looked at me and said, "*Ah ju-go han hancho ka! Itchee go koo.*" (Ah is Squad Leader. 159.) "You honest man. No searcho." I was dumbfounded. And relieved, as I realized all my conversations with him and the *Nippon-go* for English lessons exchange had paid off.

After the search, about twelve men were beaten up out on the square. Three were dragged off to the Japanese guard-room and punishment cells. Half an hour later, "Tiffy" Sheppard and I were sent for by Major Crossley. He looked very worried. He told us one of the men, Daley, had been caught with a diary, and that the diary contained bits of news and rumours we had brought in from the mine.

Later the Major was sent for by Tahara, the Japanese Orderly Officer. The 2nd-in-Command, "Flash Harry" and Lt Suzuki were present at his interrogation. He was told that as Captain Imamura was away from Kinkaseki, "Flash Harry" was now Officer-in-Charge. Further, there had been a serious breach of rules. A hidden diary had been found, and it contained recent war news. The Jap officers demanded to know if the prisoners had a hidden radio in the camp.

The Major of course replied that there was no radio. How could we possibly store it or have a source of power, he asked them. The questioning went on. They told the Major that in the diary were references to "The Christian", "Goldie", "Pan-Face", "Scotch Jock", and that these were obviously code names as they were connected with information on the progress of the war! the Major explained that these were nick-names of people the prisoners knew in the mine who sometimes told them bits of war news. Then they wanted to know which of the prisoners knew enough Japanese to talk to these informants in the mine. Eventually, the Major was sent away to make a list of "nick-names" of all Japanese or Formosans with whom the prisoners had contact.

The Major told us he had sent for us as we would probably be questioned soon. He warned us to be very careful in our replies and to stick to the same story. He said no one had had access to Daley since he was in the Japanese guardhouse. We had no idea what he had told the Japs. He thanked God that this diary had been found after the mine had stopped working. And at least all the news we were getting must be accurate and up to date, he added cheerily. It must be if they thought we had a secret radio in the camp.

"Tiffy" and I were later interrogated by both "Flash Harry" and "Suzuki". They wanted to know about our knowledge of *Nippon-go* and who we had spoken to in the mine. We were both knocked about and "bashed", but nothing as serious as the beating and ill-treatment I had received the night of the air raid.

Later, the Major showed us the list of "nick-names" he intended to submit. It contained all sorts of names, but of course none of the real "nick-names".

Three days later poor Daley was released from the punishment cells, his face a mass of cuts and bruises. He had to be carried to the hospital. He had been beaten and tortured. As I was, he had been forced to kneel while they stood on a bamboo behind his knees and then his ankles. Obviously Daley had not talked. If he had, "Tiffy" Sheppard and I would have been quickly arrested, questioned, tortured, and maybe executed.

After the war when I returned on War Crimes Investigation with Major Crossley, we discovered how very lucky we were. "Flash Harry" and Suzuki, in admitting the torture of Daley, told the court they did not call in the dreaded *Kempeitai* (Military Police) or report the matter higher for two reasons. First, the mine was closed and the whole camp moving, so they reasoned the source of news was cut off. Second, the Commander, Captain Imamura, was away at that time, getting instructions and looking at sites for a new prison camp. They were afraid of the consequences for them if the Commander, Jap HQ, or the *Kempeitai* had been informed.

So by a miraculous piece of timing, the mine closing and Imamura being away, we were saved, and the method of our "news service" was still not known to the Japs.

Major Wheeler knew the consequences if caught and had kept his diary safely hidden all along. His brief entries at that time must have hidden deep fears and emotions. Yet they show his true character, his never thinking of himself, only of others:

March 14th 1945

Still we go on. Since the 9th work has stopped in the mine, for how long or for good, we don't know. It will be a good thing for the men, now that the last few days have been warm and sunny.

Three men are in the ice-box — two for stealing and one for we don't know what, something to do with a diary?

Americans still visit the island daily but we have not seen or heard much lately — the siren is wailing as I write.

Sick calls on but I have less to do of course with the men not working. Captain Seed seems to be holding his own. Some improvement in Captain Stewart. Some eleven seriously ill in the

193

hospital. Food has been cut with no work, and vegetable greens only.

In the next few weeks there were more rumours from the guards that parties would leave soon for other camps. Major Wheeler was again told to pick out two groups of sick prisoners and made up lists. Without knowing where they were going, how far, or if any transport would be provided, this order put both Major Wheeler and Major Crossley in a terrible dilemma. Most of the sick would certainly die if the journey was anything like that coming to Kinkaseki. As two parties were called for, every effort was made to save the worst cases to last, and these two letters below are evidence of the pitiful condition of these men. These desperate attempts failed. Captain Stewart and most of the men listed died in the next few weeks at their new camps.

To: The Commander

Sir,

In my capacity of Medical Officer I feel it my duty to bring the following points to your notice.

1. The following Officer and men:
Officer No. 447 — Captain Stewart, men nos. 31, 942, 952, 988, 1004 were classified amongst the sickest in the camp. Captain Stewart can only walk short distances and is extremely weak, and had it not been as easy to look after him in the officers' squad he would have been in hospital for the past three or four months. If he is made to travel other than as a sick man he is unlikely to survive.

The men, though somewhat stronger, are in very little better condition.

2. No.954 was admitted to hospital with jaundice yesterday. Although he is not acutely ill at the moment the condition will almost certainly increase in severity before he recovers.

3. None of the cases taken from the isolation ward are at present acutely ill but many of them may still be carrying dysentery bacilli.

I am, Sir,
Yours respectfully,

Medical Officer

To: The Commander

Sir,

In continuation of my letter dated 20.2.15, I understand that five may be struck off the list as unfit to travel. It appears, however, that Capt Stewart is not included. I, of course, do not know under what conditions the men will travel or to where, but since the sickest men are remaining I presume the party will not be going to a hospital.

As the party now stands, Capt Stewart is more seriously ill than any other man, and I strongly feel that I would be failing my duty if I did not take this final opportunity of clearly stating that, in my opinion, Capt Stewart will almost certainly die if he is made to undergo anything more than a short journey with proper attention during it, and on arrival at his destination.

Yours respectfully,

B.M. Wheeler Medical Officer 20.2.17.

Into these parties more of my close friends and signal section would go: Frank "the Colonel" Buttifant, "Willie" Coates, Jim Gibson, George Smith, Frank "Joe" Haslam, that unquenchable Boltonian, and Cpl. Len Savage. I was sorry to see these go. They were all great characters. "The Colonel" was in fact just a Signalman. In the early days he was given this nick name with my section. His slow Norfolk speech, his bearing, and the fact that he always seemed to be able to avoid "spit and polish" parades had given him this nick-name. Jimmy Gibson, my driver who had survived that terrible "scratching operation" by Captain Seed, was still a very sick man. Willie Coates, one of my replacements for the men lost at Slim River, was a cheerful Yorshireman. George Smith had the dubious honour of being twice sent to the mine as he had left on one of the first "thin men" parties only to return later. He deserved to survive — and did.

Then Major Wheeler was ordered to leave with the last of the two "sick parties". It was fitting. He was a sick man himself, worn out and exhausted. Still, he argued to be allowed to stay. He pointed out that if he went there would be no doctor left at Kinkaseki (Capt Seed was leaving along with the worst cases). As always, the Japanese were adamant. Wheeler had to go and accompany the second party. Major Crossley placated him by telling him he was travelling with the sickest. Jokingly, he added, "That's what you get for protesting too much!"

The departures of the two parties were sad affairs. The worst, of course, was the last. It contained 86 men, the two Captains, Seed and Stewart, Major Wheeler, and two of the medical orderlies, Parker and Perrera. All of them should have been on stretchers, but only 12 were allowed to be carried. The rest had to hobble along on improvised crutches. It was a pathetic sight: broken down skeletons of what were once men. They had been broken by malnutrition, beatings, ill-treatment and that hell-hole — the mine. We said our emotional farewells, gave and received our handshakes, hugs, tears, and the usual promises to meet after "it's all over". George Harrison made a farewell card out of scrap paper to give to "Doc" Wheeler. Signed by all who could, it said:

Better by far you should forget and smile
Than you should remember and be sad.

We were now left with only Cpl Dave Donnelly, of the RAMC, and Regimental Medical Orderlies Joe Wallace, George Harrison, "Josh" Thompson and Bernard Fisher, to look after the sick. No doctors! The camp strength was now down to approximately 300. We felt miserable and deserted, wondering what fate had in store for us. At least we still had the Major, and while we had him, we had hope. With him we also had some good officers, Capt J.E. Franke, Lt J.T.N. Cross, Lt K.A.W. Davis, Lt Robert W. Hellyer, and Lt Lewis.

We were all that was left of nearly 1,000 men who had come through Kinkaseki since 1943 to work in the mine. Out of the original 524, there were just 89 left. We were the survivors, the supposedly fittest. We looked at each other there on the parade ground that day. Of my original signal section I still had Leslie Davis, "E.J." Morris, Jimmy Craig, Eric Clack, and another of the replacements from Slim River, L/Cpl Mick Mcloughlin. Eric looked far from fit, his legs blown out with beri-beri. I could not understand why he had not gone with the same party as George Smith.

In my old squad I was lucky to still have with me "Big Sam" Lockhead, Jim Brown, Archie McPhail, Fred Norbury, and "Tiffy" Sheppard, my news-sheet stealing partner. We survivors of the original party clung together. One of the old "one-bars" had joked with me when I came back after that close call with death from worms, saying, "Your bones made of iron". We all had a pride that we had survived the mine, but apprehension filled us about what was to come.

We were told that in the next few days we would be leaving Kinkaseki for "Red-Crossu Campo". "Napoleon" told me that this camp was "very rovery" and in the mountains. He said you could swim and catch fish in a river, and we could grow food. It sounded like Heaven to us. However, we were old birds by now, and I confided my worries to the Major that we might just be marched off into the mountains to be finished off if the Americans landed.

CHAPTER 16

The Japanese Dig In

Our camp was to be cleared of all stores and rice. We prisoners were to carry it to a small mineral railway-line about three miles from the camp. Each day for the next three weeks we would carry goods to the railhead. The Major immediately protested that this was heavy labour and we should be given our original rice ration back. After the usual face slapping for his impertinence and a period of arguments, "Flash Harry", still Commandant in the absence of Imamura, agreed, much to our relief. To carry the big bags of rice and stores, we split into syndicates of two or three, each man carrying a little to try to ease the burden. The Japanese and Formosan sentries were spaced out along the road at intervals to watch us. They watched mainly from high ground. It was an amazing sight, the 300 of us spaced out, struggling along the uphill road. Although it was hard work we felt in good spirits. We were outside the camp and on the road again for the first time in over two years — it was exhilarating. The effect of the walk back after delivering the stores to the railhead was wonderful. We felt like animals freed from cages — it was a fantastic feeling to be outside the walls of that camp.

If only we could manage to find or steal a newspaper, we thought, to tell us how the war was really going. Luck again was with us. At the railhead there were civilian workers checking the stores we unloaded. It was now late April and getting warmer, and they had removed their outer clothing. Sure enough, out of one of the pockets was sticking a folded up news-sheet. This time though, I was beaten to it by one of the brave "light-fingers" of the camp, T. Timlin, ex-Gordon Highlanders. He swooped in and "nicked it" in a second.

That night Jim Bingham, Major Crossley and I worked on the Japanese text. There was great news. The Russians and the Allies were closing in on Berlin! The war in Europe must be nearing its end. We hoped and prayed it was, and that the whole weight of the Allied war effort would then turn on our oppressors - the Japs. The camp buzzed with that news all night. I sat with "E.J." and Les Davis for a long time talking of our prospects. We were joined by Jim Craig and "Plonka" Clack. Of my original signal section, only we remained from those 36 who had assembled in Scotland. Was it only four years ago? It seemed like a dream of another world.

In a few more weeks we had man-handled all the stores down to the railhead. The Major informed me we were all to leave Kinkaseki soon. He had been given the same story as I, "A Red Crossu camp in the mountains". To his question — how far away we would have to march, what work we would do, etc., he had received the usual: no answer. The Major said that an advance party of l00 of the fittest men would go first. The remainder would follow in two groups. the Major had decided to send Sgt. Bingham and myself on the first party as Sgt. Bingham was his Administration Assistant and I was the Senior Squad Leader.

After Jim Bingham had left the hut, the Major discussed the mass execution threat. He hoped we would all be together if that time came. He then gave me instructions on what he thought I should try to do if we were separated.

On the night of l5th May, the "boot store" was opened and we were told either to find our original boots or fit ourselves out with what we could find! We were like a kid with a new toy, eager to put those boots on after nearly 2½ years of wooden platforms or canvas rag shoes. We would have to leave camp at 2:30 am to march to Zeho, the railway station over the mountains, our original detraining point. As he shook hands with Jim Bingham and I wishing us luck, the Major told us the interpreter had said the second party would leave on 30th May and the last party on 16th June.

Everyone was up to see us move off in the dark on what was fortunately a fine night. As we marched out of the gates in our "Blighty boots", we passed the guard-room for the last time, and bitter memories flowed over me. Loaded down with our kit, wooden rice-buckets, and odd stores the Japanese had given us to carry, we were at first elated as we marched up the rough mountain road past "Boot Hill". The memories of so many of our comrades, now laying there, reached up to us. I encouraged Les and "E.J.", both struggling along with me.

"We're on that road, at last, away from that bloody mine. Think of it. It's our first steps to freedom!"

However, we soon found that in our weakened state, climbing that mountain road in boots we had not worn for 2½ years was killing our feet. Those of us who had socks were wearing the ones we were issued years ago, patched and worn to holes. Others without socks were in a worse state. I could tell by the pain that my feet were blistering as we stumbled over the rough road.

Our camp guards were accompanying us under the command of Sgt. Major Tatsuo Furuo, known as "The Beast". He was a vicious disciplinarian, who lashed out with his sheathed sword at the guards, cursing, shouting and screaming. He pushed relentlessly to keep us moving. Whenever we tried to rest or adjust our loads, we were hit or kicked. All our exhilaration and relief was being beaten out of us. As my feet ached and burned and I gasped for breath, I remembered that first journey and Johnnie Griffiths, the first death caused by the march to Kinkaseki.

At long last we reached the top. But there was no stop. They drove us downhill with their rifles, clubbing and incessantly screeching, "*Kura, Kura. Nani sura ka. Bugeiroo!*" Dawn was breaking and we could see in the distance the little hamlet of Zeho, the railway lines glinting. Suddenly, our feet touched a smooth surfaced road. The effect was tremendous, easing the pain on our tortured feet and bodies as we ceased stumbling over the pot-holes and stones of the mountain road.

We arrived at the station at about 6:30 and were ordered to "*Yasumay*", collapsing where we were. We had been marching non-stop for four hours, and our first thoughts were for our feet, everyone pulling off their boots. Everyone's feet were the same, a mass of blisters, some broken and bleeding. My old grey army socks were stuck to my feet with dried blood. We used a little of the precious water from our bottles to wash our feet and lay back exhausted. Typical of the Japanese, our train was not due until 8:00! There had been no need for the forced march.

As we recovered and looked around the buildings near the station, we took satisfaction from the clear signs of the bombing and strafing of even this remote area.

The train came, and with our spirits back after the two hours rest we did not need any second orders from our guards to clamber aboard. We were excited, chattering like children going on a picnic or being let out from school. They packed us on to the wooden seats, but amazingly gave no orders for the wooden shutters to be closed as we set off. It was marvellous to look out on the villages and paddy fields, to see normal people again. We even waved and shouted. But they all stared sullenly back. They looked cowed and frightened. One of our guards told us our destination was Taihoku, the capital city. As we neared the city, there was more and more evidence of the bombing by the Americans. Nearly every building showed signs of it. Some factories were smashed completely. We had heard the bombing from Kinkaseki, but to see the results really raised our morale. Cheered, we wondered just how long Japan would be able to stand up to this. If this was what the Americans were doing to Taiwan, what were they doing to mainland Japan? The more I saw, the more I wondered how long before the Americans would land. I tried not to think of the possible massacre.

At last we drew into the main station and were hustled off the train. As usual, we were assembled, counted, and marched off, nearly at a run, to cries of "*Hyaku, hyaku*" and "*Speedo, speedo*". It was about 10:30 and a beautiful clear blue sky and hot sun beat down on us. The city looked to be expecting an attack. Bodies of troops were everywhere, the shops shut and sand-bagged. Very few people stopped and looked. Everyone seemed to be on the move, loaded with goods. Many groups of people were pushing trailers or two wheel trolleys loaded with furniture. There was an air of tension.

"Looks just like Singapore in the weeks before the attack," said E.J. "God, they must be expecting an air raid or invasion the way they are preparing." As we turned into a street leading to a small station, all around us were signs of destruction. In our joy and interest at seeing the scenes, we forgot our tiredness and burning feet.

This time there was no waiting. We were pushed into what was obviously a suburban train and it set off towards the outskirts of the city. There were mountains ahead. Again our guards did not bother to close the wooden shutters. Our eyes eagerly took everything in. We could see streams of vehicles, people, and people pushing trolleys, all heading for the hills. As we got closer we could see why. In the hillside were caves containing factories and stores. Troops were everywhere, fully armed.

201

We came to a halt at the end of this narrow suburban line. Ordered off the train, we marched through a narrow market street and on to the pebble beach of a wide river. Downstream we could see a long, thin, pedestrian suspension bridge leading to the opposite bank and mountainous country. In front of us were primitive ferry boats operated by men with long poles. We were told to sit and eat the cold rice we had carried with us, our last *bento* from Kinkaseki. Again we removed the boots which were playing havoc with our feet. Luckily, some of us had our old canvas mine shoes left and gladly tied these on.

Just as we were getting down our first mouthfuls of rice we heard sirens and bells, and before us a scene of complete panic took place. Everywhere we looked people were running. Our guards quickly drove us under the trees and ordered us to lie face down, eyes closed, and not to look or we would be shot. They showed us they meant business by loading their rifles, slamming the bolts, and laying down so as to cover us from every angle. Over the planes came, but we took a chance and had quick peeps at the silver shapes of our allies in the sky. We waited for the shock of the bombs, but they were heading for the city we had just left, "Thank God they came late," Les shouted to me, "Otherwise, we might have been killed by our own allies!"

The bombs fell over the city we had just traversed, one long series of explosions. It seemed as though all those high flying, four-engined bombers had dropped their bombs at the same time. This was the method of bombing we would experience for months. It was called "carpet bombing", but we called it "the Yanks pulling out all plugs!" They certainly pulled all plugs that morning, as we felt the earth shake where we lay.

As soon as they flew off, we were hustled to our feet and harangued by a Japanese sergeant we had not seen before. He was very stocky with small, piggy eyes and, by his manner, one to avoid. He told us we were to march to our new camp "in the mountains", waving his arm vaguely behind him. First he said "*Oru mei* go store carry rice and *branketsu.*" His emphasis and pronunciation of "blankets", the "r" for an "l" as all Japanese did, earned him the nickname "Blankets".

We were marched back into the village to a store where we picked up sacks of rice, some big baskets of vegetables, two large iron rice boilers, and one bale of blankets. Lying alongside this pile of goods were eight stretchers made of two bamboo poles each, criss-crossed with bamboo strips. The two rice boilers were lashed onto two bamboo poles with green bamboo strips. The rice sacks were either loaded on stretchers, two bags each, or given one to a man. Gus Wyllie of the 155 and I were ordered to pick up a stretcher with two rice bags.

We set off in a long line, "Blankets" and some guards leading. Those carrying individual loads went first, the eight stretchers loaded with the rice- sacks next, and the two iron boilers last. Our own Sergeant Major from Kinkaseki, "The Beast", dispersed Formosan sentries along the column and brought up the rear.

We straggled through the village and over the pedestrian suspension bridge which, we noted with pleasure, showed much evidence of bomb splinters. Shortly after crossing this river, the Tamsui, we turned onto a track leading into the countryside and the mountains. Over the first half-mile we passed through thousands of wooden shacks occupied by people who had fled from the bombing in the city.

Gus and I soon began to tire under the strain of carrying the sacks of rice and our kit, which we had piled together on the stretcher. Our arms were aching and the sweat poured off our bodies as the sun climbed to its hottest at midday. The bamboo poles making up the shafts of the stretcher were too thick to grip properly. Gus said, "First *yasumay* we get, Taff, I've an idea to make this a bloody sight easier."

After about an hour of staggering along under this weight, we reached the others waiting for us to catch up. The column was halted and we flopped down exhausted. Gus said "Come on, Taffy. Let's smash the handles and bind them smaller. It will be easier to grip." The idea sounded good. We smashed the bamboo ends between two stones, bound them with some of our old rags of clothing, and, using old respirator case straps, made slings for our shoulders. We were not given a long rest and as we set off again the straps around our shoulders and easier to grip handles seemed a great boon.

On we went, the path gradually becoming rougher and narrower. It led up a valley flanked by hundreds of paddy-fields. The march then became a nightmare, the stretcher jolting and swaying under its load, the straps cutting into our shoulders, and the split bamboo shafts becoming agony to grip. The journey seemed endless. We were just staggering on like automatons, the sun seeming to get hotter and we thirstier, every mile.

Our guards were suffering too. Loaded down with their packs and rifles, their tempers got worse as the continual shouts of "*Hyaku, hyaku!*" and "*Speedo, speedo!*" came from "Blankets" and "The Beast".

As each halt was called, we discovered how unlucky we had been. The men carrying the individual loads were always halted first to wait for the stragglers with the stretchers to catch up. The leaders' rest, therefore, was always longer. We stretcher parties of rice-sacks and boilers had only a brief period before the column was ordered up again. Still, when we saw the gang carrying the rice-boilers, four men to a stretcher, we realized how fortunate even we were. Those big heavy boilers must have been agony to carry, and "the Beast" was lashing out at these poor men, flogging them back to their feet after only five minutes. How lucky we had been not to get a boiler!

The nightmare journey continued, now winding up on rougher tracks into the hills. The river flowed on our left as we turned and twisted. Then two of our Formosan guards collapsed and had to be assisted by others.

The journey's torture increased as we staggered upwards. We would jog-trot like coolies to get away from the ill-tempered guards, then flop until we heard their yells. Eventually, we reached a small farmhouse on a cliff overlooking the river hundreds of feet below. It was mid-afternoon, and we were in a pitiful condition. The kind peasants in the house, after giving the Japanese and Formosan soldiers food and water, called us to drink from their well. We were later to discover we were only half-way to our destination. Thus, this farm house became known as "The Half-Way House."

The last to stagger in for this welcome rest had been the rice-boilers party. One of their stretchers had already broken under the strain and they were carrying the boiler by its sharp rim, two on each end. They were in a shocking state. We tried to improve our loads and bathed our aching bodies in the cold water from a stream pouring out of the ubiquitous bamboo pipe. To our incessant questions of "How much farther?" and "Where is the camp?", we received, "*Moh skoshee*" and

204

an arm waved to the mountains above us. "Little more, the bastards," moaned Gus. "Christ, Taff! We must have carried this bleeding rice sack nearly six miles!"

On again, we were hit and pushed to stagger and stumble on. All I could see now was the back of Gus's head and shoulders in front of me. The track got worse. It was overgrown, sometimes going over rough bamboo bridges. The trees, bamboo thickets, and brush now frequently had to be hacked and cleared for us to get through.

As we staggered on, all we could hear behind us were the screams of "the Beast" and the blows of his stick on the backs of the poor lads carrying those boilers.

Gus and I continued our carry in the same way. Once clear of the guards and their rifle-butts, we flopped, resting until we heard the guards approach from behind. Then we staggered to our feet to continue. How we continued that nightmare, I will never know. Only the punches, hits, and kicks of our ill-tempered guards forced us on, up and up, into the mountains.

At long last and just as the sun was sinking, we staggered into a clearing containing two huts made of bamboo and attap (long grass roofs). As we fell to the floor exhausted, we saw Imamura, our old Kinkaseki Camp Commander, sitting in one of the huts watching us. He was smiling, sipping tea.

It was nearly 8:00 . We had been carrying those loads over that terrible journey since mid-day. The last to straggle in were the "boiler-men", both stretchers long broken. They had climbed, slipped, and made their way, carrying those rice-boilers by their rims. If our condition was pathetic, their's was worse. Beaten all the way by "the Beast", they were all in a state of collapse. Among them was poor Les Davis from my section. I made my way down to him and he fell into my arms.

Imamura lined us up and gave us a brief speech. He said this place would be our home in future. "If you want food, you grow food. If you want house, you build house. No food, no house, you oru die here." His voice rose as he waved his stick in the air. "There is nothing here. You have job from tomorrow to build camp."

We were shown an area of grass and told if we wanted beds, we had to cut the long elephant grass all around. All we wanted was to lie down where we were. Everyone was aching and exhausted. Our shoulders lacerated and bruised, our hands and feet blistered and cut, we were pitiful remnants of the exhilarated men who had left Kinkaseki at 2:30 that same morning.

After a short rest we roused ourselves and found a stream nearby to wash in. We were allowed to light fires, set up the boilers, and were given enough rice to make one small ball each.

We slept where we were, utterly exhausted, until the nightly air raids of heavy bombers passing overhead to Taihoku woke us. We lay awake nursing our broken bodies, listening to the rumble and crash of the explosions, feeling every explosion was a blow of revenge for our miserable condition.

CHAPTER 17

Jungle Camp

Thus, in a clearing we called the "Jungle Camp", began the last phase of my captivity. The official report compiled by Major Crossley in October, 1945, described it as follows:—

Jungle Camp

With the new camp commenced a phase which was to be as bad, if not worse than anything we had experienced. Conditions generally were extremely grim; the living accommodation consisted of huts built of grass, cut and erected by the men under the instructions of the Taiwan soldiers. Severe beatings then became the order of the day, and food was shorter than ever.

The site of this camp was in the mountains known as the Taihoku Heights, and partly on a long disused and over-grown tea plantation. The nearest transport stopped at Shinten, 11 to 12 miles away. It was only possible to reach the camp by a mountain path. This path was for the most part rough and steep. It must be understood that all equipment, stores, blankets, 300 60 kg sacks of rice, Jap office equipment, etc. was carried from Shinten to the camp between 1st June and 20th July. The loads allotted to each man for the march up were anything from 40 to 60 kg. The beatings meted out on these marches were numerous and severe. Such building materials, sand, cement, etc. as were required in the construction of the camp had to be transported in the same manner.

The main work was to clear large expanses of land which had become virtually jungle, and plant sweet potatoes. Headquarters, Taiwan laid down a programme which ordered that the camp had to be completed by 20th July, and 16,000 sweet potato plants had to be planted per day from 2nd June. The latter part of this programme was a physical impossibility and the Japs on the spot knew it, but the order had been given, and they set out to drive the men to the limit and beyond.

The Major's report to Intelligence in October 1945 conveys a brief summary of those last four months. Those who were there said it was their worst experience as prisoners of war. Certainly, we were never hungrier, worked harder, or beaten more.

That first morning when we woke, stiff, aching, and sore, we took stock of our situation. There were only a few sergeants and no officers to guide us. As always, we were at the mercy of the Japs. We found we had two new Japanese to terrorize us at this camp. The first was Lt Tamaki, a fat, English-speaking officer, who had commanded Heito Camp previously. We heard from men who had been in Heito that he had boasted he would fill his cemetery. He did. His camp had been closed after the Americans had bombed it, the bombs killing more than 50 prisoners. Tamaki loved to show off his English, delighting in mimicking any phrases which caught his ear.

The other terrorist was a Japanese Corporal, thin faced with a small moustache, who we nick-named "The Tashee Corporal" because of his moustache. He had an evil look which fitted his temperament.

That first morning we were paraded, Tamaki told us that we would work to build huts for the rest of the Kinkaseki camp men who would be following us very soon. Only two prisoners would be allocated to tend the fires and cook the rice ration.

Work on building the huts started immediately. We were split into four groups, one party to go into the undergrowth on the mountain for bamboo, one to go for tree trunks as uprights for the huts, one to gather long grass to make roofs, and the fourth to clear sites for the huts.

I felt lucky to be detailed that first morning to stay on the camp site. The selection for this group was simple: those barefoot, their feet a mass of blisters from the march, stayed. We found ourselves working under the control of Tamaki. We nicknamed him "the Madman" because of his frequent tantrums, interposed with periods of calm when he would talk quietly in English.

We were given the usual chunkels and baskets to cut and remove earth, creating terraces and a better path to the camp entrance. Tamaki, watching our attempts at work with our sore hands, aching bodies and shuffling steps while carrying the baskets of soil, went crazy. He threw off his shirt and worked like mad for two minutes, chopping up the ground, filling and throwing baskets of soil. He was the first Japanese officer I ever saw take off his shirt in front of us. He jumped up and down in rage when we protested we could not work at that pace. To the pleas of the prisoners that they were "*Byoki toksan*" (very sick"), he whined, "*Nani byoki toksan*", imitating us.

With the Taiwanese sentries standing over us, Tamaki occasionally visiting our group, and even Imamura watching at times, we were worked continually. Any sign of slacking or request to *benjo* (go to the toilet — just a hole we had dug about twenty yards away), meant a "bashing". As the parties came back from the mountainside laden with tree trunks, long bamboos, or bundles of elephant grass, we realized we had been the most fortunate. They related how they had been marched into the mountains, been given axes or hand scythes, and told to cut bamboo, trees, or grass. All had had a terrible time and bore cuts from the branches, bamboo, and long sharp grass. The grass cutting party had fared the worst. In charge was "The Tashee Corporal" who had beaten up every man in the party. They all came back that night exhausted. Most had had to climb into the jungle for up to three miles to do their work. Then loaded down they had trudged back.

The meals were pitiful compared to Kinkaseki. There was only a watery soup made of *ensai*, a tasteless green vegetable top, and just enough rice for a ball as big as your fist. We were told that first night that no one could be "sick" as at Kinkaseki. Imamura told us again, "No work, no eat. Oru men die. Does not matter".

The work went on. Our "Madman" party cleared areas, made holes for uprights, and, under the guidance of two civilian Taiwanese, built the huts. Only a few nails were used, in the main supports. Everything else, cross members and rafters of bamboo, was tied together with thin green bamboo strips.

The bundles of long elephant grass brought back by the "grass-cutting" party were stock-piled, ready for roofing. The "Tashee Corporal" had evolved a cunning quota system for his gang. Only after a number of bundles were cut was his group given a *Yasumay*. He pushed up the required quota each day until all the prisoners agreed to work at the same pace.

Our only attempt to improve conditions met complete failure and more beatings. Jim Bingham and I decided to write a letter to Imamura pointing out the weakened state of all the men, the small rations after the mine, and the inordinate amount of work required.

The following morning when "the Madman" was detailing the work parties, Jim stepped forward and handed him the note. The "Madman" read it and went into a terrible rage. He jumped up and down, pulled out his sword, and I thought he was going to cut Jim down. Stepping forward, I tried my limited *Nippon-go*, but it just made matters far worse. We both got bashed. Then Tamaki called another man out of the line and asked him, "Do you know what is in this letter?" Being scared, he replied, "No." This gave Tamaki more excuse to bash us, and he called Jim a liar for saying he was protesting for all the men.

Tamaki then threw off his cap, put back his sword, and sarcastically mimicked British soldiers. Adopting a cowed posture, he whined in a plaintive voice, *"Byoki, byoki, sukoshee meshee"* (Sick, sick, little food).

That morning convinced Jim and I that our only hope of improving conditions would come when the Major arrived with the rest of the Kinkaseki men. The work went on, and after a week we had roofs to sleep under and a place to store our kits and blankets. We were told by Imamura that three huts had to be up by May 31st, as the second party from Kinkaseki would arrive then.

Our only solace in those days was the daily flights of American planes passing overhead to bomb Taihoku. At night we listened with pleasure as we heard the raids go in. Those first 15 days at the jungle camp were a nightmare. We were worked from just after dawn until the sun set. Imamura was determined to have those three huts built.

At last the day we had been working for came. It dawned with a clear blue sky and hot sun. Suddenly, at about mid-day, over came the Americans in far greater numbers than we had ever seen before. The sky seemed full of big silver four-engined bombers, and below them there were flights of smaller, strange looking, split-tailed planes. The warning shouts from the sentries soon gave us their name and type. *"Koshoo kayo! Tai-ee! Abunai-O! B nee-ju shee! P sam-ju hatchee!"* (Air-raid! Take-cover! Danger! B 24! P 38!) Those low-flying planes were P38s, and a deadly, sleek, fighting machine they looked.

Our guards that morning seemed dumbstruck by the sight of this immense armada roaring overhead. Tamaki, standing over us, started to back away, shouting to us, "No American plane, all Nippon, all Nippon!" However, as soon as he had backed about ten yards, he turned and ran for the cover of the trees. He was clearly scared stiff. Our feelings of joy gave way to worry as we realized that if the Major and the men from Kinkaseki had left at the same time as us, they would be crossing Taihoku at this very time. Even where we were, 12 miles away, the rumble from the bombings was intense. We prayed and hoped that wherever our comrades were, they would be safe.

When they arrived that evening, exhausted as we were after the long march from Shinten, there was great excitement. We greeted each other and exchanged news of the biggest air-raid we had seen. They had been on the river-bank in the same position we were three weeks earlier when the bombs began falling. The Major told me they had also seen what appeared to be leaflets dropping from the planes. We told the situation, described the problems with Imamura, Tamaki, "The Beast", "Tashee Corporal", and the guards, all of whom seemed to be getting worse tempered each day.

The Major told us he really believed we were on the "last leg" of our captivity. The increasing number and intensity of the bombings probably meant an imminent invasion by the Americans. He believed the real reason for our move from Kinkaseki was to move us inland away from the coast.

Two days later the Major made his first attempt to re-instate the Kinkaseki camp system of "White Cards". Imamura refused to see him, and Tamaki, who clearly wanted to show he was in charge of building the camp, flew into his usual tantrum. He knocked Major Crossley's cap off with a blow to the head. The Major's glasses went with his next swing. What infuriated Tamaki even more was that the Major simply picked up his battered old service cap and his glasses, put them back on again, took a pace back, and saluted. He then told Tamaki, quietly and firmly, "There is only one way to finish this camp properly: you and I will have to co-operate."

"*Nani-ka* co-operate!" Tamaki exploded. Again he struck the Major. The Major simply stood still, riding the blows. Clearly, Tamaki wanted to knock him down in front of us. He then put his foot behind and pushed him to the ground. At this there were angry shouts from all of us watching. The Major quickly called out, "Steady everyone. Don't move!" The sentries around Tamaki had raised their rifles and bayonets. It was a very tense few minutes. The Major stood up, dusted himself, and said, "Very well, Lt Tamaki. We shall see." He turned and ordered us to proceed on work parties.

The incident ended, but that night the Major sent for those of us left from the original committee and told us we clearly had to be very careful from now on.

Imamura, a changed man from Kinkaseki days, now wandered around the camp-site, frequently using his stick on prisoners, something he never did at the mine camp. He ordered that the remainder of the camp huts had to be built and all the camp-stores at Shinten to be carried to the Jungle Camp within the next 30 days.

They finally agreed that the Major be allowed to detail the work parties. This meant that the sickest men could be put on the most suitable working parties away from the worst of our task-masters. But as there was very little difference between the work parties, it was very difficult.

The work parties were as follows:

Town Party: March to Shinten, the light-rail head, each day and carry back stores, rations, etc.

Timber, Grass, Bamboo Party: Go into the surrounding jungle and collect timber, grass or bamboo as required to construct the huts.

Cultivation Party: Reclaim jungle land and plant sweet potatoes.

Tamaki Party: Do the construction work in the camp directly

under Lt Tamaki (this party was later called "M" party — "M" for "Madman").

Farming Party: Cultivate a small area to plant peanuts and tomatoes. Chosen by the Japs.

The Major, aided by Cpl Donnelly and two American officers, tried to move the men around between these parties. One of the American officers was a medical officer, luckily for us. The Americans had become attached to our group at Shinten. Every night the Major would talk to the squad leaders and try to put men who were sick on parties where they could be "covered" by their comrades.

The work went on at a tremendous pace each day. Every party had its beatings, the severity depending upon the temper of the guards, but mainly on the NCO in charge. Most men wanted to get on the "town party". At least on that group you were out of the camp all day. The freedom felt on the long walk down, the chance of some extra food and the possibility of stealing something at the store near the rail-head amply compensated for the long slog back carrying the heavy loads.

The worst party was the Timber, Bamboo, or Grass party. These parties under the "Tashee Corporal" seemed to collect the worst of our Taiwan guards. "Tashee" always wanted more timber or bamboo collected, and always pushed the quota up for bundles of grass cut. This forced hard labour, the constant harassment, beatings, and poor rations were having a worsening effect on everyone. Men looked terrible; eyes sunken, shoulder blades protruding from their backs as if the skin would break, rib cages exposed. All were like living cadavers. At night, with no lighting except the moon, we just lay down exhausted. Many men were beginning to show signs of mental disorder. I wondered if we would survive the few months we hoped were all there was left of the war. Completely cut off now from civilization, with no news, starving, slaving all day in the sun, more and more men were cracking under the strain.

One night Les Davis, who now slept alongside me on the dried grass floor, came back from the "Tashee Corporal's" party in a pitiful state. Les was a strong character whom nothing seemed to shake previously. The battle in Malaya, the mine, all he had taken in his quiet way. Now a skeleton of about 90 lbs., he came in that night and collapsed. His

213

shoulders and arms were cut and bruised. He had fallen under the load of a tree trunk in the river when crossing and then had been beaten by "Tashee" and the guards when cleaning his wounds in a stream later. He fell into my arms sobbing. "They said I was on a *Yasumay*" he blurted. That night I cradled and comforted Les, joined later by "E.J." and Jim Craig. We talked about only one thing — surviving until the end came.

In the next few days a beating on the grass cutting party produced our first lunatic at the Jungle Camp. The following excerpts from the official Intelligence Report compiled after the war give some idea of conditions in the following weeks:

Jungle Camp

5th June, 1945
    During the morning a party was employed cutting elephant grass used in the construction of the huts. In charge of this party was a Jap sergeant, Nakajimi; at midday, when it was time to return to camp for lunch, the men were lined up and those who, in the opinion of this sergeant, had not done enough work, he ordered to be beaten by the Taiwan guards. Among the men so punished was Corporal Flynn. One particular Taiwan guard, who appears before in this report and was known to us as the "Nasty Carpenter", proceeded to hit Flynn on the head with the handle of a sickle until he fell unconcious. He was picked up by two men and carried back to the camp. At 1300 hrs the Jap Sergeant called for his working party, and was somewhat put out when he found that his party was one man short. The PA was called for and went to investigate, whereupon he found Corporal Flynn in his billet being held down by two men, and raving. This was explained to the Jap Sergeant by the PA and the sergeant adopted a threatening attitude and ordered the PA to have the man carried out onto parade. This the PA refused to do, and after a good deal of shouting, the party moved off minus Corporal Flynn. The Doctor was then called to the sick man, and stated that he was suffering from a manic depression of the brain caused by the blows on the head. It was necessary to put two orderlies to watch over Flynn, who was by this time becoming very violent. Immediately letter as under was submitted to the Camp Commander by

"I wish to bring the following points to your notice. This morning on the grass cutting party (*Kaya kaya*) the men were first told to collect four bundles each before returning to camp. Later one of the sentries told the men to collect 15 bundles each before lunch. When the men paraded to return to camp all those who had done only seven or eight bundles each were beaten very hard over the head with the handle of a sickle. About 1300 hrs in the camp one of the men who had suffered this mistreatment showed signs of irritation to the brain and medical attention was necessary. The Doctor considers that this might lead to serious consequences. This instance is typical of the treatment which all prisoners have received during the last few days. The majority of men have all been kicked, beaten and shouted at unmercifully. We have now been PoWs for almost 3½ years which is in itself a big strain on the nervous system. There is no doubt whatsoever, if present maltreatment continues, there will be many more cases like today's. For the past year or so we have been treated reasonably and we cannot think of any reason why there should be a sudden change in the treatment. As Commander of the Camp we appeal to you, Sir, to give us the same fair treatment which you have always previously given to us.

(sgd)

J.F. Crossley (PA)
5.6.45.

Later Major Crossley was sent for by Lt Tamaki and screamed at in the usual Jap manner for some twenty minutes. Not satisfied with this Lt Tamaki again called Major Crossley and repeated the dose for about ten minutes.

6th June

Major Crossley and Capt Schneider USMC, were called for by Lt Tamaki who proceeded to beat both these officers, knocking them to the ground. During this interview Lt Tamaki said that if Flynn attempted to walk out of the camp he would be shot. Later, the Doctor and the PA asked for a further interview, at which it was agreed that Flynn might remain on his bed and two orderlies remain with him. A demand that Cpl Flynn by tied up with rope was refused by the two officers, and a

215

counter proposition that he be removed from the camp to a proper hospital was made. After this Lt. Tamaki asked that a Medical Report on Flynn be made for the Commander, but that it must not include details as to how Flynn received the injuries, and also must be submitted through Lt Tamaki. The following report was submitted:

Insane Prisoner

1.   No ll05 Cpl J. Flynn, 2 squad, has for the past five days been suffering from a mental illness which has close resemblance to a manic depressive psychosis. He is not aware of his present surroundings and has alternating periods of depressed and violent activity. He believes people are plotting to harm him. He has tried to wander away from the camp and it has been necessary to maintain a 24-hour guard over him to keep him from doing so.

2.   Because of the inadequate facilities for treatment of this case at this camp, because of the undesirability of having him escape, and because he might remain in this condition for many weeks or even months, it is requested that this man be moved to a camp where facilities to treat this type of case are available.

(sgd)

Leo Schneider
Capt US
Med Corps 11.6.45.

As is pointed out at the beginning of this section beatings were the order of the day, and a day never passed without two or three really brutal beatings and many others of lesser magnitude. Only a few incidents will be detailed on the days they occurred, as we go on.

23rd June

Bentley is now very sick with pneumonia. The Doctors have been trying all day to get drugs. This afternoon they were given the following remedy for pneumonia. Dig up 10 worms, wash them, cut in half, boil, and administer the soup to the patient. This is as far as the Jap medical staff will go at the moment.

24th June
Still no drugs for Bentley. In spite of repeated efforts by the doctors. Bentley died this afternoon. Jap SM very amused.

25th June
The Officers decided to ask to be allowed to accompany the work party with a view to doing something, if possible, to intervene in the beating incidents. It was agreed that two officers per day accompany the party, and we were allowed to brew tea for the men.

30th June
Situation pretty grim. Food very short, very little vegetables. Constant daily beatings and, what is more wearing, the interminable shouting of, "Speedo, Speedo", the word used by the Taiwan Guards to spur on the men to work harder, are having disastrous effects on the men's health, both mentally and physically.

7th July
Black day at cultivation. Commenced work 0720; break 0920-30. Lunch 1155; recommenced work 1300; break 1530-43. Work finished 18:10. Work party reached camp 1840. The SM (Furo) really "went to town". He felled six or seven men. Broom came in for the worst of his fury, being knocked to the ground five times, and on each occasion he was kicked viciously whilst on the ground.

The daily "town party" was now the work group every prisoner tried to get on. The "Half-Way House" peasants always took pity on the prisoners. It was worth getting on that party just for the sweet potato given by these kind people. Also, there was always the chance of a "niggle" at the sacks of rice or baskets of vegetables carried back by the party. A "niggle" meant opening a hole in the sack or basket and stealing the odd vegetable and a handful of dry rice.

The Major put me on the "town party" in the hope that I would see a news-sheet lying about near the store. Only once was I lucky. That day we were to collect goods near the small station that served the rail-head. Our guards left us to get some cold drinks, and I persuaded a Taiwan civilian to give me a newspaper. I pleaded "*Benjo. Kami*

217

kudesai." (Toilet. Paper please) Without knowing what he handed me, I was delighted to find it was that day's news-sheet.

On arrival back in camp we were always searched, but we were old hands now, and all had a method of hiding something and fooling the guards. That night Jim Bingham worked with the Major by the light of a bean-oil lamp to interpret the sheet.

The great news was that it appeared the Americans had landed on Okinawa, north of Taiwan. There were stories of planes being shot down and American ships being sunk, all near the Japanese mainland. A description of a bombing-raid and self-blasting (*Kamikaze*) attacks by their "Wild Eagles" on targets in Okinawa convinced us we had been by-passed.

This was wonderful news for us. The Major said to me, "At last, real hope we may survive. If the Yanks go for the mainland after Okinawa, they may not land here, and the Japs won't carry out their plan to kill us."

It gave me a tremendous lift to go from hut to hut giving out "the griff" that night. Others in my hut, "Tiffy" Shepherd, Timlin, and Archie MacPhail, all agreed to try to steal news-sheets on future "town parties". I slept better that night than any since the day we had left Kinkaseki. We were back in business with the "news service".

A few days later, however, we had a set-back when four men, all from my hut, were caught stealing food on the "town party". They were first beaten unmercifully and then marched down to the guard hut at the camp entrance. Four posts were hammered into the ground. They were then tied to these by the wrists and ankles. We were paraded and told they would stay there night and day until they had paid for their crime.

Lt Suzuki and the guards then took turns beating them and punching their faces. They left them there hanging on those posts, being bitten constantly by the maddening mosquitoes which swarmed around their blood-stained faces and bodies. On the second day we were allowed to feed them a ball of rice twice a day and give them a little water. Daley, the man who had survived the ordeal at Kinkaseki over the illegal diary, was in the worst condition. He looked to be dying.

That night after appeals by the Major, they were cut down and carried to a portion of the hut called "the hospital". Their arms and legs, swollen with beri-beri, were cut and marked by the cruel ropes that had bound them. Daley was found to have a broken jaw. The American doctor and our dedicated orderlies set his jaw and bound him up. The Japanese insisted they return to their normal huts. The next day, as Daley could not speak, I had to put him in number one position at *Tenko* (roll-call). When I shouted *Bango* (number) for the Orderly Officer, Les Davis started with *Nee* in the normal *Itchee, Nee, San* (One, two, three) numbering. Poor Daley was number one in my *Tenko* until the end came. To feed him we had to make his rice ball into a pulp and poke it into his mouth. He had an amazing spirit and survived.

With the arrival of the last party from Kinkaseki, more men were sent on "cultivation party", and a big drive was made to bring all the stores from Shinten.

My luck held at the Jungle Camp, and, due to my knowledge of *Nippon-go*, "The Madman" Tamaki decided one day I was to be his *hancho*. This meant I would be on the "in-camp party" every day. We worked with the two Taiwan *daiku* (carpenters) and, using the materials carried in, built more huts. We had to measure out supplies, make holes for the up-rights, cut and shape timbers, cut and lay bamboo, split up green bamboo as binders, and generally act as "coolies".

One day Tamaki announced to my party, "Today we build most important house for camp!" I thought we were going to build a hut for the Commander or the Jap office. In typical Tamaki style, using theatrical gestures, he went on, "Most important house in camp, is *unka* (dung) house!" He howled with glee at his own joke. Still with mirth he went on, "*Unka* house is *benjo*. British soldier always *byoki, gerri-gerri*. Go *benjo, toksan*!" Crouching down like a prisoner using the latrine pits, he imitated a prisoner with diarrhoea or dysentery. "Why you think most important house in camp?" he continued like a comedian with an audience. "Because of Circle Theory. Circle Theory," he explained, giggling as we looked on dumbfounded, "First British prisoner make *unka*. Second, put *unka* on sweet potatoes to grow. Give potato tops to pigs. Make fat. Pigs fat, kill. Pork for Nippon soldier. Nippon soldier become strong then for fighting. Nippon soldier give little pork British prisoner. Very kind. British prisoner, very thin. Eat but cannot digest. So more *gerri-gerri*, more *unka*. You see?" he laughed. "First *gerri-gerri*. Then *unka*. Then vegetables. Then pork. Then more *gerri-gerri*!" He roared at his logic. "Understand? Ka," he shouted. "Circle Theory! Circle Theory! Now we build most important house in camp!"

We were now convinced "the Madman" was named correctly. No sane person could ever have thought up such a depraved scheme under those bizarre conditions.

Timlin now made an important discovery. One Japanese news-paper was being brought back every day by the "town-party" guards. The NCO in charge in camp would always take it to the Commander's hut. I asked all of the party to watch the Japanese and Formosan guards' huts to see if the newspaper ever reached there. L/Bdr Joe Wallace, "Wee Joe" as he was known, agreed to help. He was kept in camp to nurse those prisoners who were now even past walking (literally dying in the hospital hut). The Japs had insisted, however, that the Medical Orderlies had to "work" also. They had been given bamboo brushes to sweep up around the huts. While sweeping up around the Jap huts, Joe occasionally saw a newspaper. Between us we would then plot how to get our hands on it during the day. Sometimes it would be left lying on the bamboo sleeping platform the guards used. While Joe would keep look-out, I would creep into their hut and make the grab. One time while the off-duty Jap guards were sleeping, Joe poked his brush though the window and swept the news-sheet to a position where he could grab it. On another occasion he told me the newspaper was in the Jap store-hut. That night as I was carrying back the chunkels into the hut I saw the paper. Next load I carried in, I put a rag over my shoulder under the chunkels. Tripping when near the newspaper, I fell, dropping the rag and chunkels to cover the precious sheet. Despite a *Kura* and *Bugeiroo*, accompanied by punches for my stupidity from the Jap in charge, I was delighted to pick up my rag and the news-sheet!

Others managed to steal news-sheets occasionally on the "town party". The bulletins we were able to put out after Jim Bingham translated them were worth all the scares and risks. As before, just the news that "a paper is in" was a tremendous boost for the camp. The faces around me would eagerly hang on every word as I gave out the "griff" in those pitch-black huts at night. This gave me the morale lift I needed to carry on from day to day, even though I knew I was lucky to have an in-camp job. They suffered hell from the work and beatings on the outside parties.

The Intelligence report gave details of some of the more important events in the period that followed:

14th July.
The Commander made the following speech to the work parties (especially referring to the Town Party) before they left the camp this morning.

"Today you are going to town and will bring back foodstuffs for you to eat. Your rations are no less than any other Nippon person, and even though you may be hungry it is no excuse to steal. When you steal it brings shame on your country. There is a proverb in our Army which says that a soldier must never admit hunger, even when he is hungry he must smile and pretend his stomach is full. The loads you are asked to carry are very small. Any normal Japanese person will carry three times as much as you do. Even on cultivation the work you are doing is only equal to the work of a Japanese child or woman. (The loads were never less than 30 kg and more usually 40 to 60 kg. The distance of the carry was some ll to 12 kilometres up a rough mountain track, usually with only two short rest periods allowed.)

19th July, 1945.
A special drive was made to complete the transport of stores from Shinten to the camp and 100 men were employed. The march back on this day grimmest ever. Among the supplies brought back were 30 sacks, each containing four individual Red Cross parcels (British), dated 1942. Each man carried two sacks — 15 of the 100 men carried these Red Cross supplies, the remainder (85 men) being used to transport Nippon Army stores. The Commander himself accompanied this party and it was apparent that he intended to get the maximum out of the prisoners. The loads were more abnormal than usual and the beatings en route were more severe. He himself (the man who said he disagreed with beating and stopped it at Kinkaseki) used his walking stick frequently on the march. The majority of the 100 men reached the camp physically exhausted and almost mentally deranged.

The following day, for the first time since arriving at the Jungle Camp, we were given a half-day's rest and 60 Red Cross parcels. It

221

worked out to roughly one between five men. They had been packed in Bermondsey, London, on 29th April, 1942, over three years before. Some of the tins were rancid as they had been damaged, but we were like animals and divided up the contents, revelling in the long forgotten tastes of chocolate, bacon, cheese, and sugar.

"Think of it," said E.J. Morris to me. "The lucky bastard PoWs in Europe get one of these to themselves monthly!" It was our crazy sense of values. To be a PoW of the Germans or Italians would have seemed to us to be heaven! That afternoon we washed with real soap in the stream that passed our camp, each of us in a sharing group using a thin quarter of a piece. We called it a "Blighty wash".

The Japanese refused to issue the other 60 parcels and told us, "They are being kept for an emergency."

"We know what emergency they have in mind too, don't we Sergeant," the Major said to me that night. Always when he and I met alone we knew each other's thoughts, still sharing the awful knowledge that even when freedom came we might be massacred.

The mad rounds of work went on. The huts were now all up and the stores carried back from Shinten. Every man possible had been put on "cultivation parties". "The Madman" decided his party should join the "farming party", and we were marched out into the mountains. Our destination was a little farm about a three mile trek away where jungle was being cleared to grow peanuts. We were worked pitilessly in the hot sun, clearing the undergrowth, stacking it for burning, and digging the ground for planting. Our Taiwan guards, chased by Tamaki, watched us constantly, always shouting, "*Speedo, Speedo*", and ready to bring their bamboo staves down on our backs at any minute.

Our only joy was the daily procession of American bombers flying overhead. Our only respite came when tropical rainstorms made work impossible. We prayed for heavy rain even though we got soaked. The rains also kept the Jap guards in their huts.

The camp had no fence. The jungle was our fence. They knew we were too weak to escape. At night when it rained we were allowed to build a fire in the centre of the hut to dry our rags of clothing or blankets. Our huts had no sides or backs and the roofs were poorly thatched so the rain would pour in, the fire doing little good. We used it, however, to "brew-up" what we called "Jungle Soup". In each hut we had our "mucking-in" groups. Each had a tin to brew-up hot water and whatever else could be boiled over the fire. My group was Les Davis, Gus Wylie, and Jim Brown. In the dark we would creep out into the jungle and, if possible, go to the cultivated plots kept by peasants, grabbing anything. Anything we believed edible, leaves, grass, etc., went in to supplement the two rice balls a day. We would just grab what we could, crawl back into camp, and put it into the tin, which another of the group had filled from the stream. All of us shared. All took their turn and contributed what they could to the green boiling mess we called our jungle soup. Looking back now, I realize we were near to animals in our approach to life, just hanging on! Sometimes we caught a frog or a small lizard. Anything that moved, we ate. One day Les Davis came back from a working-party, carrying three hornets he had caught wrapped in a leaf. They went in our "soup" that night, boiled up with our "jungle greens". A native on "cultivation party" had told us they were good to eat.

Then we had a boon. Jim Brown was put in charge of the pigs which "the Madman" was raising for their pork supply. Each day Jim had to go to the Japanese cook-house to collect their leavings for use as pig swill. The pigs never saw the best of the leavings! Jim shared them with us. He merely topped up the tin with water in case the Japs checked before he reached the pigs.

Meanwhile two more men had joined poor Cpl Lynch, all mentally deranged and put in a bamboo cage at one end of the hospital hut. One, L/Bdr Smith, had to be tied down. He had started to wander the camp naked, screaming abuse and swearing. Other times he would say, "I am God, come back." The scene at the hospital hut was bedlam. Cpl Donnelly, Fisher and Wallace were nursing with nothing except words of encouragement. We had our inevitable deaths. They were buried in hastily dug graves bearing a bamboo cross, in a little clearing outside the camp.

Daley in my hut, his jaws clamped together, continued to survive. Every morning as he stood in the roll-call his eyes blazed defiance, while Suzuki, who had broken his jaw, was highly amused at this arrangement.

223

The Japanese officers, NCOs, and guards all seemed determined to step up their beatings. Punishments grew in intensity; devilry seemed to have taken over. They, like us, were becoming more like animals. They knew they were losing the war and did not care what happened any more.

A few days later on the "peanut planting" gang, Tamaki showed his madness again. We were starting to plant out the peanuts and the temptation to pop them in our mouths was irresistible. The first men caught were beaten-up by the guards, who also told Tamaki. Predictably, he went into a rage and shouted, "Any prisoner caught eating, is stealing, and would be killed!"

Next day while the group I was with were cutting the undergrowth and stacking it to burn in bonfires, Tamaki seemed to be quite docile, happily poking at the fires with a long bamboo pole. Suddenly, two men from the "planting party" were brought up to where we were working. They had been caught with peanuts in their mouths. Tamaki screamed and shouted, bashing at them with his smoking bamboo pole. "You British prisoner thief, you should die. Burn you," he ranted. The guards holding them then pushed them towards the fire at his bidding. Thankfully, "the Madman" had another of his quick changes of temper and laughed. Then he said, "No burn, just cook." The unfortunate pair were forced to stand on the downwind side of the fire, getting the full heat of the flames as well as the smoke until Tamaki was satisfied they had suffered enough.

The only two advantages of being on the "peanut" party were the kindness of the natives who lived in the little huts nearby and the view from the mountainside. Now hundreds of "*B nee ju shees*" (B29s) and "*P san ju hatchees*" (P38s) swept over us daily. We could see them clearly, circling unopposed over Taihoku, and "pulling their plugs". Sometimes they dropped long lengths of silver paper which adorned the trees like Christmas decorations. We now know this was to confuse Japanese radar, but our scared guards thought it might explode or burst into flames. The Japanese would send hundreds of soldiers to carefully collect this tin-foil. Using long bamboos, they would remove it very gingerly from the branches.

On one "town party", we had a very narrow escape crossing the pedestrian suspension bridge at Shinten. We were right in the middle of the bridge when six P38's swooped down the valley firing their machine-guns and making a bomb run at the bridge. To them we must have looked like a bunch of coolies with an escort of Japanese soldiers. We flung ourselves on the ground and hid behind the steel uprights. Luckily the machineguns, cannon-fire, and bombs all missed. The close sight of those fearsome, split-tailed machines gave us a tremendous thrill.

Our loads felt lighter as we struggled back to the camp that evening. I had been lucky again in using my "*Benjo kami*" (toilet-paper) plea to obtain a news-sheet. The paper was translated that night by Jim Bingham, and it indicated that heavy raids were taking place on Japan. There were also reports of land fighting and sea battles around Okinawa, but the paper said the American attacks had all been repulsed.

August came and with it more frequent rain storms, making work on the "cultivation" and "peanuts" parties more difficult. Tamaki decided to cut his party in half, and I found myself lucky enough to be put back in-camp.

Starting on the 30th of July, all the sick men "in hospital" who could stand were made to work. These men could not even walk to the cultivation areas. Some sorted out sweet potatoes. The men in my gang were made to sit outside and break up green bamboo into thin pieces for the construction of sleeping platforms. I was put on this detail. The Japanese said if enough were made, we could construct sleeping platforms in our huts also. Our huts were sometimes awash at night during heavy rainstorms, and these platforms were therefore badly needed. The platforms were very simply constructed, just bamboo supports with cross lengths a foot off the ground, covered over with split green bamboos. We started first in the hut which contained the so-called "hospital" and the cage at the end for our maniacs. They were pitiful to see. Scarier was to look around in your own hut at night and see those you had known for three years acting strange as well.

Major Crossley's notes stated:

9th August
    It is noticed that many more men are showing mental strain. Some are behaving in quite peculiar ways.

And so it went on, with beatings every day — the two most serious offenders are the Jap Sergeant Major Furo and Sgt. Nakajima, always aided and abetted by the Taiwan soldiers.

Those of us who survived those last four weeks are convinced we were walking on the narrow edge between man and animal. All of us looked ghastly, eyes sunken, mere skeletons, covered with rashes, sores, or cuts which would not heal. Others too far gone to save were blown-up with beri-beri, legs and testicles like balloons. Many had long gone past caring to clean themselves or even "force the rice down". At that jungle camp Dave Donnelly, Bernard Fisher, Joe Wallace, George Harrison and Josh Thompson, our medical orderlies, really gave service which was "over and above the call of normal duties". Only those who survived such a camp, with men dying of every disease from dysentery to famine to oedema, will understand.

"Gus" Wylie was now with me on the "platform-building" party. Poor Gus, so sick he could not stand, spent his days breaking up green bamboos. As he and I were in the first hut built for prisoners, it was at the lowest part of the mountain covered by the camp. The mountain was terraced and our hut was on a slight rise that formed a lip on the terrace. It backed up the water and therefore was the last hut flooded. Major Crossley decided that after the hospital had got its platform, each hut would be provided in turn with ours last. This meant three huts would receive their platforms before our squad. One day when he was very low I tried to cheer him up. I said, "Gus, don't worry. We'll never sleep on these platforms we're making!" He asked, "Why?" I replied, "Because this bloody war will end before we reach our hut." Gus smiled, but grumbled back, "No way. It will go on this winter and that'll be the end of us!"

Gus was in the same frame of mind as many — totally depressed. It seemed nothing you said or did now could shake them out of their mental state.

On the 16th August we had started work on one side of our hut, driving in the supports and placing the long bamboo poles along the top to be covered with split green bamboo slats. Work went on normally all day. At the lunch break I went up to the officers' hut. There I found the Major, the American doctor Captain Schneider, and Cpl Donnelly reviewing the gloomy prospects for the hospital. It was a depressing conversation. It was clear that we could not survive much longer on these rations. With no drugs for the dying, their end was not far away.

Suddenly at about 4 o'clock we heard people shouting, "The cultivation party is in!" There was an excited buzz of voices. The first man I met, "E.J." Morris, said to me, "Sarge, we think THE WAR IS OVER!" I hurried up to the officers' hut to speak to Cross and Hellyer, who had accompanied that party to boil water for drinking. Then I heard their excited story.

Instead of being taken to the usual place to clear the jungle, they had been taken to a patch already cultivated and told to "weed the plants." The guards, instead of standing over them with sticks and "bashing" out with the usual cries of "*Speedo, speedo*", had left them alone. They had walked to the top of the field and sat under the trees with the Jap Sergeant Major, seeming not to care. Very soon all the prisoners were doing nothing, just sitting on the ground between the rows of plants pretending to work. Then a Taiwan farmer came out of the trees and beckoned Lt Cross, indicating the war was finished. He pointed to the sky and said, "No aeroplanes today, you see."

At lunch time a Formosan guard told them, "There will be a *Yasumay* day tomorrow". At three o'clock they were ordered to stop work and fall in to march back to camp. Lt Cross asked the Jap Sergeant Major, "Why are we going back early?" The sergeant cursed at him and pointing to a cloudless blue sky said, "Rain coming." Lt Cross was convinced something very strange was happening. He was optimistic, hoping there were peace negotiations or an armistice.

When the "peanut party" came in half-an hour later, we just stopped work. It was all like a dream. The Jap and Taiwan guards didn't care. All of them except the sentries had suddenly withdrawn to their own area of the camp.

There was much talk and speculation. More excitement when at about 6:30 pm we saw all the Japanese and Taiwan soldiers parading in their best uniforms. They went out of the camp to a clearing nearby, far enough away that we could not see or hear. Three of us from my hut decided to take a chance and sneak through the trees to at least watch. They were all drawn up, rifles with fixed bayonets. There was much saluting and bowing as Imamura read from a piece of paper. We could not catch the words, but it reminded us of the days back in Kinkaseki when Wakiyama had read out the "Imperial Rescript". Their faces were impassive, and we could not tell what that paper contained. It was clearly something very important. We now waited impatiently for *tenko* that night. However, there was no indication at *tenko* of anything different, "Flash Harry" and the guards checked each hut as usual. Then at 7:30 pm he gave us the good news. "*Yasumay* tomorrow," he said. Our spirits rose. Something must have happened. We returned to our huts with the exciting news, all praying and hoping that we would hear no American bombers that night.

Very few slept that night. We went from hut to hut, visiting friends, talking until dawn, watching and listening, speculating on what could be happening.

Major Crossley's record for those two days was:

16th August

Men go to work as usual, but instead of going to the patch of land commenced last night, they were taken to a plot already cultivated and planted and told to weed. No shouting — gentle work — almost dream conditions, after what they had had. Something strange afoot! Many rumours. Lunchtime one man told by a Chinese "War finished yesterday". Taiwan guard says "Holiday tomorrow". Later a Taiwan farmer tells us (Lt Cross) "War finished 12 o'clock yesterday". Work stopped at 3 o'clock. They know nothing in camp. Two men are released from the guard room, one after only two days, and he had committed "sabotage". The Nippon Army properly dressed and on parade at 1915 hrs. We are not sure what it is all about. The Nips announce a holiday for tomorrow, and the camp wonders!

17th August

A day of speculation. Is it or is it not? We all wait for the work detailed for tomorrow. At 1810 hrs it comes — "Work as usual, except for cultivation, which is only to be for half a day". Reason given — "the time for planting sweet potatoes is over and you will only be required to weed the land you have already planted."

For me it was a day of watching the Japanese for any indication of what the truth was and hoping to see a news-sheet being read. As it was a "*Yasumay* Day" there was no excuse to go near the Japanese huts and we were careful to keep our distance. Most of us laughed and joked as we washed and dried our tattered and patched khaki drill shirts and shorts in the stream or sat under the small waterfall. We revelled in doing nothing. Most of us had worn these same clothes when we were taken prisoner 3½ years previously. All watched the clear blue sky and listened, now dreading to hear the American bombers. We knew if they came the war was definitely still on. I washed and pressed out by hand "Basher" Gore's shorts. I had inherited them when he died. These I had decided I would "wear to freedom", when that great day came.

As the day went on we worried more that this was just a rest day and tomorrow it would all start again.

That night we squad leaders gathered at the usual time at the Major's hut for the work to be detailed. We were crestfallen. It was bad news, work parties as usual. But the cultivation would be for only a half-day and no digging. Returning to the huts, we sat in the dark still speculating over what was happening. All that was left of my old signal section sat together. "Don't worry," I told them. "Something is definitely happening. No air-raids for two days and the cultivation party only weeding; there must be peace negotiations in progress." Others argued against it. If the war was really over, they reasoned, our rations would be better and they would be looking after our dying. We all decided we would watch and listen again that night. Very few slept. We squatted on the grass near the hut door, looking up at the sky wondering, praying all would be quiet again.

After what seemed an endless night, dawn broke. Out of the early morning mist came the usual bucket carriers with the rice and watery soup. It was the same ration as usual. As we sat in the gloom and ate our rice the depression mounted. Gus said, "It's a load of balls. They can't be talking peace. The war's nay over, the bloody ration's the same! Now its *tenko* as usual."

Just as we finished *tenko* I heard shouts, "Stay in your huts! Stay in your huts!" Jim Bingham was running down the path from Major Crossley's hut. Then in a buzz of excitement there was another shout, "All work parties except town are cancelled. Stay in your huts!" Jim looked at me, grinned, and put his thumb up. Through the mist I could see Major Crossley and Lt Cross walking down the path towards the

229

first hut. We stood up as if for roll-call, watching their progress until they walked into our hut. As they came in I called everyone to attention and, after years of habit, bowed Japanese style. The Major, Lt Cross, and Sgt. Jim Bingham stood in the door. The Major looked at me, a faint smile on his lips, and spoke to all, "I have been informed this morning by the Camp Commandant, Capt Imamura, that peace negotiations have been opened on 14th August between Great Britain, America and The Japanese Empire. While the war is not exactly over, peace reigns, and the commandant hopes we will soon be free men."

The Major and the others immediately walked out. For a second there was silence. Then the truth sank in and we all turned to each other, embracing, shaking hands, crying and talking at the same time. Only certain phrases were said, each over and over again. But mostly, "We've made it! We've made it!" Les and I hugged each other. "E.J." and Jimmy Craig came running in from the next hut. We four all stood, crying and embracing. "We've survived! We lasted out! We've made it!" Later Les and I did what so many others did, sank to the dried grass on the floor and thanked God for our deliverance from that life of hell. Now there was no cheering, no shouting, just a numbness, an unbelief that it was really all over. Gus Wylie came to me, shook both my arms with his bony grip, and babbled, "Christ you were right, Taff! We're no goin' to sleep on those bamboo beds!"

An hour later the "town party" left with quite a send-off. The Japanese sentries and Taiwan guards took no notice as we joked and shouted at the "town party", "Don't forget to come back!"

Then a work party was called for to collect wood for the fires and Sgt. Brodie was put in charge. He was told by the accompanying sentries he could give the orders on how much wood to collect and when to return to camp!

Two hours later all squad leaders were sent for and told we would be issued 200 grams of crystallized brown sugar and a piece of soap. This would be the first piece of soap issued by the Nips in three years. "The war must be over now," we all agreed.

It appeared Major Crossley, to use our PoW language, had been "on his bike" trying to improve our situation. He had sought an interview with the Commandant and recorded in his official report what took place.

Questions	Answers

Food

1.	What is the position on bean paste, eggs, kill[ing] the bullock [ox] for meat.	Permission required from PoW HQ.
	Over 40 Hospital patients dying from beri-ri.	Commander will do his best.
	The Red Cross Parcels? Today or tomorrow.	
2.	Sweets	Yes, sugar today.
	Cigarettes	None.
	Matches	Burners will be allowed.
3.	Boots still in store	Yes, issue today.
4.	Cemetery (1 officer & party to tidy graves etc.)	Yes, after lunch today.
5.	Church Service of Thanks-giving	Yes at 1400 hours.
	"The King" to be sung.	No, not allowed.
6.	Concert at 1800 hours.	Yes.
	Roll Call at 1930 hours.	Yes.
7.	Rules and Regulations.	Remain the same. Extremely severe punishment for stealing.

As the day went on, we revelled in the freedom of no work parties and a piece of soap. Most spent the day like the one before, washing their bodies and clothes in the stream and playing in the waterfall. The soap seemed to have gone to everyone's head. Lather was everywhere. We washed and washed as if we were trying to clean away all the filth, dirt, and disease of the past years.

At 2 o'clock we gathered for the most moving service I have ever attended in my life. Lt Cross asked me to lead the singing of "O God our Help in Ages Past". He prayed and thanked God for our survival and peace at last. He then read Psalm 107, certain verses ringing out. The Jap interpreter watched over those skeleton figures' heads.

O give thanks unto the Lord, for he is good: for his mercy endureth forever.

Let the redeemed of the Lord say so, whom he hath redeemed from the hand of the enemy.

And gathered them out of the lands, from the east, and from the west, and from the north, and from the south.

They wandered in the wilderness in a solitary way; they found no city to dwell in.

Hungry and thirsty, their soul fainted in them.

Then they cried unto the Lord in their trouble, and he delivered them out of their distresses.

And he led them forth by the right way, that they may go to a city of habitation.

Oh that men would praise the Lord for his goodness, and for his wonderful works to the children of men!

For he satisfieth the longing soul, and filleth the hungry soul with goodness.

Such as sit in darkness and in the shadow of death, being bound in affliction and iron;

Because they rebelled against the words of God, and contemned the council of the most High:

Therefore he brought down their heart with labour; they fell down and there was none to help.

Then they cried unto the Lord in their trouble, and he saved them out of their distresses.

He brought them out of darkness and the shadow of death, and brake their bands in sunder.

We listened as those words, written centuries ago in praise of God's deliverance, described our situation so well. We had truly been brought out of darkness and the shadow of death. Death, though, was still with us. One more was to die that day, and many more before they could return to their homes and loved ones.

During the afternoon the Japanese Medical Sergeant called for the American doctor and our orderlies, asking for a report on the sick. He wanted to know how many would be unable to walk if the camp had to move. He was told at least 20 to 25 could not and would require transport. The Jap sergeant then asked them to, "Please get these men well as soon as possible." He was told that without nourishing food and drugs this was impossible. He then promised to release Red Cross drugs he had been holding, apologizing that he did this because he did not know how long the war would last and was saving them in the interest of the prisoners!

That night the rice ration improved slightly and some greens brought back by the "town party" made the soup a little thicker. Our concert was a sing-song which continued after *tenko* in my hut. "E.J." and my friends had gathered, and we few Welshmen sang old hymns as well as army and patriotic songs. Suddenly, as we were really letting the chorus of "Rule Brittannia" and "Land of Hope and Glory" rip out, the interpreter burst in. He was obviously very annoyed, demanding we stop and ordered me as Squad *Hancho* to follow him to see Major Crossley. After a very heated exchange the Major told him many of my squad were Welsh and singing Welsh hymns as thanks for peace. The interpreter finally went away, muttering angrily in Japanese. So ended our first day with the knowledge that the war was really over. Again we slept little, excited as we were.

Next morning the Major put me on the "town party" with instructions to report back all I saw and try to obtain a newspaper. As we made our way down that long track and got nearer to Shinten it became clear that all the temporary wooden houses were being abandoned. All around us civilians were on the move back to Taihoku. They waved to us and smiled. Everyone appeared happy and relaxed. Our guards took no notice as some handed us rice cakes and water. Despite looking everywhere, I had no luck for a newspaper. Even with our loads of vegetables, we were a light-hearted party that reached camp later that evening.

The good news that greeted us was that the Japs had agreed to give out what was left of the Red Cross parcels the next day. They were in as sorry a state as the others, and also stamped "London, 29th April, 1942". A number were so badly damaged that nothing inside was edible, but the rest were distributed, one parcel between every six men.

There was much discussion in my squad of how best to use the contents. We decided to pool everything edible. First of all, the 2 oz. bags of tea were collected together to make a special cup of "Blighty Char" about mid-morning. At the same time we ate the biscuits and little pieces of cheese. Half the meat-tins (meat and vegetable, ham and tongue, bacon, fish and meat pastes) were tipped into a container and mixed into a covering for the rice at lunch time. Even the empty tins were not wasted. We swilled out the interiors with boiled water and served the greasy result as soup!

For the evening meal we repeated the process and used the tins containing sweet puddings, again mashed-up and rationed out to each man. After that day of improved rice rations, sweetened English tea, and the Red Cross supplies, we felt wonderful and, for the first night since the 15th, slept soundly.

In the next two days two incidents occurred which brought us back to the reality of the precarious existence we still had to endure. Some of the braver spirits of the camp had slipped through the jungle to cross the river to trade blankets or steal from the natives' vegetable plots. The first we knew of it was the sound of rifle shots and shouting in the distance that night.

On the 20th the Commandant ordered that the "town party" carry back to Shinten the bales of blankets, boxes of soap, and 30 sacks of rice. Major Crossley immediately protested and sent in the following letter:

Sir,

I wish to protest against the work which prisoners are now being called upon to perform.

Every single man in this camp is in a very poor state of health and today we had great difficulty in finding 60 men strong enough for the town party. In the opinion of the Doctor no men are fit for this work, and today they have been ordered to carry down to town the following articles: 7 boxes of medical stores, 30 30-kg bags of rice, 7 boxes of soap.

I submit, Sir, that this is having further detrimental effect on the health of the prisoners. Would you please clarify the position and inform us what work is likely to be expected in the near future with regard to the evacuation of this camp.

As you will probably already know, 30 men will have to be carried out on stretchers and that alone will present a very difficult problem.

Signed J.F. Crossley, Major RA.

The reply to this letter was delivered verbally. "The answer is simple. You are still Prisoners of War," said the interpreter. The Major told him the letter should be kept as an official protest.

Later that day the Commander sent for the Major and in a quite different manner said a number of stores had to be carried to Shinten, but that he would see the loads were made as light as possible.

The following day the Japs agreed that the old water buffalo which had been used to pull the plough on the farm could be killed for food. "Big Sam" Lockhead slaughtered it with a sledge hammer. The Japanese took the best of the meat, but still the bones, entrails, etc. made a good stew.

Finally on the morning of 23rd August we heard the news we had been waiting for: we were leaving the Jungle Camp at last. The Major called us squad leaders to a meeting and told us the situation. He said 20 of our comrades could not walk. We would have to make bamboo stretchers and carry them. He proposed to call for 80 volunteers to carry the sickest of the camp. The rest of the sick would be like "walking wounded", helped along on the journey, one to each of the remaining men. The move would be in two groups. The stretcher party with the doctor and medical orderlies would go first. One hour later the "walking party" would follow. The Japs, he told us, had promised boats on the river near the "Half-Way House" to take us the rest of the journey to Shinten.

235

We returned to our huts and broke the news to our squads. We called for volunteers. Instead of the 80 required, 110 offered to carry. My old "Madman Party", experienced in splitting and plaiting green bamboo, now set to work making stretchers. They had many helpers. The Japs provided two canvas strechers, so we had to make 18 more. That day there was one less to carry. He just could not hang on to life.

CHAPTER 18

Killed by Food

Early next morning each carrying party of four went to the hospital with a stretcher to collect their loads. It was a misty morning, promising a fine hot day, and we were in high spirits, anxious to get away from that place.

My partner and I were to carry Lance Bombardier W. Vacher, once a strapping six-footer in the Lanarkshire Yeomanry, but now a wasted skeleton of a man, his testicles and legs swollen up with beri-beri. He was a cheerful Cockney who had been with us since the original party had reached Kinkaseki, and I was glad I was carrying him. We loaded our small packs on to the stretcher beside him and carefully wrapped the handles with our shirts to avoid rubbing our shoulders with the rough bamboo. To the cheers of the No.2 party which would follow us, we moved off in single file at about 6:30 am, at last leaving that camp. The day we had prayed for, hoped for and dreamed of for years had arrived. We were on the journey home.

The going, though all downhill, soon got rough and difficult, especially where the sloping paths became steep, or twisted and turned through the undergrowth. The rough timber and bamboo bridges over the culverts and streams were a nightmare to cross. Our progress got slower and slower. Frequently we had to put down several stretchers and all concentrate on getting one at a time over these dangerous crossings. As the sun rose, so did the sufferings of the men, especially those on the stretchers. Each bump and jar must have been agony for them. We bearers soon felt the strain, and it was obvious to Captain Francke in charge of our party that we would never keep ahead of the second group as planned.

We had hardly progressed three miles when the No. 2 party came through us. They were the "walking sick", and they too looked in a bad way. The Major was accompanying that party and stopped a moment to cheer us up. We changed over some of the worst of the stretcher bearers with some of the helpers of the "walking sick". Once they were ahead, we pressed on through the undergrowth and jungle, blindly jogging along with our uncomplaining burdens. Turning a corner about a mile before the "Half-Way House", we came across a man I recognized. His name was Bird and he was slumped against a tree. He told us he had dropped out of the No.2 Party to go to the toilet, that he had dysentery, and was too ill to go on.

"Old Vach", as we knew L/Bdr. Vacher, did not hesitate to suggest that if two could help him, he would try and walk and the other two could carry Bird. This was a very gallant and self-sacrificing act, typical of many prisoners. Walter Vacher, with his swollen legs and running ulcers, struggled on between two of us, his arms over our shoulders while the others picked up Bird. On we went, changing the burdens every hundred yards until we finally reached the clearing overlooking the river and the farm-huts we called the "Half-Way House". Here the other teams were resting. Again, the kind Taiwan civilians who lived there gave us food and water. Our medical orderlies went round from stretcher to stretcher, doing what they could to make the patients more comfortable for the remainder of the journey.

Then the blow fell. Lt Suzuki, who had accompanied our party, said, "No boats available here. Have to go further down river." The river twisted and turned down the valley to Shinten and ferry boats would shorten the distance considerably. But there were two more crossing points where we had seen boats in the past and where we hoped there would be boats on that day.

Captain Franke argued with him, but to no avail. Suzuki just shouted and yelled, "Moh skoshee," pointing down the valley. Again typical, the promise of boats was not being kept and the agony of that journey would be prolonged. We set off again at about midday, slowly stumbling down the path until we reached level ground alongside the river. The first ferry point for boats was reached at about three o'clock, but only two boats were waiting. Each could take only five stretchers. The carriers and the rest would have to continue the long march around the curve of the river to Shinten. Captain Francke made the selection. As we were still carrying both Bird and Vacher in relays, we were among the ten chosen for the shorter journey by boat. We were poled across the river by an old man and a boy, and then continued our march through paddy-fields until we reached another crossing-point. Again this ferry saved a couple of miles. Eventually, after a stiff climb and a tortuous descent, we could see in the distance the suspension bridge at Shinten. There was a long straggling column of prisoners crossing the bridge. Our "walking sick" party had arrived.

On we marched, the going now easier, but our burdens seemed heavier as our shoulders, legs, and bodies were wracked with pain and exhaustion. Through the small villages we staggered, the inhabitants looking on with obvious sympathy, many coming forward with water and gifts of fruit. It was another of those days of which I sit and wonder how we struggled on, especially for that last mile. We reached Shinten about an hour after the remainder of the ten stretchers who had gone the long way round.

Here we loaded onto Japanese open army trucks. Heavy rain started to fall, and we set off in convoy heading into Taihoku. The lorries moved off at a fast rate over roads which were pot-holed from the constant air-raids. Our patients on the stretchers screamed out in pain as they were jolted and thrown about. We tried to help them by sitting them up and holding them off the metal floor of the trucks, but the journey was agony for them. At last we reached our destination, a two-storey wooden building in a place called the Matsuiyama area, an outer suburb of Taihoku. As we unloaded our stretchers, we saw that their occupants were in a wretched, dying condition, several unconscious. As we put them down our doctor and medical orderlies told us the tragic news: two were dead! One of them was "Plonka", Eric Clack. He had survived the Malayan campaign, two tours at the mine camp, and then the Jungle Camp. And he had died ten days after what was to become known as "VJ day". It was so tragic.

Despite the terrible journey and the deaths, we recovered our spirits quickly. That night there was as much rice and soup as we wanted, though the rice tasted and looked mouldy. For the first time the Japs issued some solid food — black musty biscuits — and more crystallized sugar. We fell on these like wolves, not thinking of the consequences. The result? Early next morning, most of us had diarrhoea.

Our excitement ran even higher the next morning when we discovered on the roof of our billet a large sheet with the letters PW clearly painted. The Major was told by the Commandant that this had been agreed with the Allies, as American planes would soon come to drop food supplies.

Major Crossley quickly took the initiative to, as he always put it, "keep our moral ascendancy over our captors". He requested an interview and submitted a letter as follows:

Sir,

I consider that in the position we find ourselves our two comrades who have just died are entitled to and should be given a funeral with military honours and a service conducted by an ordained priest. I therefore request the following:

1. Two British flags for wrapping the coffins.
2. A trumpet or bugle so that our own trumpeter can sound the "Last Post" and "Reveille."
3. That Capt the Rev. T. Pugh now at No. 6 PoW Camp is allowed to come and conduct the service.

Signed J.F. Crossley, Major RA
(1 & 3 were refused, 2 was granted).

The Major took Sgt. Bingham with him for this interview. The sergeant kept a shorthand record of the following exchanges:

Major Crossley	"Do you still consider we are PoW?"
Commander	"Yes, still the same.
Major Crossley	"Then in the light of what we saw and were told coming here yesterday, I must disagree. I consider we are British and American troops under the protection of the Nippon Army"
Commander	"We differ."
Major Crossley	"Do you think it right that British and American officers should still be saluting Nippon and Taiwan privates?" (This question had to be repeated three times. In the end the reply came)
Commander	"This rule is relaxed."

Major Crossley	"There are only six latrines for 340 men. These are not enough. May we be allotted more of the existing latrines or have more dug?"
Commander	"I will look into it".
Major Crossley	"The rice we have been issued in this camp is the worst type we have been asked to eat since becoming PoW. Many men cannot eat it because of its roughness and it is causing stomach troubles".
Commander	"This rice has been in store and is the only rice we can get. Perhaps you are not cooking it correctly."
Major Crossley	"Could the Nippon cook give us instructions?"
Commander	"Yes."
Major Crossley	"May I again bring up the question of the sick men. Three men have died since the Armistice and we have four dangerously ill."
Commander	"I am going to HQ now and will do everything I can. A Nippon Army doctor will visit."

After this interview Major Crossley issued the following order:

Officers will in future salute the Camp Commander only. All other ranks will salute Nippon Army officers only.

Later our own carpenters were given box wood to make two coffins. We also received a Jap army trumpet for our use. After lunch we assembled for a short service over the rough coffins. Volunteers were called for to take them to be buried. After the privations of the march from the Jungle Camp, very few were fit to carry the coffins. We were told they would be buried in the hills. However, those who could still walk in my signal section readily volunteered. They and comrades of Gnr Biggin, the other poor chap who had died, made up a party of 20.

The survivors of my signal section were L/Cpl Mick McLoughlan, "E.J." Morris, and Jimmy Craig. The others who volunteered for this duty were "Big Sam" L/Sgt. Lochhead, "Old Screwtop" Sgt. Davy Dewsnap, Willie Muir, Pat Dobbie, Peter Bolton and Charles Carter. I noted their numbers on the back of my last work sheet at the Jungle Camp: 159, 357, 116, 339, 138, 142, 533, 296, 578, 353.

Lt Tamaki, accompanied by an escort of Japanese and Taiwan sentries, led us outside the camp where we found a bullock cart we could load the coffins on. We moved off through the streets of Matsuiyama, a pitiful procession watched by curious civilians. After about two miles we turned off into the paddy fields. Taking it in turns, we carried the wasted bodies of our two comrades. At last we reached a Chinese cemetery where we dug the graves. We made two rough crosses and Lt Cross said a prayer. Then, for the first time in many years, we heard the plaintive notes of "Last Post" and "Reveille". Our bugler played beautifully.

As we returned to the main road, thousands of Taiwan civilians were lined up, attracted by the sounds of the trumpet. When they caught sight of us they yelled and cheered, clapping their hands. It was obviously a display of sympathy and friendship towards us. We drew ourselves up and got into step, whistling proudly, our heads up, shoulders back, marching smartly in our rags of uniforms. The crowds grew thicker and began pressing forward with fruit in their hands. Our guards, especially "the Madman", became very annoyed. They screamed and shouted, and brandishing their rifles and bayonets pushed the crowd back. This action caused us to smarten up even more and break into old marching songs such as "Tipperary" and "Pack Up Your Troubles". The crowd reacted joyously to our singing, and began yelling and cheering. Eventually Tamaki had enough. He drew his sword and yelled orders causing our guards to charge at the people, forcing them back.

We ignored this confusion and marched on down the road and back to camp, leaving Tamaki and his sentries trying to disperse the crowd which wanted to follow us. This display of friendship to us and hostility to the Japanese up-lifted us, especially after that sad funeral.

Next day we held a Thanksgiving Service and, for the first time, were allowed to sing our National Anthem, "The King". I have heard it sung on many a solemn occasion, but never with the emotion it caused that day. The skeletons of what were once strong fit soldiers stood to attention in their rags, tears streaming down their faces.

Later that day the Major called us squad *hanchos* together. From now on, he told us, he was taking over command of the camp. Those of us who were NCOs were to make or mark our ranks on our arms. There must be strict discipline, he emphasized, and we must prevent any man going outside the fence. We were under our own Army Regulations. He said he would appoint an Orderly Officer and Duty Sergeant daily, and anyone appointed to a duty would wear a white cloth around his arm. There would be one roll-call a day, taken by him tonight, and done British Army style.

When we told our squads, some men grumbled, "It's the old bullshit, all over again! You fucking sergeants and officers can't wait until we are free." There were always the moaners. The vast majority, though, welcomed this sensible move by the Major. I especially knew it was only his leadership and strong sense of discipline that had got us this far in one piece.

Roll-call that night was really amusing for the Major and us. Some of the Squad Leaders called their squads to attention with the Japanese *Yotskee* and bowed! Years of being forced by beatings to report in *Nippon-go* had made it a habit.

Major Crossley's report of the next day's tragic events went as follows:

28th August
At about 1630 hours American planes B-29's appeared above Taihoku. At frequent intervals loads of Red Cross goods could be seen dropping not far from our camp. At 1730 they appeared to notice us — one plane flew directly overhead at a very low altitude and dropped parachutes twice — about 1,000 metres south of our camp. The first dropping of goods in the immediate vicinity of the camp took place about 30 minutes later. These parachutes landed about 100 metres east of the billet, and in so doing killed two civilians. The second dropping landed some 50 metres north of the billet harmlessly. The third landed on top of the billet making five large holes about 10 metres in diameter. The

heavy containers as well as the timber broken by the impact inflicted injuries on a number of men and rendered our only building partially habitable. The fourth landed to the south of the billet and wounded several more prisoners. The fifth drop landed on the fence, breaking it down — Casualties 2 civilians killed, 3 prisoners of war killed, 5 severely injured, 16 injured.

Casualties were removed to hospital: A roll-call of the camp was taken and the building put out of bounds until it was light enough to see what damage had really been done to the main structure. The men spent the night outside. It should be mentioned here that the behaviour of the men during this trying incident was exemplary; also that the Nippon Army did not interfere in any way. One Medical Officer and two Medical Orderlies allowed to accompany the casualties to the hospital."

That was a day we would never forget. Planes were circling in the distance, dropping supplies with parachutes on what we guessed were other PoW camps and seeming to ignore us. We waved, shouted, and ran about pointing to the PW markers on our roof, praying they would see us. At last one B29 spotted us and came so low we could see the crew waving. The Major's account gives the simple report, but those minutes of terror and tension had to be lived to be understood. As soon as we saw what happened on the first drop, civilians crushed to pulp by the heavy containers, we knew what to expect. Each time the plane came in to drop, the group I was with tried to run out of the line of the falling containers. The plane was so low the parachutes weren't opening and the huge metal containers came crashing down like unexploded bombs. I was running towards the hut with others to try and reach the screaming patients inside when the fourth drop caught our group. The container swept past me and I was bowled head over heels by the parachute trailing behind, my pals scattered like nine-pins.

I think at that moment I must have gone berserk as I thought this was the ultimate insult, to be crushed and killed by food from one's friends after suffering and starving from one's enemies. The next thing I remembered was Major Crossley yelling and swearing at me, something I could not recall him ever doing before. He had all us squad leaders quickly organized and detailed four parties of 20 men each. One party was ordered in to help the medical orderlies, another to clear up the debris in the billet. My group and the other party were to go outside the fence and gather in all we could of the supplies.

The scene on the road outside the camp was carnage. The heavy containers had hit the road and ploughed into the crowds of watching civilians, bursting on impact. There were mangled bodies and wounded lying about, and children crying, bleeding. The mob instinct for food, though, had already taken over. As fast as they could, these hungry civilians were picking up and plundering the precious food supplies.

My gang, consisting mostly of my old squad of sergeants and NCOs, was wonderful. They worked like beavers picking up tins and manhandling the huge containers back into camp. A group of us had to fight off some of the more determined civilians who were grabbing all they could.

We worked on as it got dark, picking up every last tin or packet we could find. Back in the camp the Major had got the Japs to agree to take the injured to the civilian hospital. All our other sick were lying outside the hut. The scene was lit by three huge bonfires of broken timber from the billet. Three still forms covered in blankets lay apart. They and those who were maimed or terribly injured were the price of our food.

The Major and our other officers set up a small command post, lit by an old bean oil-lamp, and organized the cooks to make drinks and meals with the supplies that had been dropped. As we came in exhausted, each of us was given a mess-tin of sweet milky cocoa and told that for the first time there would be no rice tonight!

After a roll-call, the Major addressed us and thanked us for our conduct. He told us to remember the price we had paid for the food dropped, but to understand that in the time remaining until we were freed it would save more lives than it cost!

He also told us that in one of the containers a message had been found telling us they would be back in two days to supply us with more food. We sank down around the fires that night enjoying helpings of meat and vegetable stew, the first meal without rice in $3\frac{1}{2}$ years. American cigarettes and matches were then given out. We lay back, exhausted by the day's events, sleeping on the bare ground with the luxury of a full stomach.

The next day was spent assessing the damage and trying to make as much of the billet habitable as possible. We removed the PW sign from the roof and, even with one end of the billet completely smashed and the upper floor sloping, we got most of the camp under cover that day.

Our three comrades who had paid with their lives for our food and supplies were buried that afternoon next to Biggs and Clack on the hill-side.

The Major sent for me that night and told me that as I was the Signal Sergeant he hoped I could find a way to stop the planes from "bombing" us. We decided to try flashing at them with a glass or tin lid and to tear the white parachutes into strips and lay them so as to spell out "DON'T DROP". I told the Major that I would try to contact the planes first by flashing and, if that didn't work, by semaphore. With the help of Sgt. Brodie and others, early next morning we then put out the signs alongside the wrecked billet. Using the old containers, we built a small platform for me to stand on at the end of the sign. From there I would try to communicate with the planes.

When they appeared next morning there were three. They came in and began circling, trying to decide where to drop. The Major lined up all the men in three ranks along the road outside the camp boundary. I was on my own, standing on the platform of containers, armed with a tin lid and two big pieces of white parachute to be used as flags. The Camp Commander, Tamaki, and the remaining Japs ran past me into the air-raid shelters at the end of the compound. I flashed with the tin lid first and then waved frantically with the flags, hoping they would see me and the "DON'T DROP" sign.

At last one of the B29's came out of formation, banked, and headed straight for our camp. Now I was desperate. I dropped the lid and started signalling in semaphore, "DON'T DROP, DON'T DROP, DON'T DROP". On came the plane. I could see its bomb bay was wide open. I shut my eyes and held my breath, praying they would not drop. As it roared low over my head I opened my eyes and could see the containers, attached to the parachute cords, ready to fly out.

Now I breathed again and, as it banked away, signalled "DON'T DROP, THREE MEN KILLED, DROP OUTSIDE CAMP." I continued repeating this message and, as it circled again, I was rewarded with an "R" flashed by a signalling lamp. With his signal light flashing, he came down low and I could see the crew.

He flew off, much to our relief, and joined the others who all released their parachutes in an area which appeared to be over the town. Then back one came, circled low over our camp, signaled "R" again, and dropped a streamer message.

As he flew off I felt tremendous relief. Tamaki and the Japs emerging from the air-raid shelter actually shook my hand and said I was "*Jotoh*!" It made my day when we found that in the message dropped was a note asking for the me to get in touch with the crew "when you are State-side". It also gave the number and name of base of the squadron. They were based on Saipan.

Later that afternoon a Jap army lorry drew into camp loaded up with the parachute containers. The planes had made their drop in and around the civilian jail, injuring several prisoners. These containers not only had food, but badly needed medicine, hospital supplies, clothing, and boots. Our meals that day were again without rice!

Next day Major Crossley was ordered to a conference at the HQ Camp. There he found the senior officers from each of the island's prison camps, including Col Kilpatrick, the senior British officer left alive on Taiwan (from No. 4 Camp), and Captain Gibbons, representing No. 6 Camp. They told of arrangements being made for a surrender ceremony in Tokyo, and the possibility of a contact team of Allied officers being dropped by parachute. Better arrangements were secured for the sick, and it was agreed that each camp would be supplied with a radio to receive world news. An agreement was also reached for communication between the prison camps and a new site for future air drops.

That night the radio arrived and Major Crossley gave me, as Signal Sergeant, the privilege of tuning it in. It was an unforgettable scene. Everyone was inside the big billet. It was lit by bean-oil lamps (the electric circuits were smashed during the food-drop) and all were crowded around as I twiddled with the controls trying to pick up the English World News. Everyone's ear was cocked as I got scraps of American bulletins. Then suddenly the Westminster chimes sounded and that world-famous voice said, "This is London calling, B.B.C."

All of us began crying at that first sound of home and freedom. We heard news of prisoners being released everywhere — Java, Sumatra, Singapore, Thailand — and of the assembling of the fleets of the United States and Britain in Tokyo Bay. We looked all around at each other. "E.J." Morris said to me, "Sarge, don't they know we are here on Taiwan?"

Suddenly there was a loud creaking of the sloping, broken floor on which we were crowded. The Major realized the danger and ordered me to switch off while everyone quickly got outside. In our excitement to hear the broadcast we had all forgotten the precarious condition of the floor, which might suddenly collapse if remaining timber supports cracked under the strain of our combined weight.

The following day two incidents took place which were a delight to all. First, a Jap army truck arrived loaded with baskets of vegetables and, for the first time, the Taiwanese soldiers did the unloading themselves. Then later, a large party of Jap soldiers arrived to dismantle the air-raid shelters at the end of the compound. We had the luxury of standing and watching Japanese and Taiwan soldiers working. Despite the Major's strict orders to keep away and avoid incidents, a crowd gathered to watch, delightedly crying out, "*Speedo, speedo.*"

On the 2nd September Col Kilpatrick arrived at our billet with the news that a contact team had parachuted in and were at PoW HQ. He told us they had informed him that every effort would be made to get us off Taiwan immediately after the surrender ceremony was held in Tokyo Bay. He warned us to be very careful and avoid incidents with the Japanese and the Taiwan civilians. Emphasizing that our position was not yet secure, he said no one yet knew what the Japanese Army on Taiwan would do when the surrender came. We all knew of their boast that they would never surrender.

That night we were suddenly struck by a typhoon. Its torrential rains and howling winds further damaged our wooden billet and we all lay on the floor as boards and debris flew around. Nothing, though, could now shake our spirits. The war was over. It was only a question of time before we would be free. We joked with Capt Schneider, the American doctor, betting that the British Navy would come and get us before the American Fleet.

The next morning at about 11 o'clock a line of Japanese staff cars drew up outside the camp entrance. Out stepped what was obviously a group of senior staff officers, resplendent in full uniform with riding boots, swords, and white gloves. With them we saw Col Kilpatrick.

The Major lined us up and the Japanese Commander-in-Chief of all PoW Camps made an incredible speech. He told us he hoped we would return to our native countries soon and be good "ambassadors for the Great Nippon". He went on to say that he was sorry if we had been beaten or ill-treated, but we must understand that this was not done by true Japanese soldiers, but by Taiwanese recruited soldiers.

How a demonstration or incident did not develop I will never know. Everyone was fighting to control themselves. It was only because we were still surrounded by fully armed soldiers that we were held in sway.

He quickly saluted the Major and led his entourage smartly back to the cars.

The next day the Major sent for us squad leaders and told us he was going to demand the surrender of all Japanese arms and we were going to take over! I thought he was crazy and would get us all killed, but the look in his eyes told me and others it was no use arguing. He marched in to Imamura and told him, "I am no longer Major Crossley, Senior British Officer in this prison camp. I am Senior Officer Commanding Allied troops in this area, awaiting evacuation." In an amazing scene the arms and ammunition were meekly handed over, everything counted, and a receipt given. It was unbelievable, our arrogant, bestial captors of just a week ago handing over their arms and authority to us, a ragged bunch of skeletons.

The Major decided that afternoon that we would mount our own armed guard at the gate that night. He told us to pick volunteers who could be trusted to carry out strict orders. We sergeants left thinking there would be moans from the men about more "bullshit". Instead we were overwhelmed with volunteers. The Major's orders for the guards were simple; no Japs or Taiwanese allowed in the camp unless he gave instructions, and no prisoners allowed outside the camp. He warned again about the danger of incidents.

That night he told us sergeants we should form our own mess and elect a President. The meeting that followed showed that old camp loyalties and habits died hard. Although there was a Warrant Officer and sergeants senior to me in the camp, I was elected "President". The WO asked me to carry on as *hancho*. My first job was to find a sergeant to take the first guard duty. There was no difficulty. It was great to see the effort the men chosen to be guard made with their clothing. All of us watching sensed the historic occasion; prisoners-of-war mounting guard with arms surrendered from the Japanese.

Our compound was besieged by hundreds of civilians the next day. Many of us started to barter Japanese army blankets left behind for fruit and eggs. Some brisk trading took place until the arrival of a lorry of the now not so dreaded Military Police, the *Kempeitai*. The civilians ran, but they showed by their shouts their resentment and hatred of the Japanese who had occupied Taiwan for more than 50 years. Again, we revelled in the luxury of tasty, large meals without rice. The main problem was that our stomachs could not take the solid, richer foods, and nearly everyone was troubled with diarrhoea. That afternoon we were saddened to hear of the death of Private Kerr of the Cambridgeshire Regt, who had been a cheerful character in the mine and jungle camps.

Next morning, 5th September, at about 7:30 we saw American planes from aircraft-carriers circling overhead. They were circling low and the Major ordered me to quickly put out our "don't drop" ground strips just in case. A message from the HQ PoW Camp came that a plane had dropped a note asking all camps to put out location signs. The message also brought the tremendous news that American destroyers were going to attempt to enter Keelung harbour that day.

L/Sgt Brodie of the 155th RA, I, and others went outside the camp to a clearing on the opposite side of the road. Using the PW sign and some strips of parachute we made an arrow pointing to the camp. Not long after we had finished we were spotted and the planes began swooping down low over our position. We waved, shouted and jumped up and down, excitement filling us. Planes circled all day. We heard later they had been ordered to do so to keep our morale high. Our spirits required no boosting. The news that the American Navy was near had rocketed our spirits into orbit.

CHAPTER 19

The Marines Carry Us to Freedom

At about 3 pm that afternoon our liberators came. I was washing under the tap when a convoy of Jap Army lorries led by a Jap staff car flying a huge "Stars and Stripes" flag came heading into our camp. A group of American Marines armed to the teeth and led by an American officer got out of the car. With shouts and whoops, parties of other Marines jumped out of the lorries and came running into the camp.

This was it, the moment we had waited and prayed for. We rushed at them, shaking hands, holding them, laughing and shouting. "For Christ sake, take it easy boys. We're gonna get you out, right now!" one of them said. One big sergeant got hold of me and said, "Come on. Point out all the bad bastards to us now!" He had a camera. "You're too late. They've all gone!" I replied.

The Major was trying to get order out of this chaos and called for all squad leaders to assemble. He told us we were to get ready to leave immediately. We were the first camp to be evacuated.

The Americans shouted to us, "Just assemble outside the camp. Don't take anything, just walk out as you are." We really had nothing to carry except what was left of the Red Cross medicines and the food supplies. Despite their yells of "Get outside, leave everything!", it was too hard for us to leave food behind after our experiences. Many men grabbed their packs and started to fill them with tins still left in the store. "For God's sake you crazy Limies," a big Marine said to me, "Leave it. Shit, there's tons of food where you're going!" To us they all seemed huge, like giants from another planet wearing uniforms and helmets we had never seen before.

Within a half-hour of their arrival we were lined up outside the camp, all except for the very sick who could not walk, and the doctor and two

251

medical orderlies. Near the camp ran a railway line and along came an engine with four passenger coaches. We were told to "Climb aboard for freedom!" We needed no second bidding. Kept back by the cordon of Marines was a huge crowd of civilians and the Japanese and Taiwan soldiers. All our promises to cut up the Japs and take revenge on our guards were forgotten in that rush to go home. The worst of our captors, "The Sergeant Major," "Tashee Corporal", "The Madman", "Sanitary Syd", and Suzuki had all disappeared after we left the Jungle Camp.

As the train drew out we waved the Union Jack from our windows. We had made it with the red, white, and blue parachutes that had been attached to our supplies. Others had streamers made from the same. As we pulled out Major Crossley, defiant as ever, was waving his fist at Imamura. "Don't forget me, Imamura!" he shouted. "I **am** coming back. I'm coming back for all you bastards!"

The civilians cheered us, and at every crossing and the frequent halts, crowds gathered. Satisfied we were on our way to freedom, we threw out tins of food and cigarettes to their clutching hands. At last we drew into Keelung Station and saw the results of all the bombing raids we had heard since late 1944. The town was a shambles, destruction everywhere. There seemed to be hardly a building untouched. Slowly we were shunted through the station. Then upon seeing ships and two Americans destroyers, we realized we were being carried right to the dock-side. We were going to leave from the very quayside we had arrived at in November 1942. So many months and lives ago!

As we shunted slowly forward we saw a wonderful sight. The Marines and sailors had cordoned off the dockside with barbed wire, and the gaps were covered with armed sentries and machine-guns. Every gun on the destroyers was manned, and hundreds of sailors were cheering and waving their caps to us. As we passed through the cordon we saw a group of Japanese officers turned back with rifles and bayonets. This got a cheer from us.

The train stopped opposite the destroyers and, as we climbed down, the sailors swarmed off the ships towards us. They picked us up like babies. I was picked up by what seemed a giant of a man. He was crying, saying, "Christ the bastards! What have they done to you?" As I was carried up the gangway of the destroyer I will forever recall looking over his shoulder at a rubbish bin with pieces of white bread on top. I thought, "This is it. I'm really free at last. There is bread, thrown away as waste."

As we sailed out of Keelung harbour that evening I stood on the deck with Les Davis and George Smith. We looked at the receding coastline, shook hands, and vowed that wherever we were later in life, we would remember this day and each other. At ten o'clock that night we had a hair-raising transfer to two aircraft-carriers via small boats in quite a choppy sea. As we pulled alongside, we were lifted out by brawny sailors and carried up the gangway to be deposited in a brightly-lit hangar. Here the ship's band was playing. As I was greeted and asked to say my name, rank, and number into a microphone, the band broke into "Bless Em All, Bless Em All. The Long and the Short and the Tall." Those were my sentiments, and I did not quibble as I was told I would be stripped, bathed, and my head cropped. "Sorry," the Petty Officer said to me, "you're lousy, pal!"

With a minimum of fuss two sailors were assigned to each of us as we got on board. My constant nurse and companion later asked me for a souvenir of my captivity. I gave him a Japanese 10 Yen note I had picked up. He in turn gave me one of his identity discs which I still treasure. It reads, "Richard Writer Fredricks, 380882, p T 5/42, USMCR A."

Divested of our rags, showered, shaved, and hair cut, we were handed a sailor's cap, shirt, trousers, slippers, and taken below. The whole of the hangar deck of the USS Block Island had been cleared and each of us had a mattress and blankets provided. The crew had given up theirs for us.

After recovering, I asked the Marine Sergeant assigned to me to allow me to go up on deck so I could look back at the coast of northern Taiwan. He could not understand why, but my persistence made him agree. I just wanted to look at those mountains which held that hell-hole camp of Kinkaseki and its tunnel, so nearly our tomb. As I stood silently, I prayed fervently and gave a few simple words of thanks. I had survived!

The survivors of Kinkaseki and the Jungle Camp were all put together on cots near the medical area so that treatment for our many

253

ailments could start. We were given newspapers and magazines and shown films. We learnt about the tremendous battles in Russia, "D-Day", and the amazing "A" Bombs that had saved our lives. We also learnt of the massacre of PoW prisoners in the Philippines. For the first time we all realized how lucky we were that our island, Taiwan, had been by-passed and the Americans had landed on Okinawa.

Arriving in Manila Bay, we saw evidence everywhere of the tremendous power of the American war machine. As we sailed in, on every side we could see destruction and sunken ships, evidence of the bitter fighting and weight of bombs which had led to the occupation of that city. We were efficiently moved to a huge hospital camp by convoys of ambulances. Here we were told that their one object was to get us fit enough to travel home, and that transport was being arranged.

In our hospital beds we were questioned by American Intelligence officers. I told them the story of the food drop, my luck in contacting the B-29, and showed them the names of the aircrew. It was typical of the American kindness, generosity, and concern that, to my astonishment, a week later those very men were brought to my bedside. Quite off-handedly they told me they had flown down from Saipan when they had received the news that our camp survivors were in Manila. The miracle, I discovered, was that there was only one man in the three B-29s who could read my signals. He had learnt his semaphore as a lad in the Boy Scouts! They were even more surprised when I told them I was the only man in that camp who could send semaphore, and I had learnt mine in the Boys' Brigade!

The only sour note in that period of bliss in the American hospital camp was a visit from a very pompous British officer. He was not interested in our hardships. He wanted to know how much money we had been paid by the "detaining power". This question, the way he phrased it, and the use of the words "detaining power" for those Japanese bastards we had called all sorts of other words struck us as very funny. His attitude, I regret to say, was typical of many of the young British officers we were to meet before we reached home. Needless to say, he left our ward with some really choice replies to his inept and pompous questions and his regimental manner.

While in this hospital camp we also had the great news that the party that left our camp in March 1945 had reached Japan safely. Survivors had been seen. Every day now new prisoners arrived in the hospital by plane from Japan, some bringing bits of news of our old comrades.

Major Crossley came to say good-bye to us. He had been ordered home and was going by air so as to report to the War Office as soon as possible. We were very sad to say farewell to this man we had been through so much with, and who had been such an inspiring leader over those terrible years.

We left Manila on board the "Empress of Australia", which had come from Hong Kong with a load of released prisoners and internees. Straight out of hospital beds, we had expected to be assigned bunks in cabins on this liner. But we had a rude shock: we were allocated an ordinary troop-deck with sling hammocks. We were told we were under the OC Troops on this ship and that discipline would be enforced. Then the Ship's RSM read us out the orders and told us that all "upper decks", occupied by internees, officers, etc., were "out of bounds", as were certain recreation decks and public rooms.

Our reaction was instantaneous outrage. We told him what he could do with his regimental orders and that in no way were we going to accept being confined after our experiences. There was a near riot as he threatened the usual Army penalties if we broke regulations by "straying" onto other decks. The cry went up, "That's bloody typical. We were captured by the Japs, released by the Americans, and now re-captured by the British!"

After an uncomfortable first night at sea when most of us slept on the deck rather than in the hammocks, we were a rebellious lot the next morning. We decided to see the OC Troops en masse to try and obtain cabins. We had been told there were plenty empty.

The OC agreed to see a deputation from the approximately 150 of us who had come aboard at Manila. I was elected as one representative. It reminded me of the delegation to see the Nips at Kinkaseki! The OC listened sympathetically, but then explained these were standard "ship's orders" on the carrying of troops and, despite our experiences, we were "troops in transit."

As we came out of his office, two of our party immediately went and walked on the upper decks while the rest of us went to tell the boys the result. When we found out later that both of them had been put on a charge for being "out of bounds" on the upper decks, we all agreed to stand together. Now in a thoroughly mutinous mood, we decided if one of them was punished, we would all stand outside the OC Troops office in demonstration.

At 11 o'clock that morning they were put "on charge" to appear before the OC Troops for "conduct prejudicial to good order and military discipline, etc." At that time we all lined up in the ship's lobby area outside the OC's room. They came out smiling. The officer had told them "in the circumstances the charge would be dropped", and consideration would be given to our requests for more freedom on the ship. Later that day we were told all "out of bounds" areas of the ship were lifted and we were free to walk anywhere. The attitude of the authorities on that ship was typical of the lack of imagination and generosity towards us that our own officers and commanders had, and that we were to find so often on the way home.

However, there were sterling examples of the opposite approach from other officers and individuals, who really cared to help us and seemed to have some idea of what we had been through. At Singapore came on board a woman in Red Cross uniform slacks and shirt, heading a group of "brass hats". She was Lady Mountbatten, Edwina, the wife of the Supreme Commander, Far East. "What do you boys need the most?" she asked. "Have you any complaints? I have some idea what you have suffered as I have seen first-hand some of the camps you have left." (We discovered later she had in fact dropped in by aircraft to some of the worst camps in Java.)

We quickly explained our situation on the mess decks and asked for newspapers and magazines. We were hungry for news. She came down to our mess deck and we could tell from her face that she was not pleased with our accommodation. After her visit we were moved to a far more spacious area, mattresses were provided and, best of all, 200 sailors (due for home leave) were put on board to look after us.

Lady Mountbatten, we learned later, appeared at all sorts of places in the Far East where prisoners and internees were being evacuated. Her husband had sensibly put her in charge, giving her full authority to cut "red tape" and get the prisoners and internees on their way home as soon as possible.

We steamed home via Colombo, where we were further treated in hospitals. Then on to Suez where we obtained winter British uniforms. Nearing the coast-line of England at last, we were told we would be delayed landing at Liverpool "because of a dock workers' strike". Sure enough we were anchored outside the Mersey for another 48 hours while arrangements were made with the unions to berth us!

If those men on strike could have heard the comments of the impatient ex-PoWs longing to get home, some after seven years away, they would have been shamed. When the unions were told our ship contained ex-PoWs and internees, they agreed to handle our berthing! We came alongside the crowded quay-side with raucous shouts of "Don't dirty your fucking hands!" and "Leave her, we'll bloody jump ashore!" going to the men handling the lines.

As we tied up, streams of officers came on board. Soon names of men to report to the OC Troops office were being called out on the loud-speaker. My name was called, as were those of many Kinkaseki survivors, and we waited to be interviewed, one at a time. All of us were given personal news of a sorrowful nature. It was done as nicely as possible by Red Cross officials who were trying to soften the blow of a sad home-coming. Some men had news of the deaths of wives. In one case a man had lost his whole family in the blitz on London. Others had tragic news that their wives had gone to live with other men or gone through marriages believing them long dead. Many of us had been posted "Missing, believed killed" before Singapore fell. The majority had simply been posted "Missing". I was shattered by my news, though it was not as bad as some had had to face. The good part was my father and brother were on the quay to meet me.

Hurrying back on deck I searched the mass of up-turned faces, but could recognize no-one. Suddenly an officer in a trench coat waved his cap at me. It was the Major. Bless him, he had not forgotten "his boys". He was there to welcome us home.

I eventually met my father and brother and talked briefly to the Major. He told me he would have to go back to the Far East "soon" and would be in touch with me.

The next two weeks were a blur of family re-unions, sadness, and happiness. The sad part was to find that being "Missing, believed killed" for nearly five years meant that I was a ghost to many people. I found it difficult to talk to or eat with people. I sweated easily and could not control my emotions, crying if I went to a cinema or heard certain music.

When Len Savage reached Great Britain, he immediately came to my home town of Cardiff looking for me. We had an emotional meeting at the station. He saw the state I was in and took me back with him to his home in Watford. He also found it was difficult to talk and relate to family and relatives. We both went to a farm near Land's End where he had stayed pre-war during motorcycle trials. Here some wonderful people, Mr. and Mrs. Humphries, seemed to sense we wanted to be left alone. We walked, swam in the sea (in December), and puttered around the small farm at Trevescan. Neither of us wanted to go home for Christmas, not even to see our worried families. But under the Humphries' persuasion, we left. I wrote in their visitor's book, "Out of a hell, I found a heaven in Trevescan."

Arriving home on Christmas Eve, I found a letter from Major Crossley telling me he had been ordered back to the Far East for war crimes investigations. Would I list the Japanese and Formosans I thought should be prosecuted and, if necessary, come back with him to help, he asked. With my mixed up emotions and inability to sleep or eat meals with the family, I jumped at this chance to get away again. That night I wrote to the Major giving my list of all the nick-names and proper names (those I knew) of the *hanchos*, guards, and officers I felt should be prosecuted. The Major agreed with my list, but because many of those named were mine *hanchos* he did not know, "I would have to volunteer" to go back with him.

Major Crossley, Lt Cross, and I were interviewed in the War Office, all promoted (for our conduct in prison camp, we were told), and briefed on our task. We were to fly back to Singapore as soon as possible. We were told our mission would be:

(1) To identify and assist in the apprehension of Jap and Taiwan war criminals.
(2) To give evidence against them and assist in any prosecutions.
(3) To give all the assistance we could to War Graves recovery teams in locating burial sites.

We were given a few more days leave to settle personal affairs, and a date and time to report back to London. I used those days to visit the family of "Basher" Gore and return his signet ring. This was a sad and trying experience. Though I had several other items to return to families of my section and friends, I could not face them then. On my last day, I plucked up enough courage to travel 20 miles from my home to return a photograph of a wife and baby given to me by a dying man in Kinkaseki. He was not one of my section, but a fellow Welshman who suffered terribly from hammer floggings before he died. I had promised him I would return this treasured photograph. How I regretted that journey.

I knocked on the door of the house and a little girl answered. She took one look at me in my uniform, turned, and shouted, "Mummy, Mummy! I think Daddy's come home!" It was terrible, this poor woman had still not been told. No definite news had come through yet. She had been hearing of PoWs arriving home and kept hoping and waiting, telling her little girl, "One day soon Daddy will come home!" I had the awful job of telling her he would never come home again. I didn't tell her how he had died. Thankfully, her parents lived very near and I waited until she brought them to meet me. I pleaded excuses, promising to return as they did not want me to leave. But I never went back again.

How true what Major Wheeler wrote on 27th January, 1945: "How little a list of casualties tells the real story of war."

The Major, Lt Cross and I returned to the Far East. My own family thought I was crazy, volunteering to go back. Looking back now I am certain we were not normal or rational, but were any of us who came back from that? Could anyone be, having experienced such cruelty and deprivation?

Our journeys, escapades, and adventures in arresting Japanese War Criminals and giving evidence at the many trials can be left perhaps to another book.

When we returned we found the old camp was in ruins, the huts stripped. I decided to poke about in the rubbish left where the Camp Commander and Japanese officers had lived. Someone had made a major mistake and not burnt the old camp records. We found them, soiled but intact and readable. After working all evening and long into the early hours of the next morning, our interpreters discovered among them the only surviving copy of the written order to massacre all PoWs if the Allies landed. Kinkaseki will go down in history as the only place where this evidence was found. I was deservedly lucky and I am proud to say that I found it. Below is a copy of the translation:

Document No. 2701
(Certified as Exhibit "O" in D.c. No. 2687)

From the Journal of the Taiwan POW Camp H.Q. in Taihoku
entry 1st August, 1944

(entries about money, promotions of Formosans at Branch camps, including promotion of Yo Yu-toku to lst Cl Keibiin — 5 entries).

The following answer about the extreme measures for POWs was sent to the Chief of Staff of the 11th Unit (Formosa POW Security No. 10).

"Under the present situation if there were a mere explosion or fire a shelter for the time being could be had in nearby buildings such as the school, a warehouse, or the like. However, at such time as the situation became urgent and it be extremely important, the POWs will be concentrated and confined in their present location and under heavy guard the preparation for the final disposition will be made.

The time and method of this disposition are as follows:

(1)   The Time.

Although the basic aim is to act under superior orders, individual disposition may be made in the following circumstances:

(a)   When an uprising of large numbers cannot be suppressed without the use of firearms.

(b)   When escapes from the camp may turn into a hostile fighting force.

(2) The Methods.

    (a) Whether they are destroyed individually or in groups, or however it is done, with mass bombing, poisonous smoke, poisons drowning, decapitation, or what, dispose of them as the situation dictates.

    (b) In any case it is the aim not to allow the escape of a single one, to annihilate them all, and not to leave any traces.

(3) To: The Commanding General
      The Commanding General of Military Police
      Reported matters conferred on with the 11th Unit,
      the Keelung Fortified Area H.Q., and each
      prefecture concerning the extreme security in
      Taiwan PoW Camps."

In the early morning of the day after the find, I thanked God that the Americans had dropped the atomic bombs on the Japanese Empire. The present day marchers at "Ban the Bomb" demonstrations, often led by chanting Japanese monks, with their slogans of "Remember Hiroshima and Nagasaki", forget what the cost would have been if those bombs had not been dropped. They have no concept of the mentality of our captors, our oppressors. What if the Americans had not dropped it and the Japanese had had time to develop it themselves?

On each anniversary of the dropping of the bombs, the media covers the Japanese memorial ceremonies and stresses the victims still dying or suffering as a result. Nothing is written or said of the hundreds of thousands of lives saved as a result of the quick end those bombs brought to that terrible war. Very little is written and scant attention paid to the thousands of ex-PoW's and internees who have died since 1945 as a direct result of their captivity and ill-treatment at the hands of the Japanese. There are thousands still under constant treatment in hospitals and mental institutions, in homes for the blind, etc., as a direct result of their captivity more than 40 years ago. What is written of the hundreds of thousands of civilians murdered by the Japanese Army? What would they have done if they had invaded the US?

The survivors came back changed men, with severely different sets of values on life and its meaning. My great friend G.P. Adams in his book "No time for Geishas" said, "The experience of almost four years as a prisoner in Japanese hands had an effect on one's sense of values like that of the sea upon a piece of driftwood, stripping away all that is soft, leaving only the hard lines of grain".

These words are so true. We all came back "marked men", either physically or mentally. Nothing would be the same again.

Living in the Far East in Hong Kong, I have been able to visit most of the cemeteries where the remains of thousands of PoWs were collected for burial. Many have stones with their names and regiments and a simple message from the next of kin. But thousands are simply marked, "Known only to God". Others are just names on the "Missing in action" memorials.

Of the men of Kinkaseki I have traced 356 who have individual headstones at Sai Wan Bay Cemetery, Hong Kong. Others are buried in Japan at Yokohama, and many more merely recorded "missing" on the Kranji memorial at Singapore.

When I visit the cemetery in Hong Kong I look at their ages, from 19 to 28 on average, and realize how very lucky I was to survive. It gives me strength to make my life as worthwhile as I can, to try and obtain recognition of what these PoWs endured, and to procure reasonable compensation or pensions for those still suffering as a result of their sacrifices.

We who are left meet as often as possible, at least at yearly reunions. Our motto is "To keep going the spirit that kept us going."

A Final Word

All during my captivity we were encouraged to "take care of our health", so we would be good "Ambassadors for Nippon" when we returned home. I come as an ambassador for the PoWs of Nippon. I seek not revenge, but recognition and compensation. Germany has paid and is paying for the soldiers it held prisoner and civilians it killed and/or tortured. Japan has not paid one penny. German war criminals are still sought out and punished. Japanese war criminals have the equivalent of a pardon. Some Jap war criminals are millionaires who are even now exploiting people in their own nation and the people of the country that saved me. (Not all rich people exploit, but these war criminals I know of do.)

Nuclear weapons are a terrible thing. But what happened to the citizens and soldiers at Nagasaki and Hiroshima was, for most of them, quick and painless. Those on the fringes died in varying degrees of slowness and agony, but the worst were over it within a few weeks, months at most. True, some still suffer. But daily, we were "bashed", harangued, starved, humiliated, intimidated, tortured, and forced to do hard labour in that hell-hole. Our health was ignored, ridiculed. This went on for over two and one-half years at Kinkaseki. At the jungle camp the work was under better conditions, but the food, medical care, beatings and harrasment were worse. We have suffered since then from physical and mental disabilities, the direct result of this treatment at the hands of our cruel and vicious captors. When we returned we found we had lost wives, parents, children, and friends to the allies of these sadists. They showed none of the concern a human being feels for a fellow human being. A large number of our tormentors escaped with little or no punishment. Unless we could prove a direct murder, they were not executed, even though they indirectly caused the deaths of many then and the shortened lives of all they held captive. Those who went to jail lived under conditions that we would consider luxurious and were soon free. Some are now rich men.

Again I admit that nuclear weapons are a terrible thing. But without that terror our oppressors would not have surrendered. Their code of *bushido* is the thinking of a neurotic, insane mentality. Logic could not prevail on them. Without the bombing of Nagasaki and Hiroshima, I and my comrades would have remained their slaves and victims for years, only to be murdered as the Allies landed. The citizens of a country bear the responsibility for their leaders, dictator or democrat. Napoleon acknowledged it with plebiscites. The citizens of Germany elected Hitler. The Soviets believe their system is the best available. The ruler must have the consent of the ruled. When a people choose or allow their leaders to hide the truth and/or commit attrocities out of apathy or fear or laziness or short sighted self-interest, they are foolishly putting off till tommorrow what they should face today. Like a note at the bank, it always comes due with interest added.

I feel no remorse for what the Americans did to Japan. I only regret they did not do it sooner. Where are the annual messages of condolences, rituals, newspaper and TV articles to the dead and my comrades and the wives, children, and relatives of those who died stopping these monsters? Why do you not thank the men and their leaders who saved the lives of your fathers and brothers, and many of your mothers and sisters, by quickly ending a war wrought by an insane and blood-thirsty war machine? I saw the bodies of Chinese men, women, adolescents, and babies shot by members of the Japanese regular army for no reason other than that they opposed the Nippon army and were Chinese.

The Japanese of today should not be punished for the wrongs of their ancestors. And many of their ancestors would have been shocked if they had known of our treatment. Nor will it do any good to extract retribution from the surviving citizens who allowed this atrocity to form and finally to take place. Just give we that survive the dignity and respect we deserve. Quit adding to our mental torture by ignoring our suffering and, insult to injury, publicly decrying our saviours while bemoaning the fate of those whose labour supported our sadistic, pitiless captors. The Allies rebuilt Japan and Germany and Italy. Nobody rebuilt our lives. The tears and nightmares will remain till death. I'm willing to forgive. None of us should forget.

Appendix A

Copy of a letter written by Lt. L. Henry Taylor to his son, Frederick H. Taylor (Ricky), age 8.

Lt. L. Henry Taylor, USNR
USS Thos. J. Gary, D E 326
FPO San Francisco, Calif.
7 September 1945

Dear Ricky:

Just recently, the Navy told all of us that our personal letters would not be censored any more. That means that I can share my experiences and life with the other members of the team — you, Kathy, and particularly Mother have contributed far more to it than I. For we are a very close team. You haven't had a home of your own. I know you have missed having your own things around you — also I think I am saying you and Kathy have missed me — I know Mother has. Perhaps she has worried about me sometimes. All of that was hard. I haven't been able to tell any of you very much about what we are doing — the safety of ships and the war required us to say nothing. The team has been entitled to know more but conditions of war denied them the right. Knowing that all of your are interested in what I am doing and now that censorship has lifted, I will try to tell you something of the past week.

Why am I writing to you, the youngest member of the team, this first time I am able to tell of our operations? Well, Rick, I want to brag a little and although I feel somewhat uncomfortable telling you what we have been doing, I know that if I were writing to Mother, I would tone the story down. I don't want to tone it down. You like to play guns, — well, I have been playing guns too — not real guns, just playing, you understand. I have been wearing my hoister with Grandpa's. 45 Colt just as you wear your. 45 holster. My gun has been loaded bu there has been little idea it was anything but play. You, too, have been particularly interested in Japs with their buck teeth, their long swords which they almost trip on. Well, Ricky, I want to tell you about these things and the game I have played lately. You would like a story — consider this one. (It is a true story, though.)

Ricky, ask Grandpa Taylor if he remembers spanking me one day in Pomeroy for walking on the thin railing of the bridge over the creek near the school. The jeweler that lived up Main St. had seen me showing off above the creek and he told Dad. Both were worried over my safety, though they had no need to. Well, I suppose that some of that streak is still in me because I have enjoyed participating as fully as I could in recent activity. I don't know just why I am this way — Mother's tales of your diving make me think you feel this same way. Kathy's exploits make me fear she has some of that streak.

Ricky, you must let the rest of the folks share this letter. Well, we had been sweating it out down in Leyte Gulf, P.I., where there were hundreds of our ships. The aircraft carriers which are in our group were waiting too. You know, our DEs are to protect and guard the carriers and to pick up any planes that hit the water, etc. I musn't get started on that part of the job now or my story would be too long.

We pulled out of the Philippines and started North to join in the liberation of Korea, Shanghai, etc. I believe we were to protect the large group of mine-sweeps that were sweeping a lane up through dangerous waters so that troops could get through. This was on 29 August. You'll have to ask Mother about mines and mine-sweeping-she can tell you. They are like big bombs that are placed under water to blow up ships that don't know where they are. Usually, there is a crooked lane through such a field but only an accurate chart shows a ship where to go. Even then mine-sweeping vessels continually go back and forth over the secret lane to sweep up and bring to the surface any mines that may have drifted into the safety zone. Some of these mines have points all over them like a prickly ball. They are abou ten feet under the water where you can't see them and they will blow up a ship if it touches them Others. explode magnetically when a ship passes near them, and there are newer kinds. Enough about mines.

Well, a typhoon started down around the Philippines, and moving six or seven knots it began to curve towards where we wanted to go. Will you ask Mother about a typhoon it is just like a tornado only bigger and with wind whirling in a counter-clockwise direction north of the Equator. Winds blowing up to one hundred and twenty or thirty knots circle the center and the bad storm is from one to two hundred miles in diameter. We were south of Okinawa and we all knew the rule that when we faced the wind the storm center was on our right. We maneuvered to keep away from the storm center. The carriers bounced and rolled, both of them — they thought it was very rough. To us on the Gary it wasn't bad at all since the North Atlantic used to be as rough through an entire trip as this was. It was difficult to eat and sleep but not too bad.

We felt very badly one day when Lt. Comd. Victor Gain, a doctor on one of the carriers, was swept overboard from the bow of the carrier by a wave. The Finch, one of our ships, found him face down in the water about an hour later. They tried for several hours to pass his body by breeches buoy back to his own ship but the sea was too rough. The Admiral directed the Finch to conduct the burial services. Just as the sun was going down in the red western sky, this officer was buried at sea. All ships dipped their colors and on the Gary, we stood at attention facing the Finch which was several miles away. It was a solemn moment, the fourth life this particular carrier had lost since we had joined them. After the war was supposed to be over, it made us particularly sad.

The next day our orders were changed and we got a new job. Conditions were uncertain — we knew little of obstacles to be encountered but it sounded good. We fueled from a carrier — they pass oil to other ships through a big rubber hose. We were tossing quite a bit. At one time a wave swept over the carrier's forecastle and seriously injured two men. I took some pictures of the operation and most of them that follow in this story. I did get wet once when water swept over the deck but the camera didn't get wet. Ricky, this seems a long time ago but really it was only four days ago.

We watched the storm center carefully. On the second of September, Mother's birthday and the day when the surrender document was signed, the typhoon began to move north of Formosa and we started to work over that way. The fueling spoke of above was on the next day. Ricky, I know that since it will be in the newspapers and magazines that it is all right for me to tell you what we were to do and how we did it and what small part you Dad had in it all.

We, our small group of destroyer escorts, all ships I have ridden in our division, and the two small carriers were to go into Formosa and get things established so that others could come in. We were to carry off the prisoners of war on Formosa or at least to open it up so that other ships could come in. Intelligence didn't give us too much to go on. We did know that there were mine fields, both those of the Japs and our own, around the port which was selected. We knew where our mines were — not where the Japs' were. No mine-sweeps were to be provided. We knew where the Jap prison camps had been located for holding men from Bataan, Singapore, Malaya and other places and the approximate number of Japs.

The exact temper of the Japs was not known — we were to go in on Sept. 5, 1945, the third day after V-J day. On the afternoon of 4 Sept., it was decided that my boss, Commodore Johnson, would take the Gary and one other ship, the Kretchmer, into arrange for the transfer of the prisoners. My Commodore was to be in charge of all arrangements. The carrier would send planes over us to look for mines and submarines and learn what they could about the ships in the harbour or suicide boats. They also wanted to have a display of force before our destroyer escorts came in so they sent as many planes as possible over the land. We didn't know how willing the Japs would be cooperate.

On Tuesday afternoon, we sent our motor whaleboat over rough waters to get fifteen marines and four officers from the carrier. I got pictures of them coming aboard with their packs, tommy guns, pistols, rifles, etc. Two of them brought camera equipment. This rather disappointed me because the Commodore had promised me I could go ashore with the Marines — I was to be the only Navy officer from our group in first and I was to take pictures. The Colonel of Marines agreed I could go anyway. I loaded up Dad's. 45 and got the camera all set. I had only five rolls of film so had to take pictures sparingly.

I had the 2200 to 0200 watch so didn't go to sleep before 0230 in the morning but tried to find out what we were going to do. It seems that mine fields were the worst hazard. They wanted me to give them assurance that we could negotiate them safely with the use of our Sonar gear, which is my department. Tuesday night, I felt fairly sure though it would be hazardous. The Gary was to go first in column, the Kretchmer following five hundred yards behind in the water we had proved safe. The carriers and the other two ships here would stand off Formosa about thirty or forty miles while we went in.

Well, I got to sleep at 0230 or 2:30 A.M. Wed., 5 Sept., and we went to General Quarters at 0500 or 5:00 A.M. We had left the carriers two hours before. I am Officer of the Deck at General Quarters and also I was responsible for deciding when we should maneuver the ship when an underwater object which might be a mine was located a short distance ahead.

We did make many turns with the Kretchmer following us. Proceeding at slow speed, we traveled with all hatches of the ship closed tightly so if we did hit, water wouldn't flood all of the ship. Planes came over head and called us to report what they saw ahead. We passed one floating mine three hundred yeards abeam and fired on it to sink it. It wouldn't explode so a plane was called in to dive on it and sink it after we had passed on further along. You know, Ricky, when I woke up Wed. morning after my three hours'sleep I felt quite exhilarated and was confident we could get through the mine fields without trouble.

As we approached Kiirun (or Kielung) the port on the north eastern tip of Formosa, we constantly tried to get in touch with the Japanese radio station. We thought that a small Allied group of three or four men were already in and negotiations for release of Prisoners of War started. When the town and harbour were visible, we at last got the Jap radio and made them understand they were to send a pilot — we were about three miles out then. They were told to have the ranking officer present when we came in. Planes called and told us that there were several fast speed boats in the harbor but no warships. The Japs told us in broken English they would send a pilot in one hour.

We waited. Finally a small boat or tug flying the Jap flag came out. We couldn't get her to come alongside to put a man on us. She'd come up near and then dart away motioning us to follow her. Not taking any chances on treachery, we wouldn't and insisted they send a man over. They lowered a small boat and sculled it over with a little scared Jap in it. He was scared to death. He came aboard and up on the bridge and indicated on the chart where we were to go. He wasn't a pilot but we went on in following the small tug. As we passed into the harbour we were greatly relieved. We had passed the mine menance. Rick, our bombers had simply flattened Kiirun. The small harbour was filled with sunken ships, buildings lining it were flattened. A few Chinese junks with sail spread passed near by. Hundreds of Japs were visible in the rubble covered streets. A pilot boarded us inside end we went in to dock by a building and dock not completely destroyed by bombs. We turned around in the small space and tied up bow out so we could get away fast if necessary. All guns were manned.

As we passed down the harbour a green camoflaged Jap sub-chaser was tied up on our port side. About six officers on its bridge snapped to attention as we passed less than 2000 yards away. Then they broke out cheering. It wasn't until then that we recognized them as Allied officers in the Jap boat. We rendered them honors by facing the ship and saluting.

We came into the dock to tie up. About six Jap officers were waiting with their huge swords, their braid, etc. There were many Jap soldiers bowing and scraping around them. I took their picture, Rick hope you can see it soon.

The first group to rush aboard — of course, we wouldn't let the Japs come on — was a mixed group. A British Major who had been a prisoner of war for four years, an American Captain who had been a P.O.W. for over three years from Bataan, a third British P.O.W. from Malaya and a little man whom I later found was the Mayor of Foochow, China.

Well, Rick there were three other officers, two army and one Navy that were not P.O.W., but had come over three days before from China on a Jap sub-chaser. None had known we were coming in. The Amercian officer that had been a prisoner rushed aboard first. With tears in his eyes and a face full of emotion he said, "This is my first chance to set foot on American soil in four years." The rest of the group came aboard and went into the wardroom for conference.

The Japs waited impatiently on the dock for about an hour. We posted guards along the dock, searched the warehouse nearby for treachery and an armed group from the Kretchmer in their motor whaieboat went up and down in the harbour on the water side their machine guns ready in case of trouble. Planes from the carriers, four at a time roared by low overhead. All of us were just pumping the officers who had been prisoners. They gave us information. These men who had suffered so much were still full of spirit though they were physically half starved and weak. All of the prisoners on Formosa, over twelve hundred of them, were in the north and arrangements had already been started to move those strong enough to be moved.

The Japs came aboard, wearing their huge swords which almost dragged on the ground. I got a picture, hope it was good. The conference lasted until about three P.M. I took a few pictures before the conference broke up while two Jap Naval officers were discussing charts, etc. We found that our intelligence had been faulty and we had negotiated a mine field. The Jap Lt. (j.g.) that had gone to school in Palo Alto, Calif said a number of time, "Very dangerous! very dangerous!" when we showed our course coming in.

The Navy Capt. (Jap) agreed to have five sets of charts showing the exact position of Jap mine fields in our hands by 1700 (5:00 P.M.). The Jap who was head of Prison Camp #4 at Taihoku, the captol and largest city of Formosa, was an evil looking fellow.

I was ready to go with the Marines. It looked as if they would have no trouble at all by now. They shoved off at 1600 (4:00 P.M.) to go to the P.O.W. Camp #4. The Commodore asked me to stay. The Marines would stay ashore. We were to take two shiploads of P.O.W. back through the mine field. The Marines went in Jap trucks.

AT 4:15 the Commodore wanted to cross the small harbour to request further charts. We were to assist a group of two English cruisers and one destroyer to come in the next day. All this happened just yeaterday. It seems longer ago than that. It was Wed., 5 Sept. Before I forget it, Rick, this might interest you. I guess it's true although I haven't checked it. One of the American officers, the one who was not a prisoner but who came over in the Jap sub-chaser, said that the Thomas J.Gary, D.E. 326, our ship, was the first American man-of-war to enter a Formosa port since Commodore Perry's time and it was exciting for me to be Officer of the Deck as we came in.

Well, as I started to say, at 4:15 P.M. the Commodore and I set out to visit the Jap headquarters. I had the ship's camera over my shoulder and Dad's. 45 Colt loaded in my holdster with two extra clips in my belt. I told the Commodore I was quite a shot (I wonder) and so I went as his guard and also as his staff.

We went over in the motor whaleboat and a Jap almost fell out of his boat as he saluted when we landed. We left all the men in the boat and walked about a block to the headquarters The natives were fascinating and we were a sight for them and the soliders. An old man looked just like the doll of Kathy's with the hands that shake, only he was in rags.

We entered the almost demolished building as men snapped to salute at the entrance. The Captain's office was spacious and airy (all windows had been blown out). We sat down and smoked. Cap. Fujio was in a white sport shirt, navy green pants. His big sword was lying on his desk. He was Naval Commandant of the port. The Commodore made him understand that Lt. (j.g.) Nishimura, the Jap with some schooling in the U.S. was needed as interpreter. He came in and was told that the British cruisers and a destroyer would be in tomorrow. More charts were required, also pilots for us that evening and the next day. Only four pilots were available. He agreed to comply. We went back out through the barbed wire fence and back to the motor whaleboat and ship.

Things were working out so smoothly. Bless the old man, the Chinese mayor of Foochow. I took him for a Jap at first. He is a prominent Nationalist of China and has helped over nine hundred Americans to escape the Japs. He was partially responsible for this small committee that had come over from China on the Jap sub-chaser on V-J day and so well had they progressed that at 1700 (5:00 P.M.) the train pulled in alongside the dock with three hundred and fifty prisoners of war, mostly British.

Rick, out of over twelve hundred prisoners here, only half a dozen had been in Jap hands less than three and one half years. Well, you can imagine the feelings of those first three hundred and fifty as the train pulled up and came alongside our ship. Planes had dropped them clean clothing. Most of them could stand. A few were carried on backs of stronger ones. They fell into formation. Rick, I walked along talking to them and taking a few pictures. One of our boys threw an unfinished sandwich off the fantail. A Britisher said, "Three days ago, we'd have gone in the water for that." The British major in charge just stared at the potatoes the boys got out of the bins.

Well, Ricky, I'm not going to try to tell you the stories of hunger, starvation, brutality, despair and hope that poured out of these men's lips, men from Bataan, Corregidor, Singapore, Thailand, Hong Kong, etc.

A hundred and seventy-five came aboard each ship. We got underweigh. This time also we went out at General Quarters. Our charts and pilot knew where the mine fields were. We saw several floating mines and encountered what I thought to be a few under water but we avoided them. It was dark when we got back to the carriers.

Then, as motor whaleboats from all the ships transferred all the P.O.W.s to the two carriers for the next four hours, I had a chance to talk further with the officers and men, mostly British and Australians, who had suffered so much.

Ricky boy, those men were wonderful. Their bodies were only skin and bones but their eyes were bright for the most part. Many couldn't stand up, legs and feet were swollen with beri-beri where there was muscle left to swell but they could smile and joke. Ricky, they'll live again, most of them. One American Capt. and I talked for several hours. He has done much and worked constantly to try to keep his fellow men alive. He should be home in a month or two — have Mother look him up. Tell him I'm the one that showed him the pictures of Seaside, that was on the ship that carried him away from the Japs. Dr. Leo Schneider — his wife, Mrs. Rae Schneider, 335 S.W. College, Portland [Ore.] He wasn't sure where his wife is now in Portland but this address may get him.

The sea was calm. Ropes were placed around each man's life jacket as he descended the ladder to the boats so that the weak ones would not fall. Very weak ones, my it was pitiful, were stretched out in bunks in C2021 and they were lashed on stretchers and lowered into the life boats, carried over that way and hoisted onto the carriers.

For the first time at sea, lights were showing so we could effect the transfer. Always, you know, from sunset to sunrise, not a light can show anyplace at night. The men on the ship worked like beavers — no opportunity for sleep or rest. The whole ship smelled — it was delightful, though, Rick, these men were free and could eat and live again. Oh yes, their meal on the ship, roast beef, potatoes, bread, butter, soup — it was heaven for them.

Well, by midnight, all were safe on the carriers. I had the 2200 to 0200 watch again. Believe me, I was so tired I could have fallen on my face. I even felt cranky and barked at my Junior Officer of the Deck when I shouldn't have. I suppose there had been some nervous tension during the day which I hadn't realized that had tired me.

We started in at six A.M. again yesterday morning with all four of our D. E.s, the Finch and the Brister coming along. The Gary led the way back over water which had been found safe the night before. The other three followed in column behind us. At General Quarters again, I was kept busy on the bridge. We had a Jap pilot that had come out with us the previous night. There was no worry.

Ricky, and the rest of you, I've just returned from the fantail where I exchanged information with English boys hungry for words of the past four years. They have been largely in the dark. They told me stories too. I was just going to take pictures of them when we began to fire at a floating mine and they all left their improvised tent. I must go on watch now. — Above, I started to tell you something of yesterday. It was one of the fullest and most interesting days I have ever had. Maybe tonight I can write more to all of you.

Well, here I am again. We have just received quite a commendation from our Admiral and Admiral Kincaid, Commander of the 7th Fleet. I'll send a copy of it to you.

Well, Ricky, and of course the rest of you. (It is easer to dramatize this for you, Ricky.) we picked up a few mines but got into the harbour by 0900 yesterday, Thurs., 6 September. We knew that the British cruisers and the destroyer were due later in the day. We had sent out pilots and proper charts to bring them in.

Captian Fujio, Jap Naval Commandant, was waiting on the dock. We turned around and headed out, our four ships now end to end along the dock. My Commodore requested a car from the Jap, also Lt. (j.g.) Nishimura to act as interpreter. He and I were to drive forty miles to the big prison camp where all P.O.W.s of Formosa were concentrated. The car came, a 1937 Buick.

Ricky, it was a lark, really it was. I felt kind of bad because none of the other officers or men could leave any of the ships. The Japs met us, a driver and the Lt. with his fancy ivory handled dagger with a gold covered leather case. They bowed and scraped and the Commodore and I got into the rear seat, the Japs in the front and off we went. The

Commodore was unarmed. I had the trusty. 45 Colt of Grandpa's, the camera and about eight cartons of cigarettes. That drive had just thousands of sights. If I were to write a book, I couldn't cover all the pictures. Added to it was the amazement of the Japanese army and people as they recognized us as we passed by. I can't begin to give you the pictures but they included practically all that one expects of China or Japan.

We left the pier and started down paved roads, dodging rubble of buildings and bomb craters For the first time began seeing the natives. Believe me, they were a sight and they found us so. Thousands of babies were everyplace. The small babies are all carried on their mother's back in slings. I saw one poor baby with just its head in a sling. All along the highway for the two hour trip there, people by the hundreds of all ages and descriptions were plodding the highway on foot, on ox-carts, on rickshaws, on bicycles. Many coolies carried tremendous loads on poles on their backs. Huge carts were loaded with furniture or produce or coal and struggling men pulled them. I saw one Jap Army group we passed that were struggling up the hill with nothing but hand carts.

Just out of town, we passed through a long tunnel. Then every place along the road were caves where the Japs kept their ammunition, air raid shelters, etc. We saw the rice paddies for miles with Japs or Chinese working in the water. Water buffaloes were every place, some lying in water up to thie knees, some just lying completely covered up to the eyes, some working in plowing with a stick plow. White birds of some sort of crane stood out against the green of the rice. In streams we passed, women in slips squatted and washed their clothes on the rocks. In the villages, which had water-filled gutters, they washed their clothes in the gutters. Everywhere there were people and children by the hundreds. One group of six year olds trudged up the highway, each with a chair.

We passed just a few feet from their homes and could see them squatting there in squalor. When they saw us, they were excited. Most boys from eleven or twelve up to old men were in soldiers' uniforms. All sergeants and officers carried those huge swords We passed temples and ducks, haystacks with pointed tops, grass homes, brick homes, bamboo thickets, sugar cane. We saw little boys standing naked by the roadside, still smaller ones with a circle cut out of the seat of their pants goint to the toilet without having to bother too much. Adults also went to the toilet by the roadside. The women dressed in just a shift for the most part and all except the very young were mothers or in such a state. We passed temples, village after village. Always the road was crowded with moving people. Our horn honked almost continuously.

When about two-thirds of the way there, we saw the train approaching with about nine hundred men for us. I stuck my head out of the car and waved. You should have seen those men. Ricky, you and Kathy and Mother would have been repaid for you long wait for your own home. They cheered and waved. Of course the cheers weren't for me — they were going to freedom and they were happy.

A few miles further along, we met Col. Cooley of the Marines and the English Major and others that had been on the ship the previous day. The Marines had left and all P.O.W.s that could be moved were out of the camp. Their car had an American flag flying so we recognized it and hailed them. We said we were going to the prison camp and asked the way. Also we enquired about buying souvenirs. One of the men had 100 yen which he lent to the Division Commander. We headed on, just the two of us and it was a regular picnic.

This letter is boring you, I know, I must cut it short, soon I hope to be able to tell you about it. We came into Taihoku, the capital of Formosa and its largest city. it was really quite a beautiful c ity of a quarter of a million people, but many of its beautiful buildings had been bombed. Many of the buildings looked like our state buildings or most were bombed.

We drove up a boulevard with palm trees lining it and abou two miles outside of town came to the prison camp. Ricky, one can never see a sight like that and think that war is anything but horrible. We had heard plenty of the officer in charge. He had been inhuman and cruel, kicking and beating his prisoners who through lack of food were mere skeletons. When the Japs were ready to call quits, couldn't be too nice to the men. He knows he's a war criminal and you can bet he'll pay. Tales of him make one's blood curdle. We drove in to find the camp almost deserted. The Jap commanding officer, "Baggy Pants," and his assistant came up, Guards surrounded the place.

Most of the men we couldn't move were in a hospital. They had hospital treatment only four days before we arrived. Two died from assorted weaknesses while we were there. I sauntered through the prison camp itself. In one room a dozen living skeletons suffering from dysentery greeted me. Their buddies through these sufferings were going out, yet they could smile and talk. I took a picture of them. Then I sauntered down the dirty, ramshackle building to a room where T.B. patients lay too weak to move much and just skin and bones. They joked and talked with me. I asked if I could take their picture. They covered up boney legs. After I finished one many said smiling, "You won't have much trouble labeling this pjicture — just call it the TBs."

Just as the Commodore and I were ready to leave, a contingent of American Air Corps doctors arrived. They had just landed in the nearby airport. How wonderful that they could come when these poor men needed them so. Understand we weren't in the hospital — there were worse there. The Jap driver and the Jap Lt (j.g.) drove us to the "Hall of Justice" (does Japan have one?). It was a marble building. Officers walked by, all with swords, and stared at us — we stared back. How I would have liked to get one of those swords for Grandpa Taylor. I couldn't. We were trying to find out how much yen were worth and we wanted to buy some presents. Our interpreter coldn't get any money. We went down into the center and found a shop. They didn't have much. We had only 150 yen between us and nobody seemed to know what a yen was worth. Well, we went into another shop and I got you a snakeskin wallet, a camphor box and a little carved figure for Mother and Kathy. I didn't have a yen left to buy anything for Mother and Dad.

The Commodore and interpreter went into another shop. Ricky, I went out on the street and stood on the sidewalk. You have no idea what an attraction I was, the first free American they had seen. I smoked and watched the Japs and people of Formosa. Soldiers just gaped and passed on, girls, women, and children gathered somewhat and stared. Did I feel like a big shot wearing that. 45. It was fun to be the only armed "army of occupation" in that capitol city of Formosa. Ricky, wasn't that a swell game and it's true, the gospel truth. The Commodore and I were having a swell time. But we had to rush back to the ships.

At 1530 we got back. Our four ships were loaded with the nine hundred men. Only 163 hospital cases were left on the island and good care had just arrived by plane. The two English cruisers and the destroyer were in the harbour. Men too weak to walk were secure in the bunks below. A tent was improvised on the fantail.

Rear Admiral Survaes of the Royal British Navy arrived in his barge. He was piped aboard and greeted by Commodore Johnson. I got his picture. He greeted the many British subjects aboard. He had arrived too late. Escort Division Fifty-Seven was ready to leave with all the moveable war prisoners in Formosa. The Admiral passed each of our four ships and waved to the men lining the rail.

We got underweigh. As we approached the first of the big British cruisers, we faced port at attention and at the whistle signal we rendered honors to the British ships. Ricky, it was a thrilling moment and a real lump came into my throat. The British broke into tremendous cheers and they swept those cruisers — those cheers to the men of Bataan, Singapore, Burma, and all came in unison, time after time. They made part of the difficult separation from Mother, Kathy and you easier. I can't describe the intensity of those cheers or their meaning.

Again the Gary led out of the harbour, the other three ships following. The British remained. With all eyes alert for floating mines, with the gear in operation which I have spent so much time on, we went out and then we were free of the mine fields. We secured from General quarters. [sic] I wandered around and talked to the men, two hundred and fifty aboard. All the officers were with us. In an hour and a half we were by the carriers and eight motor whaleboats transferred men to the carriers. At 2300 all but those we were carrying on to Manila were transferred. Many were litter cases so that transfer was rapid.

My heart was wrung as I talked to the men. Once, I was moved terrifically. I was overseeing Compartment 202 where the men too weak to stand were lying. One had gone up the ladder to the head and asked me to help him down. Looking at skin and bones is touching, but I had no idea until I put my arm around this man to lift him down the ladder. I was afraid my hands would go through his ribs to crush his heart and lungs. There was nothing there but he had spirit — he was free.

To all of you — the amazing thing to me is these men haven't been crushed. They sparkle, they will be men again.

Tonight we travel with the ship lighted. Dad, the lights are coming on again all over the world. Our passengers had a restful night, they ate real food.

There is so much I haven't said; my hand is cramped from writing. I haven't had much sleep. I had the 0000 to 0400 watch last night and got up after three hours of sleep.

Let me close with a dispatch that came to us over the radio this afternoon. Tomorrow I'll be in Manila and will mail this. Before forget, tried to get word of Donald and failed. [Donald Dodd, U.S. N., cousin of L.H. Taylor, missing at Corregidor. He was never found and was presumed dead.]

Here is the dispatch and it does mean something. From the Admiral of our task force to all ships — quote: "For evacuating prisoners of war from Formosa, you were nothing short of sensational. Every officer and man in your ship deserves resounding applause for shoving your noses into Kiirun before the occupation in a most worthy cause; the handling of passengers and their care, like everything else, was done in the American way — there is no better."

From Admiral Kincaid, commanding officer of the Seventh Fleet: "Your proven and determined action in Formosa even under difficulty certainly was a magnificent and difficult performance and a Godsend to our prisoners. Well done." Adm. Kincaid.

Well, Ricky, this has been a long story of these past few days. I hope you're not too tired. You, Kathy and Mother, have shared so very much in this. I have had my play with guns, with buck-toothed, squatty Japs with long swords. What a grand opportunity we had to participate.

I am tired. I'm ready to come home to Mother's arms, to play with you and Kathy. Give my love to Mother. Squeeze and kiss her for me. Give a hug and kiss to Grandma and Grandpa Taylor, to Grandma and Grandpa Ruby, and to Kathy.

Lots of love,
Your Dad.

Liberated P.O.W'S and the crews of U.S. Destroyers are cheered by the British Cruisers *H.M.S.* *"Belfast"* and *H.M.S* *"Bermuda"* on the second day's evacuation from Taiwan in Keelung Harbour.

The U.S.S. "Gary" alongside Keelung Harbour, Taiwan. The First Japanese Officers are allowed on board for conference led by "Baggy Pants".

Second day of the evacuation Keelung Harbour Taiwan. U.S.S. "Kretchmer", "Brister" and "Gary" loaded with liberated P.O.Ws.

Conference in ward room Japanese Officers meet American Officers for first time face to face in peace Col. Cooley U.S. Marines and Commander Johnson U.S. Navy arranging evacuation that day of the first out, the Kinkaseki survivors.

8TH DIVISION

AUSTRALIAN IMPERIAL FORCES
Headquarters

Administrative H.Q.

General Base Depot

2nd Echelon

Command Pay

Depot & Field Cash Offce

8th Divn & Base Postal Units

ROYAL AUSTRALIAN ARTILLERY

2/10 Field Regt R.A.A.

2/15 Field Regt R.A.A.

4th Anti Tank Regt R.A.A.

ROYAL AUSTRALIAN ENGINEERS

H.Q. Royal Austn Engrs

2/10 Field Coy. R.A.E.

2/12 Field Coy. R.A.E.

2/6 Field Park Coy. R.A.E.

AUSTRALIAN ARMY SERVICE CORPS.

H.Q. A.A.S.C.

No 1 Coy. A.A.S.C.

No 2 Coy. A.A.S.C.

Dett 2/2 Res. M.T. Coy.

3 Reserve M.T. Coy.

4 Res. M.T. Coy.

8 Div. Amm. Sub Park

8 Supply Persnl Sec.

9 Supply Personnel Sec.

1 Field Bakery Sub. Sec.

AUSTRALIAN DIVISIONAL ORDNANCE

2/3 Ordnance Store Coy.

22 Indep. Bde Gp Ordnce W/Shops

22 Bde Gp Ordnce Field Park

27 Indep. Bde Ord. W/Shops

27 Bde Gp Ord. Field Park

2/10 Ordnance Workshops

2/10 Ordnance Field Park

8th Div. Salvage Unit

8th Div. Mobile Laundry and
forward decontamination Unit

69 Light Aid Dt

73 L.A.D.

74 L.A.D.

84 L.A.D.

85 L.A.D.

86 L.A.D.

87 L.A.D.

88 L.A.D.

8th Div. Mobile
Bath Unit

AUSTRALIAN DIVISIONAL SIGNALS

AUSTRALIAN DIVISIONAL PROVOST
Including Detention Barrack Room.

22ND AUSTN INF. BDE	27TH AUST. INF. BDE
Headquarters	Headquarters
2/18th Inf. Battn	2/26 Inf. Battn
2/19 Inf. Battn	2/29 Inf. Battn
2/20 Inf. Battn	2/30 Inf. Battn

DIVISIONAL TROOPS
2/4th Aust. M.G. Battn

8TH DIVISIONAL MEDICAL CORPS

10 Aust. Gen. Hospital	No 2 Conv. Depot
Philanthrophic Personnel	2/4 C.C.S.
13 Aust. Gen. Hospital	2/2 Motor Amb. Convoy
Austn Army Nursing Serv	2/3 Motor Amb. Convoy
3 Adv Depot Med. Stores	2/9 Aust. Fd Amb.
8 Div.˜ Mob. Bactl Laby	2/10 Aust. Fd Amb.
17, 18, 25, 27, 32, 33, 34 Dental Units	2/5 Field Hygiene Secn

ATTACHED TROOPS

Johore Volunteer Engineers
44th IND. INF. BRIGADE 45th IND. INF. BRIGADE.

HEADQUARTERS
MALAYA COMMAND

7
H.Q. HONG KONG GARRISON

8th Coast Regt. R.A.

12th Coast Regt. R.A.

5th H.A.A. Regt. R.A.

1st Hong Kong Regt. R.A.

22nd Fortress Coy. R.E.

40th Fortress Coy. R.E.

Hong Kong Volunteer Defence Force

H.Q. MAINLAND BRIGADE

2nd Bn. The Royal Scots

5th/7th Rajputana Rifles

2nd/14th Punjab Regt.

H.Q. ISLAND BRIGADE

1st Bn. The Middlesex Regt.

Royal Rifles of Canada

The Winnipeg Grenadiers

All personnel

of

Burcorps,

Chindits,

14th Army and

South East Asia

Command

6
H.Q. SINGAPORE FORTRESS

7th Coast Regt. R.A.
9th Coast Regt. R.A.
16th Defence Regt. R.A.
3rd H.A.A. Regt. R.A.
5th S/L Regt. R.A.
35th L.A.A. Regt. R.A.
30th Fortress Coy. R.E.
35th Fortress Coy. R.E.
41st Fortress Coy. R.E.
1st A.A. Regt. I.A.
1st H.A.A. Regt. H.K.S.R.A.
Jind Infantry I.S.F.
2nd H.A.A. Regt. H.K.S.R.A.
Kapurthala Infantry I.S.F.
3rd L.A.A. Regt. H.K.S.R.A.

H.Q. 1st MALAYA BRIGADE

2nd Bn. The Loyal Regt.
1st Bn. The Malay Regt.
2nd Bn. The Malay Regt.

H.Q. 2nd MALAYA BRIGADE

1st Bn. The Manchester Regt.
2nd Bn. The Gordon Highlanders.
2nd/17th Dogra Regt.

H.Q. S.S.V.F. BRIGADE

1st Bn. S.S.V.F.
2nd Bn. S.S.V.F.
4th Bn. S.S.V.F.

AIRFIELD DEFENCE TROOPS

1st Bahawalpur Infantry I.S.F.
1st Hyderabad Infantry I.S.F.
1st Mysore Infantry I.S.F.

5
H.Q. PENANG FORTRESS

11th Coast Regt. R.A.
36th Fortress Coy. R.E.
5th/14th Punjab Regt.
3rd Bn. S.S.V.F.

H.Q. L. of C. AREA
H.Q. F.M.S.V.F.

1st Bn. F.M.S.V.F.
2nd Bn. F.M.S.V.F.
3rd Bn. F.M.S.V.F.
4th Bn. F.M.S.V.F.
Armoured Car Coy. F.M.S.V.F.

JAVA & SUMATRA TROOPS

'B' Sqdn. 3rd Hussars
6th H.A.A. Regt. R.A.
77th H.A.A. Regt. R.A.
21st L.A.A. Regt. R.A.
48th L.A.A. Regt. R.A.

MALAY STATE FORCES

Johore Infantry
Johore Volunteer Engineers
Kelantan Volunteer Force
Kedah Volunteer Force
Perak River Platoon
Sultan Idris Coy.

4
H.Q. 9th INDIAN DIVISION

5th Field Regt. R.A.
88th Field Regt. R.A.
42nd Field Park Coy. S. & M.

H.Q. 8th INDIAN BRIGADE

19th Field Coy. S. & M.
2nd/10th Baluch Regt.
1st/13th Frontier Force Rifles.
3rd/17th Dogra Regt.

H.Q. 22nd INDIAN BRIGADE

22nd Field Coy. S. & M.
5th/11th Sikh Regt.
2nd/12th Frontier Force Regt.
2nd/18th Royal Garhwal Rifles.

H.Q. 12th INDIAN BRIGADE

122nd Field Regt. R.A.
15th Field Coy. S. & M.
2nd Bn. The Argyll and Sutherland Highlanders.
5th/2nd Punjab Regt.
4th/19th Hyderabad Regt.

H.Q. 44th INDIAN BRIGADE

6th/1st Punjab Regt.
7th/8th Punjab Regt.
6th/14th Punjab Regt.

H.Q. 45th INDIAN BRIGADE

7th/6th Rajputana Rifles.
4th/9th J.A.T. Regt.
5th/18th Royal Garhwal Rifles.

H.Q. 28th INDIAN BRIGADE

2nd/1st King George V's Own Gurkha Rifles (The Malaun Regt.).
2nd/2nd King Edward VII's Own Gurkha Rifles (The Sirmoor Rifles).
2nd/9th Gurkha Rifles.

This Order of Battle has been prepared by Mr J.J. Ashworth of Cleveleys, a member of the Military Heraldry and Military Historical Societies who served with 14th Army. Due to the need for economy with this programme and the lack of the official information, it has not been possible to include all the Units with which some of our members served until capture. Our sincere apologies to all those concerned -- their efforts and subsequent sufferings need no reminders to their comrades--in--arms.

3

H.Q. 3rd INDIAN CORPS

H.Q. 11th INDIAN DIVISION

3rd Cavalry (I.A.)
100th Light Tank Sqdn.
137th Field Regt. R.A.
155th Field Regt. R.A.
80th A/Tk. Regt. R.A.
85th A/Tk. Regt. R.A.
43rd Field Park Coy. R.E.
23rd Field Coy. Royal Bombay S. & M.

H.Q. 6th INDIAN BRIGADE

22nd Mountain Regt. (I.A.)
17th Field Coy. Royal Bombay S. & M.
2nd Bn. The East Surrey Regt.
1st/8th Punjab Regt.
2nd/16th Punjab Regt.

H.Q. 15th INDIAN BRIGADE

3rd Field Coy. King George V's Own
  Bengal Sappers and Miners.
1st Bn. The Leicestershire Regt.
2nd/9th J.A.T. Regt.
1st/14th Punjab Regt.
3rd/16th Punjab Regt.

AUSTRALIAN IMPERIAL FORCES

SARAWAK & BRUNEI TROOPS

2nd/15th Punjab Regt.
Coastal Marine Service.
Sarawak Rangers.

All R.A.P.C., Pioneer,
Intelligence and
Education Corps
Personnel.

2

H.Q. 18th BRITISH DIVISION

118th Field Regt. R.A.
135th Field Regt. R.A.
148th Field Regt. R.A.
125th A/Tk. Regt. R.A.
287th Field Coy. R.E.
288th Field Coy. R.E.
560th Field Coy. R.E.
251st Field Park Coy. R.E.
18th Bn. the Recce Regt. (5th Bn. The
  Loyal Regt.).
9th Bn. The Royal Northumberland
  Fusiliers (M.G.).

H.Q. 53rd INFANTRY BRIGADE

5th Bn. The Royal Norfolk Regt.
6th Bn. The Royal Norfolk Regt.
2nd Bn. The Cambridgeshire Regt.

H.Q. 54th INFANTRY BRIGADE

4th Bn. The Royal Norfolk Regt.
4th Bn. The Suffolk Regt.
5th Bn. The Suffolk Regt.

H.Q. 55th INFANTRY BRIGADE

5th Bn. The Bedfordshire and
  Hertfordshire Regt.
1st Bn. the Cambridgeshire Regt.
1st/5th Bn. The Sherwood Foresters.

All Chaplains,
Doctors, Dentists
and Personnel
of
R.A.M.C. and
R.A.D.C.
Units.

All Personnel
of
Supply, Ordnance,
Signals, Provost
and
A.C.C. Units.

FLEET AIR ARM

ROYAL MARINES

ROYAL AIR FORCE

The Royal Marine survivors of H.M.S. "Prince of Wales", H.M.S. "Repulse"
and other sunken ships combined with what was left of 2nd Bn. The Argyll
and Sutherland Highlanders to fight as "The Plymouth Argylles."

Appendix B

Nominal rolls of those imprisoned at Kinkaseki Camp, Taiwan, compiled and preserved by Sgt. Jim Bingham of the 155th Field Regt (Lanarkshire Yeomanry) RA. One is by regiments, incomplete, probably compiled mid 1944. The other is a full list of names, giving ranks, Japanese camp numbers, and the dates of death or leaving on "Thin-Man" parties where known.

This record kept on stolen Japanese work sheets in pencil is not a complete list of those who passed through, died or survived at Kinkaseki. Checks made by the author suggest it was compiled in mid-1944, therefore names of early sick "thin-man" parties may not be on these lists. Sadly also, many of the names recorded died either at Kinkaseki or later at the Jungle (Yama) Camp or at other P.O.W. camps in Taiwan or Japan.

Camp No.	Name	Rank	
1	Adams. J.	Gnr	Left 20.8.43 Shirakowa Died
2	Adamson. J.J.	Sigmn.	Died 14.12.42
3	Agass. E.	L/Cpl	Left 20.8.43 Taihoku
4	Albone. H.J.	Gnr.	Left 8.11.43 Taihoku
5	Allardyce. A.	L/Cpl.	*
6	Anderson. M.L.	Capt.	Left 20.8.43 Died
7	Anderson. W.G.	Sgt.	Died 13.1.45
8	Andrews. E.G.	Gnr.	Died 23.3.43
9	Angus. G.	Bdr.	Left 21.2.45 ?
10	Appleton. J.A.	Gnr	Left 21.2.45 ?
11	Askew. H.	L/Bdr.	Left 13.11.43 Heito
12	Atinson. D.F.H.	Sgt.	Left 20.8.43 Taihoku
13	Aylward. P.B.	Bdr.	*
14	Badgett	Capt.	Left 20.8.43 Shirakowa
15	Baigent. G.	Gnr.	*
16	Bailey. E.	Gnr.	*
17	Baillie. T.W.	Gnr.	Left 25.10.44 Shirakowa
18	Baker. A.W.	L/Bdr.	Left 20.8.43 Taihoku
19	Baker. B.N.	Sgt.	Left 13.11.43 Heito
20	Barber. G.	Sigmn.	Died 29.1.45
21	Barker. H.	Gnr.	Died 3.3.43
22	Barnes. E.	Gnr.	Left 20.8.43 Taihoku
23	Barnes. F.V.	Gnr	Died 18.1.45
24	Barrett. H.G.	R.S.M.	Left 13.11.43 Heito
25	Barrie. W.	Gnr	Left 21.2.45 ?
26	Barritt. C.	Gnr	Died 13.1.43
27	Bartelot. R.	Capt.	Left 20.8.43 Shirakowa
28	Bartholomew. A.E.	Gnr	Left 20.8.43 (Died)
29	Batrick. W.	Gnr	Left 8.11.43 Taihoku
30	Beaument. A.	Gnr	Left 20.8.43 Taihoku
31	Beaumont. S.	Bdr.	Left 21.2.45 ?
32	Bell. D.T.	L/Sgt	*
33	Bell. H.N.	Gnr	Left 25.10.44 Shirakowa
34	Bell. J.M.	Gnr	Left 20.2.45 ?
35	Benson. C.	Gnr	*
36	Bentick. J.H.	Gnr	Left 21.2.45 ?
37	Bentley. J.	L/Bdr	Died 24.6.45
38	Beszant. S.	Pte.	Left 8.11.43
39	Bidwell. H.A.	Gnr	Left 8.11.43 Taihoku
40	Biggins. S.	Gnr.	Left 30.3.45 Taioku

*Indicates soldier remained at Kinkaseki until moved to Kokutsu 15th May, 1945.

41	Bilham. L.	Gnr.	Left 8.11.43 Taioku
42	Bingham. J.	Sgt.	*
43	Bird. J.C.	Gnr.	*
44	Black. J.	L/Bdr	Died 11.3.43
45	Blair. D.	Gnr	Left 22.3.45 Shirakowa
46	Blair. W.B.	L/Bdr	Died 6.2.45
47	Blakely. J.	Gnr	*
48	Blezzett. B.	Gnr	*
49	Boughey. J.G.	Cpl.	Died 21.2.43
50	Bowers. A.R.	Gnr	Left Shirakowa
51	Brain. K.H.G.	Gnr	Died 28.12.42
52	Brandon. W.J.	Gnr	*
53	Brazier. J.L.	L/Cpl	*
54	Brennan. J.	Bdr.	Left 13.11.43 Heito
55	Brentnall. R.	Gnr.	Left 20.8.43 Taihou
56	Brewster. W.	Bdr	Left 22.3.45 Shirakowa
57	Briggs. L.G.	Gnr.	Left 20.8.43
58	Brodie. J.	L/Sgt	*
59	Brooke. E.		Left 25.10.43 (Died)
60	Brookes. W.S.	BSM	Left 13.11.43
61	Brookes. K.G.	Gnr	Left 20.8.43 Taioku
62	Brown. G.M.	Gnr	Died 6.4.43
63	Brown. H.	Gnr	*
64	Brown. J.	L/Sgt	*
65	Brown. W.M.G.	Lieut	Left 21.2.45
66	Bruce. D.	L/Bdr	Left 3.11.43 Taioku
67	Bruce. E.	Gnr	Left 8.11.43
68	Brunton. G.W.	Bdr	Left 20.8.43
69	Buchanan. R.	Gnr	Left ? (Died)
70	Buckham. J.	Gnr	*
71	Buckton. T.E.	Gnr	Left 21.2.45 ?
72	Bunting. J.	Pte	Left 22.3.45 Shirakowa
73	Burgess. J.	Gnr	Left 8.11.43 Taioku
74	Burnhill. W.	Gnr	Left 8.11.43 Taioku
75	Burns. H.	Gnr	Died 8.2.45 Taioku ?
76	Buttifant. F.I.	Sigmn	Left 30.3.45 Taihoku
77	Calder. W.	Gnr	Left 13.11.43 Heito
78	Caldow. J.	Gnr	*
79	Callaghan. D.	Gnr	*
80	Callan. R.	Gnr	Left 20.8.43 Shirakowa
81	Calland. D.	L/Bdr	Died 5.2.43
82	Cameron. R.M.	Gnr	Left 25.10.44

83	Cameron. W.G.	Gnr	Left 21.2.45
84	Cameron. W.J.R.	Gnr	Left 22.3.45
85	Campbell. A.	Gnr	*
86	Campbell. G.	Gnr	*
87	Campbell. W.	Gnr	*
88	Campion. F.	Sigmn	Left 20.8.43 Shirakowa
89	Cant. B.	Gnr	Left 20.8.43 Shirakowa
90	Carey. R.E.	L/Bdr	Left 20.8.43 Taioku
91	Carlyle. I.	L/Bdr	*
92	Carmichael. A.	Genr	Left 21.2.45 ?
93	Carr. A.	L/Bdr	Left 13.11.43 Heito
94	Carroll. H.A.	Gnr	Left 22.3.45
95	Carrol. J.	Gnr	Left 13.11.43 Heito
96	Carruthers. W.	Gnr	*
97	Carson. B.	L/Bdr	*
98	Cartwright. D.	Gnr	*
99	Chadwick. A.	Pte	Left 8.11.43 Taioku
100	Channon. C.J.	Cpl	Left 8.11.43 Taioku
101	Chivers. W.H	Gnr	Left 21.2.45 ?
102	Christie. R.H.	L/Bdr	Left 25.10.44 Shirakowa
103	Clack. E.A.	Sigmn	Died 25.9.45
104	Clark. W.S.B.	L/Bdr	*
105	Clingan. W.	Genr	Left 20.8.43 Taioku
106	Coates. W.H.B.	Sigmn	Left 22.3.45 Shirakowa
107	Collins. F.C	Genr	Left 13.11.43 Heito
108	Coogan. A.	Genr	Left 13.11.43 Heito
109	Cooke. R.T.W.	BQMS	Left 13.11.43 Heito
110	Cooper. G.A.	L/Bdr	Left 13.11.43 Heito
111	Cousin. J	Sgt	*
112	Cowan. J.	Gnr	Died 8.2.43
113	Cox. J.	Gnr	Left 5.12.44 Taioku
114	Cragg. M.J.	Gnr	Left 25.10.44 Shirakowa
115	Craig. D.	L/Bdr	Left 13.11.43 Heito
116	Craig. J.	Sigmn	*
117	Cresswell. J.	L/Sgt	Left 20.8.43 Shirakowa
118	Cross. J.T.N.	Lieut	*
119	Crossley. J.F.	Major	*
120	Dalgliesh. G.	Gnr	Left 25.10.44 Taihoku
121	Daly. R.W.	Gnr	*
122	Davey. J.S.	L/Bdr	Left 22.3.45 Heito
123	Davidson. T.	Gnr	Left 13.11.43 Taohoku
124	Davies. A.	Gnr	Left 20.8.43
125	Davies. D.	Gnr	*

126	Davies. E.B.	Lieut	Left 20.8.43 Shirakowa
127	Davies. J.A.	L/Cpl	Left 21.2.45 ?
128	Davis. E.G.	Sgt	Left 21.2.45 ?
129	Davis. I.	Gnr	Left 20.8.43 Taioku
130	Davis. K.A.W.	Lieut	*
131	Davis. L.E.	Sigmn	*
132	Day. F.	Gnr	Left 20.8.43 Taioku
133	Dell. R.	L/Bdr	Left 20.8.43 Taioku
134	Denny. C.	Gnr	Left 8.11.43 Taioku
135	Denton. R.O.	Gnr	Left 30.3.45 Taioku
136	Devere. E. Frank	Gnr	*
137	Dewar. W.	Gnr	Left 30.8.43 Taioku
138	Dewsnap. D.J.	Sgt	*
139	Dickson. A.	Gnr	*
140	Dickson. W.J.	Gnr	Left 8.11.43 Taihoku
141	Dixon. J.M	Pte	Left 8.11.43
142	Dobbie. P.H.	Gnr	*
143	Docherty. R.	Gnr	Left 25.10.44 Shirakowa
144	Dodds. T.	Gnr	Left 8.11.43
145	Donaldson. L.A.	Sgt	Left 25.10.44 Shirakowa
146	Donnelly. H.H.	Gnr	Left 20.8.43 Taihoku
147	Donnelly. T.	Bdr	Left 13.11.43 Heito
148	Douglas. J.W.	Gnr	Died 25.1.44
149	Douglas. J.C.	L/Bdr	Left 22.3.45
150	Downie. A.	Bdr	*
151	Downie. J.	L/Bdr	*
152	Downs. A.K.	Gnr	Left 20.8.43 Taihoku
153	Dubock. H.	BSM	Left 21.2.45
154	Duncan. A.	Gnr	Left 20.8.43 Taihoku
155	Dunsmure. W.	Bdr	Left 13.11.43 Heito
156	Edgar. P.F.	Gnr	*
157	Edwards. C.J.	Gnr	Left 21.2.45 ?
158	Edwards. G.	Gnr	*
159	Edwards. J.O.	Sgt	*
160	Edwards. S.A.	Gnr	*
161	Ellerby. G.	L/Bdr	Died 18.12.42
162	Embury. G.	L/Bdr	Left 22.3.45 Shirakowa
163	Fairbrother. E.B.	Gnr	Died 27.11.44
164	Farmer J.A.	L/Sgt	Left 13.11.43 Heito
165	Farmer J.C.	L/Bdr	Left 20.8.43 Taihoku
166	Fasson. J.C.H.	Lt/Col	Left 20.8.43 Shirakowa
167	Ferguson. A.	Gnr	Left 20.8.43 Shirakowa
168	Ferguson. D.J.	Gnr	Left 21.2.45

169	Fergusson. J.	Bdr	Left 21.2.45
170	Field. A.	Pte	Died 10.2.43
171	Fisher. B.W.J.	L/Bdr	*
172	Fisher F.C.	Gnr	Left 20.8.43 Shirakowa
173	Fitzgerald. J.A.	L/Bdr	*
174	Flanagan. W.J.	Gnr	*
175	Fleming. W.	Gnr	Left 21.2.45 ?
176	Fletcher. W.	Gnr	Left 20.8.43 ?
177	Flux. F.	Gnr	Left 8.11.43 Taihoku
178	Foot. A.	Gnr	Left 8.11.43 Taihoku
179	Ford. G.P.	Lieut	Left 20.8.43 Shirakowa
180	Ford. J.	L/Sgt	Left 21.2.45 ?
181	Forrest. W.W.	Gnr	*
182	Foster. F.	Gnr	Left 8.11.43 Taihoku
183	France. B.A.	Lieut	Left 20.8.43 Shirakowa
184	Francke. J.E.R.	Capt.	*
185	Fraser. P.	Gnr	Left 20.8.43 Taihoku
186	Freeman. S.	Sgt	Left 20.8.43 Taihoku
187	Freeman. W.	Gnr	Left 20.8.43 Taihoku
188	Frew. S.	Gnr	Left 20.8.43 Taihoku
189	Gale. R.	Gnr	Left 20.8.43 Taihoku
190	Guardhouse. J.	Gnr	Left 20.8.43 Taihoku
191	Germany. E.R.	Gnr	Left 22.3.45
192	Gibson. W.McG.	Sigmn	Left 22.3.45 Shirakowa
193	Gilboy. D.S.	Sgmn	Left 20.8.43 Taihoku
194	Giles. A.L.	Gnr	Left 21.2.45
195	Gill. F.	Sigmn	Left 20.8.43 Taihoku
196	Glencross. W.	Bdr	Left 21.2.45
197	Glendinning. R.	Gnr	Left 13.11.43 Heito
198	Goodman. R.G.	L/Sgt	*
199	Gordon. T.	Gnr	Left 20.8.43 Taihoku
200	Gore. H.M.	L/Sgt	Died 22.12.42
201	Gotobed. J.	Gnr	Left 8.11.43 Taihoku
202	Gough. B.	Bdr	*
203	Gowland. C.	Gnr	*
204	Graham. J.	Gnr	*
205	Grant. D.	Gnr	Died 10.7.43
206	Green. J.	Gnr	*
207	Griffiths. J.F.	L/Cpl	Died 6.11.42
208	Griffiths. T.	Gnr	Left 13.11.43 Heito
209	Grundy. G.	Bdr	Left 23.10.44 Kagi
210	Gunn. A.	Gnr	Died 18.12.42
211	Gunn. L.	Gnr	Left 21.2.45

212	Guscott. S.	Gnr	*
213	Guthrie. J.	Gnr	Left 20.8.43
214	Haines. J.J.E.	Bdr	Left 21.2.45
215	Halstead. R.A.	Gnr	Left 22.3.45 Shirakowa
216	Hands. J.A.	Gnr	Left 13.11.43 Heito
217	Hanford. D.	Sigmn	Left 20.8.43 Shirakowa
218	Hardy. K.	Gnr	Left 8.11.43 Taihoku
219	Harley. D.B.	Gnr	Left 20.8.43 Taihoku
220	Harrington. W.	Gnr	Died 27.12.43
221	Harrison. J.V.	Gnr	Left 20.8.43 Shirakowa
222	Harrison. T.	L/Sgt	Left 21.2.45
223	Harrod. D.E.	Gnr	Left 21.2.45
224	Hart. F.T.	L/Bdr	Left 25.10.44 Kagi
225	Harvey. D.A.	Gnr	*
226	Haslam. F.	Sigmn	Left 21.2.45
227	Hay. W.L.	Gnr	*
228	Haynes. G.W.	L/Sgt	Left 20.8.43 Taihoku
229	Haynes. H.	Gnr	Left 22.3.45 Shirakowa
230	Healey. P.J.	Gnr	Left 22.3.45 Shirakowa
231	Heaver. L.A.	Sgt	Left 21.2.45
232	Hellyer. R.W.	Lieut	*
233	Henderson. S.	L/Sgt	Left 20.8.43 (Died)
234	Henderson. S.	Gnr	Left 20.8.43 Taihoku
235	Hiddleston. A.	Gnr	Left 25.10.44 Kagi
236	Hiddleston. D.M.	L/Bdr	Left 20.8.43 Taihoku
237	Higgins. R.P.	Gnr	Left 20.8.43 Taihoku
238	Higham. J.	Gnr	Died 5.11.44
239	Hill. H.	Lieut	Left 20.8.43 Shirakowa
240	Hill. N.	Gnr	*
241	Hinton. G.N.	Lieut	Left 20.8.43 Shirakowa
242	Holdsworth. F.	Gnr	Left 21.2.45
243	Holmes. F.	Gnr	Died 13.10.43
244	Holt. W.G.	Gnr	*
245	Hook. G.	Gnr	Died 29.3.43
246	Hooks. D.J.	Bdr	*
247	Hope-Johnston P.W.	Capt	Left 20.8.43 Shirakowa
248	Hopkins. G.L.	Gnr	*
249	Horton. G.	Gnr	*
250	Houston. A.	Sigmn	Left 8.11.43 Taihoku
251	Hudson. H.A.	Lieut	Left 20.8.43 Shirakowa
252	Hufton. R.	Gnr	Left 20.8.43 Taihoku
253	Hughes. B.	Gnr	Left 20.8.43 Taihoku
254	Hugo. J.W.	Lieut	Left 20.8.43 Shirakowa

255	Hunt. I.	Gnr	*
256	Hunter. J.	Gnr	Left 30.3.45
257	Ingram. H.	Gnr	Left 20.8.43 Taihoku
258	Irving. W.	L/Cpl	Left 20.8.43 Taihoku
259	James. K.	Gnr	Left 20.8.43 Taihoku
260	Jennison. T.	Gnr	Left 20.8.43 Taihoku
261	Jess. H.S.	Gnr	Left 22.3.45 Shirakowa
262	Johnson. J.	L/Bdr	Left 21.2.45 (Died)
263	Jones. E.	Bdr	Left 20.8.43 Taihoku
264	Jordan.	Pte.	Died 2.2.43
265	Joy. L.R.	L/Bdr	*
266	Kane. J.	Gnr	*
267	Kappelhof. J.	Sigmn	Died 12.1.43
268	Keith. J.	Gnr	Left 21.2.45
269	Kelso. F.	Gnr	Left 20.8.43 Taihoku
270	Kennedy. M.	Gnr	Left 8.11.43 Taihoku
271	Kennedy. R. (Padre)	Capt	Left 20.8.43 Shirakowa
272	Kepple. M.	Lieut	Left 20.8.43 Shirakowa
273	Kerton. R.H.M.	Gnr	Left 20.8.43 Shirakowa
274	Kilvinton. N.	Gnr	Left 20.8.43 Taihoku
275	King. J.R.	Gnr	Left 25.10.44 Shirakowa
276	Kingsland. J.	Sgt	*
277	Kirk. L.	Gnr	Left 21.2.45
278	Kirkby. W.	Gnr	Left 21.2.45
279	Kramer. E.G.	Gnr	Left 25.10.44 Shirakowa
280	Lang. W.R.	Gnr	*
281	Langford. T.E.	Gnr	*
282	Lapsley. R.	Gnr	Left 20.8.43 Shirakowa
283	Larkin. F.	Gnr	*
284	Lawson. G.	Gnr	Left 20.8.43 Taihoku
285	Lawton. W.	Gnr	Left 8.11.43 Taihoku
286	Leaman. G.	Gnr	Left 20.8.43 Taihoku
287	Leamer. W.	L/Bdr	Died 10.12.44
288	Ledwidge. V.	Gnr	Left 13.11.43 Heito
289	Lemm. J.	Gnr	Left 8.11.43 Taihoku
290	Levett. C.	L/Bdr	Left 20.8.43 Taihoku
291	Lightowler. D.	Gnr	Died 5.11.43
292	Limb. R.	Gnr	Left 8.11.43 Taihoku
293	Lindley. F.S.	Gnr	Died 16.5.45
294	Lindsay. J.N.R.	Gnr	Left 20.8.43 Shirakowa
295	Livingstone. A.	Gnr	Left 21.2.45
296	Lockhead. S.	L/Sgt	*
297	Lowing. F.S.	Gnr	Left 20.8.43 Taihoku

298	Lowther. C.S.	BSM	Left 21.2.45
299	Lowther. M.	Gnr	Left 20.8.43 Taihoku
300	Lunness. L.	Sgt	Left 21.2.45
301	Macauslan. J.	RQMS	Left 13.11.34 Heito
302	Mackenzie. J.	Capt	Left 20.8.43 Shirakowa
303	Mackie. R.	Gnr	Left 31.5.45
304	Mian. T.	Gnr	*
305	Manley. H.	Gnr	Left 20.8.43 Taihoku
306	Markham. W.	Gnr	Left 20.8.43 (Died)
307	Marriott. J.	Gnr	Left 20.8.43 Taihoku
308	Marshall. J.M.	Gnr	*
309	Marshall. W.	Sigmn	Left 20.8.43 Taihoku
310	Marson. J.	Gnr	Left 8.11.43 Taihoku
311	Martin. A.W.	Gnr	Left 21.2.45
312	Martin. A.A.	Gnr	Left 20.8.43 Taihoku
313	Martin. W.J.	Sgt	Left 21.2.45
314	Mather. J.	Bdr	Left 25.10.44 Kagi
315	Mathewson. J.	Gnr	Left 20.8.43 Taihoku
316	McAdam. R.A.	Pte	Left 30.3.45 Taihoku
317	McAllister. J.	Gnr	*
318	McAusland. J.M.	Sgt	Left 20.8.43 Shirakowa
319	McCallum. D.	Gnr	Left 13.11.43 Heito
320	McCallum. J.W.	Gnr	Left 8.11.43 Taihoku
321	McCartney. J.	Gnr	Left 13.11.43 Heito
322	McCredie. W.	Gnr	Left 13.11.43 Taihoku
323	McCutcheon. J.	Gnr	Left 22.3.45 Shirakowa
324	McDill. W.	L/Bdr	Left 20.8.43 Taihoku
325	McEwan. J.	Gnr	*
326	McGhie. F.D.S.	Gnr	Left 21.2.45
327	McGhie. R.G.	Gnr	Left 21.2.45
328	McGill. A.	Gnr	Left 21.2.45
329	McGuinness. J.L.	Gnr	Left 21.2.45
330	McIntosh. A.	Sigmn	Left 20.8.43 Taihoku
331	McIntyre. T.	Gnr	Left 13.11.43 Heito
332	McKay. H.	Gnr	Left 20.8.43 Taihoku
333	McKew. F.	Bdr	Died 2.12.42
334	McKnight. J.B.	Lieut	Left 20.8.43 Shirakowa
335	McLean. A.	Gnr	Left 20.8.43 Taihoku
336	McLean. I.G.	Lieut	Left 20.8.43 Shirakowa
337	McLean. J.	Gnr	Left 13.11.43 Heito
338	McLeod. J.A.	Gnr	Left 25.10.44 Kagi
339	McLoughlin. M.G.	L/Cpl	*
340	McPhail. A.	Sgt	*

341	Medlock. A.	Gnr	Left 8.11.43 Taihoku
342	Melrose. R.G.	Gnr	Left 21.2.45
343	Merridan. A.T.	Gnr	Left 21.2.45
344	Miles. R.T.	L/Sgt	Left 6.12.44 Taihoku
345	Millership. H.	Gnr	Killed 1.2.43 in mine
346	Milne. W.	Gnr	*
347	Mitchell. O.B.	Sgt	*
348	Mitchell. H.	Bdr	Left 20.8.43 Shirakowa
349	Money. F.T.	Gnr	Left 20.8.43 Taihoku
350	Moorhouse. F.	Gnr	*
351	Moran. J.	Gnr	Died 7.4.43
352	Morley. W.J.	Gnr	Left 22.3.45 Shirakowa
353	Morris. E.J.	Sigmn	*
354	Morrison. D.O.	Gnr	Left 21.2.45 Shirakowa
355	Motley. R.A.H.	L/Bdr	Left 20.8.43 Shirakowa
356	Mouland. C.H.	L/Sgt	Left 21.2.45
357	Muir. W.	Gnr	*
358	Mulliner. E.	Sgmn	Left 20.8.43 Shirakowa
359	Murgatroyd. J.	Sgt	*
360	Murphy. J.J.	Gnr	*
361	Myson. E.	Gnr	Left 20.8.43 Shirakowa
362	Napier. W.E.S.	Lt.Col.	Left 20.8.43 Shirakowa
363	Nash. R.S.	Gnr	Left 21.2.45
364	Norbury. F.	Bdr	*
365	Notley. W.R.	Gnr	Left 21.2.45
366	Offord. F.	Pte	Died 9.3.43
367	Ogden. J.A.	Gnr	*
368	Olsen. S.	Gnr	Left 8.11.43 Taihoku
369	Ostler. J.A.	Gnr	*
370	Pannell. G.	Gnr	Left 20.8.43 Taihoku
371	Parry. G.	Sgt	Left 20.8.43 Taihoku
372	Parsons. S.F.	Gnr	Left 21.2.45
373	Paterson. J.	Gnr	*
374	Paterson. W.J.	Bdr	*
375	Paterson. I.	L/Cpl	Died 12.2.43
376	Peacock. T.W.	L/Sgt	*
377	Pedley. I.C.	Major	Left 20.8.43 Taihoku
378	Pelling. J.A.S.	Bdr	Left 25.10.44 Kagi
379	Perman. G.	L/Bdr	Left 20.8.43 Taihoku
380	Pestell. J.G.	Gnr	Died 22.2.43
381	Peters. C.V.	L/Sgt	*
382	Pett. K.E.	Gnr	*
383	Philipps. J.	Bdr	Left 25.10.44 Kagi

384	Pickles. S.	Gnr	Died 24.1.45
385	Plumridge. L.	Gnr	Left 21.2.43
386	Popple. C.	L/Bdr	*
387	Porteous. P.B.	Lieut	Left 20.8.43 Shirakowa
388	Powell. J.	Gnr	Died 25.11.43
389	Pryke. A.G.	L/Bdr	Left 25.10.44 Kagi
390	Puckering. L.V.	Bdr	Left 13.11.43 Heito
391	Rae. H.	Gnr	Left 25.10.44 (Died)
392	Ramsay. S.	Gnr	Died 21.1.43
393	Rankin. C.	Sgmn	*
394	Rawlingson. W.H.	Gnr	Left 8.11.43 Taihoku
395	Reid. G.	Gnr	Left 20.8.43 Taihoku
396	Readman. W.	Gnr	Left 8.11.43 Taihoku
397	Reeve. H.	Gnr	Left 20.8.43 Taihoku
398	Roberts. A.	Sgmn	Left 20.8.43 Shirakowa
399	Roberts. E.W.	L/Bdr	Left 30.3.45
400	Ronaldson. P.H.D.	Lieut	Died 9.1.43
401	Rook. F.W.	Capt	Left 21.2.45
402	Ross. W.	Gnr	Left 21.2.45
403	Rossiter. T.	Gnr	Left 22.3.45 Shirakowa
404	Rowney. W.T.	Gnr	*
405	Ryder. T.	Gnr	Left 20.8.43 Taihoku
406	Sams. R.J.	Gnr	Left 20.8.43 Taihoku
407	Sanderson. G.B.	Major	Left 20.8.43 Shirakowa
408	Sanderson. W.	Gnr	Left 20.8.43 Taihoku
409	Sargent. A.G.	BSM	Left 8.11.43 Taihoku
410	Savage. L.V.	Cpl	Left 21.2.45
411	Scarborough. E.	L/Sgt	Left 21.2.45
412	Scott. G.	Gnr	Left 8.11.43 Taihoku
413	Scott. J.	Gnr	Left 22.3.45 Taihoku
414	Scott. J.	Gnr	Left 25.10.44 Kagi
415	Scott. W.	Gnr	*
416	Scullion. P.	RSM	Left 13.11.43 Heito
417	Sears. F.	Gnr	Left 21.2.45
418	Seed. P.G.	Capt	Left 22.3.45 Shirakowa
419	Sephton. R.	Sgt	Left 25.10.44 Kagi
420	Sewell. E.R.A.	Capt	Left 22.8.43 Shirakowa
421	Shaw. J.	Sgt	Died 16.12.42
422	Sheldrick. E.F.	Sgmn	Left 21.2.45
423	Shelvey. D.A.	BSM	Left 21.2.45
424	Shephard. R.A.	L/Sgt	*
425	Shephard. E.	Gnr	*
426	Shepherd. E.	Gnr	Left 20.8.43 Shirakowa

427	Shields. W.	Gnr	Left 21.2.45
428	Shipley. L.C.	Gnr	Left 30.3.45
429	Sibley. N.A.H.	Bdr	Left 13.11.43 Heito
430	Sim. J.D.	Gnr	Left 20.8.43 Taihoku
431	Slater. W.	Gnr	*
432	Smith. A.	Gnr	Left 8.11.43 Taihoku
433	Smith. D.D.	Lieut	Left 21.2.45
434	Smith. G.H.W.	Sgmn	Left 20.8.43 Shirakowa
435	Smith. H.	Gnr	Died 24.8.43
436	Smith. J.	L/Bdr	*
437	Smith. J.M.M.	Gnr	*
438	Sorrell. P.	Gnr	Left 13.11.43 Heito
439	Southerton. H.H.	Gnr	*
440	Speed. H.	Bdr	Left 20.8.43 Taihoku
441	Spooner. R.	Gnr	Left 13.11.43 Heito
442	Spurrier. A.W.	Gnr	Left 8.11.43 Taihoku
443	Stanhope. T.E.	Gnr	Left 20.8.43 Shirakowa
444	Stevenson. J.D.McK	Bdr	*
445	Stevenson. W.	Gnr	Left 13.11.43 Heito
446	Stewart. G.M.	Major	Left 20.8.43 Shirakowa
447	Stewart. J.H.F.	Capt	Left 20.3.45 Shirakowa
448	Stockford. R.	Gnr	Left 20.8.43 Taihoku
449	Stone. S.D.J.	Gnr	Left 8.11.43 Taihoku
450	Strong. C.C.	L/Bdr	*
451	Swan. G.E.	Gnr	Left 22.3. 45 Shirakowa
452	Swan. W.	Gnr	Left 13.11.43 Heito
453	Sweeney. D.	Gnr	Killed 18.8.43 in Mine
454	Sweeney. T.A.	Gnr	Left 21.2.45
455	Tabeart. F.	Capt	Left 20.8.43 Shirakowa
456	Tait. J.	Sgt	Left 13.11.43 Heito
457	Taylor. J.	Gnr	Left 20.8.43 Taihoku
458	Taylor. L.V.	Gnr	Left 20.8.43 Taihoku
459	Telfer. J.M.	Sgmn	Left 21.2.45
460	Terry. E.	Gnr	Left 21.2.45
461	Thackaberry. G.	Gnr	*
462	Thomas. F.	Sgt	Left 30.3.45
463	Thompson. R.	L/Bdr	Left 20.8.43 Taihoku
464	Thompson. R.W.	Gnr	Left 20.8.43 Taihoku
465	Thornton. J.E.	Gnr	Left 25.10.44 Kagi
466	Titherington. T.A.	Sgmn	*
467	Topping. K.G.	Gnr	Left 20.8.43 Taihoku
468	Topping. J.	Gnr	Died 8.2.43
469	Tough. R.	L/Bdr	Left 20.8.43 Taihoku

470	Townley. W.	Gnr	Left 20.8.43 Taihoku
471	Travis. N.S.	L/Bdr	Left 22.3.45 Shirakowa
472	Trim. J.J.	Gnr	Left 20.8.43 Taihoku
473	Tuck. S.H.	Gnr	Left 25.10.44 Shirakowa
474	Turner. J.	Gnr	Left 8.11.43 Taihoku
475	Turner. M.	Gnr	Left 20.8.43 Taihoku
476	Tuthill. G.W.T.	Gnr	*
477	Vacher. G.W.	Gnr	Left 30.3.45
478	Vacher. W.M.	L/Bdr	*
479	Vanstone. R.H.	Gnr	Left 8.11.43 Taihoku
480	Vere. A.	Gnr	Left 25.10.44 Shirakowa
481	Viccars. J.V.	L/Bdr	*
482	Waldron. T.	Gnr	Left 8.11.43 Taihoku
483	Walker. A.	Gnr	*
484	Walker. W.	W/Ol	Left 13.11.43 Heito
485	Wallace. T.	L/Bdr	*
486	Walsh. H.	Gnr	Left 20.8.43 Taihoku
487	Ward. E.	Gnr	Left 20.8.43 Taihoku
488	Ward. T.B.	Gnr	*
489	Warner. J.	Gnr	Left 20.8.43 Taihoku
490	Warnock. H.	Gnr	Died 19.12.42
491	Warwick. R.D.	Sgt	Left 21.2.45
492	Watson. A.	Gnr	Left 20.8.43 Taihoku
493	Watson. B.	Gnr	Left 13.11.43 Heito
494	Watson. J.L.	Sgt	Left 22.3.45
495	Watson. T.	Sigmn	*
496	Waugh. J.D.	Sgt	Left 21.2.45
497	Wearing. G.W.	Gnr	*
498	Wearing. T.S.	Gnr	Died 14.12.42
499	Weedall. E.	Gnr	Left 20.8.43 Taihoku
500	Weighill. F.	RQMS	Died 18.2.43
501	Wheeler. A.F.	Sgt	Left 20.8.43 Taihoku
502	Whitbread. R.L.	Gnr	*
503	White. C.F.	Gnr	Died 25.1.45
504	White. C.J.	Gnr	Left 8.11.43 Taihoku
505	White. G.	Gnr	Left 8.11.43 Taihoku
506	White. J.G.	L/Bdr	Left 21.2.45
507	Whitehead. H.	Gnr	Left 31.2.45
508	Whitehead. J.	Gnr	Left 20.8.43 Taihoku
509	Whitfield. G.H.	Pte	*
510	Williams. A.M.	Gnr	Died 24.10.43
511	Williams. D.	Gnr	Left 20.8.43 Taihoku
512	Williams. E.	Gnr	Left 21.2.45 Taihoku

513	Williams. G.H.	Gnr	*
514	Williams. K.	Gnr	Left 20.8.43 Taihoku
515	Williamson. W.B.	Gnr	*
516	Wilson. B.	Gnr	Left 20.8.43 Taihoku
517	Wilson. S.W.	Gnr	Left 20.8.43 Taihoku
518	Wiseman. J.	Gnr	Left 20.8.43 Taihoku
519	Wright. G.R.	L/Bdr	Left 20.8.43 Taihoku
520	Wylie. T.	Gnr	*
521	Wyllie. J.S.	BQMS	Left 8.11.43 Taihoku
522	Wyllie. T.C.	Bdr	*
523	Pereira. F.P.	Pte	Left 22.3.45 Shirakowa
524	Hunter. G.	L/Sgt	Left 21.2.45
525	Bayliss.	L/Cpl	Left 20.8.43 Taihoku
526	Corp. J.	L/Cpl	*
527	Davies. T.J.	L/Cpl	*
528	Emmett. J.H.	L/Cpl	*
529	Bailey. A.	Pte	Left 21.2.45
530	Baillie.	Pte	Left 8.11.43 Taihoku
531	Baxter. B.	Pte	*
532	Bird. H.	Pte	Left 8.11.43 Taihoku
533	Bolton. P.	Gnr	*
534	Buckley.	Pte	Left 8.11.43 Taihoku
535	Coverdale. C.	Pte	*
536	Dootson. J.	Tpr	Left 21.2.45
537	Grimlley. L.	Pte	*
538	Leggett. B.E.	Pte	Killed food drop 29.8.45
539	Morgan.		Left 20.8.43 Taihoku
540	New. G.	Gnr	Left 22.3.45 (Died)
541	Parkins. J.	Pte	Left 21.2.45
542	Pounder.	Pte	Left 8.11.43 Taihoku
543	Quinn. D.	Pte	*
544	Reynolds. R.	Pte	*
545	Rigby. R.E.P.	Pte	Died 13.8.43
546	Rowland. M.S.	Tpr	Left 6.12.44 Taihoku
547	Spurr. T.	Pte	*
548	Stafford.	Pte	Left 8.11.43 Taihoku
549	Wilson. R.	L/Cpl	*
550	Winstanley. J.A.		Left 22.3.45 Shirakowa
551	Turner.		Left 20.8.43 Taihoku
552	Wright. J.T.	Gnr	Left 21.2.45
553	Yore.	Pte	Left 8.11.43 Taihoku
554	Young. R.	Pte	Left 21.2.45
555	Donnelly. D.H.	Cpl	*

556	Parker. T.	Pte	Left 22.3.45 Shirakowa
557	Thompson. J.	Pte	*
558	Archer. W.	Gnr	Left 6.12.44 Taihoku
559	Ashley. H.	Sgmn	Left 25.10.44 Kagi
560	Ayscough. W.A.	Gnr	Left 21.2.45
561	Baker. J.	Sgmn	Left 30.3.45 Taihoku
562	Barratt. W.	Sgmn	*
563	Barrow. A.	Bdr	Killed in mine 26.1.44
564	Bean. L.W.	CSM	Left 21.2.45
565	Beeby. E.A.	Gnr	Left 31.5.45
566	Benfield. G.	Sgmn	Left 6.12.44 Taihoku
567	Birtwistle. G.E.	Gnr	*
568	Bishop. E.A.	L/Sgt	*
569	Bishop.	R.S.M.	Left 13.11.43 Heito
570	Blackham. H.G.	L/Sgt	Left 21.2.45
571	Bosi. I.	Sgmn	*
572	Bowkett. H.Y.	Cpl	*
573	Bradley. H.M.	Sgmn	Mine Death 11.10.44
574	Bramford.	L/Cpl	Left 13.11.43 Heito
575	Brompton. D.F.	Sgmn	Left 30.3.45
576	Browell. J.	Sgmn	Left 30.3.45
577	Bruton. S.F.	CQMS	Left 21.3.45
578	Carter. C.F.	Gnr	*
579	Campbell. G.	L/Cpl	Left 21.2.45
580	Catton. J.	Gnr	*
581	Carson. J.	Bdr	Left 13.11.43 Taihoku
582	Carter. A.J.	Sgmn	Left 25.10.44 Kagi
583	Cassidy. D.	Gnr	Left 21.2.45
584	Clarke. E.A.	Gnr	*
585	Collins. J.M.	Gnr	Left 6.12.44 Taihoku
586	Collingwood. W.	Gnr	Left 22.3.45 Shirakowa
587	Cornthwaite. J.	Gnr	*
588	Coouper. J.P.D.	Sgmn	*
589	Cripps. R.E.	L/Bdr	*
590	Crocker. W.S.	Gnr	*
591	Curry. W.	Pte	*
592	Cutler. B.I.	Gnr	Left 21.2.45
593	Daley. C.	Gnr	*
594	D'arcy. G.R.	L/Bdr	Left 22.3.45 Shirakowa
595	Dare.	Gnr	Left 13.11.43 Heito
596	Davies. L.J.	Gnr	*
597	Deegan. M.	CQMS	*
598	Edwards. R.	Sgmn	*

599	Elliott. A.T.	L/Sgt	Left 25.10.44 Kagi
600	Essay. N.I.T.	Sgmn	Left 21.2.45
601	Ewing. A.C.	Sgmn	*
602	Finn. W.H.H.	Gnr	Left 21.2.45
603	Foster. A.J.	Gnr	*
604	Gettie. J.	Gnr	*
605	Gibbons. J.	Sgmn	Left 25.10.44 Kagi
606	Gill. J.M.	Gnr	*
607	Guest. W.	L/Bdr	*
608	Harrison. G.W.	L/Bdr	*
609	Hayde. W.E.	Sgmn	Died 14.1.44
610	Haynes. W.F.	L/Bdr	Left 22.3.45 Shirakowa
611	Henderson. G.	Sgmn	Left 25.10.44 Kagi
612	Hill. W.L.	Gnr	Left 21.2.45
613	Holmes. F.	L/Cpl	*
614	Holmes.	Gnr	Left 13.11.43 Heito
615	Howe. J.T.	Gnr	Killed food drop 29.8.45
616	Hunt. C.S.	Cpl	Left 21.2.45
617	Irvine. J.S.	Gnr	Left 21.2.45
618	James. J.W.	CQMS	Left 30.3.45 Taihoku
619	Ker. T.McD.	Bdr	Left 6.12.44 Taihoku
620	Kingate. W.	Gnr	Left 21.2.45
621	Marshall. J.C.	Gnr	Left 21.2.45
622	May. F.W.	Bdr	Left 21.2.45
623	May. R.	Gnr	*
624	McGill. R.	Gnr	Left 21.2.45
625	Miller. J.	Gnr	*
626	Molyneaux	Sgmn	Left 3.11.43
627	Morgan. S.L.	Gnr	Left 6.12.44 Died
628	Moule. B.J.	L/Bdr	*
629	Mrirhead. J.E.	Gnr	Left 21.2.45
630	Newman. W.T.	Sgmn	Left 21.2.45
631	Noble. W.A.	Bdr	Left 25.10.44 Kagi
632	Oaff. L.S.	L/Bdr	Left 25.10.44 Kagi
633	O'Toole. T.F.	Sgt	Left 6.12.44 Taihoku
634	Painter. F.	Gnr	*
635	Perrett. F.J.	BQMS	*
636	Perry. C.	Gnr	Left 22.3.45 Shirakowa
637	Perrin. J.H.	L/Bdr	*
638	Pullinger. C.A.	Sgt	Killed in mine 25.11.43
639	Ratcliffe. D.W.	Gnr	*
640	Reynolds. G.H.	Bdr	Left 22.3.45 Shirakowa
641	Richards. M.F.	Gnr	Left 21.2.45

642	Ritchings. J.D.	Bdr	Left 22.3.45 Shirakowa
643	Rivers. E.	Gmn	Left 25.10.44 Kagi
644	Roberts. J.	Gnr	Left 30.3.45 Taihoku
645	Robinson. T.F.J.	Gnr	Left 25.10.44 Kagi
646	Rogers. W.J.	Sgt	Left 21.2.45
647	Ross. R.W.	Gnr	Left 21.2.45
648	Rotherforth. F.	L/Bdr	Left 21.2.45
649	Russell. D.	L/Bdr	Left 21.2.45
650	Scargill. J.C.	Gnr	*
651	Scott. L.G.	Cpl	Left 25.10.44 Kagi
652	Scriven. R.G.	Gnr	Left 13.11.43 Heito
653	Shorto. W.K.	Sgmn	Left 25.10.44 Kagi
654	Simpson. A.J.	Sgmn	Left 30.3.45
655	Slater. C.	Sgmn	Died 8.12.43
656	Stone. J.	Gnr	*
657	Stratford.	Sgmn	Left 13.11.43 Heito
658	Telford. J.	Gnr	Left 21.2.45
659	Thomas. R.N.	BSM	Left 22.3.45 Shirakowa
660	Tufrey. R.W.	L/Cpl	Left 21.2.45
661	Walker. J.	Sgmn	*
662	Wallace. R.	Sgmn	Died 25.1.45
663	Ward. R.V.	L/Bdr	*
664	Warwick. W.F.C.	Sgmn	Left 25.10.44 Kagi
665	Watson. M.	Sgmn	*
666	Webber. S.A.	Sgmn	Left 30.3.45
667	Webster. G.W.	Sgmn	*
668	Wersby. L.	Gnr	Left 25.10.44 Kagi
669	West. H.	Sgmn	Died 13.1.45
670	Wheatley. T.	Gnr	Left 25.10.44 Kagi
671	Wheeler. B.M.	Major	Left 22.3.45 Shirakowa
672	Whyatt. J.C.	Gnr	*
673	Willders. L.S.	L/Bdr	*
674	Wilson. M.W.	Gnr	Left 21.2.45
675	Wilson. W.	Gnr	*
676	Winder. R.	Sgmn	*
677	Woodburn. E.B.	Cpl	*
678	Yeats.	Sgmn	Left 13.11.43 Heito
679	Birks. E.	CSM	Left 21.2.45
680	Cameron. A.	Sgt	Left 22.3.45 Shirakowa
681	Duell. A.E.	L/Sgt	Died 29.12.44
682	Lowndes. G.L.	Sgt	Left 22.3.45 Shirakowa
683	Parkes. J.	L/Sgt	Left 25.10.44 Kagi
684	Pearson. L.	Sgt	*

685	Pickles. T.A.	L/Sgt	Left 25.10.44 Kagi
686	Slack. B.	L/Sgt	Left 22.3.45 Shirakowa
687	Woodage. P.D.	Sgt	Left 21.2.45
688	Aspinall. J.	Cpl	Left 25.10.44 Kagi
689	Barry. J.	Bdr	*
690	Bell. G.H.G.	Bdr	Left 25.10.44 Kagi
691	Bemstead. F.W.	Cpl	*
692	Dorse. J.G.	Cpl	Left 22.3.45 Shirakowa
693	Locke. J.A.	Cpl	*
694	McFarlane. W.G.	Bdr	*
695	Simpson. J.S.	Cpl	Left 30.3.45 Taihoku
696	Wildinson. J.P.	Cpl	*
697	Durrant. E.	L/Cpl	*
698	Gee. J.A.	L/Bdr	Left 22.3.45 Shirakowa
699	Hockley. D.G.	L/Cpl	Left 25.10.44 Kagi
700	King. G.	L/Cpl	*
701	Kingston. C.	L/Cpl	Left 21.2.45
702	McFarlane. A.	L/Cpl	*
703	McLernon.	L/Bdr	*
704	McLoughlin. S.	L/Cpl	Left 21.2.45
705	Smith. A.	L/Cpl	Died 18.5.44
706	Street. A.S.	L/Bdr	Left 21.2.45
707	Turnbull. P.	L/Bdr	Left 22.3.45 Shirakowa
708	Whittall. A.	L/Cpl	Left 21.2.45
709	Adcock. R.	Gnr	Left 21.2.45
710	Aldred. D.	Pte	Left 25.10.44 Kagi
711	Allen. F.J.	Tpr	Left 25.10.44 Kagi
712	Auger. H.W.	Gnr	Left 21.2.45
713	Baker. F.W.	Gnr	Left 6.12.44 Taihoku
714	Bamsey. A.E.J.	Pte	*
715	Barnes. J.	Pte	*
716	Beresford.	Pte	Left 13.11.43 Heito
717	Bridges. W.A.	Pte	*
718	Burch. E.P.H.	Spr	Left 21.2.45
719	Byford. L.E.	Pte	Died 21.9.44
720	Chambers. W.E.	Gnr	Left 22.3.45 Shirakowa
721	Clark. K.G.	Gnr	Died 19.12.44
722	Cloeman. P.	Gnr	*
723	Darby. B.D.	Spr	Left 22.3.45 Shirakowa
724	Davison. G.	Fus	Died 4.3.45
725	Day.	Gnr	Left 13.11.43 Heito
726	Denyer. H.R.	Pte	Left 21.2.45
727	Dixon. J.P.	Spr	Left 21.2.45

728	Down H.F.	Spr	Left 21.2.45
729	Eardley. L.	Gnr	Left 30.3.45 Taihoku
730	East. E.J.	Gnr	*
731	Eldridge. W.H.	Gnr	*
732	Fletcher. J.W.	Pte	Left 22.3.45 Shirakowa
733	Fowler. J.V.	Pte	Left 22.3.45 Shirakowa
734	Greenwood. S.	Pte	*
735	Grubb. C.	Pte	Left 21.2.45
736	Harrison. L.R.	Gnr	Left 25.10.44 Kagi
737	Hart. L.J.	Gnr	Left 21.2.45
738	Higgins. A.	Gnr	*
739	Hill. D.	Gnr	Died 3.4.44
740	Hill. J.R.	Spr	*
741	Hooper. R.J.	Spr	Left 21.2.45
742	Jackson. A.	Spr	Left 22.3.45 Shirakowa
743	Jones. L.B.	Gnr	*
744	Kelly. R.	Gnr	*
745	Kerr. A.R.	Pte	Died
746	King. E.	Gnr	*
747	Lawton. A.	Spr	*
748	Marshall. A.C.	Pte	*
749	McAlpine. G.	Spr	*
750	McArthur. J.	Pte	*
751	Miller. M.G.	Spr	Left 21.2.45
752	Moushi. A.O.	Gnr	Died 8.12.43
753	Mulrainey. T.	Gnr	*
754	Murray. J.	Gnr	Left 21.2.45
755	Owens. W.	Spr	*
756	Parkes. L.R.	Spr	*
757	Payne. H.G.	Spr	Left 22.3.45 Shirakowa
758	Peach. W.	Pte	Left 30.3.45 Taihoku
759	Prescott. J.	Pte	*
760	Preston. D.	Pte	*
761	Randall. E.J.	Spr	Left 22.3.45 Shirakowa
762	Rawsthorne. J.	Tpr	*
763	Richardson. E.E.	L/Cpl	*
764	Riley. L.	Pte	Left 30.3.45 Taihoku
765	Roe. C.F.	Pte	Left 21.2.45
766	Rooney. M.A.	Spr	*
767	See. A.H.	Pte	Left 25.10.44 Kagi
768	Sillett. F.G.	Spr	*
769	Southgate. W.G.	Pte	Died 18.3.45
770	Stevenson. R.	Pte	*

771	Strongie. J.	Pte	*
772	Togher. J.	Gnr	Left 21.2.45
773	Upton. R.E.	Spr	*
774	Watson. G.	Spr	Left 6.12.44 Taihoku
775	Watts. A.P.	Pte	*
776	Wood. J.	Spr	Left 22.3.45 Shirakowa
777	Woods. A.	Pte	Left 25.10.44 Kagi
778	Young. J.	Pte	Left 21.2.45
779	Allen. R.	L/cpl	*
780	Atkins. J.A.	Gnr	Left 21.2.45
781	Bagnall. A.W.J.	Spr	*
782	Baker. H.	Gnr	Left 8.11.43 Taihoku
783	Bannister. H.	L/Cpl	*
784	Barlow. E.	Gnr	Left 22.3.45 Kagi
785	Bailey. T.W.	Pte	Left 22.3.45 Shirakowa
786	Beardsworth. B.	Pte	Killed food drop 28.8.45
787	Bennett. H.	Pte	Died 10.1.45
788	Black W.A.	Pte	Left 21.2.45
789	Blease. H.	Pte	Left 22.3.45 Shirakowa
790	Blowers. J.W.	Pte	*
791	Bodell. W.	L/Cpl	Left 25.10.44 Kagi
792	Bortoft. J.	Pte	*
793	Broome. N.J.	Cpl	*
794	Brown. J.	Tpr	Left 22.3.45 Shirakowa
795	Butters. W.J.	Pte	*
796	Carter. A.W.	Pte	Left 25.10.44 Kagi
797	Carter. E.	Pte	*
798	Cheeseborough. F.	Gnr	Left 25.10.44 Kagi
799	Cherry. H.G.	L/Sgt	*
800	Claridge. S.	Pte	Died 8.2.44
801	Condon. W.	Sgt	Left 21.2.45
802	Cooper. H.	Pte	Left 25.10.44 Kagi
803	Copping. R.	Pte	*
804	Corfield. D.	Tpr	Left 21.2.45
805	Cox. J.W.	Gnr	Left 21.2.45
806	Daulby. W.	L/Cpl	Left 21.2.45
807	Dennison. C.		Left 13.11.43 Heito
808	Derbyshire. W.	Tpr	Left 21.2.45
809	Dougan. M.	Pte	*
810	Dunn. J.	Marine	Killed in mine 22.6.44
811	Forbes. J.M.	Pte	Left 21.2.45
812	Fossey. H.	Pte	*
813	Gallagher. M.F.	L/Cpl	Left 25.10.44 Kagi

814	Goldring. A.	Gnr	Left 22.3.45 Shirakowa
815	Griffiths. T.H.	Cpl	Left 22.3.45 Shirakowa
816	Hayles. H.W.	Cpl	Left 25.10.44 Kagi
817	Hansard. G.W.	Pte	*
818	Hardwick J.E.	L/Cpl	Left 30.3.45 Taihoku
819	Heathcote. W.R.	L/Cpl	Left 30.3.45 Taihoku
820	Hickman. E.	Gnr	*
821	Hillditch. H.	Pte	Left 21.2.45
822	Hiscock. G.	L/Cpl	Left 22.3.45 Shirakowa
823	Hitchen. L.T.	Cpl	*
824	Horsfall. G.	Gnr	Left 21.2.45
825	Housego. E.C.G.	Pte	Left 25.10.45 Kagi
826	Hughes. T.A.	L/Cpl	Left 21.10.44
827	Hume. A.	Pte	*
828	Hynes. J.	Pte	Left 22.3.45 Shirakowa
829	Fletcher. J.	Cpl	*
830	Ingram. J.	Pte	*
831	James. N.	Pte	Left 22.3.45 Shirakowa
832	Jones. H.	Bdr	Left 25.10.44 Kagi
833	Kinniburgh. R.S.	Sgmn	*
834	Kirk. F.	Pte	Left 22.3.45 Shirakowa
835	Knight. C.R.	L/Cpl	Left 8.11.43 Taihoku
836	Knight. R.	L/Cpl	*
837	Lamb. J.B.	L/Bdr	Died
838	Langridge. C.H.E.	Gnr	Left 21.2.45
839	Lawrance. R.H.	L/Cpl	*
840	Livingstone. S.	Pte	*
841	Loskey		Left 8.11.43 Taihoku
842	Lovett. H.	L/Cpl	Left 30.3.45 Taihoku
843	Luck. J.	Gnr	Left 13.11.43 Heito
844	Martin. A.	L/Sgt	Left 22.3.45 Shirakowa
845	McGregor.J.	L/Cpl	Died 4.11.44
846	McShane. W.	Pte	Left 21.2.45
847	Millman. W.	L/Cpl	Left 21.2.45
848	Mills. G.	Pte	Left 21.2.45
849	Milne. R.	L/Cpl	Died 22.8.45
850	Morris. G.W.	Pte	Left 30.3.45 Taihoku
851	Nash. W.	L/Sgt	Left 21.2.45
852	Oldham. N.	Gnr	*
853	Oswin		Left 13.11.43
854	Perkins. A.	Pte	*
855	Pollard. E.E.	Sgmn	Left 25.10.44 Kagi
856	Poole. A.J.	Pte	Left 13.11.43 Heito

857	Porter. E.	Pte	Left 22.3.45 Shirakowa
858	Presland. W.J.	Pte	Left 21.2.45
859	Roast. G.E.	Gnr	*
860	Robertson. W.A.	Pte	Left 21.2.45
861	Robinson. A.	Pte	*
862	Seaton. A.J.	Spr	Left 30.3.45 Taihoku
863	Shearer. A.J.B.	Gnr	*
864	Singleton. W.	Gnr	Killed in mine 22.6.44
865	Soutar. W.	Gnr	Left 22.3.45 Shirakowa
866	Stalham. C.W.	Pte	Left 21.2.45
867	Street. T.	Pte	*
868	Swindlehurst. J.	Sgmn	Left 21.2.45
869	Taffs. F.	SA	Left 6.12.44 Taihoku
870	Tiffney. D.	Gnr	Left 25.10.44 Kagi
871	Tonne. A.F.	Pte	Left 21.2.45
872	Tracey. A.A.	Spr	Died 13.1.45
873	Wallwork. A.	Pte	Left 25.10.44 Kagi
874	Waring. H.	Spr	Left 25.10.44 Kagi
875	Wilson. H.	Gnr	*
876	Winsper. H.V.	Pte	Left 22.3.45 Shirakowa
877	Worthington. J.	Gnr	Left 21.2.45
878	Wragg. J.A.	Gnr	Left 21.2.45
879	Armstrong. P.	Gnr	*
880	Avins. H.	Gnr	Left 21.2.45
881	Bird. C.H.C.	L/Bdr	*
882	Bradburn. R.	Sgmn	Died 18.10.44
883	Bradlley. F.	Sgmn	Died 11.10.44
884	Brant. H.J.	L/Cpl	Left 21.2.45
885	Brewster. F.J.T.	L/Cpl	*
886	Burton. J.	Cpl	Died 10.1.45
887	Casey. J.	Gnr	Left 25.10.44 Kagi
888	Clark. R.C.	Gnr	Left 25.10.44 Kagi
889	Colton. J.J.	Gnr	*
890	Croucher. A.E.	Sgmn	Left 21.2.45
891	Crummy. G.A.	Sgmn	*
892	Dibble. A.H.	BSM	Left 21.2.45
893	Earley. J.	Gnr	Left 25.10.44 Kagi
894	Foster. P.	Sgmn	Left 21.2.45
895	Goodwin. A.J.	Gnr	*
896	Harding. J.	Gnr	*
897	Hewitson. J.H.	L/Cpl	Left 21.2.45
898	Hill. P.S.W.	Gnr	Left 21.2.45
899	Hitchen. F.B.	L/Bdr	Left 22.3.45 Shirakowa

900	Humphries. A.	Gnr	Left 25.10.45 Kagi
901	Jones. A.E.	L/Cpl	Left 21.2.45
902	Leadbeatter. A.J.	L/Bdr	Died 18.11.44
903	Linton. L.A.	Sgmn	Left 25.10.44 Kagi
904	McCoy. P.J.	Gnr	Left 21.2.45
905	McKay. J.L.	Gnr	Left 22.3.45 Shirakowa
906	McKay. G.	Sgmn	Left 25.10.44 Kagi
907	Mathews. A.R.	Sgmn	Left 25.10.44 Kagi
908	Maynard. A.H.	L/Bdr	Left 21.2.45
909	Neale. R.E.	L/Cpl	Left 21.2.45
910	Pester. A.E.	Sgmn	Left 21.2.45
911	Percy. E.T.T.	Gnr	Left 6.12.44 Taihoku
912	Quilter. G.C.	Bdr	Left 21.2.45
913	Roberts. T.E.	Sgmn	*
914	Rogers. L.	L/Bdr	Died 3.6.44
915	Rothery. H.	Sgmn	Died 7.5.44
916	Rowlands. F.W.	Sgmn	*
917	Rowe. R.O.	Gnr	Left 25.10.44 Kagi
918	Russell. L.	Gnr	Left 21.2.45
919	Rylatt. G.W.	Sgt	Left 6.12.44 Taihoku
920	Scott. W.	L/Sgt	Left 25.10.44 Kagi
921	Stevenson. J.H.	Sgmn	*
922	Waghorne. A.D.	Gnr	Left 25.10.44 Kagi
923	Walker. A.	Sgmn	Left 21.2.45
924	White. J.A.	Gnr	Left 21.2.45
925	Wood. H.	Sgmn	Left 6.12.44 Taihoku
926	Wood. S.	Sgmn	Left 23.3.45 Shirakowa
927	Wright. F.	Gnr	Left 22.3.45 Shirakowa
928	Young. R.	Sgmn	Left 21.2.45
929	Chapman. G.W.	L/Sgt	Left 22.3.45 Shirakowa
930	Cull. H.J.	L/Sgt	Left 30.3.45 Taihoku
931	Harris. L.J.	Sgt	Left 22.3.45 Shirakowa
932	Haskins. W.J.	L/Sgt	Left 25.10.44 Kagi
933	Chatt. H.	Bdr	*
934	Cox. V.	Cpl	Left 30.3.45 Taihoku
935	Davison. E.	Cpl	Left 21.2.43
936	Hawtin. E.	Cpl	Left 23.3.45 Shirakowa
937	McDonald. W.	Bdr	Died 9.2.45
938	Wilson. B.J.	Cpl	Left 25.10.44 Kagi
939	Daglish. J.G.	L/Bdr	Left 22.3.45 Shirakowa
940	Gibbins. E.	L/Bdr	Left 22.3.45 Shirakowa
941	Hall. A.E.T.	L/Bdr	Left 25.10.44 Kagi
942	Hunt. E.W.	L/Bdr	Left 21.2.45

943	Knight. F.A.W.	L/Bdr	Left 25.10.44 Kagi
944	Amos. R.A.	Gnr	Left 21.2.45
945	Atkinson. F.J.	Pte	*
946	Auty. H.	Tpr	Left 21.2.45
947	Baker. E.J.	Gnr	Left 21.2.45
948	Barford. F.C.	Gnr	Left 21.2.45
949	Barton. E.	Tpr	Left 21.2.45
950	Bastin. R.G.	Gnr	Died 10.3.45
951	Biggin. T.A.	Gnr	Died 24.8.45
952	Clarke. C.E.	Spr	Left 22.3.45 Shirakowa
953	Cooper. E.	Pte	Left 30.3.45 Taihoku
954	Crouthers. A.	Gnr	Left 21.2.45
955	Cullup. L.	Gnr	Killed 10.1.45 in mine
956	Davies. D.B.	Pte	Left 21.2.45
957	Derbyshire. T.	Pte	Left 22.3.45 Shirakowa
958	Dickinson. S.	Spr	Left 25.10.44 Kagi
959	Dodds. S.	Gnr	Left 25.10.44 Kagi
960	Edney. F.R.	Spr	*
961	Ellis. W.	Pte	Left 30.3.45 Taihoku
962	Elwell. I.W.	Gnr	*
963	Evens. A.G.	Pte	Left 30.3.45 Taihoku
964	Fern. G.	Pte	*
965	Findley. J.	Spr	*
966	Garrett. G.	Pte	*
967	Green. C.J.	Spr	Left 21.2.45
968	Gregory. G.E.	Pte	Left 21.2.45
969	Hannan. J.	Spr	*
970	Harrington. S.J.A.	Gnr	Left 25.10.44 Kagi
971	Hennessy. J.J.	Tpr	Left 21.2.45
972	Higgins. J.	Tpr	*
973	Holding. G.	Tpr	Left 21.2.45
974	Howard. R.C.	Spr	Left 21.2.45
975	King. B.G.	Spr	Left 22.3.45 Shirakowa
976	Latham. G.	Pte	*
977	Lay. G.A.	Spr	Left 21.2.45
978	Leslie. K.	Sgmn	*
979	Long. G.E.	Pte	Left 21.2.45
980	Maltby. J.	Pte	Left 21.2.45
981	Marrion. A.W.	Spr	Left 25.10.44 Kagi
982	Marshall. J.R.	Gnr	Left 22.3.45 Shiragawa
983	Middleton. R.	Pte	*
984	Millburn. J.	Gnr	Left 25.10.44 Kagi
985	Moffat. D.F.	Gnr	*

986	Morgan. C.	Spr	Left 21.2.45
987	Mutch. J.	Pte	*
988	Parsons. J.W.	Pte	Left 21.2.45
989	Price. F.R.	Sgmn	Left 30.3.45 Taihoku
990	Rush. M.	Pte	Left 21.2.45
991	Slade. E.	Gnr	*
992	Slater. N.	Spr	Died 1.2.45
993	Spence. F.	Pte	Left 25.10.44 Kagi
994	Stevenson. F.G.	Pte	Left 21.2.45
995	Symonds. F.G.	Spr	Left 25.10.44 Kagi
996	Talbot. V.	Fus	*
997	Teasdale. J.	Gnr	Left 21.2.45
998	Tennant. W.	Gnr	*
999	Walker. T.	Pte	*
1000	Washbrook. C.	Pte	Left 21.2.45
1001	Westacott. J.	Pte	*
1002	Wheatley. W.S.	Gnr	*
1003	Wileman. G.W.	Spr	Left 21.2.45
1004	White. W.	Sgt	Left 21.2.45
1005	Birch. D.E.	Cpl	*
1006	Farbon. R.S.	Bdr	Left 25.10.44 Kagi
1007	Gardener. A.J.	Bdr	*
1008	Greening. J.C.	Bdr	Left 22.3.45 Shirakowa
1009	Harrison. D.W.	Cpl	*
1010	Rawding. E.	Cpl	Left 21.2.45
1011	Stringer. S.G.	Bdr	Left 25.10.44 Kagi
1012	Telfer. W.	Cpl	*
1013	Young. W.L.	Cpl	Left 22.3.45 Shirakowa
1014	Cadley. W.	L/Cpl	Left 30.3.45 Taihoku
1015	Dixon. R.V.	L/Bdr	Left 21.2.45
1016	Garrett. H.S.	L/Cpl	Left 21.2.45
1017	Griffiths. W.	L/Bdr	Left 21.2.45
1018	Hughes. C.	LAC	Left 21.2.45
1019	Roberson. H.S.	L/Cpl	Left 21.2.45
1020	Ross. W.	L/Cpl	*
1021	Tanner. G.R.	L/Bdr	*
1022	Astill. H.	Pte	Left 25.10.44 Kagi
1023	Bagwell. R.	Sgmn	*
1024	Baker. F.	Pte	*
1025	Bentley. F.	Pte	Left 25.10.44 Kagi
1026	Bugg. H.	Pte	*
1027	Butterworth. J.	Pte	Left 22.3.45 Shirakowa
1028	Cooper. W.E.	Pte	Left 21.2.45

1029	Cross. R.	Tpr	*
1030	Davies. J.	Pte	Left 21.2.45
1031	Dick. W.G.	Pte	*
1032	Dobson. J.R.	Pte	Left 25.10.44 Kagi
1033	Ellis. L.J.	Tpr	Left 25.10.44 Kagi
1034	Follon. A.J.	Pte	Left 25.10.44 Kagi
1035	Forham. L.	Pte	Left 25.10.44 Kagi
1036	Foster. G.J.	Sgmn	*
1037	Fox. A.R.	Pte	Died 26.1.45
1038	Franklin. W.G.	Pte	Left 25.10.44 Kagi
1039	Gibbons. H.H.	Pte	Left 21.2.45
1040	Godwin. G.C.	Pte	Left 21.2.45
1041	Gough. J.	Pte	*
1042	Gregory. H.	Pte	Left 21.2.45
1043	Hammersley. R.E.	Pte	Left 21.2.45
1044	Harris. B.	Tpr	Died. 6.12.44
1045	Hills. H.S.	Pte	*
1046	Hindle. C.J.	Spr	Left 21.2.45
1047	Horsler. C.	Pte	*
1048	Kaye. R.	Spr	Died 9.12.43
1049	Keeley. J.H.	Pte	*
1050	Kilbridge. A.E.	Pte	*
1051	Lemmer. L.R.	Pte	*
1052	Lewis. S.J.	Spr	Left 22.3.45 Shirakowa
1053	Mawdsley. F.I.	Gnr	Left 21.2.45
1054	McLaughlin. B.	Pte	*
1055	Morgan. A.D.	AC1	Left 21.2.45
1056	Owen. T.	Pte	Left 22.3.45 Shirakowa
1057	Peatfield. J.	Pte	*
1058	Poole. L.S.	Pte	*
1059	Preston. E.	Gnr	Left 21.2.45
1060	Quinn. J.E.	Gnr	Died 19.1.45
1061	Reed. R.J.	Pte	*
1062	Robinson. H.L.	Pte	Left 25.10.44 Kagi
1063	Roscoe. A.	Pte	Died 29.11.44
1064	Scammell. J.	Pte	Left 25.10.44 Kagi
1065	Shaw. E.S.	Pte	*
1066	Smith. T.	Pte	Left 25.10.44 Kagi
1067	Soper. F.J.	Spr	*
1068	Staniforth. E.	Tpr	Left 25.10.44 Kagi
1069	Stoves. J.R.	Pte	Left 22.3.45
1070	Tetley. S.	Pte	Left 25.10.44
1071	Thomson. R.	Gnr	Died 11.12.44

1072	Tuttle. J.L.	Pte	Left 21.2.45
1073	Wann. W.	Pte	Left 21.2.45
1074	Webb. F.	Pte	*
1075	Williamson. B.	Spr	Left 30.3.45 Taihoku
1076	Weston. J.W.	LAC	Left 22.3.45 Shirakowa
1077	Winchester. H.F.	Tpr	Left 21.2.45
1078	WInter. W.	Pte	Left 25.10.44 Kagi

Numbers 1079 to 1100 Not Allotted.

1101	Johnson. E.A.	S/Sgt	Left 21.2.45
1102	Raynis. A.J.	S/Sgt	Left 21.2.45
1103	Smith. W.B.	Pfc	Left 21.2.45
1104	Kondrasiewicz. J.P.	Pfc	*
1105	Flynn. J.	Cpl	*
1106	Murphy. J.	L/Cpl	*
1107	Hodgson. G.E.	Pte	*
1108	Hodson. F.	Tpr	Left 30.3.45 Taihoku
1109	Timlin. T.	Pte	*
1110	Dean. B.	Pfc	Left 21.2.45
1111	Poole. C.A.E.	Pte	Left 21.2.45
1112	Whitmore. G.R.	Pte	Left 21.2.45
1113	Clack. E.A.	Sgmn	Died 25.8.45
1114	Harrison. J.V.	Gnr	*
1115	Kerton. R.H.M.	Gnr	Left 22.3.45 Shirakowa
1116	Lindsay, J.N.R.	Gnr	*
1117	Smith. H.W.G.	Sgmn	Left 22.3.45
1118	Jauney. E.	AC2	*
1119	Walters. R.A.	Gnr	Left 21.2.45
1120	Howard. W.E.	Pte	Left 21.2.45
1121	Gandy. C.F.	OMS	*
1122	Farnell. C.H.	BSM	*
1123	Forrester. R.C.	Sgt	*
1124	Pring. C.J.	Sgt	*
1125	Altham. J.	Bdr	*
1126	Beaney. W.E.	L/Bdr	Left 22.3.45 Shirakowa
1127	Bramley. E.V.	L/Cpl	*
1128	Hirst. G.	L/Bdr	*
1129	Rowe. H.G.	L/Cpl	*
1130	Schofield. R.	L/Cpl	*
1131	Stevens. R.	L/Bdr	*
1132	Anderson. E.W.	Gnr	*
1133	Angus. P.C.	Gnr	*

1134	Blain. G.	Gnr	*
1135	Bret. R.H.A.	Gnr	*
1136	Burmingham. J.A.L.	Sgmn	*
1137	Furbank. H.	Gnr	*
1138	Heard. G.M.	Gnr	*
1139	Henson. J.	Gnr	*
1140	Hughes. F.K.	Gnr	*
1141	Kay. F.W.	Gnr	Left 22.3.45 Shirakowa
1142	Miller. J.	Sgmn	*
1143	Morris. W.J.	Gnr	Left 22.3.45 Shirakowa
1144	Robinson. A.	Sgmn	*
1145	Sporton. S.F.	Sgmn	*
1146	Vickerstaff. N.S.	Sgmn	*
1147	Warbrick. G.H.	Gnr	*

80TH ANTI TANK REGT R.A.

OFFICERS	MAJOR CROSSLEY J.F.	LT. DAVIS K.A.W.	
	LT. HELLYER R.W.		
	LT. CROSS J.T.N.		
W.O.	B.S.M. DUBOCK. H.		
SGTS	LUNNESS L.		
	MARTIN W.J.		
	THOMAS F.		
L/SGTS	HOULAND C.		
	PEACOCK T.W.		
	PETERS C.V.		
	SCARBOROUGH E.		
	SHEPHERD R.		
BDRS	ANGUS G.	PELLING J.A.S.	
	AYLWARD P.B.	PHILLIPS J.	
	BREWSTER W.		
	GRUNDY G.		
	HAINES J.J.E.		
	HOOKS D.J.		

L/BDRS

ALLARDYCE A.
BENTLEY J.
CHRISTIE R.H.
CLARK W.S.B.
DAVEY J.S.
EMBURY G.

FISHER B.W.J.
HART F.T.
JOHNSON J.J.
JOY L.R.
LEAMER W.
PRYKE A.G.

ROBERTS E.W.
SMITH J.
STRONG C.C.
TRAVIS N.

GNRS

APPLETON J.A.
BAIGENT S.G.
BAILEY E.
BARNES F.W.
BELL H.W.
BENSON C.
BENTICK J.H.
BIGGINS S.
BIRD J.C.
BLAKELY J.
BLESSET B.
BOWERS A.R.
BROWN H.
CALLAGHAN D.
CAMERON R.M.
CHIVERS W.M.
CRAGG M.
DAVIES D.E.
DENTON R.
DEVERE F.
EDWARDS C.I.

GILES A.L.
GOWLAND C.
GUNN L.
GUSCOTT S.
HALSTEAD R.
HAYNES H.
HARROD D.E.
HEALY P.
HIGHAM J.
HILL N.
HOLDSWORTH F.
HORTON G.
HUNT I
HUNTER J.
KEITH J.
KING J.R.
KIRK L.
KIRKBY W.
RAMER E.J.
LANG W.R.
LANGFORD T.E.
LIVINGSTONE A.

MOORHOUSE F.
MORLEY W.J.
MORRISON D.O.
MUIR W.
MURPHY J.J.
PARSON S.S.
PETT K.E.
RAE H.
ROSS W.
ROSSITER T.
ROWNEY W.T.
SEARS F.
SHEPHERD E.
SHIPLEY L.C.
SLATER W.
STONE J.
SWEENEY T.A.
THACKABERRY G.
THORNTON J.E.
WHITE C.J.
WHITEHEAD H.
WYLIE T.

GNRS	EDWARDS G. EDWARDS S.A. FAIRBROTHER E.S. FERGUSON D.J. FLANAGAN W.J. FORREST W.	MAIN T. MARTIN A.W. McALLISTER McGill A. MERRIDAN A.T.	FURBANK H. GOTOBED J. HARRISON J.V. KERTON R.H.M. LINDSAY J.N.R.
OFFICERS	Ditto SIGNAL SECTION	Ditto RAOC SECTION	
W.O.			
SGTS		COUSIN J.	
L/SGTS	BELL D.T.		
BDRS			
L/BDRS		BRAZIER J.L.	
GNRS	BUNTING F. RANKIN C. TELFER J.M. TITHERINGTON T.A. WATSON T.		
SGM.		WHITFIELD G.H. BUNTING J.	

	R.A.S.C.	R.A.O.C.	R.A.M.C.
OFFICERS			CAPT. LEWIS C.V.
W.O.			
SGTS		CONDON W.	
L/SGTS			
CPLS	FLETCHER J. HAYLES H. TELFER W.	BROOME N.J.	DONNELLY D.H.
L/CPLS	ROBERSON M.S.		
PTES	BLACK W.A. FOX A.R. HYNES J. MORRIS G.W. STOVES J.R. TONNE A.F. WANN W. MORRIS G.W.	DOBSON J.R. YOUNG R.	PARKER T. PEREIRA F.R. THOMPSON J.

155 FIELD REGT R.A.

OFFICERS
CAPT. STEWART J.H.F.
L.T. BROWN W.H.G.

W.O.
B.S.M. LOWTHER G.S.
B.S.M. SHELVEY D.A.

SGTS
ANDERSON W.S.
BINGHAM J.
DAVIS E.G.
DEWSNAP D.J.
DONALDSON L.
HEAVER L.A.
McPHAIL A.
MITCHELL C.B.
MURGATROYD J.
SEPHTON R.
WARWICK R.D.
WATSON J.L.
WAUGH J.D.

L/SGTS
BRODIE J.
BROWN J.
FORD J.
GOODMAN R.G.
HARRISON T.
LOCHHEAD S.
MILES R.T.

BDRS
DOWNIE A.
FERGUSION J.
GLENCROSS W.
GOUGH B.
MATHER J.
NORBURY F.
PATTERSON W.J.
STEVENSON J.D.M.
WYLLIE T.C.

L/BDRS

BLAIR W.B.
CARLYLE I.
CARSON B.
DOUGLAS J.C.
DOWNIE J.
FITZGERALD J.A.
POPPLE C.
VACHER W.M.
VICCARS J.V.
WALLACE J.
WHITE J.G.

GNRS

BAILLIE T.W.
BARRIE W.
BLAIR D.
BRANDON W.J.
BUCKHAM J.
BUCKTON T.E.
BURNS H.
CALDOW J.
CAMERON W.
CAMERON W.J.R.
CAMPBELL A.
CAMPBELL G.
CAMPBELL W.
CARMICHAEL A.
CARROLL H.A.
CARRUTHERS W.
CARTER C.F.
CARTWRIGHT D.

GRAHAM J.
GREEN J.
HARVEY D.A.
HAY W.L.
HIDDLESTON A.
HOLT W.G.
HOPKINGS G.L.
JESS S.
KANE J.
LARKIN F.
LINDLEY F.
MACKIE R.
MARSHALL J.M.
McCUTCHEON J.
McEWAN J.
McGHIE F.D.S.
McGHIE R.G.
McGILL R.

PLUMBRIDGE L.
SCOTT Jas.
SCOTT J.
SCOTT W.
SHIELDS W.
SMITH J.M.M.
SOUTHERTON H.H.
SWAN G.E.
TELFORD J.
TERRY E.
TUCK S.H.
TUTHILL G.W.T.
VACHER G.W.
VERE A.
WALKER A.
WARD T.B.
WEARING G.W.
WILLIAMS E.

COX J.
DALGLEISH G.
DALY R.W.

McGUINNESS J.L.
McLEOD J.A.
MELROSE R.G.

WILLIAMS G.H.
WILLIAMSON W.B.
HUFTON R.

GNRS

DICKSON A.
DOBBIE P.H.
DOCHERTY R.
EDGAR P.F.
FLEMING W.
GILL J.M.

MILNE W.
NASH R.
NOTLEY W.R.
OGDEN J.
OSTLER J.A.
PATERSON J.A.
PICKLES S.

	Ditto SIGS SECTION	Ditto R.A.M.C.
OFFICERS		CAPT SEED P.G.
W.O.		
SGTS	EDWARDS J.O.	
L/SGTS		
CPL	SAVAGE L.V.	
L/CPLS	DAVIES J.A. McLOUGHLIN M.G.	
SGMH	BARBER G. BUTTIFANT F.J. COATES W.K. CRAIG J. DAVIS L.E. GIBSON W.McG HASLAM F. MORRIS E.J. SHELDRICK E.F. CLACK E.A. SMITH H.W.G. GILBOY D.M. CILL T.	

5 FIELD REGT R.A.

OFFICERS

W.O.
B.S.M. THOMAS R.N.
B.S.M. FARNELL C.H.
B.S.M. DIBBLE A.H.

SGTS
BQMS PERRETT F.J.
O'TOOLE T.F.
PRING C.J.
RODGERS W.J.

L/SGTS
BISHOP E.A.
BLACKHAM H.G.

BDRS
ALTHAM J.
KER T.Mc.D.
MAY P.W.
REYNOLDS C.H.
RITCHINGS J.D.
QUILTER G.C.

L/BDRS
BEANEY W.E.   HIRST G.   RUSSELL D.
BIRD C.H.C.   HITCHEN P.B.   STEVENS R.

WARD A.V.
WILLDERS L.S.

PAINTER F.

CRIPPS R.E.
D'ARCY G.R.
GUEST W.
HARRISON G.W.
HAYNES W.F.

LEADBEATTER A.S.
MAYNARD A.H.
MOULE B.J.
PERRIN J.H.
ROTHERFORTH F.

GNRS

ANDERSON E.W.
ANGUS P.C.
ARCHER W.
ARMSTRONG P.
AVINS H.
AYSCOUGH W.A.
BEEBY E.A.
BIRTWISTLE G.E.
BLAIN G.
BRADLEY H.M.
BRETT R.H.A.
CASSIDY D.
CATTON J.
CLARKE E.A.
COLLINS J.M.
COLLINGWOOD W.
COLTON J.J.
CORNTHWAITE J.

HILL P.S.W.
HILL W.L.
HOWE J.T.
HUGHES F.K.
IRVINE J.
KAY F.W.
KINGATE W.
MARSHALL J.C.
MAY R.
MILLER J.
McCOY F.J.
McKAY J.L.
MORGAN S.L.
MORRIS W.J.
MUIRHEAD J.E.
PERCY E.T.F.
PERRY C.
RATCLIFFE D.W.

GNRS

CROCKER W.S.
CROUCHER A.E.
CUTLER B.I.
DALEY C.
DAVIES L.J.
FINN W.H.H.
FOSTER A.J.
GETTIE J.
GOODWIN A.J.
HARDING J.
HEARD G.M.
HENSON J.

RICHARDS M.F.
ROBERTS J.
ROSS R.W.
RUSSELL L.
SCARGILL J.C.
WALKER A.
WARBRICK G.H.
WHITE J.H.
WHYATT J.C.
WILSON M.W.
WILSON W.
WRIGHT F.

Ditto SIGNAL SECTION

OFFICERS

W.O.

SGTS

L/SGTS

BDRS

L/BDRS   HOLMES F.
TUFREY A.W.

SGMN.   WEBSTER G.W.
WEST H.
WINDER R.
WOOD H.

SPRS
SGMN

PAYNE H.G.
RANDALL E.J.
ROONEY M.A.
SEATON A.J.
SILLET F.G.
SLATER W.
SOPER F.
SYMONDS F.G.
TRACEY A.
UPTON F.E.
WARING H.
WATSON S.
WILEMAN G.W.
WILLIAMSON B.
WOOD J.

9TH, 11TH IND. DIV. SIGNALS

OFFICERS

W.O.
CQMS BRUTON S.F.
DEEGAN M.

SGTS
JAMES J.W., C.Q.M.S. (F of S.)
RYLETT S.W.
CQMS BRUTON S.F.
DEEGAN M.
PULLINGER C.A.

L/SGTS

CPLS
BOWKETT H.V.
HUNT C.S.
SCOTT L.G.

L/CPLS
BRANT H.J.
BREWSTER F.J.T.
NEALE R.E.
ROWE H.G.

SPRS
ASHLEY H.G.
WALLACE R.

SGMN

BAKER J.
BARRATT W.
BENFIELD G.
BOSI I.
BRADBURN R.
BRADLEY F.
BROMPTON D.F.
BROOKE E.
BROWELL J.
CARTER A.J.
COUPER J.P.D.
CRUMMEY G.A.
EDWARDS R.
ESSAY N.I.T.
EWING A.C.
FOSTER P.
HAYDE W.E.
LINTON L.A.
MATTHEWS A.R.
NEWMAN W.T.
PESTER A.E.
ROBERTS T.E.
ROWLANDS F.W.
SHORTO W.K.
SIMPSON A.J.

WARWICK W.F.C.
WATSON H.
WEBBER S.A.
WOOD S.
YOUNG R.
BURMINGHAM J.A.L.
MILLER J.
ROBINSON A.
SPORTON S.F.
VICKERSTAFF N.S.

STEVENSON J.H.
WALKER J.

	6TH H.A.A.	5TH S.L.	I.A.	2ND H.K.S.R.A.
OFFICERS				
W.O.				
SGTS				
L/SGTS				
BDRS	YOUNG W.L.			
L/BDRS		DIXON R.	LAMB J.B.	
GNRS.	DAVIES J. HANSARD G.W. (RAOC)	CLARK H.G.		

	2ND BTN GORDONS	2ND ARGYLLE & SUTHERLAND.	1ST BTN MANCHESTERS
OFFICERS			
W.O.			
SGTS	CAMERON A.		
L/SGTS			
CPLS	SIMPSON J.S.	FLYNN J.	LOCKE J.A.
L/CPLS	EMMETT J.H. MILNE R. ROSS W.		ALLEN R. GANNISTER H. DAULBY W. DAVIES T.J. HEATHCOTE W.R. WHITTALL A.T.
PTES	DOUGAN M. FORBES J.M. GRUBB C. HUME A. McARTHUR J. McSHANE W.	McLAUGHLIN B. QUINN D. ROBERTSON W.A.	BENNETT H. BORTOFT J. BUTTERWORTH J. COOPER E. COPPER W.E. COVERDALE C.

MIDDLETON R.
MUTCH J.
STEVENSON R.
WALKER T.
YOUNG J.
BIRD H.
TIMLIN T.

DAVIES D.C.
ELLIS W.
GIBBONS H.H.
GODWIN G.C.
GOUGH J.
OWEN T.
PORTER E.
REED R.J.
RILEY I.
RUSH M.
STALHAM C.W.
STEVENSON F.C.
STRONGIE J.
HODGSON G.E.
ELLIS W.

	2ND BTN E. SURREYS	5TH BTN BEDS & HERTS
OFFICERS		
W.O.		
SGTS		
L/SGTS		
CPLS		BIRCH D.
L/CPLS		
PTES	CURRY W. HILLS G. HOWARD W.E. POOLE G.A.E.	FOSSEY H. FRANKLIN W.G. HOUSEGO E.C.G. LIVINGSTONE S. SEE A.H.

	9TH BTN R.N.F.	18TH BTN RECONNAISSANCE CORPS
OFFICERS		
W.O.		C.S.M. BIRKS E.
SGTS		HARRIS L.J.
		PEARSON L.
		WHITE W.
L/SGTS		HUNTER G.
CPLS		ASPINALL J.
		HITCHEN L.T.
		WILKINSON J.P.
L/CPLS	KING G.	CORP J.
		GALLAGHER M.F.
		GARRETT H.S.
		MURPHY J.
PTES	DAVISON G.	ALDRED D.
	TALBOT V.	ALLEN F.J.
		ATKINSON F.J.
		AUTY A.
		PEATFIELD J.
		PRESCOTT J.
		RAWSTHORNE J.
		RUSCOE A.

BAILEY A.
BAKER F.
BARNES J.
BARTON E.
BAXTER B.
BEARDSWORTH B.
BENTLEY F.
BLEASE H.
BROWN J.
BUGG H.
CORFIELD D.
CROSS R.
DERBYSHIRE T.
DERBYSHIRE W.
DENYER H.R.
DOOTSON E.
ELLIS L.J.
GREENWOOD S.
GREGORY H.
GRIMLEY L.
HARRIS S.
HENNESSY J.J.
HIGGINS J.
HILLDITCH H.
HOLDING G.

ROWLAND H.S.
SMITH T.
SPENCE F.
STANIFORTH E.
STREET T.
TETLEY B.
WALLWORK A.
WASHBROOK C.
WILSON R.F.
WINGHESTER K.F.
WINSTANLEY J.A.
ROBINSON A.
HODSON F.

	2ND BTN CAMBRIDGERS	1ST BTN CAMBRIDGERS	4TH BTN NORFOLKS
OFFICERS			
W.O.			
SGTS			
L/SGTS			
CPLS			
L/CPLS			KNIGHT R.
PTES	KERR A.R.	HORSLER C.	ASTILL H.
	MARSHALL A.C.	TUTTLE J.L.	BAILEY T.W.
	PARSONS J.W.		BLOWERS J.W.
	SOUTHGATE N.G.		BUTTERS T.W.J.
			DICK W.G.
			HAMMERSLEY R.E.
			LONG C.E.
			WINTER W.
			SCAMMELL J.

	5th BTN NORFOLKS	6TH BTN NORFOLKS
OFFICERS		
W.O.		
SGTS		
L/SGTS		
CPLS		
L/CPLS		
PTES	LEGGETT B.E. PRESLAND W.J. WEBB F.	KILBRIDE A.E.

	1ST 5 SHERWOODS	4TH BTN SUFFOLKS	5TH BTN SUFFOLKS
OFFICERS			
W.O.			
SGTS	LOWNDES G.L.		
L/SGTS	SLACK B.		
CPLS	DAVIDSON E. HAWTIN L.G.		
L/CPLS	RICHARDSON E.E.	HOCKLEY D.G. HUGHES T.A.	DURRANT E.
PTES	CARTER E. COOPER H. COPPING R. FLETCHER J.W. FOLLON A.G. GARRETT G. GREGORY G.E. INGRAM J. JAMES N.	BYFORD L.E. BAMSEY A.E.J. BRIDGES W.A. FORDHAM L. FOWLER J.V. PERKINS A. ROBINSON H.L. SCAMMELL J. WATTS A.P.	HILLS H.S. KIRK F. POOLE L.S. SHAW E.S. WINSPER H. YORK

WOODS A.

LATHAM G.
MALTBY J.
PARKING J.
PEACH W.
PRESTON D.
ROLE G.F.
SPURR T.
WESTACOTT J.

	85TH A/T REGT R.A.	125TH A/T REGT R.A.	7TH COAST REGT R.A.
OFFICERS			
W.O.			
SGTS	WOODAGE P.D.		
L/SGTS	PICKLES T.A.	DUELL A.E.	
BDRS	JONES H. GARDENER A.J.	BARRY J. BELL G.H.G. CHATT H.	
L/BDRS	GEE J.A. GRIFFITHS W.	DAGLIESH J.G. GIBBINS E. KNIGHT F.A.W.	
GNRS	KELLY R. TOGHER J. BARLOW E. HARRINGTON S.J.A. THOMSON R.	BAKER F.W. CHEESEBOROUGH F. COLEMAN P. CROUTHERS A. HIGGINS A. MARSHALL J.R. HOFFAT D.F. NEW G.	ADCOCK R. EARDLEY L.

OLDHAM N.
ROAST G.E.
TEASDALE J.
WHEATLEY W.S.
WORTHINGTON J.

	88 FLD REGT R.A.	118 FLD REGT R.A.	135 FLD REGT R.A.
OFFICERS			
W.O.			
SGTS			
L/SGTS			CHAPMAN G.W.
BDRS			
L/BDRS			STREET A.S.
GNRS	GOLDRING A. HARRISON L.R. PRESTON E. QUINN J.E.	AUGER H.W. KING E.	ELDRIDGE W.H.

	Ditto SIGS SECTION	137 FLD REGT R.A.	148 FLD REGT R.A.
OFFICERS			
W.O.			
SGTS			
L/SGTS			
BDRS		BEAUMONT S.	FARSON P.S. GREENING J. McDONALD W. MCFARLANE W.G.
L/BDRS			HALL A.E.T. HUNT E.W. McLERNON D. TANNER G.R.
GNRS	PRICE F.R.		AMOS R.A. ATKINS J.A. BAKER E.J. BARFORD F.C. BASTIN R.G. BOLTON P.

CHAMBERS W.E.
EAST E.J.
ELWELL I.W.
HART L.J.
HICKMAN E.
HORSFALL G.
JONES L.B.
LANGRIDGE C.H.E.
MAUDSLEY F.I.
MILLBURN J.S.
SLADE E.
SOUTAR W.
TENNANT W.
WRAGG J.A.
SHEARER A.J.B.
WRIGHT J.T.

	3RD IND. CORPS PROVOST	11TH IND. DIV. PROVOST
OFFICERS		
W.O.		CSM. BEAN L.W.
SGTS		
L/SGTS		
CPLS		BURTON J.E. WOODBURN E.B.
L/CPLS	MCGREGOR J.	CAMPBELL G. HEWITSON J.W. JONES A.E. BRAMLEY E.V. SCHOFIELD R.
PTES		

	9TH COAST REGT R.A.	H.Q.R.A. 11TH DIV.	H.Q.R.A. 18TH DIV
OFFICERS			
W.O.		QMS GANDY C.F.	
SGTS			
L/SGTS			
BDRS		STRINGER S.G.	
L/BDRS			LAMB J.B.
GNRS	COX J.W. MURRAY J. TIFFNEY D.	GERMANY E.R. WHITBREAD R.L.	WALTERS R.A.

	3RD A.A.	35TH L.A.A.	89TH L.A.A.
OFFICERS			
W.O.			
SGTS			
L/SGTS			
BDRS			
L/BDRS	TURNBULL P.		
GNRS	BIGGIN T.A. MULRAINEY T.	REYNOLDS R. (RAOC) WILSON H.	WHITMORE G.R.

KEELEY J.
LEMMER L.R.

	R.E.	MOBILE BATH UNIT	R.C. of SIGNALS
OFFICERS			
W.O.			
SGTS			
L/SGTS	CULL H.J. NASH W. PARKES J.		CHERRY H.G. MARTIN A.
CPLS	BENSTEAD F.W. COX V. DORSE J.G. GRIFFITHS T. WILSON B.J.		HARRISON D.W. RAWDING E.
L/CPLS	BODWELL W. CADLEY W. KINGSTONE C. HARDWICK J.F. LAWRANCE R.H. LOVETT H. MACFARLANE A.		HISCOCK G. MILLMAN W.

MCLOUGHLIN S.

FERN G.

BAGWELL R.
FOSTER C.J.
KINNIBURGH R.
POLLARD E.
SWINDLEHURST J.
LESLIE K.

SPRS
SGMN

BAGNALL A.W.J.
BURCH E.P.H.
CLARKE C.E.
DARBY B.D.
DICKINSON S.
DIXON J.F.
DOWN H.F.
EDNEY F.R.
EVANS A.G.
FINDLAY J.
GREEN C.J.
HANNAN J.
HILL J.R.
HINDLE C.J.
HOOPER R.J.
HOWARD A.C.
JACKSON A.
KAY R.
KING B.G.
LAWTON A.
LAY G.A.
LEWIS S.J.
MARRION A.W.

McALPINE G.
MILLER M.G.
MORGAN C.
OWENS W.
PARKES L.R.

	ROYAL INDIAN ARMY SERVICE CORPS R.I.A.S.C.	INDIAN ARMY ORDINANCE CORPS I.A.O.C.	INDIAN MEDICAL SERVICE I.M.S.
OFFICERS	CAPT. FRANCKE J.E.R. LT. SMITH D.D.	CAPT ROOK F.W.	MAJOR WHEELER B.M.
W.O.			
SGTS		KINGSLAND J.	
L/SGTS			
CPLS			
L/CPLS			
PTES			

INDIAN ARMY
I.A.C.C.

OFFICERS

W.O.

SGTS   FORRESTER R.C.

L/SGTS

CPLS

L/CPLS

PTES

	R.N.	R.A.F.	U.S.A.F.F.E.
OFFICERS			
W.O.			
SGTS			STAFF/SGT JOHNSON E.A. (803sd Engineers) STAFF/SGT RAYNIS A.J. (H.Q. COMMAND)
L/SGTS			
CPLS			
L.A.C. P.F.C.		L.A.C. HUGHES C. L.A.C. WESTON J.	P.F.C. DEAN G. P.F.C. KONDRASIEWICZ J.F. (Mil Police Coy) P.F.C. SMITH W.B. (194 TANK Btn)
PTES	S/A TAFFS F.	A.C. MORGAN A.D. A.C.2 JAUNCEY E.	

U.S.A. MEDICAL DEPARTMENT

Rank	Name	Number
OFFICERS	CAPT KERN C.V.	8
	CAPT SCHNEIDER L.	
W.O.		1
		1
SGTS	SGT. BRODSKY P.	14
L/SGTS		10
CPLS		28
L.A.C.	P.F.C. ENSINAS A.	50
P.F.C.	P.F.C. PARADISE B.	
PTES		235

Appendix C

List of abbreviations

ARP	Air Raid Precautions
A = T	Anti-tank
Bdr	Bombardier
BSM	Battery Sergeant Major
CO	Commanding Officer
Col	Colonel
Cpl	Corporal
DR	Despatch Rider
GOC	General Officer Commanding
Gnr	Gunner
HMS	His (Her) Majesty's Ship (indicating a Royal Navy vessel)
HQ	Headquarters
INA	Indian National Army
L = Bdr	Lance Bombardier
L = Cpl	Lance Corporal
L = Sgt	Lance Sergeant
Lt	Lieutenant
MP	Military Police
NCO	Non-commisioned Officer
o = c	Officer Commanding
OP	Observation Post
PoW	Prisoner of War
PT	Physical Training
RA	Royal Artillery
RAMC	Royal Army Medical Corps
RAOC	Royal Army Ordinance Corps
RIASC	Royal Indian Army Service Corps
RSM	Regimental Sergeant Major
Sgt	Sergeant
WO	Warrant Officer

Appendix D

Casualty Statistics of United Kingdom Force WWII

Table A1

Casualties to all ranks of the Armed Forces of the United Kingdom during the war as reported to 28 February 1946

Casualty	Total	Royal Navy	Army	Royal Air Force
Missing	41327	820	33771	6736
Wounded	277077	14663	239575	22839
Prisoner of War	172592	7401	152076	13115
Total	490996	22884	425422	42690

Source: (HMSO, 1946)

Table A2

Casualties to all ranks of the Armed Forces of the United Kingdom in the war against Germany as reported to 28 February 1946

Casualty	Total	Royal Navy	Army	Royal Air Force
Missing	35075	416	29255	5404
Wounded	260548	14360	224427	21761
Prisoner of War	135009	5518	119764	9727
Total	430632	20294	373446	36892

Source: (HMSO, 1946)

Table A3

Casualties to all ranks of the Armed Forces of the United Kingdom in the war against Japan as reported to 28 February 1946

Casualty	Total	Royal Navy	Army	Royal Air Force
Missing	6252	404	4516	1332
Wounded	16529	303	15148	1078
Prisoner of War	37583	1883	32312	3388
Total	60364	2590	51976	5798

Source: (HMSO, 1946)

Table A4

Total number of prisoners of war of the Armed Forces of the United Kingdom captured by the enemy as reported to 28 February 1946

	Total	Royal Navy	Army	Royal Air Force
Captured by Germany and Italy				
Total reported captured	142319	5629	126811	9879
Killed or died in captivity	7310	111	7047	152
Captured by Japan				
Total reported captured	50016	2304	42610	5102
Killed or died in captivity	12433	421	10298	1714

Source: (HMSO, 1946)

Published by
British Members' Council of the World Veterans Federation
Hon. Secretary: Charles Dunham MBE
1 Dillistone Court, Crunch Croft, Sturmer, Haverhill.
Tel: Haverhill (0440) 63715

Appendix E

The Japanese counting system on the board was based on five strokes. Each stroke increased the number by one. As we make a five barred gate卌, the Japanese make up their character for five — as follows: 一 for one, 丁 for two, 干 for three, 正 for four, and with the last stroke 正 five. The blackboard looked like this:

120	121	123	125	128	140	158	170	180	182	192
正	正	正	正	正	正	正	正	正	正	正
	干	正	丁	一	正	丁	一	正	正	正
		干			干			干	正